Hazard Mitigation and Preparedness

An essential text for today's emerging professionals and higher education community, the third edition of *Hazard Mitigation and Preparedness* provides accessible and actionable strategies to create safer, more resilient communities. Known and valued for its balanced approach, *Hazard Mitigation and Preparedness* assumes no prior knowledge of the subject, presenting the major principles involved in preparing for and mitigating the impacts of hazards in emergency management. Real-world examples of different tools and techniques allow for the application of knowledge and skills.

This new edition includes:

- Updates to case studies and sidebars with recent disasters and mitigation efforts, including major hurricanes, wildfires, earthquakes, and the COVID-19 pandemic.
- Summary of the National Flood Insurance Program, including how insurance rates are determined, descriptions of flood maps, and strategies for communities to help reduce premiums for residents.
- Overview of the ways that climate change is affecting disasters and the tools that emergency managers can use to plan for an uncertain future.
- Best practices in communication with the public, including models for effective use of social media, behavioral science techniques to communicate information about risk and preparedness actions, and ways to facilitate behavior change to increase the public's level of preparedness.
- Actionable information to help emergency managers and planners develop and implement plans, policies, and programs to reduce risk in their communities.
- Updated in-text learning aids, including sidebars, case studies, goals and outcomes, key terms, summary questions, and critical thinking exercises for students.
- An eResource featuring new supplemental materials to assist instructors with course designs. Supplements include PowerPoint slides, tests, instructor lecture notes and learning objectives, key terms, and a course syllabus.

Dylan Sandler serves as a Senior Planner at the New York City Department of City Planning. In this role, he manages citywide zoning changes and advises the City Planning Commission on land use policy. His areas of focus include hazard mitigation, climate adaptation, distributed energy production and battery storage, urban agriculture, industrial policy, and economic development. Following Hurricane Sandy, Mr. Sandler served as the project manager of the Resilient Industry Study, an initiative to help industrial businesses recover from damage caused by Hurricane Sandy and reduce risk during future events. He also serves as the agency's liaison on the city's Hazard Mitigation Plan. Previously, Mr. Sandler worked as a consultant supporting the National Oceanic and Atmospheric Administration to implement that National Climate Action Plan and the National Ocean Policy. In this role, Mr. Sandler facilitated communication and policy development across federal agencies focused on coastal planning and climate mitigation and adaptation. Mr. Sandler also served as a research associate at the Center for the Study of Natural Hazards and Disasters located at the University of North Carolina at Chapel Hill, where he conducted applied research regarding hazard mitigation, sea level rise adaptation, and disaster recovery planning and helped maintain the Center's website and social media. Mr. Sandler has direct experience with hazard mitigation planning at the local and state level. Working with the North Carolina Division of Emergency Management, he reviewed local plans for state and federal compliance, authored a chapter on climate change for the North Carolina State Hazard Mitigation Plan, and helped compile materials used in training sessions for hazard mitigation planners.

Anna K. Schwab is Program Manager at the US Department of Homeland Security Coastal Resilience Center of Excellence (CRC) administered at the University of North Carolina at Chapel Hill (UNC-CH). The Center focuses on conducting research associated with natural hazards and disasters, translating the findings to practice and educating the next generation of hazards scholars and practitioners. In her role as Program Manager, Ms. Schwab works collaboratively with diverse partners around the country to coordinate the research, education, and outreach projects of the Center, acts as liaison among participating principal investigators, and facilitates engagement of the CRC Advisory Board.

Prior to her current position at the Resilience Center, Ms. Schwab served as project manager and research associate at the Hazard Mitigation Planning Initiative, a partnership between UNC-CH and the NC Division of Emergency Management which provided technical assistance to local governments for the development, adoption and implementation of local and regional hazard mitigation plans in compliance with the federal Disaster Mitigation Act. Ms. Schwab also spent many years serving as a research associate and program coordinator for a variety of public service and research initiatives at UNC-CH, with her primary focus concentrating on emergency management, natural hazards mitigation, land use, law and planning, environmental and emergency management ethics, coastal zone management, sustainable development, and natural resource conservation.

Hazard Mitigation and Preparedness

An Introductory Text for Emergency Management and Planning Professionals

Third Edition

Dylan Sandler
Anna K. Schwab

Routledge
Taylor & Francis Group

NEW YORK AND LONDON

Third edition published 2022
by Routledge
605 Third Avenue, New York, NY 10158

and by Routledge
2 Park Square, Milton Park, Abingdon, Oxon, OX14 4RN

Routledge is an imprint of the Taylor & Francis Group, an informa business

First edition published by Wiley 2007
Second edition published by CRC 2017

Library of Congress Cataloging-in-Publication Data
Names: Sandler, Dylan, author. | Schwab, Anna K., author.
Title: Hazard mitigation and preparedness: an introductory text for emergency management and planning professionals / Dylan Sandler, Anna K. Schwab.
Description: 3rd edition. | New York, NY: Routledge, 2022. |
Includes bibliographical references and index. |
Identifiers: LCCN 2021020035 (print) | LCCN 2021020036 (ebook) |
ISBN 9780367635770 (hardback) | ISBN 9781003123897 (ebook) |
ISBN 9781000436006 (adobe pdf) | ISBN 9781000436020 (epub)
Subjects: LCSH: Emergency management—United States. |
Hazard mitigation—United States. | Preparedness. | Community power—United States.
Classification: LCC HV551.3 .S39 2022 (print) | LCC HV551.3 (ebook) |
DDC 363.34/70973—dc23
LC record available at https://lccn.loc.gov/2021020035
LC ebook record available at https://lccn.loc.gov/2021020036

ISBN: 978-0-367-63577-0 (hbk)
ISBN: 978-1-003-12389-7 (ebk)

DOI: 10.4324/9781003123897

Typeset in Minion
by KnowledgeWorks Global Ltd.

Access the Support Material: www.routledge.com/9780367635770

This book is dedicated to our mentor and dear friend, David J. Brower (1930–2018).

Anna and Dylan are endlessly grateful for the decades of imaginative guidance and support from Dave, the coauthor of previous editions of this text and a distinguished planner, attorney, professor, and environmental advocate. Always with a cup of coffee and an outline for a new idea in hand, Dave approached his work with clarity, creativity, and humor. He is deeply missed.

Contents

Tables

Figures

Photos

Acknowledgments

We would like to express our heartfelt gratitude to all of our editors and staff at Routledge—especially Natalja Mortensen and Charlie Baker—for their thoughtful guidance throughout this project.

Dylan Sandler would like to thank his partner, Beth Caldwell. Without her loving support and commitment to Sunday morning writing, the book would not have been possible.

Hazards and Disasters

What You'll Learn

- Types of natural and human-made hazards
- How hazards differ from disasters
- Costs associated with disasters
- The relationship between climate change and natural hazards

Goals and Outcomes

- Distinguish between hazards and disasters
- Analyze why there are more and bigger disasters
- Discuss the potential costs of a disaster scenario

INTRODUCTION

Disasters are not always natural. Of course, there are many natural hazards in the world, and there are many human-made hazards as well. But not every hazard becomes a disaster. This chapter gives a brief overview of the hazards that face our communities, both natural and human-made, and how a hazard differs from a disaster. Also covered in this chapter are the many costs—economic, social, environmental, and human costs—that are associated with hazards that affect the built environment, along with an introduction to the concept of social vulnerability. It concludes with a brief discussion of how climate change is altering some of the characteristics of the hazards we experience, both now and into the future.

1.1 HAZARDS: PART OF THE NATURAL ENVIRONMENT

This section introduces the concept of natural hazards and describes how these naturally occurring phenomena play a vital role in the Earth's dynamic equilibrium. The section also introduces human-made hazards as a potential threat to our communities.

Natural hazards are a part of the world around us, and their occurrence is inevitable. Floods, hurricanes, tornadoes, winter storms, earthquakes, tsunamis, volcanic eruptions, landslides, and other extreme events are natural phenomena that are largely beyond human control.

DOI: 10.4324/9781003123897-1

Some natural events can change the ecological environment. Consider these impacts caused by natural hazards:

- Wildfires burn forests and grasslands.
- Coastal storms erode beaches, flatten dunes, and create or fill inlets.
- Flooding inundates wetlands and marshes.
- Volcanic eruptions cover the landscape with molten rock and lava.

Despite the destruction caused by natural hazards, these occurrences are part of the natural system. Hazards have been happening for billions of years on the Earth and will continue for eons more. The natural environment is amazingly recuperative and resilient. After a hazard event, ecosystems can regenerate, and habitats are restored in time for the next generation of plant and animal life to begin anew.

1.1.1 The Earth's Dynamic Equilibrium

Many of the events we call "hazards" are in fact necessary and beneficial for natural systems and help maintain balance within the environment. Healthy natural systems maintain a balanced state over long periods of time through a series of adjustments. Change in one part of the system will be balanced by change in another part so that eventually the entire system regains equilibrium, a phenomenon referred to as **dynamic equilibrium**.

Consider the benefits that result when natural systems absorb the impact of some hazard events and readjust through dynamic equilibrium:

- Wildfires remove low-growing underbrush, opening up the forest floor to sunlight and nourishing the soil so that established trees can grow stronger and healthier.
- Flooding brings nutrients and sediment to wetlands and marshes, creating a rich habitat for a variety of plant and animal species.
- Volcanic lava and ash form fertile soils when they weather and break down, stimulating new plant growth.

These examples illustrate ways in which the environment is not only well-equipped to deal with what humans consider hazards but often requires them to renew and maintain natural systems. Among these natural processes are fluctuations in global temperatures that the Earth has experienced for millennia. Periods of extreme cold as well as periods of higher temperatures have always been part of our dynamic equilibrium. But as we will explore more fully later in this chapter, our changing climate is altering the naturally occurring ebb and flow of the Earth's systems, including alterations in the causal processes of some classes of natural hazards.

1.1.2 Types of Natural Hazards

Natural hazards can be classified according to the physical processes involved in their occurrence. Five broad categories of natural hazards are:

- Meteorological (hurricanes, tropical storms, typhoons, tornadoes, snow and ice storms, thunderstorms, etc.)
- Geological (earthquakes, volcanic eruptions, tsunamis, landslides, subsidence, etc.)
- Hydrological (floods, droughts, wildfire, etc.)

- Infectious disease (pandemic flu, vector-borne diseases, etc.)
- Extraterrestrial (meteorites impacting the Earth's surface)

Physical parameters of natural hazards include intensity and severity, measures that indicate the relative strength of a particular hazard. Hurricanes, for instance, are often categorized using the Saffir-Simpson scale, which ranks hurricanes from 1 to 5 according to sustained wind speed. Earthquakes are often described in terms of magnitude, a unit of measurement that describes the relative size at the source of the earthquake, often using the moment magnitude scale. These systems of hazard measurement are used by professional meteorologists, hydrologists, seismologists, and other scientists interested in studying and predicting natural hazard events. These scales also provide planners, emergency managers, engineers, and decision-makers at all levels with a common terminology to describe, anticipate, plan for, and manage natural hazards.

Although this book will explore many types of natural hazards, we will not discuss extraterrestrial hazards further. There have been cases of meteorites piercing the atmosphere and impacting the surface of the Earth, but these events are extremely rare and unlikely to be a direct focus of preparedness and mitigation planning.

LOCATION MATTERS

Some natural hazards occur only in certain regions of the United States. Active volcanoes are not found in New England, but in Hawaii volcanoes produce lava, ash, and steam at regular intervals. Other types of hazards are more widely distributed and can be found almost anywhere. Flooding can occur wherever water sources overflow their normal channels. In fact, flash floods can happen even in areas that experience drought most of the year, such as Las Vegas, Nevada. Still other types of hazards occur quite frequently in one part of the country but are also possible in other areas that experience them less often. For example, the risk of earthquakes in California is well documented, but less well known is the large earthquake that struck Charleston, South Carolina, in 1886. The risk of an earthquake occurring there in the near future is fairly significant.

1.1.3 Human-Made Hazards

There are two major categories of **human-made hazards**: technological hazards and terrorism. Technological hazards may be caused by accident—either through incompetence, poor planning, operator error, faulty equipment, bad weather, or some other mishap. For example, the risk of a chemical spill caused by a train derailment would be considered a technological hazard. Terrorism, on the other hand, implies an intentional act; that is, some individual or group means to cause harm to further a particular agenda, whether political, social, economic, religious, or a combination of missions. Although our understanding of human-made hazards is increasing, our ability to completely prevent either terrorism or technological hazards is still limited. We will explore human-made hazards and their effects in Chapter 5.

It is also important to note that, while it is helpful to classify different types of events into distinct categories for the sake of planning, the lines between these categories are often blurry and may change over time. For example, while infectious diseases are naturally occurring events, these can also be weaponized and used as part of a terrorist plot. Similarly, nuclear risks can exist both as unintentional hazards resulting from malfunctions of nuclear power plants or as an intentional threat from state-sponsored terrorism.

SELF-CHECK

- Define **natural hazards** and **dynamic equilibrium**.
- Discuss the beneficial functions of two natural hazards.
- Describe the differences between technological hazards and terrorism.

1.2 HAZARDS AND DISASTERS: NOT THE SAME

Natural hazards occur as part of the balance of nature, and natural environments and ecosystems can usually recover and restore themselves after a hazard event. A disaster is something different. A **disaster** results when a natural hazard takes place where humans are located and alters the normal functioning of a community or a society. A disaster is caused not just by a hazardous physical event but the interaction of that event with vulnerable social conditions, which leads to widespread adverse human, material, economic, or environmental effects. In other words, it is only when people are injured or property is damaged by a hazard that we experience it as a disaster. A similar distinction can be made for some human-made threats. For example, a vulnerability within a government database may exist for years, but it is not until a cyberattack is able to exploit the vulnerability and disrupt operations that a disaster has occurred.

1.2.1 An Official Definition of *Disaster*

The Robert T. Stafford Disaster Relief and Emergency Assistance Act is the primary legislation authorizing the federal government to provide disaster assistance to states, local governments, Native American tribes, and individuals and families. The Stafford Act defines a major disaster as:

> Any natural catastrophe (including hurricane, tornado, storm, high water, wind driven water, tidal wave, tsunami, earthquake, volcanic eruption, landslide, mudslide, snowstorm, or drought), or, regardless of the cause, any fire, flood or explosion, in any part of the United States, which in the determination of the President causes damage of sufficient severity and magnitude to warrant major disaster assistance under this Act to supplement the effort and available resources of States, local governments, and disaster relief organizations, in alleviating the damage, loss, hardship, or suffering caused thereby.

As this definition indicates, a disaster, whatever its cause, is an event of such magnitude and severity that the ability of states and local governments to cope is overwhelmed (see Photo 1.1). The threshold for determining what constitutes a disaster depends upon the resources and capabilities of states and local communities, as supplemented by relief organizations such as the American Red Cross. The patchwork of policies and regulations that makes up our system of governance has direct bearing on these resources and capabilities. Chapters 6–8 elaborate on the hazards management framework that exists in our federalist system of government. These chapters will provide information about how the federal, state, and local governments carry out their responsibilities for disaster management. It is important to note that the federal government is responsible for providing assistance only after other resources have been

Photo 1.1 Hurricane Harvey struck the United States in 2017, leading to widespread flooding, damage, and power outages, particularly in Texas. The storm caused significant damage to critical infrastructure such as hospitals, water and wastewater treatment plans, and petrochemical facilities. (Image courtesy of USGCRP Fourth National Climate Assessment. Photo credit: Staff Sgt. Daniel J. Martinez, U.S. Air National Guard.)

depleted. How strictly this policy is actually carried out is discussed in later chapters as well. The politics of extreme natural events can significantly affect the way in which disaster declarations are made and how disaster funds are disbursed from the national treasury.

1.2.2 Why Are There More and Bigger Natural Disasters?

Disaster economic losses due to disasters in the United States have increased in recent decades. It appears that the number and overall cost of major disasters is growing. In the 1990s, there were 53 disasters that each resulted in more than a billion dollars in damages. During the decade of 2000, there were 62 billion-dollar disasters. And during the 2010s, this figure spiked to a staggering 119 events of this magnitude![1]

Why are natural disasters becoming more costly? One reason that we are experiencing more disasters than ever before in our nation's history is because more infrastructure and more people are in harm's way than ever before. The rate of disasters in this country is rising at an alarming rate, because more people have chosen to live in areas exposed to coastal storms, repeated flooding, seismic activity, and other types of natural hazards, often with little or no attention to the need to protect themselves and their property. As a result, the risk of disasters occurring in the wake of natural hazards has grown over the past few decades.

Why is this happening? Part of the answer is that the population of the United States is growing. As cities and towns expand to accommodate more people, they sprawl out into areas that are potentially hazardous. For instance, many suburbs of cities in California have expanded into wildfire-prone forest, despite the well-known risk that these environments pose. Other communities are building new shopping centers and subdivisions in the floodplain, even though some of these areas have flooded in recent history. Still others are building on steep slopes where the potential for landslides is high.

Perhaps the most dramatic shift in development patterns has occurred on and near our nation's shorelines. The coastal environment can be extremely hazardous due to hurricanes, nor'easters, flooding, storm surge, erosion, and other coastal hazards, yet the shoreline continues to be some of the most desirable real estate in the country. In 2017, 94.7 million people, or about 29.1% of the total US population, lived in counties along the coastline. This represents a 15.3% increase since 2000.[2] As long as development and population growth keep expanding into hazardous areas, we can expect more and bigger disasters in the future.

HURRICANE KATRINA: AN IMPRESSIVE NATURAL HAZARD AND A CATASTROPHIC HUMAN DISASTER

Hurricane Katrina is an example of both an extreme natural hazard and a devastating disaster. This storm was not only extraordinarily powerful, but it also caused a catastrophic amount of damage and a tragic number of human deaths. As a natural hazard, Katrina had a life span in hurricane form of almost four days. During that time, Katrina made landfall twice, first as a Category 1 hurricane in Florida and then again as a Category 3 hurricane in Louisiana. It was one of the largest, most intense hurricanes in the Atlantic when it reached Category 5 status over the Gulf of Mexico. The storm produced high winds, storm surge, flooding, and tornadoes in parts of Cuba, Florida, Georgia, Alabama, Mississippi, and Louisiana and continued to produce heavy rains and flooding as it dissipated through the Mississippi Basin and Tennessee Valley.

If there had been no people or property in the path of Hurricane Katrina to experience its wrath, or if the hurricane had taken place on open ocean waters, the hurricane would have been counted as one of the strongest storms on record. But the implications of the storm would have been of interest merely to professional meteorologists and amateur storm watchers. Unfortunately, the history of Hurricane Katrina tells a very different tale. Thousands of people and structures were within direct reach of Katrina's intense rain bands, massive storm surges, and swirling winds, resulting in one of the deadliest, as well as the single costliest hurricane ever to hit the United States.

In addition to changes in the exposure and vulnerability of society to natural hazards, it is becoming increasingly clear that some natural hazard events are changing in frequency and intensity. Increasing average worldwide temperatures associated with global climate change are having far-reaching effects, from accelerating the rate of sea level rise to influencing the likelihood of weather extremes such as flooding and drought. The connection between climate change and natural hazards is discussed in more detail later in this chapter and throughout this book.

Natural hazards may also appear to be increasing in frequency because of heightened media exposure. Intense media coverage of hazard events and widespread use of social media can increase awareness of hazard losses worldwide as the documentation of news expands.[3] In past generations, when communication systems were not instantaneous as they are today, fewer people knew about natural hazards that took place outside their own communities. Today, it is not uncommon to get details, photos, and videos of disasters around the world as they are occurring.

SELF-CHECK

- Characterize the federal government's definition of disaster.
- Discuss how the conditions of a disaster differ from those of a natural hazard.
- Explain why disasters are increasing in frequency.

1.3 THE MANY COSTS OF DISASTERS

There are many different types of costs associated with a disaster. Some costs are obvious, such as the expense of repairing damaged homes and rebuilding roads and bridges. Other costs are less direct and cannot be fully calculated, sometimes not until years after the disaster has passed. Still other costs are not financial in nature, and no monetary value can be placed on them.

1.3.1 Direct Financial Costs

Disasters can be extremely expensive, whether they are caused by a natural hazard or by a human agent. When people are in danger, they must be rescued quickly and safely, then sheltered and fed. When power goes out, electricity and telephone lines must be repaired. When buildings and infrastructure are damaged, they must be rebuilt.

It costs millions, sometimes billions of dollars to remove debris, repair infrastructure, rebuild homes, and reestablish commerce and industry when a community has been hit by a disaster. Local governments are often burdened with much of the cost to reconstruct schools, utilities, fire stations, roads, bridges, and other local facilities that are damaged during a disaster. If the local and state governments cannot afford to pay for it all, the federal government may cover some of the cost of recovery and reconstruction following a large disaster, as well as the costs of short-term assistance to people who lose their homes and jobs. Federal disaster assistance programs are discussed in more detail in Chapter 6.

Who pays for these costs? Taxpayers finance the majority of activities taken on by local, state, and federal governments before, during, and after a disaster. Property owners and renters who have purchased various types of insurance may receive reimbursement for some of the costs of repairing their homes and businesses following a disaster. But when thousands of people make insurance claims all at once after a large-scale disaster, premiums for everyone, not just for those directly affected, can go up. Churches and other charities and volunteer organizations also contribute generously for disaster recovery, but this may mean that fewer resources are directed to other causes, such as reducing homelessness, supporting the arts, or serving the original mission of the organization. In other words, *we all pay for disasters*, even if we don't live in the area directly affected.

1.3.2 Long-Term Economic Costs

In addition to the direct financial costs of repair and reconstruction, other costs are often associated with disasters. Long-term economic costs can keep a community from recovering fully after a disaster occurs, even if the direct financial costs of repair and reconstruction are met.

Following a large-scale disaster that affects a major portion of a community, local businesses may close permanently, either because their capital assets (warehouses, manufacturing plants, equipment, inventory, offices, etc.) are damaged beyond repair and cannot be replaced or because the company has lost employees displaced by the disaster. Often, employees must move out of the area, either because they have lost their own homes or because they no longer have a place to work. Disruptions in the flow of goods and services impact local businesses directly and can also damage industries located outside the disaster region, for a long time. Sometimes the supply chain—both "upstream" and "downstream"—is disrupted for weeks or months on end, meaning suppliers cannot deliver raw materials and parts, while businesses are prevented from shipping out finished products. Long-term economic losses are particularly hard for small business owners and farmers, who may not have adequate savings or insurance to cover expenses and who cannot recoup their losses quickly enough to stay financially solvent.

The loss of jobs that occurs when major employers close because of a disaster can have a ripple effect throughout the community. If the job loss is severe enough, the entire economic structure of the locality can be changed permanently. Many smaller communities are dependent upon just one or two industries for their economic base, and when these are destroyed, there is no source of employment for residents. For example, towns and villages that serve primarily as tourist destinations can be devastated when a disaster obliterates the accommodations and attractions that bring visitors to the area. In turn, the local government loses its main sources of revenue from property, occupancy, and sales taxes, and no longer has means of providing services needed to support the community.

Problems arising from changes to the economic structure and employment base are compounded when municipal services are interrupted and cannot be restored quickly and efficiently. The longer utilities, schools, transportation systems, communications, and other local facilities are off-line, the more difficult it becomes for residents and businesses to return to work and commerce.

A lack of housing is often one of the most serious limitations to the full recovery of a community over the long term. When housing stocks are depleted because of an earthquake, hurricane, or other major disaster, the cost of available housing goes up, further adding to the economic burden of community residents. Building costs typically rise dramatically following a disaster, owing to a scarcity of materials, rising prices of material and labor, and a corresponding increase in demand. These high prices further limit the housing choices of new and returning residents.

1.3.3 Environmental Costs

Economic losses are not the only costs associated with hazard events. The natural environment can suffer severe damage during a disaster. Environmental damage can be the result of a human-made hazard that affects habitats and ecosystems directly, such as a chemical accident or an oil spill. The environment can also be damaged when a natural hazard causes a secondary hazard to occur, such as an earthquake that causes a gas line to rupture or a tornado that results in a chemical leak at an industrial business.

Flooding very often causes severe environmental damage when hazardous materials are released into the floodwaters. As floodwaters recede, contaminants may be carried along to surface waters (rivers, lakes, and streams) or seep into the groundwater and eventually may make their way into drinking water supplies. For example, propane, gas, chemicals, solvents, pesticides, and other harmful agents can be released if tanks, barrels, and storage containers are breached during a flooding event. Junkyards, livestock pens, meat and poultry processing plants, sewage treatment facilities, and other sources of contamination can also increase the environmental costs of a flooding disaster. For example, during Hurricane Floyd in 1999, many hog farms in eastern North Carolina were flooded when rivers and streams overflowed their banks following days of heavy rainfall. Tons of raw animal waste spilled over containment lagoons and entered the waterways of the region.

Water quality declined precipitously, endangering the health of people, livestock, wildlife, and aquatic animals and fish for a considerable length of time after the event. Despite an awareness of this risk, similar spills from hog farms occurred during Hurricane Matthew in 2016 and Hurricane Florence in 2018.

Often, with proper cleanup and handling procedures, the damage to ecosystems and habitats can be minimized, but in other cases, wildlife and vegetation are severely impacted for many years following a disaster.

1.3.4 Societal Costs

One of the most insidious effects of a disaster is the impact it can have on society. When a disaster destroys entire neighborhoods, the social fabric of the community may be ripped to shreds. Consider these possible consequences of a catastrophic event:

- Social networks that were in place to support residents are disjointed.
- A vibrant neighborhood may suddenly become a ghost town.
- Residents are often displaced and forced to live in unfamiliar locations far from family and friends.
- Children are suddenly without teachers, friends, and classmates, and the routines of school and home life are disrupted.
- Places of worship may lose their congregations, and community centers that once provided assistance to residents may be dismantled.
- Incidents of domestic violence and substance abuse often increase following a traumatic event.

1.3.5 Human Lives Lost

The death of one human being as a result of a natural or human-made hazard is one death too many. Although uncommon, the United States has experienced disasters with death tolls reaching over 1,000 people. Two of the worst events occurring in recent years have been Hurricane Katrina in 2005 and Hurricane Maria in 2017, which tragically claimed over 1,800 and over 3,000 lives, respectively.

Compared to less-developed nations, the United States and other wealthier countries tend to have fewer deaths associated with disasters than poorer nations. In fact, a study of disasters that occurred in 73 nations worldwide between 1980 and 2002 found that, despite there being no difference in the number or severity of natural hazard events between rich and poor countries, there is a substantial difference in the death tolls.[4] The Secretary General of the United Nations, Kofi Annan reported in 1999 that

> Ninety percent of disaster victims worldwide live in developing countries where poverty and population pressures force growing numbers of poor people to live in harm's way – on floodplains, in earthquake-prone zones and on unstable hillsides. Unsafe buildings compound the risks. The vulnerability of those living in risk-prone areas is perhaps the single most important cause of disaster casualties and damage.

Some recent global events demonstrate the catastrophic loss of life often seen in disasters occurring in developing nations. The 2004 Indian Ocean earthquake and tsunami, often referred to as the Boxing Day tsunami, killed more than 230,000 people in 14 countries. Similarly tragic was the 2010 Haiti earthquake with a death toll estimated at more than 300,000.

The staggering death toll of the COVID-19 pandemic points to the potential for massive loss of life from disasters. Unlike disasters made worse by poor building standards and infrastructure, the coronavirus pandemic has impacted poor and wealthy countries alike. However, the health and economic impacts—like other disasters—have been most concentrated in lower-income communities and communities of color.

1.3.6 Social Vulnerability

We have seen that across the globe, those populations with the least amount of resources are disproportionally impacted by disasters. But who are the people that make up these statistics?

There has been a significant amount of research into the topic of "social vulnerability," including attempts to identify and define the characteristics of populations that are most susceptible to the negative impacts of disaster. It is fairly clear from this work that we can dispel a popular myth about natural disasters:[5]

MYTH: Disasters kill people without respect for social class or economic status.
REALITY: The poor and marginalized are much more at risk of death than are rich people or the middle classes.

This myth-buster was made abundantly clear during the aftermath of Hurricanes Katrina, one of the deadliest events in recent US history. Those who were killed, displaced, or made homeless were disproportionately low-income African Americans who had no way to evacuate the region as the storm tore through. Similarly, while Hurricane Maria took a terrible toll on Puerto Rico, those who lost their lives were disproportionately poor and/or elderly, many of whom faced persistent lack of services such as electricity and health care for months following the storm.

The following list indicates some of the factors that can increase social vulnerability, both at home and abroad:

- Race, culture, and ethnicity
- Age
- Gender
- Disability
- Literacy
- Language barriers
- Social class
- Income disparity
- Foreign birth
- Undocumented residency status
- Domestic violence
- Substance abuse
- Mental illness
- Housing insecurity or homelessness

The population groups that fall into the above categories are not an insignificant proportion of our society. At the global level, we may add other factors to this list, such as populations displaced or otherwise impacted by genocide, war, civil unrest, famine, and drought, all of which serve to make these people disproportionately vulnerable to the impacts of natural hazards.

1.4 IMPACTS OF CLIMATE CHANGE ON NATURAL HAZARDS

Earth's climate has varied greatly in the past, but global temperatures have risen unusually quickly over the last few decades. According to reports issued by the Intergovernmental Panel on Climate Change (IPCC) and leading scientists around the world, this rise in temperature is due primarily to human-induced emissions from heat-trapping gases such as carbon dioxide. Atmospheric and ocean temperatures are higher on average than they have been in the past 1,000 years, and possibly longer. Global average temperature has risen by about 1.8°F since 1901. By 2100, it is projected to rise another 3.6–9°F, depending on how successfully heat-trapping gas emissions are reduced around the world (see Figure 1.1).[6] This phenomenon is referred to as **climate change**, a shift in the averages and/or variability of the climate that persists for decades or longer.

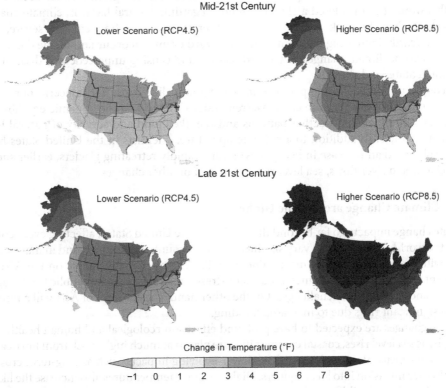

Figure 1.1 Annual average temperatures are projected to increase significantly across the United States as a result of climate change. By the end of the century, lower scenarios—reflecting greater emissions reductions—project average temperature increases across much of the country of 3–5°F. High scenario models suggest average temperature increases of 6–8–5°F. (Figure courtesy of USGCRP Fourth National Climate Assessment.)

WHAT IS THE IPCC?

Established in 1988 by the United Nations and the World Meteorological Organization (WMO), the Intergovernmental Panel on Climate Change (IPCC) is the leading international body for the assessment of climate change. The IPCC is a scientific body that reviews and assesses the most recent scientific, technical, and socioeconomic information produced worldwide that is relevant to the understanding of climate change. It does not conduct any research nor does it monitor climate-related data. Instead, thousands of scientists from all over the world contribute to the work of the IPCC on a voluntary basis.

The IPCC issues periodic Assessment Reports that review the latest climate science, as well as a series of special reports on particular topics. All IPCC reports are freely available on the organization's website: http://www.ipcc.ch/

1.4.1 Is it Weather or Is It Climate?

What does climate have to do with weather? Climate is essentially the average weather over a long period of time, often defined as a few decades. This connection has been characterized by the phrase, "Climate is what you expect; weather is what you get." A single rainstorm is a weather event, but if there are significantly more rainstorms in a given area for decades on end, this would be considered a climatic trend. Regarding natural hazards, climate change has both stacked the deck, making some weather events more frequent and severe, and added wildcards, increasing the chances that a hazard event will occur far outside the norm. For this reason, climate change is shattered records and causing unprecedented disasters in the United States and abroad.

A couple of degrees in temperature may not sound like cause for concern, but small changes in average temperature can have tremendous impacts on the dynamic equilibrium of the planet, influencing weather patterns and the likelihood and severity of natural hazards. For example, in addition to a rising temperature, scientists in the United States have already observed an increase in heavy downpours, rapidly retreating glaciers, earlier snowmelt, changes in river flows, sea level rise, and a host of other changes.

1.4.2 Climate Change around the Globe

Climate change impacts go far beyond the borders of the United States, affecting every country in the world. These impacts vary significantly from country to country, and in many cases those with fewer resources are most vulnerable. For example, many people on the African continent are projected to face increased water stress, creating significant public health, agricultural, and food security challenges. On the other hand, coastal areas of Asia will continue to face significant risks due to increased flooding.

These changes are expected to have profound effects on ecological and human health. For example, as sea level rises, coastal communities are placed at much higher risk from hurricanes and coastal storms, along with the risk of slower-evolving impacts, such as long-term erosion and saltwater intrusion into local aquifers. Higher average temperatures also increase the likelihood of drought and wildfires, placing more communities in harm's way and posing new challenges for agriculture and other industries. These and other impacts of global climate changes on existing natural hazards are explored throughout Chapters 3 and 4.

While climate change is a global issue, the impacts are felt locally, with wide variations from one community to next. Many areas in the northeast are likely to see more flooding in coming years as the number of heavy downpours increases, while wildfire risks will continue to rise in areas of the southwest that are experiencing hotter, drier days. Since it is increasingly clear that climate change influences natural hazards risks, emergency managers, resources managers, and planners will need to anticipate climate change effects on the local community to effectively respond to hazards. These efforts to address climate change within the hazards management framework are explored throughout this book.

SUMMARY

Every community faces potential exposure to hazards, both natural and human-made. Only when people are injured or killed and property is damaged by a hazard does a disaster occur. Due to patterns of population growth and development in the United States, disasters now occur more frequently than ever before. The impacts of climate change will only exacerbate the hazards we experience. Because we all pay for these disasters, directly or indirectly, it is in our best interests to prepare for disasters with responsible emergency management plans. Mitigation and preparedness strategies are critical ways of making a community more resilient against the impacts of hazards.

KEY TERMS

Climate change: A statistically identifiable change in the means and/or variability of the climate that persists for decades or longer.

Disaster: An event, potentially resulting in significant damage or injury, that exceeds the emergency response and recovery capabilities and resources of the agencies and officials responsible for its management.

Dynamic equilibrium: The Earth's natural systems maintain a balanced state over long periods of time through a series of adjustments.

Human-made hazards: Intentional or accidental occurrences caused by human activity; examples include oil spills and acts of terrorism such as bombings.

Natural hazards: Inevitable and uncontrollable occurrences such as floods, hurricanes, winter storms, and earthquakes.

ASSESS YOUR UNDERSTANDING

Summary Questions

1. Natural hazards are not the same as disasters. True or False?
2. Which of the following is an example of a natural hazard?
   a. Warehouse fire
   b. Sewage overflow
   c. Winter storm
   d. Soil spill
3. The frequency of hazards is increasing. True or False?
4. Disasters are a beneficial part of the balance of nature. True or False?
5. A disaster occurs only when human life and property suffer from damage. True or False?
6. Disasters occur most often in unpopulated areas. True or False?
7. Examples of technological hazards include:
   a. Bridge collapse
   b. Flood
   c. Bombing
   d. Tornado

8. Costs associated with disasters include:
    a. Infrastructure repair
    b. Rise in domestic violence
    c. Job loss
    d. All of the above
9. Contamination of water supplies is a possible environmental cost associated with a flood. True or False?

Review Questions

1. Natural hazards may differ from one geographic area to the next. Explain.
2. Hazards are a part of the Earth's dynamic equilibrium. Explain the role of a nor'easter on the coast of Long Island.
3. Give three possible explanations for why it appears that natural hazards are becoming more frequent.
4. How does a natural hazard differ from a disaster?
5. Disasters are increasing in frequency. Explain why.
6. Human-made hazards are another consideration for community planning. Name two types of human-made hazards.
7. How are natural hazards and human-made hazards alike? How are they different?
8. We all pay for the cost of disasters. Explain three ways we do so.
9. Some costs associated with disasters are not financial. Discuss how this is possible.

Applying This Chapter

1. Natural hazards are uncontrollable events. List three examples of hazards particular to where you live.
2. Compare the disaster potential of Missoula, Montana, versus Miami, Florida.
3. Discuss the direct and indirect costs of an oil spill in a coastal Oregon tourist town.
4. As a resident of a rural farming region of the Midwest, you've suffered through three tornadoes this year. You've faced the obvious costs of damaged crops, buildings, and equipment. Outline some of the social costs your small community may face.
5. Which members of your community should be considered for extra protection during a disaster? How will you identify this vulnerable population?

You Try It

Find Your Local Hazard

What natural hazards take place in your community on a regular basis? Are there hazards that haven't happened in a long time, yet residents can still remember "the big one" that occurred years ago? You can search for historical disaster declarations on the Federal Emergency Management Agency's (FEMA) website to learn more about major events that have occurred in your hometown or your state: https://www.fema.gov/disasters/disaster-declarations

Disasters at Home

Think about your own community or neighborhood. If a major disaster occurred where you live, what buildings and facilities could be damaged or destroyed? Who are the major employers in your city or town? What would happen if these industries and companies suddenly shut down? Could people you know find jobs nearby, or would they be forced to transfer to other areas?

REFERENCES

1. NOAA National Centers for Environmental Information. 2020. *Billion-Dollar Weather and Climate Disasters*. https://www.ncdc.noaa.gov/billions.
2. U.S. Census Bureau. July 15, 2019. *94.7M Americans Live in Coastline Regions*. https://www.census.gov/library/stories/2019/07/millions-of-americans-live-coastline-regions.html.
3. Platt, R.H. 1999. *Disasters and Democracy. The Politics of Extreme Natural Events*. Washington, DC: Island Press.
4. Kahn, M. 2005. *The death toll from natural disasters: The role of income geography and institutions*. Review of Economics and Statistics 87(2), 271–284.
5. Alexander, D. 2008. *Forty-Five Common Misconceptions about Disaster*. http://emergency-planning.blogspot.com.
6. Hayhoe, K., D.J. Wuebbles, D.R. Easterling, D.W. Fahey, S. Doherty, J. Kossin, W. Sweet, R. Vose, and M. Wehner. 2018. *Impacts, Risks, and Adaptation in the United States: Fourth National Climate Assessment, Volume II*. Washington, DC: U.S. Global Change Research Program, pp. 72–144.

2

Preparedness, Hazard Mitigation, and Climate Change Adaptation
An Overview

What You'll Learn

- Phases of the comprehensive emergency management cycle
- Differences between preparedness and hazard mitigation
- The link between natural hazards and climate change
- Characteristics of sustainable and resilient communities

Goals and Outcomes

- Assess the value of hazard mitigation and preparedness
- Identify hazard mitigation and adaptation strategies
- Describe the timing of hazard mitigation and preparedness relative to disasters
- Understand the connection between hazard mitigation, resilience, and sustainability

INTRODUCTION

As we learned in Chapter 1, we cannot stop most natural hazards from happening, nor can we fully prevent many human-made hazards from threatening communities. But we *can* take action to reduce the impacts of these hazards so that the damage is less extensive and recovery can take place quickly. This chapter introduces the concepts of hazard mitigation and preparedness as important pieces of the emergency management system in the United States. The chapter also lays the groundwork for a basic understanding of adaptation in the context of climate change and natural hazards. In addition to describing hazard mitigation, preparedness, and adaptation, we discuss some of the primary types of tools and processes that can help reduce hazard risk. This chapter then explains how actions taken to lower disaster risk can ultimately help reduce losses and associated costs and make communities more environmentally, economically, and socially stable.

2.1 THE EMERGENCY MANAGEMENT CYCLE

Comprehensive emergency management is a widely used approach at the local, state, and federal levels to deal with the inevitability of natural hazards and the possibility of human-made hazards and threats, and their potential to cause disasters in a community. The four traditional phases of a comprehensive emergency management system are **Preparedness, Response, Recovery,** and **Mitigation.** A fifth phase, **Prevention** is occasionally included in the description of the emergency management system, primarily in the context of human-made hazards. Table 2.1 outlines each of these phases.

DOI: 10.4324/9781003123897-2   **16**

Table 2.1 Phases of Comprehensive Emergency Management.

Preparedness	• Activities to improve the ability to respond quickly in the immediate aftermath of an incident.
	• Includes development of response procedures, design and installation of warning systems, evacuation planning, exercises to test emergency operations, and training of emergency personnel.
Response	• Activities during or immediately following a disaster to meet the urgent needs of disaster victims.
	• Involves mobilizing and positioning emergency equipment and personnel; includes time-sensitive operations such as search and rescue, evacuation, emergency medical care, food and shelter programs, and bringing damaged services and systems back online.
Recovery	• Actions that begin after the disaster, when the most urgent needs have been met. Recovery actions are designed to put the community back together or restore the community to a new normal.
	• Includes repairs to roads, bridges, and other public facilities, restoration of power, water, and other municipal services, and other activities to help restore normal operations to a community.
Hazard Mitigation	• Activities that prevent a disaster reduce the chance of a disaster happening or lessen the damaging effects of unavoidable disasters and emergencies.
	• Includes engineering solutions such as levees or raised roadbeds; land use planning to prevent development in hazardous areas; protecting structures through sound building practices and retrofitting; acquiring and relocating damaged structures; preserving the natural environment to serve as a buffer against hazard impacts; insurance, such as flood insurance, to protect homeowner's investment and lessen the financial impact on individuals, families, communities, and society as a whole; and educating the public about hazards and ways to reduce risk.
Prevention	• Countermeasure activities such as: heightened inspections, improved surveillance, and security operations to determine the full nature and source of the threat.
	• Law enforcement activities aimed at deterring, preempting, interdicting, or disrupting illegal activity.
	• Public health activities to detect and prevent pandemic, such as: surveillance, testing, mass immunization, isolation, and quarantine.

Although other models of emergency management are used as well, the four traditional phases of comprehensive emergency management are often illustrated in a circular pattern, signifying its cyclical nature (see Figure 2.1). We prepare for disasters before they occur. When a disaster happens, a community must first respond to that particular event and soon thereafter begin recovery. But even while the community is still recovering from one disaster, it must begin the process of mitigating the impacts of the next disaster. In fact, as we describe later, failing to incorporate mitigation into the recovery process often results in a missed opportunity.

Figure 2.1 The emergency management cycle consists of preparedness, response, recovery, and mitigation. While these are distinct phases in the diagram, the reality is that these phases often run together, and actions taken in one phase may significantly affect other phases of the emergency management cycle.

Also known as the **disaster life cycle**, this system describes the process through which emergency managers prepare for emergencies and disasters, respond to them when they occur, help people and institutions recover from them, and continually take actions to mitigate the effects of disasters on communities.

We are *always* preparing for and mitigating the impacts of disasters. These two phases are the building blocks for creating more resilient communities—communities that anticipate hazards and plan ahead to reduce losses. Interestingly, the period of recovery following a hazard event often provides unique opportunities to rebuild in a way that incorporates mitigation concepts into the redevelopment of a damaged community. In fact, the availability of government funding to carry out mitigation plans and projects has historically been the highest during the recovery phase of the disaster life cycle. New emphasis is being placed on pre-disaster mitigation activity, but the post-disaster environment continues to be one of the significant increases in funding availability and the time when some buildings and infrastructure are already being repaired or rebuilt, so the added cost of making changes to mitigate future risks may be much lower than the cost of retrofitting a structure that is in good condition. The level of technical expertise to carry out hazard mitigation activities also tends to surge in the aftermath of a disaster, so communities that are aware and proactive can often find an advantage in the midst of adversity.

2.1.1 Preparedness

Preparedness ensures that if a disaster occurs, people are ready to get through it safely and respond to it effectively. Preparedness can be characterized as a "state of readiness" to respond to any emergency or disaster. It involves anticipating what might happen during different sorts of hazard events and developing plans to deal with those possibilities. Preparedness also involves carrying out exercises, evaluating plans for shortfalls, and training and education. Although emergency managers must remain flexible and able to adapt their plans to meet immediate needs as the situation warrants, a plan or established protocol for dealing with disasters and emergencies of all sorts is crucial to a successful response. We will discuss preparedness in more detail in Chapter 11, but for now, the activities listed in Table 2.2 will give you some idea of the range of actions an emergency manager can expect to carry out prior to disaster to help citizens get ready for any type of emergency.

Table 2.2 Examples of Preparedness Activities.

Preparedness Activity	Description
Planning	All US states and territories prepare Emergency Operations Plans (EOPs). The EOP establishes a chain of command, designates responsible parties, provides for the continuity of government functions, establishes an Emergency Operations Center (EOC), and provides a road map for decision-making during emergencies. Evacuation and emergency sheltering are also important planning functions of the preparedness phase, as is the creation of backup lifeline services such as power, water, sewage, and communication systems.
Training	Emergency managers, first responders, and public officials take classes in emergency planning, disaster management, hazardous materials response, fire service management, communication systems, and other protocols to ensure that responsible organizations and individuals have the tools needed to respond effectively.
Exercises and Drills	From "tabletop" discussions of a specific problem to full-scale exercises that involve detailed disaster scenarios unfolding over several days, exercise events bring together every agency and volunteer organization that would respond in a real disaster.
Emergency Awareness and Education	Educational messages include teaching children how to make a 911 call, reminding parents to keep emergency supplies on hand, showing homeowners how to make their homes more hazard proof, encouraging people to report suspicious behavior that could be connected with a terrorist attack, and other public messages to help the broader population reduce risk.
Warning	Warning activities include the development of warning systems, emergency alert systems, social media and digital messaging, and coordination of sirens, and other emergency notification methods. Regular testing of warning and notification devices and protocols is critical.

TURN AROUND, DON'T DROWN!

An example of a very successful warning system is the placement of road signs to alert drivers to dangerous flood hazards. According to the National Weather Service (NWS), almost half of all flood fatalities occur in vehicles. As little as 6 inches of water can reach the bottom of many passenger cars and cause them to stall, and a foot of water can cause many vehicles to float. Two feet of water will float even larger vehicles like SUVs and pickups. If the water is moving, vehicles can be swept away. Driving at night during a local flood can be especially hazardous. To increase awareness of the dangers of shallow flooding, the NWS has initiated the "Turn Around, Don't Drown!" program to help communities educate residents about the dangers of walking or driving in floodwaters.

2.1.2 Federal Preparedness Programs

Preparedness activities are one element of a broader national preparedness system led by the Federal Emergency Management Agency (FEMA). The **National Preparedness Directorate** was established in 2007 following Hurricane Katrina. It provides policy and planning guidance to build prevention, protection, response, and recovery capabilities for states and local governments nationwide, including many of the strategies that enable professional first responders to carry out their preparedness duties. You can find out more about the Directorate at www.fema.gov/national-preparedness-directorate.

FEMA's public engagement and awareness campaign, Ready.gov provides a wealth of information, in both English and Spanish (listo.gov), to empower Americans to prepare for and respond to emergencies, including natural and man-made disasters. The goal of the campaign is to get the public involved and ultimately to increase the level of basic preparedness across the nation. Ready.gov urges individuals to prepare in a number of ways, including the following:

- Build an emergency supply kit
- Make a family emergency plan
- Sign up for emergency alerts
- Get involved in voluntary organizations involved in disaster response

Ready Business (ready.gov/business) is an extension of the Ready program that focuses on business preparedness, while Ready Kids (ready.gov/kids) provides tools, including interactive games, accessible information, and planning templates for educators and parents to teach children in grades 8–12 about emergencies and how to prepare them in a non-threatening, age-appropriate way.

TRAINING AND EXERCISES: DISASTER CITY

While it is important to have a well-informed and prepared citizenry, the skills of professional first responders are essential in any large-scale emergency or disaster. A critical element of a successful preparedness program relies on frequent training and exercises for first responders. There are many training facilities throughout the United States, but one of the oldest and best known is located near Texas A&M University in College Station, TX. The 52-acre training campus, known as Disaster City, includes a wide variety of emergency scenarios, complete with full-scale props such as derailed trains, collapsed buildings, leaking hazmat tanks, and other realistic disaster situations. There is even a portion of a WWII battleship to simulate the experience of fires and other emergencies that can occur aboard the large oil and gas tankers and drilling platforms. Experienced facilitators expose firefighters, law enforcement, emergency medical technicians, emergency managers, industrial workers, and others responsible for public and worker safety to rigorous, hands-on training. For more information, visit the Texas A&M Engineering Extension Service at http://www.teex.com.

2.1.3 Hazard Mitigation

Hazard Mitigation is defined as "any sustained action to reduce or eliminate long-term risk to people and property from hazards and their effects." This definition highlights the long-term benefits that effective mitigation can have. This definition also emphasizes that mitigation is an ongoing effort that communities must make on a continuous basis. The ultimate purpose of mitigation plans, strategies, and actions is to avoid placing people and property in harm's way and make structures and communities safer and stronger when avoidance is impossible or impractical.

2.1.4 The Difference between Preparedness and Mitigation

Preparedness involves the functional, logistical, and operational elements of emergency management. Although preparedness activities are carried out in advance of a hazard event, they are directed to the response and, to a lesser degree, the recovery phases of the emergency management cycle. During preparedness, we gather our supplies and make our plans for what to do when the disaster hits.

Preparedness can be visualized as the phase in which we pose a series of "what if" questions and seek to find the answers before they become reality. For instance, an emergency manager may consider various worst-case scenarios, such as:

- What if the power goes out? Do we have generators and a supply of fuel? What about telecommunications, water, and sewer service?
- What if the roads are blocked? How will we deliver needed supplies and medical services to impacted populations?
- What if our food supplies are cut off? Do we have access to water, ice, and Meals-Ready-to-Eat? Where are these supplies stored, and how quickly can they become available?
- What if there are multiple injuries? Who are our medical contacts? How will these medical providers triage and coordinate with one another? Will they need transportation, supplies, a power source, and blood?
- What if residents have to leave their homes quickly? Is an evacuation plan in place? Does it account for fluctuations in populations, such as the tourist season in a resort community? What about people who do not own cars or are not independently mobile? How do we handle residents who are disabled, ill, old, young, or illiterate?
- Are community buildings ready to serve as shelters? Are their locations clearly identified and accessible? Who opens the shelters? Are pets provided for as well?
- Are first responders ready to carry out search and rescue missions? Have they been trained to serve in disaster conditions? How will they communicate with one another?

Hazard mitigation, in contrast, is the ongoing effort to lessen the impacts of disasters on people and property through pre-disaster activities. Mitigation can take place for months, years, and even decades before a hazard event or a man-made threat occurs and continues after a disaster occurs with an eye to the future. Mitigation differs from the other phases of emergency management in that it looks for long-term solutions to prevent or lessen the impact of hazards. Hazard mitigation involves a different thought process and sometimes a different skill set, one that is oriented toward long-range policy and decision-making processes.

Hazard mitigation can be visualized as the ongoing process of asking "how can we reduce losses?" For instance, an emergency manager may ask questions about avoiding or absorbing impacts from a range of hazards and threats that they may foresee occurring in their community, such as:

- Are there specific locations that have been damaged by multiple events in the past? What is the best use of this land, and how can we ensure that life and property are not exposed to excessive risks?

- Are there certain populations in our community that are more at risk from potential hazards? What can we do to ensure that services and investments reach these members of our community to make them safer?
- Are buildings in our community constructed in a way so that they can withstand natural hazards that typically occur in these regions? What about bridges, powerlines, sewer systems, and other infrastructure?
- Are people sufficiently aware of risks in a way that encourages them to protect themselves and their assets? Do people have adequate insurance coverage in the event of damage to their homes and belongings?

One of the primary differences between hazard mitigation and preparedness is the visibility of the respective results. The benefits of mitigation often are not realized for some time—months or even years after being implemented. Success is measured by what does *not* occur, or "losses avoided." Avoidance and prevention are the outcomes of mitigation done well, outcomes that can be difficult to quantify. As a result, communities have often favored highly visible, result-oriented action in preparation for the immediacy of an emergency situation over the more deliberate, process-oriented strategy of hazard mitigation.

Unfortunately, hazard mitigation is often neglected until after a disaster actually occurs. In the case of natural disasters, history is filled with examples of communities that rebuild in the same places and in the same manner as previously, only to suffer the same perils when a strikingly similar hazard event recurs. It's natural and expected for people whose homes and businesses have been destroyed by a hurricane, tornado, or flood to want to get their lives back to normal, and they want that to happen as quickly as possible. But sometimes, rebuilding too quickly means opportunities to build back *smarter* may be missed. Hazard mitigation seeks to consciously break the cycle of destruction and reconstruction that accompanies repeat and foreseeable disasters by adapting human settlement patterns and construction techniques to reflect the threat posed by future hazards.[1]

SELF-CHECK

- List the four stages of the comprehensive emergency management cycle.
- Discuss the difference between preparedness and mitigation.
- Describe the primary preparedness tasks that Ready.gov encourages citizens to carry out.

2.2 CLIMATE CHANGE ADAPTATION

As we will explore further in later chapters, climate change has a direct effect on many of the natural hazards we deal with today. As our climate continues to change, the frequency, intensity, spatial extent, duration, and timing of weather events will change, resulting in unprecedented extreme weather events. Events that occurred only once every 30 years on an average may begin occurring every 4–5 years in the future.

The consequences of climate change are already being felt, and these consequences are likely to become increasingly significant around the world. Yet there are opportunities to decrease vulnerability and, in doing so, decrease losses from current and future disasters. In other words, climate change may increase the frequency and intensity of some hazards, but the damage caused by those hazards cannot be attributed to climate change alone—responsible public policy and private actions can reduce risk today and in the future.

2.2.1 What Can Be Done?

Responses to climate change are generally divided into two categories: **mitigation** efforts that address the "cause" of human-induced climate change—primarily through attempts to reduce greenhouse gas emissions that cause warming of the Earth's atmosphere; and **adaptation** efforts to address the "symptoms" of climate change. Neither of these efforts pursued alone can help us avoid all climate change impacts. Rather, mitigation and adaptation complement each other and, if pursued together, can significantly reduce the results of climate change.[2]

Hazard Mitigation, Climate Mitigation, and Climate Adaptation: What's the Difference?

Many words and phrases commonly used in the fields of emergency management and environmental management are not only closely related but also have distinct and meaningful differences. Understanding these nuances can be important in being able to communicate clearly about programs and policies to reduce risk.

Climate mitigation aims to reduce the forces that cause climate change, such as efforts to reduce carbon dioxide being released into the atmosphere as a result of burning fossil fuels. Climate adaptation aims to reduce vulnerability to climate change, such as building a wastewater treatment facility according to the sea level expected decades in the future. Hazard mitigation, focused on reducing vulnerability to natural hazards, shares many of the same characteristics of climate adaptation. Both are focused on identifying vulnerability to natural hazards and developing strategies to reduce that vulnerability. In fact, many of the strategies overlap between the two. So what's the difference?

For one thing, some hazards addressed in a hazard mitigation plan may not be impacted by climate change. For example, a climate adaptation plan is not likely to assume that risk associated with earthquakes is increasing, while a hazard mitigation plan will still evaluate strategies to reduce earthquake damage caused by earthquakes. Another difference is that climate adaptation may take an even more holistic view of the various ways that climatic changes are likely to occur in a given location, developing a plan to infuse this understanding into a wide range of decision-making and investments. For example, if climate change is expected to significantly impact the local ecosystem in an area, a climate adaptation plan may introduce programs that attempt to maintain biodiversity. Since hazard mitigation tends to focus more on limiting the loss of human life and reducing damage to property, hazard mitigation planning may be less focused on efforts that are solely designed to manage impacts to the natural environment.

2.2.2 The Case for Adaptation

Even if carbon dioxide emissions stopped today, we know that we are already committed to some warming of global temperatures, and that this warming will affect many of the critical services and functions that governments provide, especially at the local level. Some communities are already feeling the effects of climate change in the form of higher disaster costs and changing fauna and flora, but the high cost and damage of climate change are not inevitable. Adaptation provides an opportunity to reduce these risks.

The good news is that many adaptation actions have obvious and immediate benefits as well as long-term benefits, and they are worth pursuing in and of themselves. Adaptation strategies are generally consistent with sound environmental practice, improve the use of natural resource, and are often an effective way to increase resilience against current natural hazards.

ROOFTOP GARDENING IS COOL

Many adaptation actions also reduce greenhouse gas (GHG) emissions. Green roofs, or rooftop gardens, are actually able to cool cities, helping to adapt to the "heat island" effect of urban areas, which is only getting worse as global temperatures rise due to climate change (*adaptation*). These vegetated roofs (see Photo 2.1) also retain water during storms and reduce the amount of runoff that flows off of buildings and impervious surfaces like roads and parking lots, helping to manage flooding caused by heavy rainfall (*hazard mitigation*). At the same time, green roofs also increase the energy efficiency of buildings by providing additional insulation, resulting in lower energy demand for heating and cooling, which in turn means that less amount of carbon dioxide is released into the atmosphere (*climate mitigation*). Green roofs aren't alone in their ability to have many benefits at once. A number of the mitigation strategies discussed in this text have multiple positive outcomes.

Photo 2.1 Green roofs, like this one on City Hall in Chicago, are a good example of multi-objective building techniques, by serving both natural hazard mitigation as well as climate change mitigation purposes. The vegetation captures excess rainwater while also cooling the building, thereby reducing the building's energy consumption. (Image courtesy of TonyTheTiger/GFDL/CC BY-SA 3.0.)

SELF-CHECK

- Describe the relationship between hazard mitigation, climate mitigation, and adaptation.
- Explain why climate change adaptation is important even if steps are taken to reduce greenhouse gas emissions.

2.3 HAZARD MITIGATION AND ADAPTATION STRATEGIES

There are a wide variety of tools and techniques that a community can use to reduce the impacts of hazards on people and property while also adapting to climate change. Although every community is unique in terms of its exposure to hazards and its individual level of risk, strategies to mitigate these hazards and adapt to climate change tend to fall into common categories. Several of the key categories that we will return to throughout this text are summarized below.

Infrastructure strategies involve changes or modifications to the basic physical systems of society to make both infrastructure itself and the community that depends on it more resilient to natural hazards, man-made threats, and climate change. Examples of this type of strategy include construction of new water storage systems, burying powerlines, raising wastewater treatment plants above flood levels, and other interventions to build or retrofit critical infrastructure to reduce the chance of damage and disruption to service.

Land use strategies guide development and people out of harm's way, as well as improve design and location of development to better respond to hazard risks. Land use includes restrictions on development in flood zones, low-impact development to improve management of storm water, and urban landscaping to reduce summer temperatures.

Natural resource strategies reduce consumption of raw resources and protect ecosystems that provide essential services. For example, techniques to reduce freshwater consumption and measures to protect coastal marshes that limit storm damage would both be considered natural resource strategies.

Education strategies disseminate information to the general public and businesses about climate change and natural hazard impacts, along with information about adaption and mitigation measures. The success of many of the above strategies relies on the willing participation of community members; thus, education strategies are central to effective risk reduction.

Each of these types of strategies seeks to reduce the vulnerability of the built environment to the impacts of hazards (see Photo 2.2). Many communities use a combination of strategies to meet their risk reduction needs. Chapter 12 provides a detailed discussion of hazard mitigation tools and techniques.

2.3.1 Risk Assessment and Mapping

Before a community can implement any of its hazard mitigation or climate change adaptation strategies, it must have a clear picture of the types of hazards that pose a threat and how those hazards may impact people and property. Hazard identification is the necessary first step to reducing vulnerability; it involves a process of culling information about the community's hazard history, profiling various hazard events, and making predictions about the possibility of future hazards. The community must also determine what assets and populations are vulnerable to the hazards that have been identified, including analysis of land use patterns, growth potential, and development trends to evaluate what may be at risk in the future. Maps are a critical component of a community **risk assessment**, as they can be used to illustrate where hazards intersect with the built environment in a graphic and visual way. The analysis and maps produced during a risk assessment can help a community make important decisions about how to protect local assets and vulnerable populations. Chapter 10 explores the goals and approaches for conducting a community risk assessment, including tools commonly used by emergency managers and planners.

Most communities in the United States have an official Flood Insurance Rate Map, or FIRM, that shows the location of flood-prone areas throughout the jurisdiction. These maps indicate the likelihood that a particular area will flood over a given period of time. For

Photo 2.2 Sea Bright, New Jersey: Construction crews finish elevating this house that was damaged during Hurricane Sandy. Elevation is one way to mitigate flooding for a home situated in a floodplain. (Image courtesy of Steve Zumwalt, FEMA.)

example, the maps show the area that has 1% or higher chance of flooding during a given year (often called the 100-year floodplain), as well as showing coastal locations that are likely to experience significant waves during flooding events. These maps are used as the basis for developing ordinances that regulate the types of structures that are allowed in the community's floodplain and specify how these structures must be protected to mitigate the impacts of various levels of flooding.

2.3.2 Managing Community Growth and Development

One of the most effective approaches to hazard mitigation and climate change adaptation is managing community growth and development through land use planning and regulations, as well as controlling the quality of new structures through building codes. Local governments can use zoning and subdivision ordinances to steer development away from hazardous locations such as floodplains, seismic risk areas, landslide-prone sites, and wildfire areas. Local governments can also install infrastructure such as roads, utility lines, water and sewage treatment facilities, and other public services to avoid hazardous areas. By making hazardous areas less attractive for the development through strategic investment in capital improvements, communities can discourage building on inappropriate sites.

The choices we make regarding where and how we build determine our level of vulnerability to many natural and human-made hazards and threats. Hazard mitigation should not be seen as an impediment to growth and development of a community. On the contrary, incorporating hazard mitigation into decisions related to a community's growth can result in a safer, more resilient community and one that is more attractive to new families and businesses.

IMPLEMENTATION IS KEY

A thoughtful risk assessment will provide good information that identifies potential hazards and illustrates the impact those hazards are likely to have on the community. However, a viable risk reduction strategy relies on more than the production of colorful maps, no matter how detailed and accurate they are. Decision-makers must use the information gathered during the risk assessment to develop sound policies that specifically address the identified threats. But even that step is not going far enough—it is not until the policies implemented will changes take place that reduce the level of risk. Unfortunately, all too often, this final "action" step does not take place, and local residents remain vulnerable, despite the knowledge that danger lurks.

Tragically, this seems to be the case in Oso, Washington, where on March 22, 2014, a very large, rapidly moving landslide killed approximately 39 people, many of whom were in their homes when a wall of mud rushed down a steep slope, engulfing an entire neighborhood in a mix of earth, stones, tree trunks, and other debris. Aerial photography clearly showed the occurrence of previous landslides (an indication that future landslides were possible), identifying the area as a very high landslide risk zone. Prior to 2014, the county had considered buying up and emptying property that was later wiped out in the mudslide but decided instead to stabilize the base of the slope and leave residents where they were. Unfortunately, there were also a few restrictions on new construction in the area. It is possible that if more stringent development guidelines had been implemented based on the known exposure to landslides, the tragedy in Oso may have been avoided.

SELF-CHECK

- List four major categories of hazard mitigation strategies that can also be used for climate change adaptation.
- Describe how risk assessment and mapping help inform the hazard mitigation strategy process.
- How can land use planning contribute to a community's overall risk reduction strategy?

2.4 THE VALUE OF HAZARD MITIGATION AND PREPAREDNESS

We have learned that the goal of mitigation is to save lives and reduce property damage by encouraging the long-term reduction of hazard vulnerability (see Table 2.3). Hazard mitigation can be accomplished through cost-effective and environmentally sound actions, which, in turn, can reduce the enormous cost of disasters to property owners, businesses, and all levels of government. In addition, hazard mitigation can protect critical community facilities, reduce exposure to liability, and minimize community disruption. Preparedness saves lives and property and facilitates response operations through pre-disaster plans, training, and exercises.

2.4.1 Hazard Mitigation Pays

A fundamental premise of mitigation is that current investments in hazard mitigation will significantly reduce the demand for future expenditures by reducing the amount needed for

Table 2.3 Benefits of Mitigation and Preparedness.

Mitigation and Preparedness Benefit	Description
Reduces loss of life and damage to property	Communities can save lives and reduce property damage from hazards through mitigation actions, such as moving families and their homes out of harm's way. Mitigation and preparedness also reduce the risk to emergency workers who must rescue people during a disaster.
Saves money	A community will experience cost savings by not having to provide emergency services, rescue operations, or recovery efforts. Communities also avoid costly repairs or replacement of buildings and infrastructure.
Speeds response and recovery	By considering mitigation and preparation in advance, a community can identify post-disaster opportunities before a disaster occurs. A strategy that is thought out prior to a disaster allows the community to react quickly when the time comes.
Protects businesses and jobs	Impacts of disasters can debilitate the local economy, threatening the viability of businesses and the jobs they provide. Mitigation and preparedness can reduce disruptions, which in turn help maintain a stable economy and job opportunities.

emergency response, recovery, repair, and reconstruction following a disaster. By protecting its investment in infrastructure and capital assets, a community will enjoy cost savings over a long term. Hazard mitigation, therefore, is a fiscally responsible activity for a community to pursue. The benefits of mitigation and preparedness likewise accrue to business, industry, and other members of the private sector. By reducing losses, companies can protect their employees, their income stream, and company assets, and they are better equipped to maintain fiscal solvency and economic viability even after a disaster. Chapter 9 describes private sector mitigation and preparedness activities.

A DOLLAR FOR HAZARD MITIGATION SAVES SIX!

Many studies have evaluated the effectiveness of mitigation projects around the country. While avoiding property damage, certainly isn't the only indicator of value, these studies consistently show that mitigation has significant economic advantages, saving communities and taxpayers' money in the long run. In fact, mitigation programs, such as more stringent building codes, collectively save Americans about $3.4 billion each year.[3] According to the National Institute of Building Sciences, for every dollar invested in mitigation, the nation saves about six dollars in future losses avoided.[4]

2.5 SUSTAINABILITY AND DISASTER RESILIENCE

As hazard mitigation serves to protect the environment and reduce disaster-related costs, it can contribute to the community's long-term sustainability, supporting economic vitality, environmental health, and quality of life for the community as a whole. Climate change adaptation takes this one step further, by factoring future climate conditions into decisions made today. Sustainability is attained when decisions made by the present generation do not reduce the options of future generations. **Sustainable development** is a development that meets the needs of the present without compromising the ability of future generations to meet their own needs. Building in a way that reduces or avoids the impacts of disasters is an essential characteristic of a sustainable community.

Sustainability is a concept that can help communities of all sizes and in all locations make decisions that will lead to a better quality of life for all of their members, now and in the future. The principles of sustainability also apply to communities that find they must recover and rebuild in the aftermath of a disaster. The goal of sustainable development (and redevelopment) is to create and maintain safe, lasting communities through the protection of life, property, the natural environment, and the economy. Hazard mitigation and climate change adaptation activities are a very important part of any effort to become more sustainable.

Embracing hazard mitigation and climate change adaptation is also a key component of disaster resilience. A **disaster-resilient community** is a community or region developed or redeveloped to minimize the social, environmental, and economic losses and disruption caused by disasters. A resilient community understands natural systems and realizes that appropriate siting, design, and construction of the built environment are essential to advances in disaster prevention.[5] Resilient communities are towns, cities, counties, and states that prepare and plan for, recover from, and more successfully adapt to adverse events.[6] Actions to prepare for natural and human-made hazards and threats, and mitigate their impacts, are essential components of resilience. Chapter 13 provides an in-depth discussion of the role of mitigation and preparedness in building community sustainability and resilience.

HURRICANE SANDY RECOVERY: PROMOTING RESILIENCE THROUGH INNOVATIVE PLANNING AND DESIGN

When Hurricane Sandy devastated communities in the region, we were reminded of the importance that climate change will have in all development and planning for our communities to become more resilient and sustainable.

Shaun Donovan,
US Secretary of Housing and Urban Development (HUD)

Hurricane Sandy was unlike any storm before it. The unprecedented damage revealed the true threat that weather events posed to our communities, states, and greater region and marked a new era of public awareness that we must change our practices and thinking and way of living to address climate change and sea level rise. While everyone affected by the storm continues to push forward with the recovery process, it is clear that we cannot simply rebuild what existed before. We need to think differently this time around, making sure the region is resilient enough to rebound from future storms.

To address these challenges, in June 2013, Secretary Donovan launched Rebuild by Design, a multi-stage design competition to develop innovative, implementable proposals to promote resilience in the Sandy-affected region. After years of planning community engagement, planning, and design, several of these projects are moving forward to reduce the likelihood of disruption from future storms and flood events. To read more about the Rebuild by Design initiative, visit http://www.rebuildbydesign.org.

SELF-CHECK

- Describe at least three benefits of hazard mitigation and preparedness.
- Explain how hazard mitigation and preparedness are connected to sustainable development.

SUMMARY

Hazard mitigation and preparedness activities help communities become more resilient to the impacts of hazards, and climate change adaptation gives communities a running start to deal with the impacts of natural hazards in the future. Disaster costs continue to escalate in the United States, and we must increase our efforts to keep property out of vulnerable locations through the implementation of long-lasting and forward-thinking mitigation strategies such as natural resource protection and land use regulations to keep development out of hazard areas, and building codes to strengthen homes and businesses against hazard impacts. We have much to do in terms of preparedness as well. The loss of life and property during recent hurricanes, wildfires, blizzards, and the enormous toll of the COVID-19 pandemic in the United States and across the globe highlight the need for vast improvements in our ability to protect our population by planning for evacuations, emergency shelter, public health programs, and distribution of emergency aid to disaster survivors. These issues are explored in detail in Chapters 10–12.

KEY TERMS

Adaptation: The process of adjustment to the actual or expected climate and its effects, in order to reduce harm or exploit beneficial opportunities.

Comprehensive emergency management: Approach used to deal with natural hazards and human-caused hazards and their potential to cause disasters in a community.

Disaster life cycle: The cycle of the four phases of the comprehensive emergency management system as it interacts with a disaster event.

Disaster-resilient community: A community or region developed or redeveloped to minimize the human, environmental, and property losses and the social and economic disruption caused by disasters. A resilient community understands natural systems and realizes that appropriate siting, design, and construction of the built environment are essential to advances in disaster prevention.

Hazard mitigation: Any sustained action to reduce or eliminate long-term risk to people and property from hazards and their effects.

National Preparedness Directorate: Within FEMA, the National Preparedness Directorate provides strategy, policy, and planning guidance to build prevention, protection, response, and recovery capabilities for states and local governments nationwide. You can find out more about the Directorate at www.fema.gov/national-preparedness-directorate.

Preparedness: A state of readiness to respond to any emergency or disaster.

Ready.gov: FEMA's public outreach and education program that helps communities, businesses, families, and individuals learn about steps that they can take to be prepared for any emergency.

Recovery: Phase in the emergency management cycle that involves actions that begin after a disaster to rebuild the community; examples include road and bridge repairs and restoration of power.

Response: Phase in the emergency management cycle that involves activities to meet the urgent needs of victims during or immediately following a disaster; examples include sheltering, evacuation, search and rescue, and delivery of emergency supplies.

Risk assessment: The process or methodology used to evaluate risk.

Sustainable development: Development that meets the needs of the present without compromising the ability of future generations to meet their own needs.

ASSESS YOUR UNDERSTANDING

Summary Questions

1. Hazard mitigation can only be carried out during or after a disaster takes place. True or False?
2. Exercises and drills are a valuable component of disaster preparedness. True or False?
3. Which of the following websites is not part of FEMA's public engagement and awareness campaign?
   a. Ready.gov
   b. Ready.gov/kids
   c. Ready.gov/business
   d. Ready.gov/homeowners
4. Because residents want to recover from disasters as quickly as possible, planners and emergency managers should always make speed their only recovery goal. True or False?
5. Installing air conditioning to better cope with heat waves is a form of climate change mitigation. True or False?
6. Some climate change adaptation strategies may have immediate benefits and cost savings. True or False?
7. A resilient community is a community that prevents hazards from happening? True or False?
8. Preparedness involves anticipating what might happen during different types of hazard events. True or False?
9. Which of the following is an example of preparedness measures?
   a. Rebuilding water supply systems
   b. Conserving floodplains
   c. Training those involved in emergency situations
   d. Road repairs
10. The period following a disaster is a valuable time for implementing mitigation measures. True or False?
11. Mitigation is a way to save communities money. True or False?

Review Questions

1. What stages of the emergency management cycle do resilient communities use to try to limit the long-term impact of a disaster?
2. Citing examples, explain the difference between preparedness and hazard mitigation.
3. A comprehensive emergency management system follows four stages. Name the stages.

4. Hazard mitigation should be considered a wise investment for a community. Explain why.
5. How does hazard mitigation affect a community's decisions regarding growth and development?
6. Describe the results of research analyzing the overall return on investment for money spent on hazard mitigation.
7. Explain the difference between climate change mitigation and climate change adaptation.

Applying This Chapter

1. Compare how a town in northern Minnesota would prepare for hazards versus a town in Arizona. Which measures are consistent?
2. As the chief emergency manager in your town, you must present a proposal to the local governing board about a new federal program that requires local governments to engage in hazard mitigation activities. How will you describe what a resilient community is? What will you include in your presentation about the benefits of hazard mitigation? How will you convince the board to authorize spending local resources to reduce the impacts of hazards?
3. Explain how hazard mitigation and climate change adaptation are similar.

You Try It

Tracking a Hurricane

As an official with your local government, you have a responsibility to ensure the safety of those who live in your town. You haven't experienced a serious hurricane in decades, but one changed its track last year and narrowly missed your town. Assume that hurricane season is approaching, and outline a public announcement that will update residents about what your town has done to prepare for this year's season. The federal (NOAA) hurricane tracking website (www.nhc.noaa.gov) is an excellent resource.

Judging Resiliency

Assume you are an emergency manager in a flood-prone community. What factors will you look at to determine how resilient your community is to this hazard? How can you determine whether your community will experience a natural hazard event, so that damage is minimal and people are safe, or whether your community will suffer a disaster?

REFERENCES

1. Blanchard, W. 1997. *Emergency Management USA: Student Manual.* Emmitsburg, MD: FEMA Emergency Management Institute.
2. Bernstein, L., R.K. Pachauri, and A. Reisinger. 2008. *Climate Change 2007: IPCC Synthesis Report.* Geneva, Switzerland.
3. NOAA, Office for Coastal Management. *Hazard Mitigation Value.* https://coast.noaa.gov/states/fast-facts/hazard-mitigation-value.html.
4. Multi-Hazard Mitigation Council. 2019. *Natural Hazard Mitigation Saves.* Washington, DC: National Institute of Building Sciences.
5. The H. John Heinz III Center for Science, Economics and the Environment. 2000. *The Hidden Costs of Coastal Hazards: Implications for Risk Assessment and Mitigation.* Washington, DC: Island Press.
6. National Research Council. 2012. *Disaster Resilience: A National Imperative.* Washington, DC: The National Academies Press.

Section I
Natural and Human-Made Hazards

What are the different causes of flooding? How do we measure and communicate the severity of an earthquake? What factors influence the likelihood of wildfires? What risks do nuclear power plants pose to nearby communities? The following three chapters address these and myriad other questions by exploring a wide range of natural and human-made hazards facing the United States. We delve into the causes, characteristics, and classifications of different hazards and describe notable historical events in the United States and around the world.

Before we can take action to reduce vulnerability to hazards, it is important to fully understand common types of hazards and be able to anticipate the damage resulting from each. This chapter discusses natural hazards connected with Earth's water system, including hurricanes, sea level rise, drought, tornadoes, severe winter weather, extreme heat, and wildfires. Chapter 4 focuses on geological hazards such as earthquakes, tsunamis, volcanoes, landslides, and coastal erosion. In Chapter 5, we turn to human-made hazards, both technological accidents such as chemical spills, as well as threats that are intentional and malicious in nature.

Every community has a slightly different hazard profile, meaning the likelihood and potential severity of these hazards is not uniform from one community to the next. Sea level rise will continue to have profound impacts on much of southern Florida, while residents of a landlocked state like Oklahoma are more concerned with hazards such as tornados, flood and drought. It is also important to consider how and why the hazard profile in a given community might shift over time. For example, new development in an area can increase the quantity of stormwater runoff resulting from a thunderstorm. Some areas that have typically had sufficient freshwater over the past century may have to use water more sparingly in the future as agriculture, energy, and industry compete for waning water supplies. The following section discusses these changes, due to both climate change and human activity, and provides the foundation for communities to prepare for and mitigate risks from natural and human-made hazards.

In addition to the causes and consequences of hazards, it is important to have uniform ways of communicating about hazards. How would an emergency manager in coastal Virginia differentiate between a minor tropical storm and a catastrophic hurricane when communicating an evacuation order? How do developers and builders decide how high the foundation of a new house should be to reduce the likelihood of flooding? The following section outlines systems that are commonly used to classify and describe hazards. In addition to providing useful information for citizens and those responsible for responding to an event, widely used methods of categorizing the likelihood or intensity of hazard events are essential for designing policy and prioritizing mitigation actions that address the most significant risks to a community.

3

Meteorological and Hydrological Hazards

Hurricanes, Sea Level Rise, Floods, Drought, Wildfire, Tornadoes, Severe Winter Weather, and Extreme Heat

What You'll Learn

- The difference between meteorological and hydrological hazards.
- Characteristics and impacts of major categories of hazards, including hurricanes, wildfire, and drought.
- Types of flooding and the relationship between floodplains and floods.
- The rating systems used to measure the intensity of hazards.
- The influence of climate change on meteorological and hydrological hazards.

Goals and Outcomes

- Explore major historical meteorological and hydrological disasters that have impacted the United States and the world.
- Understand the tools and scales use to measure meteorological and hydrological hazards.
- Examine the relationship between patterns of human activity, such as development, and the potential for natural hazards.
- Assess how climate change may cause an increase in the intensity or frequency of many natural hazards.

INTRODUCTION

This chapter examines several weather-related hazards and how they can affect a community. We classify these hazards as either *meteorological*, meaning they are due to processes in the Earth's atmosphere, or *hydrological*, which result from the Earth's water systems. This chapter focuses on the following major meteorological and hydrological hazards: hurricanes, sea level rise, floods, drought, wildfire, tornadoes, severe winter weather, and extreme heat. Although wildfire is not necessarily caused by weather patterns, it is included in this chapter because certain weather conditions must be present for wildfire to occur. We discuss some of the main characteristics of these natural hazards, what to expect during the course of a

 DOI: 10.4324/9781003123897-3

hazard event, how the hazards are ranked in terms of severity, and some of the impacts they can have on our communities.

3.1 WEATHER-RELATED NATURAL HAZARDS

Between the years 1980 and 2019, there were 273 weather and climate disasters in the United States that reached over $1 billion each in damages.[1] In 2005, a single weather-related event by the name of Hurricane Katrina exceeded all of the previous disasters in this category in terms of property damage, resulting in a total estimated cost of $170 billion, and resulted in 1,833 deaths. In 2017, an extremely active hurricane season, multiple major storms struck the U.S. Hurricane Maria devastated Puerto Rico with a death toll near 3,000. Other parts of the country have experienced their share of weather phenomena – including massive flood events and devastating tornadoes in the Midwest, blizzards and ice storms in the north, and highly destructive wildfires in the western states.

These and other weather-related hazards fall into two major categories:

- **Meteorological hazards**: A weather event that occurs because of processes in the Earth's atmosphere.
- **Hydrological hazards**: A weather event that occurs as part of the Earth's water systems.

It is possible (and common) for an event to fit within both categories. The most prevalent meteorological and hydrological hazards that occur in the United States include:

- Hurricanes
- Storm surge
- High winds
- Torrential rain
- Severe winter weather
- Freezing rain
- Snowstorms
- Blizzards
- Wind chill
- Extreme cold
- Drought
- Tornadoes
- Waterspouts
- Floods
- Nor'easters
- Heat wave
- Hailstorms
- Lightning storms
- Severe thunderstorms
- Fog
- Avalanche
- Sea Level Rise

In this chapter, we focus on the hydrological and meteorological hazards that occur most frequently throughout the country, have the highest probability of causing significant damage to property, and pose the highest risk to human life and safety. The ultimate goal of learning about weather-related hazards is to be able to lessen their impacts on our communities through mitigation and preparedness activities that specifically target the conditions and likelihood of certain events in a particular area.

Throughout this chapter, we describe how these natural hazards are changing over time as a result of climate change. Climate describes the long-term average of weather conditions such as temperature, wind, and rain at a certain place. As the global climate changes, the likelihood of many weather events such as flooding or extreme heat tend to change as well. Of particular concern for many coastal communities is the effect of climate change on the ocean, including rising sea levels. It is important to note that the impacts of climate change are not identical in every community or every region. For more specific information about the likely climatic shifts in your community and the impact this has on natural hazards, contact your state climate office: http://www.stateclimate.org/.

CHOOSING A WAY OF LIFE

Awareness of the high probability of hurricanes and other coastal storms on the Atlantic and Gulf Coasts is vital to reducing the impacts of wind, waves, rain, and storm surge on properties located along the shoreline. In some coastal communities, regulations and/or personal choice have led residents to adopt various measures to protect property. In towns such as Gulf Shores, Alabama, structures are built on stilts to reduce the risk of flooding caused by hurricanes. Although these beach houses appear to be perched on top of toothpicks, the stilts are effective in elevating the first-floor of the structure above expected flood heights, offering a degree of protection during storms. Many homeowners also install storm shutters on the exterior of the building or have plywood ready to install over windows and doors when coastal storms are predicted. These prepared residents have learned from first-hand experience or from the experience of others that slab-on-grade buildings are not safe in flood-prone areas, or that merely taping windows is not an effective way of preventing damage from hurricane-force winds. These examples indicate the wide range of choices available to property owners living in vulnerable locations such as the coast; property owners can make beneficial choices if they are knowledgeable about natural hazards and their potential impacts on people and property. We will discuss these and other mitigation and preparedness tools in later chapters. For now, we will focus on the hazards' physical characteristics and their impacts on society.

SELF-CHECK

- Define **meteorological hazards** and **hydrological hazards.**
- List examples of meteorological and hydrological hazards.
- Explain why a basic knowledge of weather-related hazards is necessary for carrying out hazard mitigation and preparedness activities.

3.2 HURRICANES

A **hurricane** is a revolving mass of wind that circulates around a calm center called the **eye**, which can be 20–30 miles wide. The eye is surrounded by **rain bands** that extend in spirals outward from the center of the storm. Hurricanes are extremely powerful forces that can last for more than two weeks over water and can extend across 400 miles. Because hurricanes are large, moving storm systems, they can affect entire states, regions, or even multiple countries. Not only is coastal development affected, but areas far inland can also suffer direct impacts from hurricanes, including high winds and torrential rain.

3.2.1 Hurricane Formation

Hurricanes originate in tropical ocean waters poleward of about 5° in latitude. Thus, hurricanes are also referred to as **tropical cyclones.** Hurricanes are "heat engines," meaning they are fueled by the release of latent heat from the condensation of warm water. These conditions exist in tropical areas and supply the energy necessary for a hurricane to form. The prime season for ideal hurricane conditions lasts from June 1 through

November 30. This means the hurricane season comprises six months out of every calendar year; much of this period coincides with peak tourist season in many hurricane-prone coastal areas.

Hurricanes begin as tropical depressions. If the proper conditions are maintained, a depression can develop in a tropical storm and then intensify to full-blown hurricane status. Hurricane formation requires the following conditions:

- Sufficiently warm sea surface temperature
- Atmospheric moisture from sea water evaporation
- A low-pressure disturbance
- Weak vertical wind shear in the lowest 50,000 feet of the atmosphere

3.2.2 Hurricane Characteristics

A hurricane is a *multi-force* natural hazard made up of several distinguishing characteristics, each of which can be very destructive. The combination of features is often what makes a hurricane so dangerous. The major elements of a hurricane that cause the most damage to property and pose the greatest threat to human life include:

- **Storm surge:** Storm surges are large waves of ocean water that sweep across coastlines where a storm makes landfall. The more intense the storm, the greater the height of the water. The higher the storm surge, the greater the damage to the coastline. Storm surge has the potential to inundate coastal areas, wash out dunes, cause backwater flooding in rivers, and flood streets and buildings in coastal communities.
- **Storm tide:** If a storm surge occurs at the same time as high tide, the water height will be even greater. Storm tide is the combination of the storm surge and the normal tide. For example, a 15-foot storm surge along with the normal 2-foot high tide creates a storm tide of 17 feet.
- **Inland flooding:** As hurricanes move across land bringing torrential rains and backwater flooding from the ocean, rivers and streams often overflow their banks. In fact, a study between 1963 and 2012 found that approximately 25% of deaths related to hurricane activity have been the result of freshwater flooding.[2]
- **Water force:** During hurricanes and other coastal storms, coastal areas may experience flooding with velocity or "wave action." The force of floodwater with waves makes flooding even more destructive. The velocity and wave action can knock over buildings, destroy bridges, move debris, erode dunes, scour the shoreline, and displace and redeposit sand.
- **Wind velocity:** The higher the wind speed, the greater the potential damage. Hurricane-force winds can travel hundreds of miles inland, causing substantial damage to vegetation, buildings, and infrastructure. Hurricane-force winds can also create missiles out of loose debris such as roof shingles, tree branches, lawn furniture, and even boats and cars. Flying debris often causes more damage than the force of the wind alone.
- **Coastal erosion:** Coastal erosion is the results of coastal land being worn away by waves. It is commonly used to describe the horizontal retreat of the shoreline along the ocean. Although erosion occurs as a natural coastal process, hurricanes can greatly accelerate the normal rate of erosion along the coastline, even to the point that houses and other structures that were considered safe from ocean waves become suddenly subject to direct wave action or even fall into the sea.

MODELING STORM SURGE TO SAVE LIVES

Since 1900 storm surge-induced flooding has killed more people in the United States in hurricanes than all other hurricane-related threats combined (freshwater flooding, winds, and tornadoes).[3] Coastal engineers are working to enhance the analysis and prediction of storm surge through the use of sophisticated computer models. One such model is the Advanced Coastal Circulation model (ADCIRC), which combines rain, atmospheric pressure, and wind forecasts to predict when, where, and to what extent coastal communities will experience storm surge, high waves, and flooding. The high-resolution models provide more detail and accuracy than typical surge forecasts through the use of supercomputers capable of trillions of calculations per second. Emergency managers can use the model's results to identify which locations to evacuate as a storm approaches and to plan for mitigation and response before severe storms occur (see Figure 3.1).

When a hurricane makes landfall and traverses across the land either up the coast or inland, the types of damage that occur vary according to the dominant feature of that particular storm. Hurricane Fran, for instance, was considered primarily a "wind hurricane." When this hurricane affected the state of North Carolina in 1996, the majority of reported damage included roofs ripped off of homes; trees falling on structures, vehicles, and roadways; and damage caused by flying debris. In contract, when Hurricane Floyd hit North Carolina three years later, most of the damage was caused by severe flooding. The entire eastern third of the state experienced unprecedented high water levels, as rainfall far inland caused rivers and streams to overflow their banks, flooding homes, businesses, hog farms, sewer plants, junkyards, and other features of the built environment throughout the coastal plain.

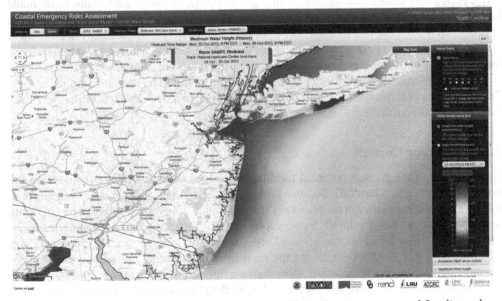

Figure 3.1 The ADCIRC coastal circulation model is used to predict storm surge and flooding as hurricanes approach the coast. (Figure accessed from Coastal Emergency Risks Assessment.)

Table 3.1 Saffir-Simpson Scale.

Saffir-Simpson Category	Maximum Sustained Wind Speed		
	mph	*meter/second*	*knots*
1	74–95	33–42	64–82
2	96–110	43–49	83–95
3	111–129	50–58	96–112
4	130–156	58–70	113–136
5	157+	70+	137+

Historically, Atlantic hurricane activity has experienced a great deal of variability. Some periods have above-normal activity, while others have below-normal activity. These fluctuations result from differences in the number of hurricanes and major hurricanes forming in the Atlantic and Caribbean each year. Hurricane seasons from 1966 to 2009 averaged 11.3 named storms each season, with an average of 6.2 becoming hurricanes and 2.3 becoming major hurricanes.[4]

3.2.3 Measuring a Hurricane: The Saffir-Simpson Scale

Hurricane severity is measured using the Saffir-Simpson Scale, ranging from 1 (minimal) to 5 (catastrophic). The scale categorizes hurricanes based upon maximum sustained winds (Table 3.1).

Categories 3, 4, and 5 hurricanes are the most potentially dangerous and are often categorized as **major hurricanes**. However, it is important to remember that hurricanes of all intensities, including categories 1 and 2 hurricanes, have the potential to cause massive property damage and pose a risk to human life. For example, although Hurricane Irene made landfall as a Category 1 hurricane in 2011, it caused extensive flood damage and resulted in approximately $10 billion in damage and 45 deaths. Similarly, Hurricane Sandy in 2012 was a Category 2 storm at its peak wind intensity but was no longer even a hurricane when it struck the New Jersey and New York area. Regardless, the storm caused catastrophic damage due in large part to its coastal storm surge, a characteristic not captured by the Saffir-Simpson scale. Table 3.2 gives examples of the types of damage that can occur with each of the hurricane categories on the Saffir-Simpson Scale.

3.2.4 Hurricane Landfall

Hurricanes have the greatest potential to inflict damage as they cross the coastline from the ocean at a point called **landfall**. Because hurricanes derive their strength from warm ocean waters, they generally deteriorate once they make landfall. This is particularly true regarding wind speed, though heavy rainfall can persist far inland. The forward speed of a hurricane can vary from just a few miles/hour to up to 40 miles/hour. This forward motion, combined with a counterclockwise surface flow, makes the right front quadrant of a hurricane the locale of the most potentially damaging winds. Slow-moving hurricanes can actually cause more damage than faster hurricanes because they spend more time in one location, dumping more rain, causing more storm surge, and subjecting the area to prolonged high winds. The worst-case scenario is a hurricane that stalls along the coast, pounding the area for hours or even days.

Table 3.2 Hurricane Category Damage Examples.

Category	Level	Description	Example
1	MINIMAL	Damage primarily to shrubbery, trees, foliage, and unanchored homes. No real damage to other structures. Some damage to poorly constructed signs. Low-lying coastal roads inundated, minor pier damage, some small craft in exposed anchorage torn from moorings.	Hurricane Humberto (2007)
2	MODERATE	Considerable damage to shrubbery and tree foliage; some trees blown down. Major damage to exposed mobile homes. Extensive damage to poorly constructed signs. Some damage to roofing materials of buildings; some window and door damage. No major damage to buildings. Coastal roads and low-lying inland escape routes cut off by rising water 2–4 hours before arrival of hurricane's center. Considerable damage to piers. Marinas flooded. Small craft in unprotected anchorages torn from moorings. Evacuation of some shoreline residences and low-lying areas required.	Hurricane Ernesto (2012)
3	EXTENSIVE	Foliage torn from trees; large trees blown down. Most poorly constructed signs blown down. Some damage to roofing materials of buildings; some window and door damage. Some structural damage to small buildings. Mobile homes destroyed. Serious flooding at coast and many smaller structures near coast destroyed; larger structures near coast damaged by battering waves and floating debris. Low-lying inland escape routes cut off by rising water 3–5 hours before hurricane's center arrives. Flat terrain 5 feet or less above sea level flooded inland 8 miles or more. Evacuation of low-lying residences within several blocks of shoreline may be required.	Hurricane Ivan (2004)
4	EXTREME	Shrubs, trees, and all signs blown down. Extensive damage to roofing materials, windows, and doors. Complete failures of roofs on many small residences. Complete destruction of mobile homes. Major damage to lower floors of structures near shore due to flooding and battering by waves and floating debris. Low-lying inland escape routes cut off by rising water 3–5 hours before hurricane's center arrives. Flat terrain 10 feet or less above sea level flooded inland as far as 6 miles. Major erosion of beaches. Massive evacuation of all residences within 500 yards of shore and of single-story residences within 2 miles of shore may be required.	Hurricane Katrina (2005)
5	CATASTROPHIC	Shrubs, trees, and all signs blown down. Very severe and extensive damage to windows and doors; extensive shattering of glass in windows and doors. Complete failure of roofs on many residences and industrial buildings; considerable damage to other roofs. Some complete building failures. Small buildings overturned or blown away. Complete destruction of mobile homes. Major damage to lower floors of all structures less than 15 feet above sea level within 500 yards of shore. Low-lying inland escape routes cut off by rising water 3–5 hours before hurricane's center arrives. Massive evacuation of residential areas on low ground within 5–10 miles of shore may be required.	Hurricane Camille (1969)

THE DANGERS OF SLOW STORMS

Hurricane Harvey in 2017 was a sobering example of the damage of slow-moving hurricanes. The Category 4 hurricane quickly weakened to a tropical storm after making landfall in East Texas, but after slowing to a crawl, many locations continued to be impacted for multiple days. After the fourth day, some communities had received more than 40 inches of rain, roughly equivalent to the average rainfall for a typical year! Hurricane Harvey was extremely destructive for a number of reasons, but the duration of its impact on many communities in Texas and Louisiana is undoubtedly a significant reason that it cost so many lives and damaged communities.

The site of hurricane landfall is notoriously unpredictable. However, the skill of tropical storm and hurricane forecasting has greatly improved with advances in technology. In 1990, the average error in predicting hurricane landfall 72 hours in advance of a storm was almost 300 miles. Today the average error in the National Hurricane Center's 72-hour prediction is 100 miles. The track that a hurricane can take once it makes landfall is also somewhat unpredictable. Inland areas far west of the Atlantic coast and north of the Gulf Coast have been devastated by the remnants of tropical storms and hurricanes as they travel with the force of forward momentum. The erratic nature of hurricanes is illustrated on the map in Figure 3.2 shows North Atlantic hurricane tracks from 1851 to 2012.

3.2.5 Hurricanes and Patterns of Human Activity

Past trends show that hurricane frequency has fluctuated in cycles of a few decades. During the period of below-average hurricane activity that lasted from 1970 to 1994, intense

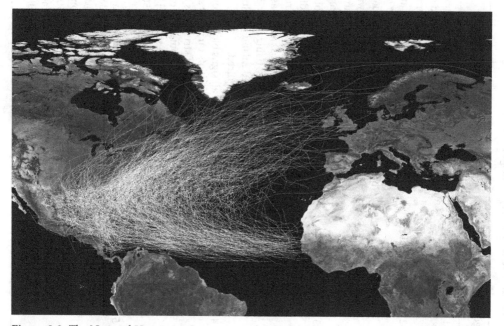

Figure 3.2 The National Hurricane Center maps the tracks of hurricanes in the North Atlantic Basin from 1851 to 2012.

development and growth occurred along the coastlines of the Atlantic Ocean and the Gulf of Mexico. Although many of the beaches and barrier islands of the Gulf and Atlantic had some development before this time, for the most part structures along the coast were relatively small-scale, single-family cottages, and the number of people living in coastal areas was much lower than today. In fact, relatively large tracts were inaccessible except by water or air, leaving extensive stretches of coastal land undeveloped.

When investors, developers, and vacationers "discovered" the pristine coastlines of states along the Atlantic and Gulf, an unprecedented boom in coastal construction began. The 1980s in particular saw a rapid expansion of development, including high-rise (and high-dollar) properties in many of the most vulnerable and fragile areas of the coast. The coinciding lull in hurricane activity served to bolster the image of the coast as a safe and lucrative investment opportunity. By the time the cycle of calm ended, development patterns in many communities were already firmly established.

Local communities and coastal states discovered that waterfront development was extremely profitable, not just for the private investor and vacation homeowner, but for the public sector as well: property tax revenues from expensive real estate contributed significantly to the local and state economies, and the multiple businesses related to tourism and other coastal industries provided jobs, further bolstering local markets. There was little incentive to curb rapid expansion and growth at that time, which set up the scenarios we are experiencing today: massive development, extensive public infrastructure, huge population numbers, and expensive investment coupled with more frequent and destructive hurricane activity. The rapid increase in property damage and loss of life that we have experienced in the last few years is due to the combination of intense hurricane activity intersecting with intense human activity along the coast.

3.2.6 Impacts of Climate Change on Hurricanes

Trends in hurricane activity are often described by changes in intensity, frequency, and the location of hurricanes. The recent trend has been toward stronger Atlantic hurricanes, with indications that climate change will continue to result in more strong hurricanes in the future. At the same time, it is possible that the overall number of hurricanes may remain stable or slightly decrease. Unfortunately, these two trends are unlikely to balance out in terms of damage, since stronger hurricanes cause exponentially greater damage than smaller storms. It is also likely that rainfall associated with hurricanes will increase over time, since a warmer atmosphere tends to hold more moisture.[5]

It is likely that climate change is shifting the location or average tracks of hurricanes further toward the poles; along the Atlantic coast, this will result in hurricanes traveling further north – such as Hurricane Irene in 2011 which caused massive flooding as far north as Vermont – and Hurricane Sandy in 2012, which had a devastating effect on New York and New Jersey. Of course, no one single event can be directly attributed to climate change, but recent large tropical storm systems may be the "wave" of the future.

WHAT'S IN A NAME?

To help identify tropical storms and track them across the ocean, the World Meteorological Organization uses six lists of names in rotation. The name of the first tropical storm of the season begins with the letter "A"; subsequent storms are named in alphabetical order, alternating between male and female names. When the alphabet is depleted, additional storms are named using letters of the Greek alphabet as occurred in 2005 when the last tropical storm of the season was named Epsilon. If a hurricane is particularly deadly or costly, its name is retired and a new name is selected to enter the six-year cycle. Recent "retirees" include Harvey, Irma, Maria, and Nate in 2017 and Florence and Michael in 2018.

SELF-CHECK

- Define **hurricane eye**, **rain band**, **storm surge**, and **landfall**.
- Name the scale used to measure hurricane activity.
- Describe four features of a hurricane that cause damage to property and risk to human life.
- Explain how climate change may affect hurricane activity.

3.3 SEA LEVEL RISE

As the earth's climate changes, global sea levels are rising due to thermal expansion of warming ocean waters, as well as the melting of ice caps and glaciers. As molecules warm, they move more quickly and take up more space. You may have experienced this phenomenon in winter when your car tires are not as inflated after a very cold night. Another easy way to visualize thermal expansion is to take an inflated balloon and hold it over a source of heat; you will see the balloon expand as the air molecules inside move more quickly. Today, the same thing is happening to our oceans at a much larger scale.

Global sea level has risen by about 8 inches since 1880, and the rate has increased in recent years – now rising about 1 inch/decade. This rate of sea level rise is greater than any other period in at least the last 2,800 years. Future predictions of sea level rise depend in part upon actions taken to reduce greenhouse gas emissions. Intermediate scenarios predict sea levels approximately 3 feet higher than they are today, while higher scenarios that assume fewer reductions in emissions predict sea levels more than 6 feet higher.[6]

3.3.1 Relative Sea Level Rise

The amount of sea level rise experienced by a particular community varies depending on local or relative sea level rise. Relative sea level rise is the combination of mean sea level rise and a number of local factors including vertical land movement (subsidence or uplift), changes in tidal ranges, changes in coastal currents, and changes in water temperature. For example, the stretch of coast from Cape Hatteras, NC to New Jersey has much higher rates of relative sea level rise than most of the U.S. Atlantic coast.[7] As a result, the coast north of Cape Hatteras is experiencing sea level rise at up to double the rate of the southern shoreline in North Carolina.[8]

3.3.2 The Impact of Sea Level Rise on Flooding and Storm Surge

The rate of sea level rise is accelerating. Thousands of square miles of low-lying land in areas of the Atlantic and Gulf coasts are at risk of both permanent inundation – when flooding events do not recede – as well as periods of punctuated flooding. Nationwide, it is expected that sea level rise will increase the 100-year floodplain by as much as 45% by the end of the century.[9]

The effects of storm surge and coastal flooding from hurricanes are also greater due to sea level rise. As seas continue to rise because of the warmer ocean expanding and melting ice sheets, the storm surge from hurricanes will ride higher upon seas and can extend farther inland, causing more damage on land. In some coastal states, sea-level rise and storm surge, combined with the pattern of heavy development in coastal areas, are already causing damage to infrastructure such as roads, buildings, ports, and energy facilities.

3.3.3 Sea Level Rise and Saltwater Intrusion

Inundation is not the only impact of sea level rise; coastal communities will also confront saltwater intrusion, failure of septic tanks, and widespread die-offs of plants and crops that are not salt tolerant. These impacts pose serious threat to coastal economies, public health, and the environment.

Saltwater intrusion is the result of seawater infiltrating freshwater aquifers. Some exchange between oceans and coastal aquifers occurs naturally due to the increased mineral content, density, and water pressure of saltwater. Coastal wetlands are at high risk due to the combined effects of sea level rise and inland droughts that reduce freshwater inflows. Damage to these ecosystems has serious implications for water quality, coastal biodiversity, and coastal fisheries. Additionally, as wetlands and saltmarsh are weakened or destroyed by sea level rise, the natural ability of marshes to absorb floodwater and storm surge declines, leaving coastal communities even more vulnerable to these hazards.

3.4 FLOODING

Flooding is the leading cause of weather-related deaths in the United States. It is the most common natural hazard in the country because of the widespread geographical distribution of river valleys and coastal areas and the longstanding attraction of human settlements to these areas. Flooding is generally the result of excessive precipitation that can occur during a thunderstorm, tropical cyclone, or other torrential rainfall. Flooding can also be caused by a dam break or levee failure.

3.4.1 Effects of Climate Change on Flooding

Climate change has a direct influence on rainfall events and subsequent flooding. Since a warmer atmosphere is able to hold more water, global warming leads to increased water vapor in the atmosphere. Storms, whether thunderstorms, rain, snow storms, or tropical cyclones, tend to have more moisture and produce more intense precipitation in a warmer climate. This increases the risk of flooding. Additionally, more precipitation is expected to occur as rain instead of snow, and snow that does fall is likely to melt earlier, increasing the risk of flooding in early spring as snow melts.

3.4.2 Floodplains, River Basins, and Watershed

Before we discuss the characteristics of flood hazards in the United States, we will introduce some of the features associated with rivers and how rivers function as part of the natural ecosystem. Quite frequently, floodwaters rise at a very fast rate because the quantity of water deposited during a particular rain event exceeds the capacity of the river channel to hold such a large volume of water at one time. Sometimes with little warning, rivers overflow their banks, flooding adjacent low-lying areas first. The flat, lower-elevation areas that typically lie to either side of a river or stream that periodically experience this inundation make up the waterway's natural **floodplain**.

- The **floodway** is the central portion of the floodplain, the area with the greatest water velocities and highest depths.
- The **flood fringe** comprises the outer areas on both sides of the floodway and is usually the area of shallower depths and lesser velocities. The flood fringe is also the area that stores water during a flood.
- A **river basin** is the land that water flows across or under on its way to a river. Just as a bathtub catches all the water that falls within its sides, a river basin sends all the water falling on the surrounding land into a central river and out to an **estuary** or the sea. River basins may also be referred to as **catchments**, because they essentially catch, or collect, the water from surrounding higher elevations.

A river basin drains all the land around a major river. Basins can be divided into **watersheds** or areas of land around a smaller river, stream, or lake. The landscape is made up of many interconnected basins or watersheds. Large river basins such as the Mississippi are made up of hundreds of smaller river basins and watersheds. Within each watershed, all water runs to the lowest point, often draining into a stream and then a river and eventually into the ocean. On its way, water that falls as precipitations travels over the surface and across farm fields, forestland, suburban lawns, and city streets as stormwater **runoff**, or it seeps into the soil and travels as **groundwater**.

3.4.3 Types of Flooding

Broadly speaking, floods fall into two categories:

- **Flash floods** are the product of heavy localized precipitation in a short time period over a given location.
- **General floods** are caused by precipitation over a longer time period and over a given river basin.

Flash Flooding

Flash floods occur within a few minutes or hours of heavy amounts of rainfall, a dam or levee failure, or a sudden release of water held by an ice jam. Flash flood waters move at very fast speeds and can roll boulders, tear out trees, destroy buildings, and obliterate bridges. In fact, because of its density, water moving at 10 miles/hour exerts the same pressure on a structure as wind gusts of 270 miles/hour.[10] During a flash flood, cars can easily be swept away in just a few feet of moving water. Heavy rains that produce flash floods can also trigger mudslides, a potentially dangerous secondary hazard.

Most flash flooding is caused by slow-moving thunderstorms, repeated thunderstorms in a local area, or by heavy rains from hurricanes and tropical storms. Although flash flooding often occurs along mountain streams where the terrain is steep, it is also common in urban areas where much of the ground is covered by impervious surfaces. **Impervious surfaces** are hard, paved areas such as roof tops and parking lots, where rainwater cannot soak through to the ground. Instead, the water flows over the surface as runoff until it reaches a drain or low-lying area. Constructed features such as roads and buildings generate greater amounts of runoff than land with natural groundcover like grass, trees, and other vegetation. Flooding can also occur when drainage channels in urban areas are unable to contain the runoff that is generated by relatively small but intense precipitation events.

TRAGEDY ON THE BIG THOMPSON

On July 31, 1976, the Big Thompson River near Denver, Colorado overflowed during an extremely heavy thunderstorm. The canyon through which the Big Thompson flows has very high, steep walls in some places, leaving little opportunity for the soil to absorb precipitation. Usually the winds above the mountains surrounding Big Thompson Canyon are strong enough to blow rainstorms away quickly but this storm was an exception. The storm moved slowly and dropped 8 inches of rain in just 1 hour in a concentrated location and dumped a total of 12 inches during its 2-hour span. As a result, a wall of water 19 feet high roared down the Big Thompson Canyon where people were camping, fishing, and exploring the canyon that afternoon. Tragically, the only egress from the Canyon floor was up its steep sides, so visitors were trapped as the wave of water rushed down the channel. Tragically, 140 people perished in this single flash flooding event.

3.4.4 General Flooding

While flash floods occur within hours of a rain event, general flooding is a longer term event that can last for several days. The primary types of general flooding are riverine flooding, coastal flooding, and urban flooding.

- **Riverine flooding** is a function of precipitation levels and water runoff volumes within the watershed of a stream or river. Periodic flooding of land adjacent to freshwater rivers and streams is a natural, inevitable, and – in the absence of human presence – desirable occurrence. When stream flow exceeds the capacity of the floodway or normal watercourse, some of the above-normal stream flow spills over onto adjacent lands within the floodplain.
- **Coastal flooding** is typically the result of storm surge, wind-driven waves, and heavy rainfall. These conditions are produced by tropical storms – including hurricanes – during the summer and fall, and nor'easters and other large coastal storms during the winter and spring. Storm surges may overrun barrier islands and push seawater up coastal rivers and inlets, blocking the downstream flow of inland runoff. Thousands of acres inland may be inundated by both saltwater and freshwater. Escape routes, particularly those from barrier islands may be cut off quickly, stranding residents in flooded areas and hampering rescue efforts.
- **Urban flooding** occurs where there has been development within the floodplain. In many areas of the country, intense development in the floodplain is a result of the use of waterways for transportation purposes when shipment by water was the major form of moving goods and raw materials. Sites adjacent to rivers and coastal inlets provided convenient places to load and offload commodities and passengers. The price of this accessibility has been increased flooding of the communities that grew up in the surrounding area. Urbanization increases the magnitude and frequency of floods by increasing impervious surfaces, increasing the speed of drainage collection, reducing the carrying capacity of the land, and, occasionally, overwhelming sewer systems.

3.4.5 Flood Mapping

Unlike some other meteorological hazards, areas prone to flooding can be mapped with relative precision, depending upon the extent and accuracy of data gathered about the waterway itself and the surrounding floodplain. Factors that are used to map flood-risk areas include:

- Proximity to the river or stream
- Amount of vegetative cover
- Soil moisture conditions
- Local historic rainfall records
- Topographic features of the area

An assessment of flooding potential requires geospatial data of these factors at a relatively small scale. We need the information at this level of detail because flood hazards vary greatly by location and type.

Flood Insurance Rate Maps (FIRMs)

Much of the flood mapping in the United States is carried out under the National Flood Insurance Program (NFIP) administered by the Federal Emergency Management Agency (FEMA). The NFIP offers federally backed flood insurance to residents in communities that choose to participate in the program by regulating development in the floodplain according to standards established by the NFIP (for a more detailed discussion of the NFIP, see Chapter 6 about the role of the federal government in hazards management).

The NFIP provides **FIRMs** to participating communities to help define the local flood risk. Digital versions of these maps are called DFIRMs. Terminology used on a FIRM includes:

- **Floodway:** the stream channel and the portion of the adjacent floodplain that must remain open to permit passage of the base flood without raising the water surface elevation by more than 1 foot.
- **100-year floodplain:** applies to an area that has a 1% chance, on average, of flooding in any given year. Despite this terminology, a 100-year flood can occur 2 or more years in a row, or once every 10 years. The 100-year flood floodplain is also referred to as the **base flood:** a national standard that represents a compromise between minor floods and the greatest flood likely to occur in a given area. The base flood provides a useful benchmark.
- **Base flood elevation (BFE):** the elevation of the water surface resulting from a flood that has a 1% chance of occurring in any given year. The BFE is the height of the base flood, usually in feet, in relation to a specific datum, such as the National Geodetic Vertical Datum of 1929, or the North American Vertical Datum of 1988.
- **Special flood hazard area (SFHA):** the land area covered by the floodwaters of the base flood is the SFHA on NFIP maps. The SFHA is the area where the NFIP's floodplain management regulations must be enforced and the area where the mandatory purchase of flood insurance applies.
- **500-year flood floodplain:** the area with a 0.2% chance of flooding in any given year.
- **Coastal high hazard areas:** coastal areas that are subject to a velocity hazard (wave action).

FIRMs also show different floodplains with different zone designations. These are primarily for insurance rating purposes, but the zone differentiation can be helpful for other floodplain planning purposes as well. For example:

- Zone A: The 100-year or base floodplain. There are six types of A zones.
- Zones V and VE: The coastal area subject to velocity hazards (e.g., wave action).
- Zone B and X (shaded): Area of moderate flood hazard, usually the area between the limits of the 100- and 500-year floods.
- Zones C or X (unshaded): Areas of minimal flooding hazard.
- Zone D: Area of undetermined but possible flood hazard.

A **Non-SFHA (NSFHA)** is an area in a moderate-to-low risk flood zone. An NSFHA is not in any immediate danger from flooding caused by overflowing rivers or hard rains. However, it's important to note that structures within a NSFHA may still be at risk of flooding. In fact, one out of four floods occurs in an NSFHA.

3.4.6 Localized Flood Risks

Most cities, towns, villages, and counties in the United State have one or more clearly recognizable flood-prone areas, usually along a river, stream, or other large body of water that are designated as the SFHAs on the community's FIRM. These flood-prone areas are targeted by several types of government initiatives to minimize flooding and its impacts. These initiatives include maps, floodplain management criteria, ordinances, and community assistance programs. However, thousands of communities also have shallow, localized flooding problems outside of the SFHA that occur because of poor drainage, inadequate storm sewers, clogged culverts or catch basins, sheet flow, obstructed drainage ways, sewer backup, or overbank flooding from small streams. These kinds of flood events can occur anywhere in a community and can result from even minor rainfall events.

Localized flooding refers to flooding outside the scope of criteria that apply to the SFHA as depicted on a community's FIRM. This includes areas within and outside the B, C, and X zones. Such floods may be referred to as:

- Stormwater flooding
- Nuisance flooding
- Poor drainage
- Ponding

If these localized floods occur infrequently, the problems are minor. However, in some areas localized flooding can be chronic, so that over the years the cumulative damage and recurring disruptions from localized flooding can be more significant than episodic flooding on major rivers and streams. The costs of insuring buildings that are subject to the repeated damage add up as well, and many property owners outside the SFHA do not purchase flood insurance. Even a few inches of water in the basement or ground flood of a building can cause expensive damage, requiring carpeting, wallboard, insulation, mattresses, and upholstered furniture to be disposed of and replaced. Studs, stairs, floorboards, and other wooden parts of a flooded building must be thoroughly cleaned and dried or discarded. Electronics, appliances, papers, and irreplaceable personal possessions (including photographs) are often destroyed. Even minimal amounts of flooding can block streets and disrupt traffic patterns, which can impact areas outside the immediate flood area. Localized flooding also poses health risks from mold and mildew that grows in wet conditions inside homes and buildings.

SELF-CHECK

- Define **floodplain, Special Flood Hazard Area (SFHA),** and **base flood.**
- List the three types of general flooding.
- Cite three factors used to map flood-risk areas.
- Describe how FIRMs are used.

3.5 DROUGHT

Drought is one of the costliest natural hazards affecting the United States. **Drought** is a period of unusually persistent dry weather that lasts long enough to cause serious problems such as crop damage or water supply shortages. The severity of a given drought depends on the degree of moisture deficiency, the duration, and the size of the affected area. However, the impacts are often a result of the combination of the natural event (less precipitation than expected) and the demand communities place on water supply. In this way, human activities can exacerbate the impacts of drought.

Drought can be classified in four ways:

- **Meteorological** drought is a departure of precipitation from normal levels. Due to climatic differences, what might be considered a drought in one location may not be a drought in another.
- **Agricultural** drought refers to a situation where the amount of moisture in the soil no longer meets the needs of a particular crop.
- **Hydrological** drought occurs when surface and subsurface water supplies are below what is considered normal for the area.
- **Socioeconomic** drought refers to the situation that occurs when water shortages begin to affect people. This can happen, for example, when water capture, storage, and delivery do not keep pace with growth and development in a community.

3.5.1 Effects of Climate Change on Drought

There are a number of mechanisms by which climate change influences the likelihood and severity of drought. There has been an increase in drier, hotter areas around the world, particularly in the subtropical band circling the globe which includes the states of Texas, New Mexico, and Arizona.[11] Climate change is also leading to wider swings between wet and dry extremes. Much like a larger bucket, a warmer atmosphere can hold and dump more water but takes longer to refill. Finally, earlier snowmelt as a result of a warming climate can further reduce water availability in the summer and fall.

3.5.2 Impacts of Drought

Periods of drought can have a wide range of environmental, agricultural, health, economic, and social consequences. Sustained lack of moisture can diminish or suspend crop production and damage wildlife habitat. Water quality often suffers during droughts since less water is available to dilute pollutants. In addition, many industrial processes and electricity production rely heavily on water supplies, and their continued operation can be jeopardized by water shortages. Drought also significantly increases the risk of wildfires (discussed in the next section).

BLOWING IN THE WIND

The Dust Bowl of the 1930s, caused by severe drought combined with unsustainable farming methods, was one of the most significant disasters the United States has faced. Following a decade of extensive deep plowing of agricultural land in the Great Plains, the drought of the 1930s caused the loose topsoil to dry out and blow away with the prevailing winds. Millions of acres of farmland were damaged and hundreds of thousands of people were forced to leave their homes in search of new economic opportunities.

With the advent of soil and water conservation districts and concerted efforts of government training initiatives, farming practices following the Dust Bowl were modernized to ensure adequate crop rotation and other forms of resource management were put in place to mitigate the impact of droughts nationwide.

Despite the revolution in farming and advances in resource conservation that were implemented after the Dust Bowl, drought continues to impact farmers and ranchers in the United States. The 2012–2013 North American Drought, caused in part by a lack of snow and reduced meltwater absorbed into the soil, is the most extensive drought affecting the United States in half a century. Roughly 80% of agricultural lands in the United States were impacted, resulting in significantly lower crop yields and reducing the national gross domestic product by an estimated 0.5–1%.

3.5.3 Drought Monitoring

A number of indicators are used to monitor and communicate drought levels. These indicators typically combine variables such as precipitation and temperature. However, since the indicators tend to be climate-based, they do not reflect changes in how drought interacts with human development, such as increasing population density or intense agricultural production that may make the effects of drought worse.

The U.S. National Integrated Drought Information System (NIDIS) was established in 2006 to provide users with the ability to determine the potential impacts of drought and associated risks. Through the U.S. Drought Portal (www.drought.gov), NIDIS makes the U.S. Drought Monitor and a range of other indices and tools available to the public.

SELF-CHECK

- Explain the differences between **meteorological**, **agricultural**, **hydrological**, and **socioeconomic drought**.
- Describe how climate change is influencing drought.
- List three impacts that drought can have on society or the natural environment.

3.6 WILDFIRES

A wildfire is an uncontrolled burning of wilderness or relatively undeveloped areas such as grasslands, brush, or woodlands. The potential for wildfire depends on:

- Recent climate conditions (e.g., drought)
- Current meteorological conditions (high temperature and/or low humidity)
- Sufficient fuel load, including dense forest undergrowth and dead timber

Hot summers with average or below-average rainfalls and extensive dry vegetative groundcover increase susceptibility to fire in the fall, a particularly dangerous time of year for wildfire.

DROUGHT SETS THE STAGE IN COLORADO

A string of wildfires devastated several areas of Colorado in the summer of 2012. The dry conditions of the preceding winter set the stage, with only 13% of the average precipitation. Summer temperatures then exceeded 100°F with relative humidity in the teens and single digits. While thunderstorms and arsonists were likely responsible for the ignition of the blazes, the difficulty in controlling the fires and the extent of damage were largely a result of the prevailing meteorological conditions. Approximately 34,500 residents were evacuated and at least 500 homes were destroyed during the fires that lasted from June through August.

3.6.1 Human Management of Wildfire

Wildfires have taken place as a natural process for many thousands of years, playing an important role in the ecological integrity of our natural environment. Human settlement has significantly influenced changes in the spatial and temporal pattern of wildfire occurrence as well as the associated risks to human life and property. Table 3.3 shows the various approaches to wildfire since early human habitation in North America.

Natural wildfires still take place on a regular basis. They can be caused by human carelessness, arson, or from lightning strikes. Other natural disturbances such as tornadoes and hurricanes can influence the structure and fuel distribution of forests, which can lead to a change in wildfire intensity and risk. Occurrence and frequency of wildfire also relies greatly upon the type of forest surrounding the community.

3.6.2 Measuring Wildfire Risk Conditions

One scale of wildfire risk conditions is measured with the **Keetch-Byram Drought Index (KBDI)**. The KBDI estimates the potential risk for wildfire conditions based on daily temperatures, daily precipitation, and annual precipitation levels on an index of 0 (no drought) to 800 (extreme drought). It is a useful tool for fire fighters, planners, and citizens in understanding the risk of wildfire.

Table 3.3 Fire Regime Time Periods.

Time Period	Fire Description
14,000–500 years ago	American Indians used fire for swidden agriculture, hunting visibility, reduction of wildfire fuel, and maintenance of trails.
500–100 years ago	European settlers used fire to maintain large amounts of permanent agricultural fields at a much greater scale than before.
Late 1800s into early 1900s	Forests were extensively logged, exacerbating conditions for common occurrence of wildfires.
1900–1950s	Response to wildfires was widespread fire suppression.
1950 to Today	Active management; natural role of fire is incorporated through prescribed burning.

3.7 TORNADOES

A **tornado** is a violently rotating column of air extending from the base of a thunderstorm. Tornadoes can also form during hurricanes. These dangerous wind events are sometimes called "funnel storms" or "funnel clouds" because the shape of the rotating column of air is typically wider at the top than at the base. Contrary to popular belief, the tornado funnel does not always touch the ground; a debris cloud beneath a thunderstorm may confirm the presence of a tornado despite the absence of a visible funnel. **Waterspouts**, which are weak tornadoes that form over warm ocean waters, can occasionally move inland to become tornadoes.

3.7.1 Tornado Formation

Tornadoes are spawned by thunderstorms and produced when cool air overrides a layer of warm air, forcing the warm air to rise rapidly. Tornadoes are usually preceded by very heavy rain and, possibly, hail. If hail falls from a thunderstorm it is an indication that the storm has large amounts of energy and may be severe. In general, the larger the hailstorm, the more potential for damaging thunderstorm winds and/or tornadoes.

As powerful as they are, tornadoes account for only a tiny fraction of the energy in a thunderstorm. What makes them dangerous is the energy that is concentrated in a small area, perhaps only a hundred yards across. The damage from a tornado is due to the resulting high **wind velocity**, or speed of the wind as it revolves.

3.7.2 The Fujita-Pearson Tornado Scale

The intensity, path length, and width of tornadoes are rated according to a scale developed in 1971 by T. Theodore Fujita and Allen D. Pearson. Under this scaling system, tornadoes classified as F0-F1 are considered weak tornadoes; those classified as F2-F3 are considered strong, while those classified as F4-F5 are considered violent.

The size of a tornado is not necessarily an indication of its intensity. Large tornadoes can be weak, while small tornadoes can be violent. Tornado intensity may also change during the lifespan of the event. A small tornado may have been larger and is at the "shrinking" stage of its life cycle.

Evidence from past tornadoes suggests that tornadic wind speeds can be as high as 300 miles/hour in the most violent events. Wind speeds that high can cause automobiles to become airborne, rip homes to shreds, and turn broken glass and other debris into lethal missiles. The most serious threat to humans and other living creatures from tornadoes is from flying debris and from being tossed about in the wind.

The Enhanced Fujita Scale

Because of limitations in the original Fujita Scale – which does not recognize differences in construction and can overestimate wind speeds greater than F3 – a team of meteorologists and wind engineers collaborated to develop the **Enhanced Fujita Scale**, which was unveiled

Table 3.4 The Enhanced Fujita Scale.

Fujita Scale		Enhanced Fujita Scale	
F Number	*3 Second Gust (mph)*	*EF Number*	*3 Second Gust (mph)*
0	45–78	0	65–85
1	79–117	1	86–110
2	118–161	2	111–135
3	162–209	3	136–165
4	210–261	4	166–200
5	262–317	5	Over 200

by the National Weather Service in 2007. The Enhanced Fujita Scale can be used to determine an "EF Number" based on 28 separate damage indicators (see Table 3.4). The damage indicators represent typical types of construction, ranging from single-family residences to multistory hotels. Depending upon the type of indicator, specific Degrees of Damage can be identified.

3.7.3 Tornado Activity in the United States

In an average year, more than 1,000 tornadoes are recorded across the United States, resulting in 80 deaths and over 1,500 injuries. The year 2011 was a particularly destructive and deadly year with 1,692 confirmed tornadoes in the United States, resulting in 553 deaths and more than 5,000 injuries. These figures are based on tornado events that are sited and reported. In less populated areas, tornado frequency may be much higher, but the events remain unobserved. Tornadoes can occur in any state but are more frequent in the Midwest, Southeast, and Southwest. Although tornadoes can occur at any time of the year, in the southern states peak tornado season lasts from March until May, while the northern states experience more frequent tornado activity during the summer. Waterspouts are more common in the late fall and winter in the southern states and along the Gulf Coast.

The Effects of Climate Change on Tornado Formation

The tornado outbreak across the southern United States in late April 2011 was deadly, devastating, and record breaking. These days, when the weather breaks records, it's natural to wonder if global warming is to blame. At this point, there is no clear long-term trend connecting climate change to tornadoes. Although some computer models do suggest that climate change could cause conditions to be more favorable for tornado formation in certain regions of the country or shift the timing of tornadoes, it is too early to know if and how tornado activity may be impacted by climate change.

2011 JOPLIN, MISSOURI TORNADO

On May 22, 2011, one of America's deadliest and most costly tornadoes tore through Joplin, Missouri and into portions of Newton and Lawrence counties. The EF-5 tornado, part of a larger tornado outbreak in late-May, was approximately 0.75 miles wide and flattened 8,400 houses, 18,000 cars, and 450 businesses in its 22.1 mile-long track. The tornado also completely destroyed St. John's Regional Medical Center and Joplin High School. In all, 189 people lost their lives from tornado-related injuries. The cost to rebuild Joplin is estimated at $3 billion.

SELF-CHECK

- Define **tornado, wind velocity**, and **waterspout**.
- Discuss the conditions required for the creation of a tornado.
- Name the scale currently used to rate tornadoes.
- Discuss the relationship between the size of a tornado and its strength.

3.8 SEVERE WINTER WEATHER

In contrast to tropical storms such as hurricanes, severe winter storms are **extratropical cyclones**. These storms form outside the tropics, are characterized by fronts, and have their strongest winds within the upper atmosphere. Unlike tropical cyclones that have a center warmer than the surrounding air, the center of extratropical storms is colder. Fueled by strong temperature gradients and an active upper-level jet stream, severe winter storms produce an array of hazardous weather conditions, including:

- Freezing rain
- Wind chill
- Extreme cold
- Snowstorms

Blizzards, which can involve a combination of all of these hazards, pack a major snowstorm into one cold, windy, low-visibility event. The following sections give a brief description of each of these severe winter weather hazards.

3.8.1 Blizzards

A **blizzard** is a snowstorm characterized by low temperatures (usually below 20°F) that is accompanied by winds that are at least 35 miles/hour or greater. In addition, there must also be sufficient falling and/or blowing snow in the air. This airborne snowfall contributes significantly to the danger posed by a blizzard, as visibility can be reduced to 0.25 mile or less for 3 hours or longer. A **severe blizzard** is considered to have temperatures at or below 10°F, winds exceeding 45 miles/hour, and visibility reduced to near zero.

Blizzard conditions often develop on the northwest side of an intense storm system. The difference between the lower pressure in the storm and the higher pressure to the west creates a tight pressure gradient, which in turn results in very strong winds. These winds combine with snow and blowing snow to produce extreme conditions. Storm systems powerful enough to cause blizzards usually form when the jet stream dips far to the south, allowing cold air from the north to clash with warm air from the south. With the colder and drier polar air comes an atmospheric temperature cold enough for the development of snow, sleet, or freezing rain. A few of the notable blizzard events in the United States are listed in Table 3.5.

Table 3.5 Notable Blizzard Events in the United States.

Name of Storm	Date	Details
The "Knickerbocker" Storm	January 1922	This blizzard took place in Washington, DC and caused the roof of the Knickerbocker Theater to collapse, killing almost 100 people.
The New York City Storm	February 1969	There was so much snow in the city that even the snow plows were buried in snow, forcing the city to employ 10,000 workers to clear the streets with shovels.
The Buffalo Storm	February 1977	Areas surrounding western New York state and Ontario, Canada were hit by a blizzard that killed 28, shut down Buffalo, and stranded thousands of people in their cars on the highway.
The Blizzard of the Century	March 1993	This storm took place across a wide area of the eastern United States, from Alabama to Massachusetts. Snowfall rates of between 1 and 2 inches/hour took place in many areas.
The Blizzard of 1996	January 1996	This January blizzard took place in the northeastern United States and was the cause of over 100 deaths.
North American Blizzard of 2010 ("Snowmageddon")	February 2010	"Snowmageddon" was a Category 3 nor'easter that dropped more than 35 inches of snow in some areas and resulted in at least 41 fatalities between the United States and Mexico.

3.8.2 Snowstorms

Snow is frozen precipitation in the form of a six-sided ice crystal, commonly known as the snowflake. **Snowstorm** is the phrase used to describe any storm with heavy snow.

Snow requires temperatures to be below freezing in all or most of the atmosphere, from the surface up to cloud level. Snow can fall when surface temperatures are above freezing and form a relatively shallow layer on the ground. Under these conditions, the snow will not have enough time to melt before reaching the ground; the snow will be quite wet and contain large flakes, the result of wet snow crystals sticking to one another to form larger flakes. Generally, 10 inches of snow will melt into one inch of water. Sometimes the snow-liquid ratio may be much higher – on the order of 20:1 or 30:1. This commonly happens when snow falls into a very cold air mass, with temperatures of 20°F or less at ground-level.

High-impact snowstorms in the Northeastern United States are ranked according to the **Northeast Snowfall Impact Scale (NESIS)**, developed by Paul Kocin of The Weather Channel and Louis Uccellini of the National Weather Service. NESIS consists of five categories of storms in descending order of severity: Extreme, Crippling, Major, Significant, and Notable. The scale rates storms that have large areas of 10-inch snowfall accumulations or greater. A score is assigned to each area affected by the snowstorm as a function of the amount of snow, the area impacted, and the number of people in the path of the storm. Because the score includes population data, the index gives an indication of a storm's societal impacts.

Table 3.6 NESIS Categories.

Category	NESIS Value	Description
1	1–2.499	Notable
2	2.5–3.99	Significant
3	4–5.99	Major
4	6–9.99	Crippling
5	10.0+	Extreme

NESIS categories, their corresponding NESIS values, and descriptive adjective are displayed in Table 3.6.

3.8.3 Freezing Rain

Freezing rain or freezing drizzle is rain or drizzle that occurs when surface temperatures are below freezing. The moisture falls in liquid form but freezes upon impact, resulting in a coating of ice or glaze on all exposed surfaces. **Sleet** is precipitation that falls as frozen water or becomes frozen before it hits the ground.

Freezing rain is caused when there is a warm mass of air in the middle altitudes between the ground and the cloud deck and a mass of freezing air near the surface. When the precipitation falls from the cloud, it will generally be snow. As it encounters the warm air it will melt to form rain. The melted snowflake then falls through the shallow freezing layer without refreezing into sleet. As the precipitation reaches ground level, it enters air at below-freezing temperatures and quickly turns to ice. As a result, when the liquid droplets encounter exposed objects at the surface they freeze upon contact.

Some ice events (up to and including ice storms) are the result of cold air damming (CAD). CAD is a shallow, surface-based layer of relatively cold, stably-stratified air entrenched against the eastern slopes of the Appalachian Mountains. With warmer air above, falling precipitation in the form of snow melts, then becomes either supercooled (liquid below the melting point of water) or refreezes. In the former case, supercooled droplets can freeze on impact (freezing rain), which in the latter case, the refrozen water particles form ice pellets, or sleet.

3.8.4 Wind Chill and Extreme Cold

A **cold wave** is an unusual fall in temperature to the freezing point or below, exceeding 16°F in 24 hours or 20°F in 36 hours. What constitutes extreme cold varies across different regions of the United States. In areas unaccustomed to winter weather, near-freezing temperatures are considered extreme cold. In contrast, the more northern and mountainous states require much lower temperatures for conditions to be considered extreme cold.

- **Wind chill factor** describes what happens to the human body when there is a combination of cold and wind. As wind increases, heat is carried away from the body at a faster rate, driving down skin temperature (which can cause frostbite) and eventually the internal body temperature (which can cause death).
- **Wind chill temperature** is a measure of the combined cooling effect of wind and ambient air temperature. Wind chill temperature is a unit of measurement used to describe the wind chill factor.

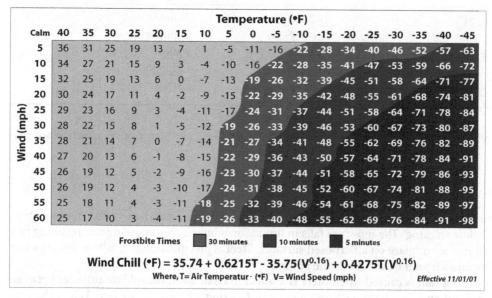

Figure 3.3 NOAA has developed the wind chill index to show how wind speed and temperature combine to create a wind chill effect, including the amount of time it can take for frostbite to occur. (NOAA National Weather Service.)

Figure 3.3 is a wind chill chart that shows the amount of time it takes for humans to develop frostbite given different wind chill temperatures (see following section for definition of frostbite).

3.8.5 Effects of Climate Change on Severe Winter Weather

Climate change is likely to impact winter weather in substantially different ways depending on the region. As temperatures rise, the atmosphere is able to hold more moisture, resulting in more intense precipitation events. In mid-winter, this may translate into heavier snowfalls and more severe winter weather, assuming that the temperature is still below freezing. However, at the beginning and end of the snow season, and in communities with winter temperatures near freezing, it is likely that the warmer temperatures associated with climate change will lead to more rainfall events rather than snow.

Over the past century, the northeastern United States has experienced a dramatic increase in one-day precipitation extremes during the cold season from October to March. This observed trend is consistent with predictions about the effects of climate change on severe winter weather.

3.8.6 Impacts of Severe Winter Weather

The dangers posed by severe winter weather are generally threefold:

- The cold wet conditions can be extremely hazardous to the health of people and animals that are exposed for prolonged periods of time.

- Driving conditions become hazardous as roads, bridges, and overpasses become slick or impassable due to accumulation of snow and ice.
- Power outages can occur when power lines are coated with ice or are knocked down by falling tree limbs.

On average, winter weather claims nearly 100 lives each year in the United States; the majority of these fatalities can be directly attributable to the impacts of winter storms. About 70% of all winter-related deaths occur in motor vehicle accidents caused by hazardous driving conditions, while nearly 25% are due to prolonged exposure to snow and cold. A significant percentage of winter weather-related deaths are due to heart attacks caused by overexertion while shoveling snow. Deaths have also occurred as a result of poisonous fumes released by generators, propane heaters, gas stoves, and charcoal grills when power outages force people to improvise alternate sources of heat and cooking for their homes. Without adequate ventilation in enclosed spaces, these devices can prove deadly within a matter of hours.

Dangers to human health from exposure to extremely cold conditions include frostbite and hypothermia.

- **Frostbite** is a severe reaction to cold exposure that can permanently damage body extremities. A loss of feeling and a white or pale appearance of fingers, toes, nose, and ear lobes are symptoms of frostbite.
- **Hypothermia** is a condition brought on when internal human body temperature drops below 95°F. Symptoms of hypothermia include uncontrollable shivering, slow speech, memory lapses, frequent stumbling, drowsiness, and exhaustion.

WINTER WEATHER DOWN ON THE FARM

Heavy accumulation of ice can bring down trees, electrical wires, telephone poles and lines, and cell phone towers, disrupting communications and power for days. The massive ice storm of January 1998 covered the St. Lawrence River Valley with a veneer of solid ice. Although the destructive storm hit a region accustomed to severe winter weather, it left more than 4 million people without electricity, including a large number of the area's farmers. Because many of these rural farms were not equipped with generators, livestock suffered (see Photo 3.1). Many lessons were learned from this event about rural emergency preparedness, planning, and action. Today, many more farms and rural homeowners have generators stored in preparation for the next winter event.

SELF-CHECK

- Define **extratropical cyclone, blizzard, severe blizzard, snowstorm, wind chill factor,** and **hypothermia.**
- List four conditions created by severe winter storms.
- Discuss the difference between a snowstorm and a blizzard.
- Name three dangers that severe winter weather pose.

Photo 3.1 Cattle and livestock had a difficult time staying warm and finding food during severe winter weather in Kansas in 2007. Farmers had to airlift hay to animals in the field. (Image courtesy of Liz/Roll, FEMA.)

3.9 EXTREME HEAT

Extreme heat, often referred to as a heat wave, is a prolonged period of excessively hot weather, which may be accompanied by high humidity. While specific definitions vary, it is generally characterized by at least three consecutive days with temperatures that exceed 90–100°F.

In addition to high temperatures, relative humidity can increase the risk of health-related problems such as sunstroke or heat stroke. The National Weather Service **Heat Index** combines the air temperature and relative humidity to estimate the **apparent temperature**, or the perceived outdoor temperature, to help emergency managers, public health workers, and individuals understand the potential risks from extreme heat.

3.9.1 Impacts of Extreme Heat

The effects of extreme heat can be profound, leading to public health emergency, damaging infrastructure, causing power outages, increasing the risk of wildfire, and may even lead to an increase violent crime. Every year, a large number of hospitalizations and deaths are connected to extreme heat. In fact, an average of 400 deaths in the United States each year are directly related to heat, a higher mortality rate than any other natural hazard in this country.[12] Older adults, very young children, and those who are sick or overweight are at a higher risk for heat-related illnesses, which include heat exhaustion, heat stroke, dehydration, and heat rash.

Additionally, public health researchers expect that heat-related mortality may be much greater because of underreporting heat as causing or contributing to death.

3.9.2 Urban Heat Island

People living in urban areas are often at higher risk than those in rural areas, particularly as stagnant warm air can trap pollutants in urban areas and cause problems for people with respiratory difficulties. Additionally, materials in urban environments like asphalt and concrete can store heat longer and gradually release it overnight, resulting in much higher nighttime temperatures than typically occur in rural areas. This phenomenon of urban areas being warmer than rural areas due to human activities is referred to as the **urban heat island** effect.

The 1995 Chicago heat wave was one of the worst in United States history. The excessively high heat index, measured as high as 125°F, led to approximately 750 heat-related deaths over a period of five days. Most of the victims were the elderly poor living in the heart of the city, many of whom did not have air conditioning or could not afford to turn it on. Fear of crime also made many older citizens resistant to opening windows and doors at night, contributing to the tragedy.

With climate change, temperatures will rise in many areas of the country, and extreme heat events are expected to become more prevalent – particularly in the Southeast. More extreme heat means:

- More intense and frequent heat waves or consecutive high-temperature days, when temperatures do not drop at night.
- An increased number of very hot days throughout the year.
- An increase in seasonal average temperatures. Future climate projections include shorter cool seasons and longer warm seasons, with an increase in average temperature during both.

SELF-CHECK

- Define **extreme heat, heat index, and apparent temperature**.
- Explain the cause of the urban heat island effect.
- Discuss the populations and groups who tend to be most vulnerable to extreme heat.

SUMMARY

This chapter covers some of the most prevalent – and destructive – meteorological and hydrological hazards of the United States. The combination of intense hurricane activity and intense human activity along the coast has resulted in greater loss of life and property than ever before. Similarly, where humans choose to live often leaves them more vulnerable to riverine, urban, and coastal flooding. Conversely, unusually dry or hot conditions can stress communities, infrastructure, and the natural environment and lead to a range of disasters resulting from drought, wildfire, and extreme heat. This chapter also covered the dangerous effects of tornadoes and severe winter weather hazards. Ultimately, a greater knowledge of all of these weather-related hazards will enable us to lessen their impacts on our lives and communities.

KEY TERMS

100-year floodplain: An area with a 1% chance of flooding in any given year.
500-year floodplain: An area with a 0.2% chance of flooding in any given year.
Base flood: The 100-year flood floodplain as shown on a community's FIRM.

Base flood elevation (BFE): The elevation of the water surface resulting from a flood that has a 1% chance of occurring in any given year as shown on a community's FIRM.

Blizzard: Snowstorm characterized by low temperatures and accompanied by winds that are at least 35 miles/hour.

Catchment: A river basin, or the area surrounding a river that collects water from higher surrounding elevations.

Coastal erosion: The wearing away of the shoreline along the ocean.

Coastal flooding: Flood event that is the result of storm surge, wind-driven waves, and heavy rainfall.

Coastal high hazard area: Areas that are subject to a velocity hazard (wave action).

Cold wave: An unusual fall in temperature, to or below the freezing point, exceeding 16°F in 24 hours or 20°F in 36 hours.

Enhanced Fujita Scale: An updated tornado index based on the Fujita scale that incorporates 28 damage indicators and degrees of damage estimates to more clearly classify tornado intensity during a tornado event.

Estuary: A semi-enclosed area where fresh water from a river meets salty water from the sea.

Extratropical cyclones: Storms that form outside the tropics; severe winter storms.

Eye: Calm center of a hurricane.

Flash flood: A flood event occurring with little or no warning where water levels rise at an extremely fast rate.

Flood fringe: The area on both sides of the floodway with lower depths and velocities. The flood fringe stores water during a flood.

Flood Insurance Rate Map (FIRM): Map of a community that shows both the SFHAs and the risk premium zones applicable to the community. D-FIRMs are digitized versions of the flood maps. Official FIRMs and D-FIRMs are issued by FEMA.

Floodplain: Low-laying flat areas that typically lie to either side of a river or stream.

Floodway: The central portion of the floodplain with the greatest water velocities and highest depths.

Freezing rain: Moisture falling in liquid form that freezes upon impact when surface temperatures are below freezing.

Frostbite: A severe reaction to cold exposure that can permanently damage its victims.

General flood: Flood event caused by precipitation over an extended period and over a given river basin.

Groundwater: The water found in cracks and pores in sand, gravel, and rocks below the earth's surface.

Hurricane: An intense tropical cyclone, formed in the atmosphere over warm ocean waters, in which wind speeds reach 74 miles/hour or more and blow in a large spiral around a relatively calm center or "eye."

Hydrological hazards: Weather event that occurs as part of the Earth's water systems.

Hypothermia: A condition brought on when the body temperature drops below 95°F.

Impervious surface: Hard areas, such as pavement or rooftops, where water cannot soak through to the ground.

Inland flooding: A hazard event where river and streams overflow as a hurricane or storm system moves across land.

Keetch-Byram Drought Index (KBDI): Scale of fire conditions that estimates the potential risk for wildfire based on daily temperatures, daily precipitation, and annual precipitation levels on an index of 0 (no drought) to 800 (extreme drought).

Landfall: The point where a hurricane crosses the coastline from the ocean.

Major hurricane: Categories 3, 4, and 5 hurricanes; often the most potentially dangerous.

Meteorological hazards: Weather event that occurs because of processes in the Earth's atmosphere.

Northeast Snowfall Impact Scale (NESIS): Scale used to characterize and rank high-impact snowstorms in the Northeast United States.

Rain band: A spiraling arm of rain radiating out from the eye of a hurricane.

River basin: The area surrounding a river that collects water from higher surrounding elevations; the drainage area of a river.

Riverine flooding: Flood event that is a function of precipitation levels and runoff volumes within the watershed of a stream or river.

Runoff: Water that is unable to soak through impervious surfaces such as rooftops or pavement.

Severe blizzard: Snowstorm with temperatures near or below 10°F, winds exceeding 45 miles/hour, and visibility reduced by snow to near zero.

Sleet: Ice pellets.

Snowstorms: Any storm with heavy snow.

Special Flood Hazard Area (SFHA): An area within a floodplain having a 1% or greater chance of flood occurrence in any given year (100-year floodplain); represented on Flood Insurance Rate Maps by darkly shaded areas with zone designations that include the letter A or V.

Storm surge: Rise in the water surface above the normal water level on the open coast due to the action of wind stress and atmospheric pressure on the water surface.

Storm tide: The combination of a hurricane's surge and the normal tide.

Tornado: A violently rotating column of air extending from the base of a thunderstorm.

Tropical cyclones: Storms that form in the tropics; includes hurricanes and other less intense storms.

Urban flooding: Flood event that occurs where there has been development within the floodplain.

Water force: The wave action of water during a hurricane that makes flooding particularly destructive.

Watershed: All the land drained by a river, stream, or lake; many watersheds make up a river basin.

Waterspout: Weak tornadoes that form over warm ocean waters.

Wildfire: An uncontrolled burning of grasslands, brush, or woodlands.

Wind velocity: The speed of wind.

Wind chill factor: As wind increases, heat is carried away from the body at a faster rate, making temperatures feel colder.

Wind chill temperature: Unit of measurement to describe wind chill factor.

ASSESS YOUR UNDERSTANDING

Summary Questions

1. Weather-related natural hazards can be classified as either meteorological or hydrological. True or False?
2. Which of the following is not a prevalent hazard in the United States?
   a. Drought
   b. Storm surge
   c. Waterspout
   d. Tsunami

3. A hurricane begins as a
   a. Waterspout
   b. Tropical storm
   c. Tropical depression
   d. Tornado
4. A hurricane's severity is measured on a scale of 1–6. True or False?
5. Hurricane velocity increases after landfall. True or False?
6. The current trend in hurricane landfalls is
   a. Steady
   b. Decreasing
   c. Increasing
   d. Difficult to determine
7. The World Meteorological Organization relies on Greek names to identify tropical storms and hurricanes. True or False?
8. A catchment is the same as a:
   a. River basin
   b. Streambed
   c. Flood hazard zone
   d. Floodplain
9. Flash flooding is common in urban areas. True or False?
10. Flood maps are created using
    a. Soil moisture conditions
    b. Topographic features
    c. Proximity to a river
    d. All of the above
11. Which of the following is the most damaging effect of a tornado?
    a. Lightning
    b. Hail
    c. Wind velocity
    d. Heavy rain
12. A small tornado can cause less damage than a large tornado. True or False?
13. Severe winter storms are tropical cyclones. True or False?
14. Blizzard conditions are characterized by extreme cold and wind. True or False?
15. Wind chill factor is
    a. A unit of measurement to describe wind speed
    b. The wind temperature during a cold wave
    c. The air temperature during a winter storm
    d. How a combination of cold and wind affects the human body
16. Frostbite and hypothermia exhibit similar symptoms. True or False?

Review Questions

1. Hurricanes can affect more than just coastal areas. Explain how.
2. When is hurricane season in the United States?
3. Hurricanes typically involve more than one destructive feature. List the six characteristic threats of a hurricane.
4. According to the Saffir-Simpson Scale, what are the hurricane categories and the corresponding levels used to describe them?
5. When a river overflows, floodwater first moves into the surrounding low-lying, flat areas. What is the name of this area?

6. Flash floods can occur in mountains or urban areas. Explain the role of impervious surfaces in a flash flood.
7. Coastal areas often face the threat of flooding. Name three different ways that coastal communities can be flooded during a storm.
8. Define a tornado. How is a tornado different from a hurricane, and how are they related?
9. Name the scale used to rate tornadoes and give the range for classification.
10. Explain how climate change may cause us to experience both more frequent flooding *and* more frequent drought, as well as seasons that may be both hotter *and* colder than we have experienced in the past.
11. Severe winter weather can be very dangerous. How does wind chill affect human safety during winter weather?
12. What are three dangers that officials must be concerned about during a winter storm?

Applying This Chapter

1. Using the list of the most prevalent meteorological and hydrological hazards in the United States, pick the 10 hazards that most apply to where you live and put them in order of most likely to least likely to occur.
2. Working with the list of 10 hazards for your community, consider the likely impact each event could have on the community.
3. Imagine that a hurricane with maximum sustained winds of 125 miles/hour were to strike your area (whether or not you live in a hurricane-prone region). Examine your neighborhood to see how it would be affected.
4. Assume you are an official of a town on a barrier beach island on the Gulf Coast. A large hotel and resort has brought much-needed tourism to the area, along with a boom in real estate development. Using the example of a real community that was hit hard by a hurricane, draft an introduction to a presentation you'll give about why development should be carefully regulated in hazard areas.
5. Assume that you are an insurance agent in an area that has not experienced serious flood damage in more than 25 years. How could you begin to convince your clients of their needs to buy flood insurance for their homes? What kind of information could you provide to them?
6. If a tornado with winds of 115 miles/hour were to hit your community, what level of tornado would it be, and what kind of damage would be likely? Which buildings would be especially vulnerable?
7. Compare the potential effects of a blizzard to those of an EF2 tornado. Which elements are different? Which are the same?
8. With wind speeds of 40 miles/hour and a temperature of 0°F, calculate the wind chill and explain what that means for someone who has left his or her broken-down car in a storm to walk an undetermined distance for help.

You Try It

Find Your Ecological Address

Even if you don't live on the waterfront, the land around your house drains into a river, estuary, or lake somewhere nearby. What river basin are you located in? Into what river or stream does your land eventually drain? Does the water running off your property enter a storm drain, a ditch, or an open field? How fast does runoff enter local streams? How much of the area is paved or covered with hard surfaces such as roads or rooftops?

Flooded with Information

Evaluate your risk of experiencing a flood where you live. Which type of flooding are you most vulnerable to? You can get more information about floods and estimate your flood risk and your insurance premium from the FEMA National Flood Insurance Program Flood Smart website: www.floodsmart.gov.

Communicating Hazard Threats

Select one threatened area or population of your community and come up with ideas for how to prepare for a potential natural hazard. For example, consider aging mobile homes that you feel could not withstand a serious wind event. What information would you provide to members of your community and how would you make it available?

Winter Storms: The Deceptive Killers

Imagine that you'll be spending a winter in Buffalo, New York, an area that can be crippled by intense lake-effect snows. Where will you be when disaster strikes? At work, at school, or in the car? A severe storm event may confine you to your home or force you to evacuate. What would you do if basic services – water, gas, electricity, or telephones – were cut off? Using the following NOAA and FEMA websites, prepare a disaster plan for you/or your family: http://www.ready.gov/make-a-plan & www.nws.noaa.gov/om/brochures/wntrstm.htm.

REFERENCES

1. Smith, A., N. Lott, T. Houston, K. Shein, J. Crouch, J. Enloe. 2021. *U.S. Billion-Dollar Weather & Climate Disasters 1980-2020*. National Oceanic and Atmospheric Administration. http://www.ncdc.noaa.gov/billions/events.pdf.
2. National Oceanic and Atmospheric Administration. 2018. Inland Flooding: A Hidden Danger of Tropical Cyclones. National Oceanic and Atmospheric Administration. https://www.noaa.gov/stories/inland-flooding-hidden-danger-of-tropical-cyclones.
3. Blake, E.S. et al. 2007. *NOAA Technical Memorandum NWS TPC5*. Miami, FL: National Hurricane Center.
4. National Hurricane Center. *Tropical Cyclone Climatology*. Miami, FL: National Oceanic and Atmospheric Administration, National Hurricane Center. http://www.nhc.noaa.gov/climo/.
5. Geophysical Flouid Dynamics Laboratory. 2020. *Global Warming and Hurricanes. An Overview of Current Research Results*. Princeton, NJ: Geophysical Flouid Dynamics Laboratory. https://www.gfdl.noaa.gov/global-warming-and-hurricanes/.
6. USGCRP. 2017. Climate Science Special Report: Fourth National Climate Assessment, Volume I. Washington, DC. U.S. Global Change Research Program https://science2017.globalchange.gov/chapter/12/.
7. Sallenger, A.H., K.S. Doran, and P.A. Howd. 2012. *Hotspot of Accelerated Sea-Level Rise on the Atlantic Coast of North America*. Nature Climate Change 2(12): 884–888.
8. Neumann, J. et al. 2000. *Sea-Level Rise and Global Climate Change. A Review of Impacts to U.S. Coasts*. Washington, DC: Pew Center.
9. Denchak, M. 2019. *Flooding and Climate Change: Everything You Need to Know*. New York, NY: Natural Resources Defense Council.
10. Emergency Management Institute. 2007. Floodplain management: Principles and current practices. Chapter 2: Types of floods and floodplains. *Academic Emergency Management and Related Courses for the Higher Education Program*. Emmitsburg, MD: Emergency Management Institute.
11. Dai, A. 2010. *Drought under Global Warming: A Review*. WIREs Climate Change 2(1): 45–65.
12. Basu, R. and J.M. Samet. 2002. *Relation between Elevated Ambient Temperature and Mortality: A Review of the Epidemiologic Evidence*. Epidemiologic Review 24(2): 190–202.

4

Geologic Hazards

Earthquakes, Tsunamis, Volcanoes, Landslides, Coastal Erosion, and Land Subsidence

What You'll Learn

- Different types of geologic hazards
- Causes of various geologic hazards
- Impacts of various geologic hazards
- Scales used to measure and rate earthquakes
- The consequence of excessive groundwater removal
- Ways that human activity may cause geologic hazards

Goals and Outcomes

- Become familiar with the terminology that applies to geologic hazards
- Compare geologic events according to magnitude and intensity
- Evaluate how certain geologic events are connected
- Compare the potential impacts of major geologic hazards on a community
- Consider effective ways to inform communities about geologic hazards
- Predict the risk of geologic hazards for an area using knowledge of past occurrences
- Evaluate decisions made about real communities based on geologic research

INTRODUCTION

Many geologic hazards share one thing in common: the buildup of pressure over time. In this chapter, we describe several geologic hazards that have serious consequences for humans. Earthquakes, which can have far-ranging and catastrophic effects, are examined in detail. The chapter also covers tsunamis, volcanoes, landslides, land subsidence, and sink holes, and the potential impacts these hazards can have on communities. The implications of coastal erosion are discussed in relation to patterns of building and human activity. Finally, the chapter also touches on ways human activity may lead to some types of geologic events, including mining, fracking, subsurface withdrawal of water, oil, and gas, as well as underground injection of wastewater.

DOI: 10.4324/9781003123897-4

4.1 GEOLOGIC HAZARDS

The Earth is composed of the core, mantle, and crust.

- The **crust** is a relatively thin layer on the surface, extending to about 5 kilometers (3.1 miles) below the oceans and about 30 kilometers (18.6 miles) beneath the continents.
- The **mantle** is the middle layer, approximately 2900 kilometers (1802 miles) thick.
- The **core** is the innermost region of the Earth, over 3500 kilometers (2175 miles) thick.

Much of the action associated with the geologic hazards described in this chapter occurs in the mantle, but it greatly affects the crust, the most brittle layer on which we live. This chapter describes geologic hazards that occur at the mercy of these shifting layers over time, posing threats to both people and property. It is important to gain at least a basic understanding of the science behind these hazards to take steps to protect our communities from their impacts.

SELF-CHECK

- Define **crust**, **mantle**, and **core**
- List five geologic hazards that are related to the Earth's shifting layers

---

4.2 EARTHQUAKES

The Greek word *seismos* means to quake; **seismology** is the study of earthquakes. Earthquakes are geologic events that involve movement or shaking of the Earth's crust and upper mantle, otherwise known as the **lithosphere**. The upper part of the mantle is cooler and more rigid than the deep mantle below it; thus, it behaves similarly to the overlying crust. The two layers together are broken into the moving plates that contain the continents and oceans. It is the movement of these thin **tectonic plates** that is so influential in an earthquake.

4.2.1 Tectonic Plate Movement

Earthquakes are usually caused by the release of stresses accumulated as a result of the rupture of lithosphere rocks along opposing boundaries, or **fault planes**, in the crust. These fault planes are typically found along borders of the Earth's tectonic plates. The plate borders often follow the outlines of the continents. The edge of the North American plate aligns with the continental border with the Pacific Ocean in the west but follows the mid-Atlantic trench in the east.

On average tectonic plates move only a few inches a year. However, when the seven large plates that encompass entire continents and giant portions of oceans move in opposing directions, a few inches can be highly significant.

The areas of greatest tectonic instability occur at the perimeters of the slowly moving plates because these locations are subject to the greatest strains from plates traveling in opposite directions and at different speeds. Deformation along plate boundaries causes strain in the rock and the consequent buildup of stored energy.

Tectonic plate activity can be thought of as a constant arm wrestling match underneath our feet, with each side exerting tremendous force against the other. Eventually the built-up stress exceeds the rocks' strength and a rupture occurs. When the rock on both sides of the fault snaps, it releases the stored energy by producing **seismic waves**. These waves are what cause the ground to shake in an earthquake.

4.2.2 Earthquake Motion

The variables that characterize earthquakes are ground motion, surface faulting, ground failure, and seismic activity. **Ground motion** is the vibration or shaking of the ground during an earthquake. When a fault ruptures, seismic waves radiate, causing the ground to vibrate. The severity of the vibration increases with the amount of energy released and decreases with the distance from the causative fault, or **epicenter**. Accordingly, damage is generally most severe at or near the epicenter, although this is not always the case.

- **Surface faulting** is the differential movement of two sides of a fracture – the location where the ground breaks apart. The length, width, and displacement of the ground characterize surface faults.
- **Liquefaction** is the phenomenon that occurs when ground shaking causes loose soils to lose strength and act like viscous fluids. Liquefaction causes two types of ground failure: lateral spread and loss of bearing strength.
- **Lateral spreads** develop on gentle slopes and entail the sidelong movement of large masses of soil as an underlying layer liquefies.
- **Loss of bearing strength** results when soil liquefies, causing buildings and other structures to tip and even topple over.

4.2.3 Aftershocks

Earthquakes can occur in sequence. The first impact is generally the strongest, but **aftershocks** or subsequent earthquakes may follow. Aftershocks usually occur within two days following the initial quake but may continue for weeks, months, or even years. Their size, strength, and frequency usually diminish with time. If an aftershock is larger than the main shock, the aftershock is redesignated as the main shock and the original main shock is redesignated as a **foreshock**.

Why do aftershocks occur? Even though the major strain between two plates is released by the initial quake, their touching edges still need to adjust to new positions to release additional pressure that has built up from movement of plates. The edges may not be able to pass each other smoothly, and this additional realignment creates the smaller shocks.

When the Earth's plates finally stop grinding against each other, the surface landscape may have changed over huge areas around the earthquake's center. This happened after the 1906 earthquake in San Francisco, California, when a piece of land 430 kilometers (267 miles) long shifted north by 6 meters (20 feet). Aftershocks can be very destructive. They are often of sufficient intensity to crumble roads, bridges, and buildings that had been weakened by the initial earth movement.

4.2.4 Rating Earthquakes: Scales of Magnitude, Intensity, and Acceleration

Seismologists use several different standardized scales to measure the severity of earthquakes. These include the moment magnitude scale, the modified Mercalli intensity (MMI) scale, and the peak ground acceleration (PGA) scale.

Measuring Magnitude

Magnitude is the most common way of measuring the strength of an earthquake. Because it is a measurement at the source of the fault, magnitude does not change as you get farther away, even if there is less shaking. A **seismograph**, an instrument that records the amplitude of the seismic waves, is used to measure an earthquake's magnitude. Multiple seismic stations, which make up a seismographic network, are able to precisely measure the magnitude of earthquakes.

Historically, magnitude was described using the **Richter scale**, an open-ended logarithmic scale that describes the energy release of an earthquake through a measure of shock wave amplitude. Although people often still refer to the Richter scale, this is an outdated method for measuring magnitude because it only measures one of multiple waves resulting from an earthquake.

The U.S. Geological Survey, the scientific agency most involved in earthquake research and measurement, currently uses the **moment magnitude scale** to measure the size of earthquakes. The moment magnitude scale, which can also be measured with seismographs, is based on the slip on a fault multiplied by the area of the fault surface that slips, which gives a better estimate of the total energy released in the earthquake.

Because these measures of magnitude use a logarithmic scale, the increase of one unit of magnitude is equivalent to an increase in 10 times the amplitude recorded by a seismograph, which in turn is equivalent to approximately 30 times the energy! For this reason, even an increase of 0.1 can have a significant impact in terms of the energy and resulting damage of an earthquake.

Measuring Intensity with the Modified Mercalli Intensity Scale

The measurement of earthquake *magnitude* does not specifically address various levels of damage that could result from an earthquake event. Damage potential is measured by **intensity**. Earthquake intensity is most commonly measured using the MMI scale, a 12-level scale based on direct and indirect measurements of seismic effects. The scale levels are typically described using roman numerals, ranging from 1 (imperceptible) to 12 (catastrophic).

A detailed description of the MMI scale of earthquake intensity is shown in Table 4.1. The MMI scale incorporates the types of damages that can be expected with various earthquake intensities (see Table 4.1).

Peak Ground Acceleration

PGA is a measure of the strength of ground movements at a given location. Unlike measures of magnitude that describe the overall energy released from an earthquake, PGA describes how hard the earth shakes at a given point. Damage to buildings and infrastructure is most closely related to the ground acceleration – both horizontally and vertically. Therefore, PGA is commonly used within the field of engineering and in the development of seismic building codes to help design structures that can withstand a given amount of ground acceleration.

4.2.5 Earthquake Impacts on People and Property

Direct impacts from earthquakes include damage to structures and infrastructure, such as buildings, pipelines, roadways, and bridges. Impacts to a community from an earthquake event can include injury and death; loss of vital services including electricity, gas, and communications systems; lost revenue and economic damages; and increased demand on public safety, health and emergency facilities, and critical government services. Secondary impacts are common following earthquakes and include fire, loss of water supply and water pressure, hazardous material releases, explosions of gas and other flammable material, and related incidents. Earthquakes can also trigger tsunamis and landslides.

Most injuries and deaths, as well as the majority of property damage from an earthquake, are caused by ground shaking. Hard, brittle structures such as buildings and roadways tend to break and crack when they are forced to move due to the underlying ground movement.

Table 4.1 Modified Mercalli Scale of Earthquake Intensity.

Scale	Intensity	Description of Effects	Maximum Acceleration (mm/s)	Approximate Corresponding Richter Scale
I	Instrumental	Detected only on seismographs	<10	N/A
II	Feeble	Some people feel it	<25	<4.2
III	Slight	Felt by people resting; like a truck rumbling by	<50	N/A
IV	Moderate	Felt by people walking	<100	N/A
V	Slightly strong	Sleepers awake; church bells ring	<250	<4.8
VI	Strong	Trees sway; suspended objects swing, objects fall off shelves	<500	<5.4
VII	Very strong	Mild alarm; walls crack; plaster falls	<1000	<6.1
VIII	Destructive	Moving cars uncontrollable; masonry fractures, poorly constructed buildings damaged	<2500	N/A
IX	Ruinous	Some houses collapse; ground cracks; pipes break open	<5000	<6.9
X	Disastrous	Ground cracks profusely; many buildings destroyed; liquefaction and landslides widespread	<7500	<7.3
XI	Very disastrous	Most buildings and bridges collapse; roads, railways, pipes, and cables destroyed; general triggering of other hazards	<9800	<8.1
XII	Catastrophic	Total destruction; trees fall; ground rises and falls in waves	>9800	>8.1

For example, older masonry buildings have a higher potential of large pieces coming off and crashing to the ground. In contrast, resilient or flexible objects are less likely to suffer breakages. Structures can fail due to both horizontal and vertical shaking. Tall buildings tend to sway or vibrate, depending upon the construction materials and height as well as their distance from the epicenter. The top floors of buildings that are located close to one another may even collide during the swaying motion triggered by a large earthquake. **Pancaking** occurs when high-rise buildings collapse in on themselves because the poured concrete flooring separates from the corner fastenings, causing the floors to drop vertically down.

4.2.6 Earthquake Experience in the United States

Earthquake risk in the United States is significant in many regions of the country. The area of greatest seismic activity is along the Pacific Coast in California and Alaska, but as many as 40 states can be characterized as having at least a moderate earthquake risk. In the past 20 years, scientists have learned that strong earthquakes in the central Mississippi Valley have occurred repeatedly in geologic past. The New Madrid seismic zone is an area of major earthquake activity that experiences frequent minor shocks. Although earthquakes in the

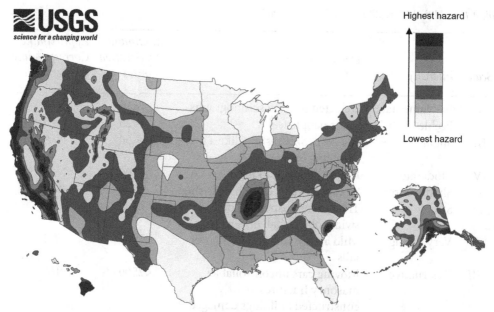

Highest hazard

Lowest hazard

Figure 4.1 The USGS provides seismic risk maps to describe the degree of earthquake risk in the United States. (USGS Earthquake Hazards Program.)

central and eastern United States are less frequent than in the western part of the country, these areas represent considerable seismic risk (Figure 4.1).

Notable Earthquakes

The United States has experienced earthquakes of all levels, some of which have caused catastrophic damage and loss of life. Of the top 10 largest earthquakes to occur in the United States, 9 have taken place in Alaska with magnitudes of 8.0 or higher. The earthquake with the second-highest magnitude in the world took place in Prince William Sound, Alaska, in 1964, with a magnitude of 9.2. This event took 125 human lives and generated a tsunami wave that reached an estimated height of 200 feet. Other significant earthquakes include:

- The *San Francisco Earthquake of 1906* occurred on April 18, 1906, at 5:12 A.M.. The epicenter was near San Francisco, and the quake lasted approximately 45–60 seconds. The quake is believed to have been between VII and IX on the MMI scale. The quake could be felt from Southern Oregon to the south of Los Angeles, and as far east as central Nevada. Reports of deaths vary from 500 to 700 people, although these figures may be underestimated. Significant damage occurred to the city as a direct result of the quake, but the event is remembered more for the devastating fires that broke out citywide following the ground shaking. Gas lines snapped, and wood and coal burning stoves overturned. Water mains broke, hampering the work of city firefighters. Firebreaks were created throughout the city by blowing up buildings and entire neighborhoods to stop the spread of the flames.

- The *Loma Prieta, California Earthquake* occurred on October 18, 1989, at 5:04 P.M., the height of rush hour, measuring 6.7 on the Richter scale, and lasting for 15 seconds. As a result of the quake, 63 deaths occurred, with over 3700 people injured. Property damage reached nearly $6–$8 billion, making this the most costly U.S. disaster up to that time. Over 1800 homes were destroyed, 2600 businesses were damaged, and 3000 people were made homeless. The two-tiered Bay Bridge and Nimitz Freeway both collapsed, crushing cars underneath and killing and trapping hundreds of motorists. Fire damage to infrastructure and buildings was extensive, gaping cracks were created in most of the main roads, and landslides were triggered in surrounding areas. Fans waiting to see the World Series baseball game in Candlestick Park rushed onto the field as the whole stadium swayed; the event was televised live nationwide until the broadcast was abruptly disconnected.

- The *Northridge Earthquake* occurred on Monday January 17, 1994 at approximately 4:30 A.M.; it measured 6.7 on the Richter scale and lasted 15 seconds. The epicenter was located 20 miles northwest of Los Angeles beneath the San Fernando Valley. Between 57 and 72 deaths and more than 9000 injuries were reported. The death and injury toll would have undoubtedly been much higher had the event not occurred on the Martin Luther King, Jr. holiday, when many commuters were at home. Nearly $44 billion in property damage occurred, with 25,000 dwellings made uninhabitable and thousands more severely or moderately damaged. The damage was so widespread that 9 hospitals were closed, 9 parking garages collapsed, 11 major roads into Los Angeles were closed, 2 bridges on the Interstate 10 Santa Monica Freeway collapsed, and countless other bridges and overpasses were damaged, paralyzing the city for weeks and severely delaying rescue and recovery efforts.

4.2.7 Earthquakes: Lessons Learned

What can we learn from these past earthquake experiences? The 1906 San Francisco Earthquake, which caused millions of dollars in damage, was considered merely ill fortune at the time. San Francisco's citizens thought little of the possibility of future quakes. The city was rebuilt following the disaster in almost identical fashion. Yet, that earthquake provided a wealth of information to scientists and, eventually, to planners and builders, about the nature of earthquake damage and the geologic processes involved. In fact, the 1906 Earthquake is considered by some scholars as one of the most significant quakes in modern history because of the scientific knowledge gained. Damage reports from the 1906 event gave an early indication of the significance of the fault, although a large horizontal displacement and the great rupture length it displayed were not fully appreciated at the time. Although the theory of plate tectonics was not developed for another half century, reports from the 1906 quake laid a sound foundation for later studies in seismology.

Subsequent earthquakes have provided even more opportunities to learn additional information about how earthquakes happen, and what types of construction design, techniques, and materials are best suited to withstand earthquake impacts. Damage reports indicate that in many of these events, structures and infrastructure (roads, overpasses, bridges, gas and pipe lines, etc.) that were constructed or retrofitted (strengthened) to handle earthquake impacts fared much better on average than older and less substantially constructed buildings and facilities. Engineers and architects have also learned that building design in earthquake-prone areas should incorporate safeguards against both horizontal and vertical shaking. Structural supports should be carefully designed to avoid potential disasters like upper floors collapsing onto the floors below or onto open space, such as parking decks, that are located on the lower levels. Much research has been conducted on transportation infrastructure (roads, bridges, overpasses, and interchanges) to discover the types of damages that have occurred to the transportation network during past quakes. Bridge performance is particularly critical because the failure of support columns can cause entire spans of highway to collapse. In California, bridges and overpasses built prior to 1971 are especially vulnerable; following the 1971 San Fernando Earthquake, standards for earthquake design and construction were toughened considerably.

CHILE VS. HAITI: HOW RICH AND POOR NATIONS EXPERIENCE DISASTER DIFFERENTLY

In 2010, two earthquakes hit in rapid succession – the first in Haiti on January 12, the second in Chile on February 27. The earthquake in Chile was far stronger than the one that struck Haiti – magnitudes 8.8 and 7.0, respectively, yet the death toll and level of property damage in Haiti were much higher. The reasons for the differing experiences are tragically simple and illustrate the value of mitigation and preparedness and the need for adequate capacity and resources for disaster relief and rebuilding.

Chile is a wealthy, developed country with a history of earthquakes, and it was better prepared, with strict building codes and robust emergency response systems. In 1960, Chile suffered the worst earthquake in recorded history, a 9.5 magnitude quake that killed thousands. As a result, people are well versed in what to do should a quake strike. Although nearly 700 people died in the 2010 quake, that number is undoubtedly much lower than would have occurred if the higher standards had not been implemented in Chile years earlier.

Haiti, in contrast, is a country with widespread poverty – its population is the poorest in the western hemisphere. Haiti has no national building code, no means of checking building safety, and there are no domestic disaster relief or recovery planning services. These factors have led to a population without the capacity to construct adequate housing and without the resources to rebuild when tragedy strikes. Haiti's death toll from the 2010 earthquake was approximately 230,000, which made it the third deadliest earthquake since 1900, behind the Indonesian quake of 2004 and one in Tangshen, China, in 1976 that killed 655,000.

Studies of past earthquakes have also shown that many injuries and deaths occur because of breaking glass, falling objects, and insecure furnishings. Fairly simple and relatively inexpensive retrofitting activities can be implemented within building to combat these dangers, such as bolting furniture to the wall, anchoring bookcases, and securing appliances like televisions and computers, so they remain stable during earthquake shaking. Similarly, some elements of building facades can be shaken loose and crash to the sidewalk during earthquakes if not designed properly. Simple modifications to building parapets and other architectural elements can go a long way in preventing injury and death related to earthquakes.

We have also learned that areas prone to earthquakes can be delineated on maps. Within these areas, seismologists can create various zones of potential earthquake severity based on the underlying geologic characteristics of the Earth. This ability to locate earthquake risk potential is critical to hazard mitigation and preparedness efforts. Seismic risk zone information is essential for steering future development away from areas that are most at risk from ground shaking and for targeting at-risk structures for retrofitting.

SELF-CHECK

- Define **seismology, lithosphere, tectonic plate, fault plane, seismic wave, ground motion, epicenter, surface faulting, liquefaction, lateral spread, loss of bearing strength, seismograph, intensity, acceleration,** and **pancaking**.
- Name three scales used to measure the severity of an earthquake.
- Describe the effects of a level VI earthquake.
- Identify the geographic areas of the United States that are potentially impacted by earthquakes.

4.3 TSUNAMIS

A tsunami is a sea wave generated by a disturbance on the seabed that displaces the overlying water. Although often referred to as "tidal waves," this name is very misleading, for the daily rise and fall of the tides has nothing to do with generating these waves. Tsunamis are primarily associated with earthquakes in oceanic and coastal regions. While less common, landslides, volcanic eruptions, nuclear explosions, and impacts of objects from outer space (such as meteorites, satellites, and "space trash") can also generate a tsunami.

4.3.1 Fast and Furious

As a tsunami crosses the deep ocean, its length from crest to crest may be 100 miles or more, yet its height from crest to trough will only be a few feet or less. Consequently, a tsunami does not capsize vessels at sea – in fact, in the open ocean, these waves are so low and broad that they pass virtually unnoticed beneath ships and cannot be seen from the air.

In the deepest oceans, such as the Pacific, a tsunami can travel very long distances – from the shores of one continent to another at the speed of a jet plane, or up to 600 miles/hour (970 km/h). When a tsunami enters the shallow waters of a landmass in its path, the velocity of the wave diminishes to just tens of miles per hour, but the height of the wave increases dramatically. In shallow waters, a large tsunami can crest to heights exceeding 100 feet (30 meters) and strike with devastating force. The word tsunami is from the Japanese meaning "harbor wave" because of the impact the waves have when they enter harbors and other narrow coastal areas.

4.3.2 Multiple Waves

Tsunamis do not strike the coastline with a single blow. As a tsunami enters the shoals, water along the beach commonly recedes from the shore before the wave hits. This water rises up offshore to form the first tsunami wave to strike the coast. Successive waves may be much bigger and hit the coast at intervals ranging from 15 minutes to several hours. Depending upon the topography of the land mass, a tsunami can reach far inland, causing damage from inundation and the force of the water rushing forward miles from the shore.

There have been reports of beachgoers who, intrigued by the unusual sight of the exposed shore as the ocean recedes, run to gather shells or rescue fish and other sea creatures left stranded as the ocean runs "backwards." This phenomenon, combined with the fact that tsunamis involve a series of waves with periods of relative calm between, has led to many deaths that might otherwise have been prevented if people had evacuated in a direction *away* from the shoreline to higher ground at the first warning signs of the impending threat.

In many cases, the first tsunami wave to hit the shore is not the biggest. At Crescent City, California, the first two waves of the 1964 Alaska earthquake tsunami swept along the coast 23 minutes apart, about 4 hours after the earthquake. These waves caused only minor flooding and gave a false sense of security to some residents, who returned to their places of business to clean up or save their merchandise. However, some of these people and a significant part of the town's waterfront then later were struck by successive waves, which were much higher. These damaging waves reached 21 feet (6.5 meters) in height. Eleven people were killed and the damage exceeded $7.5 million.

4.3.3 Tsunami Impacts

Worldwide, the impact of tsunamis has been profound and far-reaching, with deaths in the tens of thousands. The coastal areas of countries where very large tsunamis have occurred experience multiple effects, including: destruction of buildings and infrastructure; loss of livestock, crops, and food supplies; leakage of sewage, industrial waste, and hazardous materials into fresh water sources; and lost revenue from affected industries including tourism, fishing, shipping, energy, agriculture, and manufacturing.

Other impacts of tsunamis on society can include homelessness, unemployment, hunger, injuries, and disease outbreaks, as well as psychological trauma of survivors. Environmental impacts include deforestation, loss of habitat, die-off of vegetation and wildlife, wildfire, and saltwater contamination of soils. The economic, environmental, and social impacts of tsunamis can last for generations.

RECENT INTERNATIONAL CATASTROPHIC TSUNAMIS

Two recent tsunamis illustrate the devastating effects that these geologic hazards can cause. On March 11, 2011, a powerful tsunami travelling 500 miles/hour (800 km/h) with 33-foot (10 meters) waves swept over the east coast of Japan. The tsunami was spawned by a 9.0 magnitude earthquake offshore, making it the fourth-largest earthquake ever recorded. The flooding and violent shaking resulted in a nuclear emergency, in which the Fukushima Daiichi nuclear power plant began leaking radioactive steam. The triple disaster of earthquake, tsunami, and nuclear accident killed more than 18,000 people and displaced nearly half a million others.

An undersea earthquake in the Indian Ocean on December 26th, 2004 produced a tsunami that caused one of the biggest natural disasters in modern history. Over 200,000 people are known to have lost their lives. The waves devastated the shores of parts of Indonesia, Sri Lanka, India, Thailand, and as far west as Somalia on the east coast of Africa, 2800 miles (4500 kilometers) west of the epicenter. Due to the distances involved, the tsunami took anywhere from 15 minutes to 7 hours to reach various coastlines. The ability to issue warnings of impending tsunami is directly correlated with the location of the quake in relation to populated shorelines. A 15-minute window to issue an evacuation order is extremely narrow, one of the reasons that the event resulted in the deaths of thousands of residents trapped in low-lying areas as the tsunami came ashore.

4.3.4 Tsunami Hazards: A Real Risk for the United States

Scientists assess tsunami hazard based on historical evidence combined with earthquake potential. We know that devastating tsunamis have struck North America before, and the likelihood they will strike again is high. Especially vulnerable are the five Pacific states – Hawaii, Alaska, Washington, Oregon, and California. Of these, Hawaii, which is surrounded by the volcanically active and earthquake-prone Pacific "Ring of Fire," is the most exposed to tsunami impact.[1]

Tsunami hazard is moderate to very high in the Caribbean, including the American territories of Puerto Rico and the U.S. Virgin Islands. The Pacific territories of Guam, American Samoa, and the Northern Marianas experience many tsunamis, but historically these have been relatively small.

The U.S. Atlantic coast and the Gulf Coast states have experienced very few tsunamis in the last 200 years. In fact, Louisiana, Mississippi, Alabama, the Florida Gulf coast, Georgia, Virginia, North Carolina, Pennsylvania, and Delaware have no known record of historic tsunami. One reported tsunami in the Mid-Atlantic States may be related to an underwater explosion or landslide.[2]

"FREAK WAVE" IN NEW JERSEY?

In June, 2013, the National Oceanic and Atmospheric Administration announced a 6-foot wave that hit New Jersey could actually have been a rare tsunami. A weather system moving through the East Coast may have changed the air pressure enough so that waves generated by the storm behaved like a tsunami. The phenomenon is known as a "meteotsunami" – a tsunami caused by meteorological conditions, not seismic activity.

4.3.5 Tsunami Warning Systems

Since 1946, the Pacific Tsunami Warning System based at the Pacific Tsunami Warning Center in Honolulu has provided warnings of potential tsunami danger in the Pacific basin by monitoring earthquake activity and the passage of tsunami waves at tide gauges. However, predicting when and where the next earthquake, and hence tsunami, will strike is currently impossible. Once a tsunami is generated, it *is* possible through modeling and measurement technologies to forecast the arrival and impact of the tsunami, although it is difficult to make this prediction for a particular coastal location. Monitoring earthquakes gives a good estimate of the potential for tsunami generation, based on earthquake size and location but gives no direct information about the tsunami itself. Tide gauges in harbors provide direct measurements of the tsunami, but the tsunami is significantly altered by local **bathymetry** (the depth and contours of underwater ocean and lake floors), which severely limits their use in forecasting tsunami impact at other locations. Partly because of these data limitations, 15 out of 20 tsunami warnings issued since 1946 were considered false alarms because the tsunami that arrived was too weak to cause damage. Recent developments in tsunami detection – including real-time, deep ocean detectors are improving the ability to forecast and, therefore, issue meaningful warnings to coastal residents.

4.3.6 Tsunami Readiness

Although tsunamis are relatively rare, the potential for catastrophic impact makes it critical that individuals in high-risk areas are educated about and prepared for tsunamis before they strike. The NOAA TsunamiReady program helps local communities increase public awareness and engage in tsunami preparedness activities. To date, there are 16 states and territories and 192 communities in the United States participating in the TsunamiReady program. Since the NOAA TsunamiReady Program was initiated in 2001, local authorities in these states, territories, and community have drawn up tsunami emergency plans, installed sirens and other warning systems to alert people of an approaching tsunami, installed tsunami evacuation route signs and tsunami information signs along the coast and at many state parks, implemented innovative tsunami hazard educational pilot programs, and practiced tsunami evacuation drills.

4.3.7 Impact of Climate Change on Tsunamis

A tsunami hitting at high tide is more dangerous than one that hits at low tide because the water level is already elevated, allowing the tsunami to reach even farther inland from shore at higher water levels. Low-lying coastal plains are particularly susceptible to being swamped by the waves. As climate change warms the oceans, sea level rise is expected to impact coastlines throughout the world. Many of these regions are also located in areas of seismic activity and, hence, the threat of tsunami. Just as high tide gives a tsunami a "running start" when it hits the shoreline, sea level rise will similarly allow tsunami waters to flood inland from an already elevated water line, displacing more residents and causing greater damage over a larger area.

SELF-CHECK

- Define **Bathymetry**.
- Explain how tsunamis are generated.
- Describe some of the impacts of a tsunami that strikes land.
- Identify the geographic areas of the United States that are potentially exposed to future tsunamis.

4.4 VOLCANOES

A **volcano** is a vent in the surface of the Earth through which magma, gases, and ash erupt. The structure that is produced by the ejected material, usually conical in form, is referred to as a volcano as well. The word *volcano* is derived from the Latin word *Vulcan*, Roman god of the forge.

4.4.1 Reaching the Boiling Point

A volcanic eruption occurs when superheated rock under the Earth's surface rises to areas of lower pressure at the surface. During this movement, the rock undergoes a phase change from solid rock to liquid **magma** (molten rock). Volcanic action can be compared to the action that occurs when water boils and turns to steam, resulting in volume expansion. If water boils while in a closed glass container, the container does not have room to hold the additional volume and pressure buildings up. Eventually, as the temperature and pressure continue to rise, the glass will explode to release the pressure. A volcanic eruption works under the same principle, but on a far grander, and scarier, scale. The enormous amount of pressure and heat building up under the surface causes conversion of the rock to magma, and the magma expands. The result is an eruption through the most accessible escape route at the Earth's surface. Magma that reaches the Earth's surface is called **lava**. Lava temperatures can reach 1250 degrees Celsius (over 2000 degrees Fahrenheit).

4.4.2 Types of Volcanic Eruptions

There are six major types of volcanic eruptions: Icelandic, Hawaiian, Strombolian, Vulcanian, Vesuvian, and Plinian (see Table 4.2).

Some volcanoes erupt violently, while others flow more peacefully. The variation in volcanic force is due to:

Table 4.2 Types of Volcanic Eruptions.

Type of Volcanic Eruption	Description
Icelandic	Gas escapes easily and lava has low viscosity.
Hawaiian	Gas escapes easily, but lava has slightly more viscosity; builds tall peaks.
Strombolian	Smaller, more continuous eruptions; its central lava pool is easily triggered due to the pressure that builds quickly under its crust.
Vulcanian	Switch between high-viscosity lava and large amounts of ash blown out the top of the volcano.
Vesuvian	Even more violent high-viscosity lava blasts that are due to trapped gases. These gases can blow ash and rocks to great distances, either vertically or horizontally.
Plinian	The gas pressure and viscosity of the magma is so high that these volcanoes blow lava and ash laterally, or out of its side (rather than up), to relieve the pressure blockages of the throat of the volcano.

- Chemical and mineral content of the rock and magma
- Viscosity, temperature, and water and gas content of the rock and magma
- Geographic position in relation to tectonic plate edges

MOUNT ST. HELENS

Mount St. Helens in Washington State is an example of a Plinian eruption. When Mount St. Helens erupted on May 18, 1980, it erupted with such force that the top 1000 feet of the volcano disappeared within minutes. The blast sent thousands of tons of ash into the upper atmosphere. It simultaneously sent waves of lava, poisonous gas, and mud out the side and down the slopes of the mountain. Within hours, thousands of acres surrounding the volcano were blanketed with the deadly debris. More than 200 square miles of forestland were transformed almost instantly into a grey, lifeless landscape. All living creatures within miles were killed, including one geologist who had been stationed nearby to monitor the volcano's activity, and one resident who refused to evacuate the area despite official warnings. In all, 57 people died, including loggers, campers, reporters, and scientists, some as far as 13 miles from the mountain itself.

4.4.3 Volcanic Hot Spots

Areas that are prone to frequent volcanic activity are known as **hot spots**, such as the one in the Island of Hawaii. In these areas, volcanoes form when magma rises from a stationary heat source – the hotspot – beneath the Earth's lithosphere. The magma migrates up through fractures in the overriding Pacific plate and extrudes onto the ocean floor, gradually building a mountain of successive lava flows. Over time the mass accumulates until it emerges above sea level, thereby becoming an island volcano.

The Hawaiian Islands are arranged in a chain, a reflection of the relationship between the Hawaiian hot spot and the movement of the Pacific plate. The hot spot is a stationary heat source over which the Pacific plate slowly moves toward the northwest. Imagine a conveyer belt with hamburger patties slowly moving over a stationary gas flame, cooking the burgers one after another. The currently active volcanoes in the hot spot on the Island of Hawaii are Mauna Loa, Kilauea, and Loihi.

4.4.4 The Volcano-Earthquake Connection

Some volcanic eruptions are related to earthquakes occurring in the area. It is not understood what the exact triggering mechanism might be, but the subsequent volcanic activity is most likely a response to a pressure change in the magma. This could be a consequence of a change in pressure on the crust in the area of the earthquake, or possibly the severe ground shaking caused by the quake.

DOUBLE WHAMMY: A QUAKE AND A VOLCANO

The eruption of Kilauea in Hawaii in November, 1975, was directly related to an earthquake. A 7.2 magnitude earthquake, along with many aftershocks, occurred just southeast of the Kilauea volcano's caldera and within its south flank. On that occasion, the volcano erupted for over 16 hours.

4.4.5 Types of Volcanic Structures

There are several varieties of volcanic structures, including:

- **Cinder cones:** The simplest type of volcano, cinder cones have a single vent and are built of cinders. As lava erupts violently into the air, it breaks into small fragments that solidify and fall as **cinders** around the vent. Over time, these small fragments build up to form a circular cone. Cinder cones can grow to more than 1000 feet above their surroundings and have a characteristic bowl-shaped **crater** at the summit.
- **Shield volcanoes:** These volcanoes can have many eruptions from the rift zones, or fractures that are located along the flanks of their cones. Rather than erupting violently, the lava flows out of a shield volcano in all directions from its vents. These volcanoes are built almost entirely of fluid lava flows that cool as thin sheets and create a gently sloping cone. Some of the largest volcanoes in the world are shield volcanoes. The largest shield volcano (and the largest active volcano in the world) is Mauna Loa. This volcano on the Big Island of Hawaii sits over 13,000 feet above sea level, but the entire volcano measured from the sea floor rises over 28,000 feet.
- **Lava domes:** Lava domes are formed by lava piles that are too viscous, or thick, to flow far from the vent. A dome volcano grows by layering the lava upward and outward, largely by expansion from within. Some domes form short, steep-sided lava flows known as coulees. Others form spines over the volcanic vent. Domes commonly occur within the craters or on the flanks of large composite volcanoes.
- **Composite volcanoes:** Also called **stratovolcanoes**, these are large volcanoes that are also mountains. Some of the most breathtaking mountains in the world are composite volcanoes, including Mount Fuji in Japan and Mount St. Helens in Washington. Most have a central crater at the summit, but lava can erupt through fissures on the flanks of the cone or flow from breaks in the crater. These volcanoes build up over time by the fortification of the cone when the cooled lava fills the fissures and when cinders and ash are added to the slopes.

4.4.6 Impacts of Volcanic Activity on People and Property

Volcanoes can pose a serious threat to people and property. One of the most common risks associated with volcanic activity involves **lava flows**. Although lava rarely travels quickly enough to be life-threatening, it does create havoc to the natural and built environment. For example, the flow of lava from volcanoes in southern Hawaii has destroyed numerous homes and buried highways in its path. Because of its excessive heat, lava quickly burns any consumable materials it covers, including trees, houses, roads, crops, and anything else in its way. Lava flows may be slow-moving, but they are unstoppable forces. A few communities in Iceland have tried to stop the advance of lava flows using cold seawater in an attempt to change the lava from a molten to solid condition. The success of this technique is not widely recognized.

Volcanic ash also can be extremely hazardous to plants and animal life. Volcanic ash can form thick deposits on the ground, causing extensive environmental damage. The ash can contain bits of volcanic glass and can be very abrasive. Violent eruptions can bury whole communities, cause houses to collapse, clog engines in airplanes and vehicles, and create breathing problems for humans and animals. The ash plume from an erupting volcano can be dispersed a long distance by high-altitude winds, bringing similar problems to areas far removed from the eruption site.

Pyroclastic flows pose another danger to humans and are experienced in the vicinity of explosive volcanoes. A **pyroclastic flow**, also called a nuee ardente (French for "glowing cloud"), is an incinerating mixture of gas and volcanic debris, with a temperature from 700 to 1000 degrees Celsius (1300 to 1800 degrees Fahrenheit). Pyroclastic flows remain close to the ground, but they can travel downhill from the volcano summit very quickly, up to 150 kilometers (90 miles)/hour, incinerating anything in their path as they roar down the slope. One of the most famous pyroclastic flows occurred when Mount Vesuvius erupted in A.D. 79, engulfing the ancient city of Pompeii, Italy. More recently, the forest on the sides of Mount St. Helens was flattened by a nuee ardent when that volcano erupted in 1980.

Volcanic mudflows also pose a significant threat to human settlements. A mixture of water and volcanic debris, a mudflow can quickly travel downslope, burying all objects on the route downhill. Mudflows created heavy damage during the eruption of Mount St. Helens, as they traveled along stream valleys carrying trees, structures, and soils into the Columbia River below. The U.S. Army Corps of Engineers had to dredge a vast amount of debris that had been deposited in the river by the mudflow so that the river could be used for navigation following the event.

Poisonous gases from volcanic activity also pose a danger to humans and animals. Although volcanic gas is primarily made up of water vapor, other elements that may be present include carbon dioxide, sulfur dioxide, carbon monoxide, hydrogen sulfide, sulfuric acid, hydrochloric acid, and hydrofluoric acid. These toxic gases can impact urban areas and agricultural crops in the vicinity, something that occurs on the island of Hawaii fairly frequently. **Vog**, or volcanic fog, occurs a short distance downwind from the eruption site, while **laze** (lava haze) is produced when lava enters the sea and the reaction produces hydrochloric acid fumes.

ICELANDIC ERUPTION GROUNDS AIR TRAVEL

The 2010 eruption of the Icelandic Volcano Eyjafjallajökull caused enormous disruption to air travel when about 20 countries closed their airspace because of an enormous ash cloud that lingered over much of northern Europe for several days. The flight cancellations affected more than 100,000 travelers, creating the highest level of air travel disruption up to that time since the Second World War.

SELF-CHECK

- Define **volcano, magma, lava, hot spot, volcanic ash, pyroclastic flow, vog, laze, volcanic mudflows, shield volcano, cinders, cinder cones, lava dome, crater, composite volcano, stratovalcano,** and **lava flow**.
- Name the six different types of volcanic eruptions.
- Identify the United States' volcanic hot spots.
- List three risks associated with volcanoes.

4.5 LANDSLIDES AND DEBRIS FLOWS

Landslides occur when masses of rock, earth, or debris move down a slope. The major driving force behind landslides is gravity, assisted by water. Landslides vary in size from relatively small, isolated events to large, widespread ground movement and can vary in speed from a slow, gradual creep to a rapid rush of earth and debris that rages downhill. Activated by geologic hazards, rainstorms, wildfires, and by human modification of the land, landslides pose serious threats to any human-made structures that lie in their path. Landslides can impact fisheries, tourism, timber harvesting, agriculture, mining, energy production, and transportation, as well as community life.

4.5.1 Debris Flows

While some landslides move slowly and cause damage gradually, others move so rapidly that they can destroy property and take lives suddenly and unexpectedly. This type of landslide is called a **debris flow**, which can also manifest itself as a mudslide, mudflow, or debris avalanche. These types of fast-moving landslides generally occur during intense rainfall on water-saturated soil.

Debris flows usually start on steep hillsides as **soil slumps,** or slides down a slope. Debris flows can accelerate to speeds greater than 35 miles/hour. They continue flowing downhill and into channels, depositing sand, mud, boulders, and organic materials onto more gently sloping ground. Consistency ranges from watery mud to thick, rocky mud (like wet cement), which is dense enough to carry boulders, trees, and cars. Debris flows from many different sources can combine in channels, where their destructive power may be greatly increased.

4.5.2 Landslide Triggers

Torrential rainfalls such as those that occur during hurricanes or tropical storms commonly act as triggers for landslides. Several other types of hazards can also put a landslide in motion, demonstrated by the following examples:

- The Mount St. Helens debris flow was an instantaneous result of the *volcanic eruption* that took place there.
- A landslide in San Fernando, California, started as a result of a 7.5 magnitude *earthquake* in 1971.
- A string of *wildfires* that burned over 4000 acres of vegetative cover in Big Sur, California, exacerbated a landslide on California Highway 1 in 1972 after a series of torrential rainstorms.

- In 1983 land in Thistle, Utah began shifting because of *groundwater buildup* from heavy rains during the previous fall and the melting of deep snowpack from the winter. Within a few weeks, the landslide dammed the Spanish Fork River, destroying U.S. Highway 6 and the main line of the Denver and Rio Grande Western Railroad. The landslide dam caused flood waters to rise, leading to inundation of the surrounding area. The town of Thistle was completely obliterated. The Thistle landslide was the single most costly landslide event in the United States to date, with damages exceeding $400 million.
- In February 1995, a 1600-foot stretch of popular beach at Sleeping Bear Dunes National Lakeshore suddenly slid into the waters of northeastern Lake Michigan. The United States Geological Survey and National Parks Service scientists believe that repeated coastal landslides at Sleeping Bear Point may be related to *increases in fluid pressure* in the spaces between the grains of sand (pore pressure) that make up the bluff at the point. The increased amount of water likely weakened the slope, making it susceptible to the ensuing landslide.

4.5.3 Landslide Risk Areas

Areas that are generally prone to landslides include areas where previous landslides have occurred, the base of steep slopes, the base of drainage channels, and developed hillsides with steep slopes, particularly where leach-field septic systems are used. Areas that are typically considered safe from landslides include areas that have not moved in the past; relatively flat-lying areas away from sudden changes in slope; and areas at the top or along ridges. Landslide risk areas can be shown on maps, which allow emergency managers, planners, and builders to identify locations where construction should be limited or landslide mitigation building techniques can be employed.

According to the United States Geological Survey, landslides are major geologic hazards that occur in all 50 states, causing $1–$2 billion in damages per year and resulting in more than 25 fatalities annually. Notable U.S. landslides include the Canyonville, Oregon, landslide of 1974 that killed 9; the 1980 Mount St. Helens debris flow, which is the world's largest landslide; and a landslide in Mameyes, Puerto Rico in 1985 that killed 129 people during Tropical Storm Isabel.

SELF-CHECK

- Define **landslide, debris flow**, and **soil slump**.
- Identify the two forces that drive a landslide.
- List three types of land areas that are typically prone to landslides.
- Discuss the areas of the United States that are at risk of landslide events.

4.6 COASTAL EROSION

Coastal erosion is the wearing away of the land surface by detachment and movement of soil and rock fragments. Coastal erosion occurs along sandy shores and barrier islands of the Atlantic and Gulf Coasts, on the rocky coastlines and bluffs of the Pacific, as well as the shores of the Great Lakes. Erosion can occur during a flood or storm event or over a period of years through the action of wind, water, or other geologic processes. Sea level rise can also accelerate coastal erosion over time.

4.6.1 Shifting Sands, Eroding Bluffs

Wind, waves, and long-shore currents are the driving forces behind coastal erosion. In areas of sandy beach, the removal and deposition of sand permanently changes the structure and shape of the beach. Sand is transported throughout the sea and along the shore and can be transported to land-side dunes, other beaches, offshore banks, and deep ocean bottoms. Rates of coastal erosion can also be affected by human activity, sea level rise, and seasonal fluctuations.

The beach system is in a state of **dynamic equilibrium**. Constant movement transfers sand from one location to another; winter storms along the coast can remove significant amounts of sand, creating steep, narrow beaches, while during the summer, milder waves return the sand, widening beaches and creating gentle slopes. Similarly, inlets between the ocean and the sound naturally open and close over time as sand moves around the coastal system. The bluffs and cliffs of the Pacific coast experience a dynamism of their own, with wave, wind, and storm action working to wear cliff faces away slowly over time and more quickly during storm events.

Coastal erosion is a highly localized event that can take place on one end of an island and not at the other. Although much erosion takes place gradually over time, hurricanes, nor'easters, or other sudden storm events can drastically increase the amount of coastal erosion that takes place in a short period of time. **Episodic erosion** is induced by a single storm event. This type of erosion can make structures located along the shore suddenly become unstable and prone to collapse, as scouring occurs around foundation supports and undermines the building. For example, pilings or bridge foundations can become unstable if the sand beneath them erodes over time or during an episodic event.

4.6.2 Erosion Rates

The average erosion rate on the Atlantic coast is roughly 2–3 feet/year, but the states bordering the Gulf of Mexico, especially in the deltas of Louisiana, have the nation's highest average annual erosion rate at 6 feet/year. Erosion on the rocky cliffs of the Pacific coast averages 1 foot/year, although large episodic erosion occurs occasionally. The Great Lakes annual erosion rate is highly variable, ranging from 0 to more than 10 feet/year depending on a number of hydrologic and weather-related factors such as fluctuating lake levels and wave action. Rates of 25 feet/year are not uncommon on some barrier islands in the Southeast, and rates as high as 50 feet/year have occurred along the Great Lakes.

Many coastal states have **setback rules** that are based on the erosion rate along the shoreline. The erosion setback is a line, measured landward from some specified point (e.g., the first line of stable, natural vegetation), behind which construction must take place. Setbacks are designed to increase the life of a building by avoiding the wear and tear, or sudden collapse, that can happen close to the oceanfront. Setbacks and other policies to protect structures in coastal environments are discussed in more detail in later chapters.

4.6.3 Coastal Inlet Hazard Areas

Inlets are areas along the shore where ocean water flows into an estuary or sound. These channels are important for shipping, fishing, and recreation along the southern, Atlantic, and Pacific coastlines as they serve as the ingress and egress point for vessels traveling between the ocean and the inner coastal waterways. Under normal conditions, these areas are very dynamic – the mouth of an inlet typically shifts alongshore because of "everyday" erosion. During a cataclysmic event, inlets can move dramatically, or can close completely, and in some cases, entire new inlets can form. These areas can be extremely hazardous; when storm-induced erosion shifts an inlet down or up shore, houses, hotels, roads, bridges, and other structures located near the inlet are at risk. During a particularly intense storm, structures can be damaged or destroyed in a matter of hours.

4.6.4 The Effect of Climate Change on Coastal Erosion

Despite the differences in erosion potential along the world's coastlines, there has been a dramatic increase in coastal erosion over the last two decades, and this is expected to continue as sea level rises and storm frequency and intensity increase.[3] Rather than occurring over the same time scale with sea level rise, erosion of beaches and coastal cliffs is expected to occur in large bursts during storm events as a result of increased wave height and storm intensity. Because of these large events, scientific models predict that shoreline erosion may outpace sea level rise manyfold.[4] For example, in 1938 Sakonnet Point, the most seaward point in the state of Rhode Island, boasted large sand dunes that stood some 4.6 meters (15 feet) tall. Today, those dunes are nearly completely submerged during high tide as a result of the combined impact of major storm damage and increased erosional forces. While sea level rose only .4 meters during this time period, the 4.6-meter dunes have all but disappeared at high tide.[5] This example highlights the potential for erosional forces such as major storm events to outpace the rate of sea level rise.

Erosion will have significant effects on coastal habitats, which can lead to social and economic impacts on coastal communities. With the reduction of coastal habitats and the ecological services they provide, coastal communities will experience more frequent and destructive flooding, compromised fresh water supplies and smaller or fewer beaches.

SELF-CHECK

- Define **coastal erosion**, **dynamic equilibrium**, **episodic erosion**, and **setback rules**.
- Discuss the effects of episodic erosion on a beachfront community.
- Describe how climate change is likely to impact coastal erosion.

4.7 SUBSIDENCE AND COLLAPSE

Land subsidence is the gradual settling of the Earth's surface that occurs because of subsurface movement of earth materials and the resulting loss of support below ground. It usually occurs over a period of weeks, months, or years, and often happens so slowly as to be barely perceptible. **Collapse** occurs more quickly, when the land surface opens up and surface materials fall into cavities below. Collapse can take place over just a few hours. **Sinkholes** are an especially dramatic example of the collapse process. Subsidence and collapse are serious geologic hazards, posing threats to property and human life.

Subsidence is a problem throughout the world. In the United States, more than 17,000 square miles in 45 states, an area roughly the size of New Hampshire and Vermont combined, have been directly affected by subsidence.

4.7.1 Causes of Land Subsidence

Although some subsidence of land is due to natural processes, severe land subsidence is often caused by human activities, such as the removal of **groundwater** (subsurface water). Other causal factors of land subsidence include:

- Thawing permafrost
- Drainage of organic soils
- Dissolving of subsurface limestone rock
- Natural compaction of soils
- Underground mining
- Removal of oil and gas

The *construction of levees*, such as those at the mouth of the Mississippi River in Louisiana, has caused severe subsidence in Mississippi and the surrounding Gulf states. For tens of thousands of years, silt and sand were deposited by the Mississippi River when it regularly overflowed its banks. When the area was settled by humans, however, levees were built to contain the river. While levees stopped regular flooding and allowed for development and farming in some areas, they also stopped the natural replenishing of the land, leading to net loss of land and subsequent subsidence in other areas.

4.7.2 Removal of Groundwater

More than 80% of the identified subsidence in the United States is a consequence of ground-water removal. The increasing development of land and water resources means that land subsidence will likely worsen in the near future, and new problems will undoubtedly arise. When large amounts of groundwater are withdrawn from certain types of rocks, such as fine-grained sediments, the rock compacts because the water is partly responsible for holding the ground up. When the water is withdrawn, the rock falls in on itself. Land subsidence can be difficult to notice, because it can extend over large geographic areas and can take place gradually over a period of time. Eventually, however, land sinks to such a degree that houses become off-kilter, roads collapse, and flooding worsens because the elevation of the land has been lowered.

Groundwater is used to irrigate crops, to provide drinking water to municipalities, and for use in manufacturing and various industries. But the withdrawal of groundwater has depleted critical groundwater resources and created costly regional-scale subsidence in many areas of the country. In the Santa Clara Valley in northern California, early agricultural groundwater use contributed to subsidence that has permanently increased flood risks in the greater San Jose area. In nearby San Joaquin Valley, one of the single largest human alterations of the Earth's surface topography has resulted from excessive pumping of groundwater to sustain the exceptionally productive agricultural business.

Early oil and gas production and a long history of pumping groundwater in the Houston-Galveston area in Texas have also created severe and costly coastal flooding hazards and affected the Galveston Bay estuary, a valuable environmental resource. In Las Vegas Valley, Nevada, groundwater depletion and associated subsidence have accompanied the conversion of a desert oasis into a thirsty and fast-growing metropolis. Water-intensive agricultural practices in south-central Arizona have caused widespread subsidence and fissures of the Earth's surface. In each of these areas, not only have the water resources been dangerously reduced, but the action of pumping water out of the ground has also created hazardous subsidence conditions.

SUBSIDENCE CONCERNS IN COASTAL LOUISIANA

Due to subsidence, the state of Louisiana is becoming increasingly more vulnerable to destruction by coastal storms and erosion. The impact of subsidence on wetlands, the population, and coastal roads and industries in Louisiana are of major concern for residents and public officials alike.

Of particular concern is the impact of increased inundation from relative sea level rise, which causes severe wetlands loss. Indirectly, salt water intrusion kills salt-intolerant vegetation, thus making barrier islands and wetlands vulnerable to increased wave action and erosion from coastal storms and hurricanes. Since most of coastal Louisiana is comprises wetlands, the region is especially vulnerable to land loss.

As much as 50% of Louisiana's population lives in coastal areas of elevations of 3 feet or less. As population increases in the region, vulnerability to coastal storms and hurricanes also grows.

4.7.3 Mine Collapse

Mining of coal, minerals, and other ores is an important economic mainstay in many regions of the United States. However, the process of removing these materials can cause subsidence above the mines. When mining is carried out near the surface of the ground, the supporting structure for overlying rocks is removed. If too much of the supporting material is removed, the surface will collapse into the mine below, creating dangerous **collapse pits**. The danger of subsidence from abandoned coal mines is particularly acute in Pennsylvania, West Virginia, and Kentucky.

The dangers of mine subsidence can be reduced by filling in the void created when ore is removed. Leftover mining materials (mine waste) can be dumped into the mining holes to support the overlying roof. When this is impractical, sand or cement can be pumped in through access holes.

4.7.4 Sinkholes

Sinkholes are common where rock below the land surface is made up of limestone, carbonate rock, salt beds, or rocks that naturally can be dissolved by groundwater circulating through them. As the rock dissolves, spaces and caverns develop underground, creating what is known as Karst topography (named after an area in Yugoslavia where this occurs regularly). Sinkholes can be dramatic episodes of collapse, because the land usually remains intact up to the point when spaces under the Earth's surface become too large to support the upper layer of the Earth. At that stage, a sudden collapse of the land surface can occur. These collapses can be small, just a few feet wide, or they can be huge, swallowing up an entire house. The most damage from sinkholes in the United States tends to occur in Florida, Texas, Alabama, Missouri, Kentucky, Tennessee, and Pennsylvania. Sinkholes are different from soil slumps, which are the result of soil sliding downhill.

New sinkholes may result from groundwater pumping and from construction and development practices. Sinkholes can also form when natural water drainage patterns are changed and new water diversion systems are developed. Some sinkholes form when the land surface is changed, such as when industrial and runoff storage ponds are created. The substantial weight of the new material can trigger an underground collapse of supporting materials, thus causing a sinkhole.

It is very difficult to predict when a sinkhole might happen. It is critical that homeowners and local officials pay attention to clues on the surface that hint at what lies below and be particularly aware when limestone is present. Land subsidence and cracks on the surface indicate that the underlying material may have large voids, especially when the cracks occur in a circular pattern. Cracks in walls and foundations of buildings can also indicate that the ground below is becoming frail.

4.8 HUMAN-CAUSED GEO-HAZARDS

The continental United States experiences small earthquakes every day. But over the past several years, their numbers have been increasing. Geoscientists say the recent wave of small quakes may be related to human activity, including industrial wastewater being pumped into underground storage wells. Two potential trigger mechanisms may be setting off the wastewater quakes: other, large earthquakes (some as far away as Indonesia) and the activity at geothermal power plants.

Most of these little quakes in the United States are too small to feel. They tend to happen in "swarms." Geoscientists have traced some of these swarms to underground faults near deep wells that are often filled with waste fluid from oil and gas drilling. The pressure from the fluid can cause the faults to slip, resulting in earth movement. Large quakes can also cause the faults to slip, resulting in a microearthquake. The production of geothermal energy, which involves the extraction of hot water from beneath the earth's surface to produce steam-generated electricity, may also be correlated with earthquake activity.

Additionally, there is some evidence that the process of hydraulic fracturing – a method of natural gas extraction that involves injecting millions of gallons of water and chemicals deep into the earth – may also produce small earthquakes. As processes such as fracking, geothermal energy production, and the use of underground wastewater wells is on the rise throughout the country, geoscientists continue to study the potential risks of human-caused earthquakes, especially in areas near known fault lines.

SELF-CHECK

- Define **land subsidence, collapse, sinkhole, groundwater,** and **collapse pit.**
- Cite three reasons for land subsidence.
- Discuss the difference between a collapse pit and a sinkhole.
- Name two possible human-induced causes of earthquakes.

SUMMARY

The inevitable shifting of the Earth's layers over time results in equally inevitable geologic hazards. This chapter covered earthquakes and their potentially devastating effects on human life and property, particularly in areas along fault lines. We then explored the physical processes and resulting damage that can occur from volcanic activity. This chapter also discussed the risk of tsunami, landslides, coastal erosion, and land subsidence, each of which presents its own dangers and potential for death and property damage. The information on these hazards can be used by emergency managers and those in land use management to better protect communities from their potential impacts.

KEY TERMS

Acceleration: The rate at which speed of ground movement increases.

Aftershock: The smaller earthquakes that occur after a previous large earthquake, in the same area of the mainshock. Aftershocks can be very destructive and may last for days, weeks, or even years after the initial earthquake.

Bathymetry: Bathymetry is the measurement of the depth of water in oceans, rivers, or lakes. Bathymetric maps look a lot like topographic maps, which use lines to show the shape and elevation of land features.

Cinders: Lava that erupts into the air and breaks into small fragments that solidify.

Cinder cones: The simplest type of volcano; built of cinders, they have a single vent.

Coastal erosion: The wearing away of the land surface along the coast by detachment and movement of soil and rock fragments.

Collapse: When the land surface opens up and surface materials fall into cavities below.

Collapse pit: Hole created when too much supporting material is removed during mining; the surface will collapse into the mine below.

Composite volcanoes: Large volcanoes that are also mountains; also called stratovolcanoes.

Core: The innermost region of the Earth.

Crater: Bowl-shaped hole at the summit of a volcano.

Crust: The thin layer on the surface of the Earth.

Debris flow: Fast-moving landslides that generally occur during intense rainfall on water-saturated soil.

Dynamic equilibrium: In the context of coastal erosion, dynamic equilibrium refers to the process whereby sand is moved from one location to another but it does not leave the system.

Earthquake: Geologic hazard caused by the release of stresses accumulated as a result of the rupture of lithosphere rocks along opposing boundaries in the Earth's crust.

Epicenter: Causative fault of an earthquake; damage is generally most severe at or near the epicenter.

Episodic erosion: Erosion induced by a single storm event.

Fault planes: Ruptures in the Earth's crust that are typically found along borders of the tectonic plates.

Foreshock: An earthquake that occurs before a larger seismic event (the mainshock) and is related to it in both time and space.

Ground motion: The vibration or shaking of the ground during an earthquake.

Groundwater: Subsurface water.

Hot spot: Area prone to volcanic activity.

Inlet: The connecting passageway between the sea and a bay, sound, lagoon, or other enclosed or posterior body of water.

Intensity: How the damage potential of an earthquake is measured.

Land subsidence: A gradual settling of the Earth's surface.

Landslide: When masses of rock, earth, or debris move down a slope.

Lateral spread: Type of ground failure in an earthquake that develops on gentle slopes and entails the sidelong movement of large masses of soil as an underlying layer liquefies.

Lava: Magma that reaches the Earth's surface.

Lava dome: Type of volcano that grows by layering lava upward and outward, largely by expansion from within.

Lava flows: Moving lava; because of its excessive heat, lava quickly burns any consumable material it touches.

Laze: Lava haze produced when lava enters the sea and a chemical reaction produces hydrochloric acid fumes.

Liquefaction: When ground shaking causes loose soils to lose strength and act like viscous fluid.

Lithosphere: The Earth's crust and upper mantle.

Loss of bearing strength: Type of ground failure in an earthquake that results when the soil-supporting structures liquefy.

Magma: Molten rock.

Mantle: Middle layer of the Earth.

Microearthquake: An earthquake with a magnitude of less than 2.0.

Pancaking: When high-rise buildings collapse in on themselves due to earthquake shaking.

Pyroclastic flow: An incinerating mixture of gas and volcanic debris; also called nuee ardente.

Richter scale: An open-ended logarithmic scale that describes the energy release of an earthquake through a measure of shock wave amplitude.

Seismic waves: When the rock on both sides of a fault snaps, it releases this stored energy; waves are what cause the ground to shake in an earthquake.

Seismograph: The instrument that records the amplitude of seismic waves during an earthquake.

Seismology: The study of earthquakes.

Setback rules: Regulations based on the erosion rate along the shoreline. The setback is a line behind which construction must take place.

Shield volcanoes: Type of volcano that can have many eruptions from the fractures, or rift zones, along the flanks of their cones.

Sinkholes: Spaces and caverns that develop underground as the rock below the land surface is dissolved by groundwater circulating through them.

Soil slumps: Loose, partly-to-completely saturated sand or silt, or poorly compacted human-made fill composed of sand, silt, or clay.

Stratovolcanoes: Large volcanoes that are also mountains; also called composite volcanoes.

Surface faulting: The differential movement of two sides of a fracture; the location where the ground breaks apart.

Tectonic plates: Moving layers of the Earth's surface that contain the continents and oceans.

Vog: Volcanic fog; occurs a short distance downwind from volcanic eruption site.

Volcanic ash: Produced by volcanic eruption; can form thick deposits on the ground, causing extensive environmental damage.

Volcanic mudflow: A mixture of water and volcanic debris.

Volcano: A vent in the surface of the Earth through which magma and associated gases and ash erupts.

ASSESS YOUR UNDERSTANDING

Summary Questions

1. The mantle is the outer layer of the Earth. True or False?
2. Which of the following is the most brittle layer of the Earth?
   a. Mantle
   b. Lithosphere
   c. Crust
   d. Core
3. Liquefaction causes soils to lose strength and act like a fluid. True or False?
4. The Richter scale measures
   a. Shock wave amplitude
   b. Surface faulting
   c. Intensity
   d. Ground movement
5. A microearthquake has a magnitude of less than 4.5. True or False?
6. The MMI (Modified Mercalli Intensity) scale is used to judge earthquake damage potential by measuring
   a. Speed
   b. Velocity
   c. Ground movement
   d. Intensity

7. The Richter scale measures earthquakes using values from 1 to 8. True or False?
8. A Vulcanian volcanic eruption is characterized by
   a. Low-viscosity lava
   b. Large amounts of ash blown off the top
   c. Lava and ash blown out of the side
   d. Small, continuous eruptions
9. Lava that reaches the Earth's surface is called magma. True or False?
10. An area that is prone to volcanic activity is called a
    a. Hot pocket
    b. Lava spot
    c. Hot spot
    d. Lava dome
11. A stratovolcano is a
    a. Composite volcano
    b. Coulee
    c. Microearthquake
    d. Shield volcano
12. Vog is a by-product of a volcanic mudflow. True or False?
13. A debris flow can be dense enough to carry trees and cars. True or False?
14. Landslides can be caused by volcanic eruptions and earthquakes. True or False?
15. Landslide-prone areas include
    a. Bases of drainage channels
    b. Areas at the top of ridges
    c. Areas along the edge of ridges
    d. Areas that have not moved before
16. Episodic erosion takes places over a period of many months or even years. True or False?
17. Coastal erosion becomes a hazard as an increasing number of homes and structures are built in vulnerable areas. True or False?
18. Land subsidence occurs when the land opens up and surface materials fall into cavities. True or False?
19. Most of the land subsidence in the United States is a result of
    a. Mine collapse
    b. Sinkholes
    c. Groundwater removal
    d. Earthquakes

Review Questions

1. The Earth is composed of three layers. Name the layers.
2. Which factor is common among the geologic hazards covered in this chapter?
3. In which layer of the Earth does an earthquake form?
4. Explain the role of seismic waves in an earthquake.
5. Name the four variables that characterize an earthquake.
6. California is typically thought of as a particularly earthquake-prone area. Name two other areas that share the threat.
7. What is the name of the geologic event that occurs when solid rock turns to molten rock?
8. Explain what, if any, connection there may be between volcanoes and earthquakes.
9. Lava flows and volcanic ash are obvious dangers to human life and property. Name three other threats from a volcanic eruption.

10. Explain what makes a debris flow different from a typical landslide.
11. Describe how natural hazards other than hurricanes and tropical storms can affect landslides.
12. Coastal erosion is the wearing away of land surface, most notably by wind, waves, and long shore currents. Name three other causes of coastal erosion.
13. What process causes a beach profile to differ between winter and summer?
14. Removal of groundwater is the most significant cause of subsidence in the United States. What are three other actions that contribute to subsidence?
15. Explain how withdrawal of groundwater causes regional-scale subsidence in many areas of the United States.

Applying This Chapter

1. Using the geologic hazards covered in this chapter, pick those that occur where you live and put them in order of most likely to least likely to occur.
2. Imagine you live in an area that experiences an earthquake measuring 6.1 on the Richter scale. Using the MMI scale, what would be its intensity and what effects would you be likely to experience?
3. Consider the building you're in and predict its ability to withstand an earthquake that measures 5.4 on the Richter scale.
4. As an emergency manager in a town 100 miles from Washington State's Mount St. Helens, what kind of information would you provide to members of your community about the risk of volcanoes and other geologic hazards?
5. Landslides occur in all 50 states. Consider the potential for a landslide in your area. Has one occurred in the past? Where would you predict any high-risk areas to be?
6. A block of vacation homes along the shore of North Carolina's barrier islands has lost many feet of property in the past decade because of the effects of coastal erosion. What information should be presented to potential home buyers in neighboring areas that have not yet experienced such severe erosion? What should they know about regulations for building new structures?
7. Though agriculture has been responsible for a good deal of the groundwater removal and resulting subsidence, the country's growing population and its need for water (landscaping, drinking water, fire suppression, industry, manufacturing, recreating, etc.) is become a major factor. Describe an area of the country that is experiencing such a potentially hazardous boom in development. What are the community's water needs?

You Try It

Know Your Geology

As an emergency manager in your town, what resources would you use to create a map of your town's geologic high-risk areas? How would you describe the different areas of risk to a homeowner or business owner in your community?

I Feel the Earth Move

Earthquakes are a major concern in many areas of the United States. What is your community's level of risk from a quake? Use the USGS's earthquake website, at earthquake.usgs.gov, to determine when the last earthquake took place in your state. Consider how earthquake preparedness factors into your own emergency plan. Using the website, determine what you should do during an earthquake. For example, should you head for a doorway? Rooftop? Basement? Also, how are the contents of your home likely to withstand seismic activity?

REFERENCES

1. Coch, N.K. 1995. *Geohazards: Natural and Human.* Englewood Cliffs, NJ: Prentice Hall.
2. Dunbar, P.K. and C.S. Weaver. 2008. *U.S. States and Territories National Tsunami Hazard Assessment: Historical Record and Sources for Waves.* Prepared for the National Tsunami Mitigation Program by the National Oceanic and Atmospheric Administration National Geophysical Data Center and the U.S. Geological Survey.
3. Morton, R.A., T.L. Miller, and L.J. Moore. 2004. *Open File Report 2004-1043, U.S. Geological Survey.*
4. Nicholls, R.J., P.P. Wong, V.R. Burkett, J.O. Codignotto, J.E. Hay, R.F. McLean, S. Ragoonaden, and C.D. Woodroffe. 2007. Coastal systems and low-lying areas. In *Climate Change 2007: Impacts, Adaptation and Vulnerability. Contribution of Working Group II to the Fourth Assessment Report of the Intergovernmental Panel on Climate Change,* M.L. Parry, O.F. Canziani, J.P. Palutikof, P.J. van der Linden, and C.E. Hanson, Eds. Cambridge, UK: Cambridge University Press, 315–356.
5. Williams, J.B. 2007. *Proceedings of the 2007 National Conference on Environmental Science and Technology.* Greensboro, NC.

5

Human-Made Hazards
Technological Hazards, Terrorism, and Civil Unrest

What You'll Learn

- Categories of human-made hazards
- Common hazardous materials
- Ways in which hazardous materials can affect humans
- The emotional consequences of human-made hazards
- Notable human-made events in U.S. history
- Types of terrorist acts and tactics
- Ways that civil unrest can cause disorder and disruption

Goals and Outcomes

- Assess the procedures and tools to evaluate the risks of human-made hazards
- Distinguish among human-made hazards in a given situation
- Evaluate a community's preparedness for a hazard event by using an all-hazards approach
- Identify some of the potential human-made hazards in your community
- Assess the public's perception of risk from terrorism and technological hazards

INTRODUCTION

A resilient community must deal not only with recurrent natural hazards but also take action to protect itself from human-made hazards, including those that are accidental as well as hazards that are intentional in nature. This chapter introduces various types of human-made hazards and provides a short list of some of the notable human-made events that have occurred in the United States and abroad. The chapter then explores various technological hazards, including hazardous materials releases, nuclear reactor incidents, and oil spills. The chapter then discusses terrorism, cyberattacks, and mass shootings, significant intentional threats to our country. Next, the chapter explains the role and impact of civil unrest, emphasizing the importance of free expression through public demonstrations, while also describing the types of violence and damage that can occur. The chapter concludes with a description of some of the psychological effects these types of hazards may produce and a discussion of the public perception of risk associated with these hazards.

DOI: 10.4324/9781003123897-5 **94**

5.1 THE AMERICAN EXPERIENCE

When compared with the number of natural hazards such as hurricanes, wildfires, floods, earthquakes, tornadoes, ice storms, landslides, and other feats of nature that have impacted our communities in the past, the United States has experienced relatively few human-made hazards. We have one of the safest transportation systems in the world, a highly regulated nuclear power industry, and stringent laws that restrict the use of chemicals, toxins, corrosives, and other hazardous materials. Yet accidents still happen. For example, freight trains can derail, spilling chemicals over the landscape. Oil wells can develop leaks, wreaking havoc on the environment and surrounding communities. We call these and other accidental human-made hazards **technological hazards**. This chapter discusses some of the different types of technological hazards and how they can impact our communities.

This chapter also discusses intentional human-made hazards. This category of human-made hazards includes **terrorism**, which refers to intentional criminal acts carried out for purposes of intimidation or coercion. This category also includes incidents of **civil unrest**, such as protests, which can be an important part of a democratic society, but nonetheless pose risks, including injury to people and destruction of property.

5.1.1 The All-Hazards Approach

Despite the feelings of urgency we may have when we consider the threat of terrorism, along with the dangers of technological accidents and civil unrest, we must be careful to keep in mind the array of natural hazards that we know with certainty will occur in this country. We *know* that hurricanes will continue to ravage our coasts. We *know* that tornadoes will cause great damage in the Midwest. We know that communities will be flooded time and again. We know that the western states will continue to experience devastating wildfires. We know without a doubt that these hazards will take place in these regions. In our efforts to reduce the dangers posed by human-made hazards, we must not lose sight of the fact that natural hazards are a certainty. We must take care that resources devoted to homeland security are not diverted from our efforts to reduce the impacts of natural hazards through mitigation and preparedness. Our prioritization process must consider all types of hazards when we develop our risk reduction policies and strategies. This approach to dealing with both natural and human-made hazards simultaneously is known as the **all-hazards approach**.

The all-hazards approach is fully endorsed by the Federal Emergency Management Agency (FEMA), which encourages all communities to adopt mitigation and emergency operations plans that identify and assess risk from multiple sources. In many cases, actions taken to reduce risk from one type of hazard may actually have beneficial outcomes in terms of reducing risk from other hazards, and all-hazards planning allows communities to think through these co-benefits.

Each community must rank the importance of natural and human-made hazards based on its own unique characteristics. In some communities, susceptibility to a terrorist attack or technological accident is quite low. These communities will focus mainly on the natural hazards that are common in their region. Other communities, however, will find that their vulnerability to a human-made hazard is much higher, perhaps because they provide an attractive target for a terrorist attack, or because there are multiple locations or occasions where a technological accident could occur. Either way, each community will need to assess for itself what priority it should place on reducing risk from human-made and natural hazards, by assessing the probability of each type of hazard occurring in the community and factoring in the most likely consequences.

5.1.2 Significant Human-Made Events in the United States

Table 5.1 lists a few of the more dramatic events that have occurred in our nation's history. Measured in sheer numbers, the monetary impact and numbers of deaths and injuries come nowhere close to the amount of damage that has been caused by natural hazards over the years. However, these types of hazards have an emotional component that is distinct from that associated with the aftermath of a natural disaster. As an interesting exercise, try to gauge your feelings when you read the short facts listed here. Are you affected in ways that might differ from your reaction if these were events caused by nature and not by fellow humans?

SELF-CHECK

- Define **technological hazards**, **civil unrest**, and **all-hazards approach**.
- Explain the difference between human-made and natural hazards.
- Give three examples of human-made hazards.

5.2 TECHNOLOGICAL HAZARDS

From industrial chemicals and nuclear materials to household detergents and air fresheners, hazardous materials are part of the modern world. These materials are used to make our water safe to drink, generate energy, provide fuel for vehicles and machines, increase farm production, simplify household chores, aid in medical care and research, and act as key components in many of the products we use every day. As many as 80,000 products pose physical or health hazards and can be defined as *hazardous*. Each year, more than 700 new synthetic chemicals are introduced in the United States.[1] Technological hazard incidents occur when hazardous materials are used, transported, or disposed of improperly, potentially exposing the community to harmful consequences.

The types of hazardous material releases are often classified as chemical, biological, radiological, or nuclear releases, using the acronym CBRN. In some cases, explosives are added to the list, and communities will refer to these types of threats as CBRNE. Although we are discussion in this text within the section of technological hazards, it is important to note that CBRN can be the result of either accidental releases or can be caused by intentional releases such as terrorism. In many cases, the steps to mitigate risk and prepare for hazardous material releases are similar, whether they are the result of a technological failure, human error, or a criminal act.

5.2.1 Community Impacts from Technological Hazards

Technological hazards can occur at any time without warning. Hazardous materials can enter a community during any stage of the life cycle of the materials, including production, storage, transportation, use, and disposal. Even if hazardous materials are handled safely, they may be of concern if a precipitating event occurs, such as a fire or flood. Hazmat incidents can cause widespread impacts throughout a community, such as power outages, disruptions in communications, and damage to critical infrastructure. In extreme events that involve widespread dispersion of hazardous chemicals through water or air, evacuations of the affected populations may be required. If serious long-term contamination of local groundwater, surface water, or soils occurs, residents may be forced to relocate or even abandon their homes and businesses.

Table 5.1 Selected Man-Made Hazard Events in the United States.

Event	Location	Type of Hazard	Description and Impacts
Pittsburgh Synagogue Shooting October 27, 2018	Pittsburg, Pennsylvania	Mass Shooting/ Domestic Terrorism	A violent attack during a worshipping service at a synagogue, resulting in 11 deaths and 7 injuries. The perpetrator had a history of anti-Semitic beliefs and was intentionally targeting the Jewish community.
Las Vegas Shooting October 1, 2017	Paradise, Nevada	Mass Shooting	A shooter opened fire from a 32nd floor hotel suite upon a crowd attending a music festival on the Las Vegas Strip, killing 60 people and wounding 411. The incident is the deadliest mass shooting committed by an individual in modern U.S. history.
Charleston Church Shooting June 17, 2015	Charleston, South Carolina	Mass Shooting	A racially motivated, violent attack by a white supremacist targeting members of an African American church, resulting in the death of 9 people. The attack was one of the deadliest mass shootings at an American place of worship.
Fertilizer Plant Explosion April 17th, 2013	West, Texas	Technological Accident	An explosion occurred at the West Fertilizer Company's storage and distribution facility 18 miles north of Waco, TX during an emergency services response to a fire at the facility. The explosion was triggered by ammonium nitrate and resulted in at least 15 deaths, 160+ injuries, and more than 150 damaged buildings.
Boston Marathon Bombings April 15th, 2013	Boston, Massachusetts	Domestic Terrorism	Two pressure cooker bombs exploded near the finish line of the Boston Marathon, killing 3 and injuring 264 others. Three days later two suspects engaged in a firefight with law enforcement, resulting in additional deaths and an unprecedented 20 block lock down in Watertown, MA.
Deepwater Horizon Oil Spill 2010	Gulf of Mexico near Mississippi River Delta	Technological Accident	BP's oil rig *Deepwater Horizon* exploded and sank on April 20th, killing 11 oilmen, and resulting in a record breaking offshore oil spill considered the largest accidental marine oil spill in the world. The total discharge is estimated at 4.9 million barrels of oil and continues to have serious environmental, health, and economic impacts.

(Continued)

Table 5.1 (Continued)

Event	Location	Type of Hazard	Description and Impacts
Anthrax Attacks October 2001	Washington, D.C. New York City Boca Raton, FL	Terrorism of Unknown Origin	Letters containing anthrax mailed to news media offices and 2 U.S. Senators; 5 deaths, 22 infected with long-term illness; shutdown government mail service; dozens of buildings decontaminated at estimated cost of more than $1 billion.
Terrorist Attacks September 11, 2001	Dept. of Defense Headquarters (Pentagon) Washington, D.C., World Trade Center, New York City Rural Somerset County near Shanksville, PA	International Terrorism	Series of suicide attacks using hijacked airliners; 2986 deaths, thousands injured; 25 buildings in Manhattan destroyed; 1.5 million tons of debris in New York City; portion of Pentagon damaged; costs of clean-up, rebuilding, and economic losses in billions of dollars; stock markets worldwide fell; airline industry severely impacted; massive insurance claims against airlines and others; impetus for large-scale "War on Terror."
Olympic Bombing July 27, 1996	Olympic Centennial Park, Atlanta, GA	Domestic Terrorism	Politically motivated bomb attack; 1 direct death, 1 fatal heart attack, 111 injured; perpetrator Eric Rudolph captured, also charged with other bombings, and sentenced to life imprisonment.
Oklahoma City Bombing April 19, 1995	Murrah Federal Building, Oklahoma City, Oklahoma	Domestic Terrorism	Bomb made of fertilizer and other readily available materials detonated in rental truck; 168 deaths, more than 500 injured; perpetrators Timothy McVeigh and Terry Nichols captured, tried, and sentenced.
World Trade Center Bombing February 26, 1993	New York City	International Terrorism	Van with bomb driven into basement parking garage and remotely detonated; 6 deaths, more than 1000 injured; $300 million property damage.
L.A. Riots (also known as Rodney King Riots) April 29, 1992	Los Angeles, California	Civil Unrest/ Race Riot	6 days of rioting sparked when mostly white jury acquitted 4 police officers accused in videotaped beating of African American motorist Rodney King. Thousands of residents joined in what is described as a race riot, involving mass law breaking, looting, arson, murder. 50–60 deaths; more than 2000 injured; 10,000 arrests; $800 million–$1 billion in property damage.

Event	Location	Type	Description
Exxon Valdez Oil Spill 1989	Prince William Sound, Alaska	Technological Accident	Exxon oil tanker ran aground attributed to negligence of Ship's captain; 40,000 tons of crude oil spilled into ocean and spread along hundreds of miles of coastline; caused severe environmental damage and deaths of marine and coastal wildlife and plants; effects of spill still evident today; Court ordered Exxon to pay $1 billion in damages used for clean-up and restoration; disaster led to passage of federal Oil Pollution Act; Captain fined and sentenced to community service.
Three-Mile Island Nuclear Accident March 28, 1979	Near Middletown, Pennsylvania	Nuclear Power Plant Accident	Equipment malfunction, design problems, and worker errors led to partial meltdown of reactor core; small off-site release of radioactivity; no deaths; brought about sweeping changes in response training, engineering, radiation protection; caused U.S. Nuclear Regulatory Agency to tighten regulatory oversight. Today reactor is permanently shut down and de-fueled.
White supremacist attack on 16th Street Baptist Church 1963	Birmingham, Alabama	Domestic Terrorism/Civil Unrest/Race Riot	4 teenaged African American girls killed in bomb attack of church; 23 injured; riots and fires followed in city; 1 suspect acquitted of murder in 1963, re-tried in 1977, found guilty, and sentenced to life in prison; 2 more suspects tried in 2000, 1 convicted.
Great Fire of Chicago October 1871	Chicago	Accidental Fire	Small barn fire turned into raging conflagration; 300 dead; 18,000 buildings destroyed; one-third of population made homeless; city rebuilt in 2 years.

DEEPWATER HORIZON OIL SPILL

From April 20 through July 15, 2010, an estimated 210 million gallons of oil flowed into the Gulf of Mexico following the explosion and sinking of the BP Deepwater Horizon oil rig, which claimed 11 lives. In what is considered the largest accidental marine oil spill in the history of the petroleum industry, a massive response was undertaken in an attempt to protect beaches, wetlands, estuaries, marine and wildlife habitat, and the Gulf's fishing and tourism industries. While research studies continue to investigate the environmental, economic, and health consequences of the disaster, it is clear that the spill impacted thousands of marine species, resulted in physical and mental health problems for residents along the Gulf Coast, and cost the commercial fishing industry approximately $2.5 billion and the tourism industry approximately $23 billion.

5.2.2 What Makes Hazardous Materials Hazardous?

Hazardous materials are substances that, because of their chemical or toxic nature, pose a potential risk to life or health. Many of the properties of chemicals that make them valuable, such as their ability to kill dangerous organisms in water and pests on crops, pose a hazard to humans and the environment if the chemicals are mishandled. Hazardous materials come in the form of explosives, flammable and combustible substances, poisons, and radioactive materials and can cause death, serious injury, cancer, and other long-lasting health effects.

There are many definitions and descriptive names that are used for the term *hazardous materials*, each of which depends on the nature of the problem being addressed. The list that follows includes some of the definitions used by federal agencies responsible for regulating hazardous materials.

- **Hazardous Materials**: The United States Department of Transportation (DOT) uses the term *hazardous materials* to cover eight separate hazard classes, some of which have subcategories or classifications. The classes include explosives, gases, flammable liquids, flammable solids, oxidizing agents and organic peroxides, toxic and infectious substances, radioactive substances, and corrosive substances. A ninth class covers Other Regulated Materials (ORM).
- **Hazardous Substances**: The Environmental Protection Agency (EPA) uses the term hazardous substances for the chemicals that, if released in the environment above a certain amount, must be reported, and, depending on the threat to the environment, federal involvement in handling the incident can be authorized.
- **Extremely Hazardous Substances**: EPA uses the term extremely hazardous substances for the chemicals that must be reported to the appropriate authorities if released above the threshold reporting quantity. Each substance has a threshold reporting quantity.
- **Toxic Chemicals**: EPA uses the term toxic chemicals for chemicals whose total emissions or releases must be reported annually by owners and operators of certain facilities that manufacture, process, or otherwise use a listed toxic chemical.
- **Hazardous Wastes**: EPA uses the term hazardous wastes for chemicals regulated under the Resource, Conservation and Recovery Act. Hazardous wastes in transportation are regulated by DOT.
- **Hazardous Chemicals**: Occupational Safety and Health Administration (OSHA), within the U.S. Department of Labor, uses the term hazardous chemical to denote any chemical that would be a risk to employees if exposed in the work place. Hazardous chemicals cover a broader group of chemicals than the other chemical lists.

- **Hazardous Substances**: OSHA uses the term hazardous substances in regulations that cover emergency response. Hazardous substances, as used by OSHA, cover every chemical regulated by both DOT and EPA.

5.2.3 Symptoms of Toxic Poisoning

Some of the symptoms that people may exhibit after being exposed to certain hazardous materials include:

- Difficulty breathing
- Irritation of the eyes, skin, throat
- Irritation in the respiratory tract
- Changes in skin color
- Headaches or blurred vision
- Dizziness
- Clumsiness or lack of coordination
- Cramps or diarrhea
- Nausea or vomiting

5.2.4 Sources of Hazardous Materials

Many businesses and facilities throughout the United States use and store hazardous materials. Chemical manufacturers and refineries are among the industries that are well recognized as hazardous materials sites; however, hazardous materials are also present in many other locations in our communities. For example, the food processing industry may have large quantities of hazardous materials such as ammonia in the refrigeration systems of their plants, warehouses, distribution centers, and cargo carriers. Local drinking water systems, sewage treatment plants, and public swimming pools also store chemicals that are used to kill dangerous bacteria in the water, but which can be toxic if handled improperly.

Many retail commercial sites also use, store, and sell chemicals and toxic substances. Hazardous materials can be found in hardware stores, agriculture supply centers, garden shops, and in pest control businesses. Many small operations, including service stations, dry cleaners, and garages, also routinely use hazardous materials in their daily operations. Hospitals, clinics, and research universities store and use a range of biohazard, radioactive, combustible, and flammable materials. In all, varying quantities of hazardous materials are manufactured, used, or stored at an estimated 4.5 million facilities in the United States. In addition, there are approximately 30,000 hazardous materials waste sites in the country.

5.2.5 OSHA Safety Data Sheets

The OSHA sets permissible exposure levels of many chemicals for workers who may come in contact with hazardous substances while on the job. In 2012, OSHA issued revised provisions to implement the "Employee right to know" rules. The revised Hazard Communication Standards (HazCom) require that **Safety Data Sheets (SDS)** (formerly known as Material Safety Data Sheets) be available to employees for potentially harmful substances handled in the workplace. HazCom 2012 requires chemical manufacturers and importers to provide a label that includes a unified product identifier, pictogram, signal word, and hazard statement for each hazard class and category. Precautionary statements must also be provided.

The Safety Data Sheets provides workers and emergency personnel with procedures for handling or working with that substance in a safe manner and includes information such as physical data (melting point, boiling point, flash point, etc.), toxicity, health effects, first aid, reactivity, storage, disposal, protective equipment, and spill handling procedures. This information can be life-saving to first responders who may be called to the scene of a hazmat incident.

COMMUNICATING HAZARDS WITH PICTOGRAMS

As of June 1, 2015, the Hazard Communication Standard issued by OSHA requires pictograms on labels to alert users of the chemical hazards to which they may be exposed. Each pictogram consists of a symbol on a white background framed within a red border and represents a distinct hazard or combination of hazards, such as health, physical, and environmental. The pictogram on the label is determined by the chemical hazard classification. For example, the Skull and Cross Bones must appear on the most severely toxic chemicals that pose a risk of death or severe health impairment, while the environment symbol appears on chemicals that are acutely hazardous to fish, crustacean, or aquatic plants.

SELF-CHECK

- Define **hazardous materials**.
- Explain how a hazardous material becomes a technological hazard.
- Name the federal agency that sets safety regulations for workers exposed to chemicals.
- Discuss various sources of hazardous materials in a typical community.

5.2.6 Hazmat Transportation Accidents

Communities and residences located near facilities that handle hazardous materials are considered at higher risk of experiencing a hazmat incident than areas that are further removed. However, no community is completely immune, since hazardous materials are transported regularly over our highways, by water, pipeline, and by rail. Over 3.1 billion tons of hazardous materials are shipped annually, and if any of these materials are released during a traffic, train, or pipeline accident, they can spread quickly and impact a large area.

The Federal hazardous materials transportation law is the basic statute regulating the transportation of hazardous materials in the United States. The Pipeline and Hazardous Materials Safety Administration (PHMSA) within the US DOT is charged with protecting people and the environment from the risks inherent in transportation of hazardous materials by all modes of transportation, including pipelines. The PHMSA issues permits and ensures compliance of the law's provisions. The PHMSA's mission also includes preparedness and response and focuses on training of all hazmat employees involved in transport, along with planning, exercising, and enhancing capabilities.

Communities located on the known transit route of hazardous materials must take extra precautions to be ready to respond quickly in case of an accidental spill or release of chemicals during transportation. Accidents are reported directly to the 24-hour National Response Center that dispatches trained hazmat responders. Additionally, the U.S. DOT operates a 24-hour Crisis Management Center, and many state-level agencies are also on alert for transportation accidents.

HUMAN ERROR DURING TRANSPORTATION

Human error is the cause of many of the transportation incidents involving the release of hazardous materials. This was the case in the Exxon Valdez Oil Spill, where operator error was thought to have contributed to the crash of the oil tanker into a reef in Prince William Sound, Alaska, in 1989. Nearly 11 billion gallons of crude oil spilled into the bay, killing millions of fish and other aquatic animals and contaminating the water and shore of the Bay for years. The Valdez spill is considered to be one of the most devastating human-caused environmental disasters and was the largest ever in US waters until the 2010 Deepwater Horizon oil spill in terms of volume released.

5.2.7 Leaks during Storage and Disposal

There are a number of federal and state regulations that must be met for the safe and proper storage of hazardous chemicals and materials. Chemical storage buildings must be designed to contain liquid spills, leaks, vapors, and explosions to minimize risk to workers in the facilities or to the environment. Chemical storage buildings in particular must be designed to prevent the leaking of liquids into the environment. Chemical storage buildings are often constructed with steel grates and sumps in the floor of the building to collect and contain spilled hazardous chemicals. The building might also have partitions to segregate different substances.

Despite the rules and regulations imposed by the EPA, DOT, OSHA, and numerous state agencies, leaks, spills, and other accidental releases from storage facilities do occur. There is the potential for leaks and spills to go undetected for weeks, months, and even years, especially when storage containers are buried underground. Undetected leaks can cause the substances to leach further into the soil or enter groundwater, endangering residents for miles around.

Hazardous waste disposal sites are also heavily regulated by local, state, and federal authorities. Most disposal sites are located in areas far from human habitation, but problems may arise when community growth and development sprawl into areas where hazardous materials have been deposited. Most disposal sites must be lined with materials that are suitable to contain the hazardous waste deposited there to prevent leaching into the surrounding environment. However, many communities have experienced problems with leaking, abandoned, or improperly maintained and monitored sites.

Identifying the location, size, and contents of storage and disposal facilities is the first step in preparing for and mitigating the impacts of an accidental or intentional release or spill. Often, however, security concerns require that the location and other identifying features of hazardous materials facilities are not disclosed publicly due to the risk of sabotage or terrorist strike. These concerns make the job of mapping and preparedness training more challenging for the community. These concerns also highlight the importance of an all-hazards approach to emergency management at all levels of government.

DANGERS LURKING AT HOME

Despite the dangers of chemical leaks and accidents during transportation, storage, and disposal, most victims of chemical accidents are injured at home. These incidents usually result from a lack of awareness or carelessness in using flammable or combustible materials. Local poison control centers are set up nationwide to deal with accidental ingestion or spills of many types of hazardous materials; many of the calls received by these centers involve small children who have gained access to improperly stored hazardous materials such as cleaning solutions, antifreeze, and other substances that can be fatal if swallowed or touched.

Hazardous materials can also be released during routine household chores. Residents may not realize that flushing cleaning solutions and other household substances down the toilet or washing them down the sink allows these dangerous elements to enter our environment directly. The simple act of hosing down a driveway can wash oil, gasoline, and other harmful substances into the local storm water and drainage systems, where it flows into our rivers and streams and eventually enters our drinking water supplies.

5.2.8 Biological Hazards

Biological hazards can be in the form of bacteria, viruses, or other biological agents. Typically, people can be impacted by biological hazards in a few ways, depending on the type of biological material:

- **Airborne exposure**: Inhaling some biological materials can be harmful to people's health or even fatal, such as exposure to the spores that cause anthrax.
- **Ingesting contaminated food or water**: Gastrointestinal infection can result from exposure to some biological materials through food or water. For example, the bacteria *E. coli* in foods can result in widespread illness among people who consume infected food.
- **Direct contact**: Many biological diseases are spread through direct contact with infected individuals or through touching contaminated surfaces. The viruses that cause influenza are spread in this manner.

Depending on the type of biological hazard, emergency managers may work hand-in-hand with local and state public health departments and even the federal Centers for Disease Control and Prevention. As with many hazards and threats, emergency managers play a key role in coordinating across agencies and disciplines, before, during, and after an event. This may include organizing trainings, ensuring that communities have sufficient stockpiles of medical supplies and other equipment to contain biological hazards, and facilitating clear communication with the public.

COVID-19: ALL HANDS ON DECK

A novel coronavirus is leading to the COVID-19 pandemic that is unfolding around the world as this text is being written. This is one of the most significant and devastating biological disasters in modern history, infecting millions of people and impacting nearly every country around the world. Many professions and occupations are playing significant roles to slow the spread of the virus, support impacted communities, and find a cure or vaccine. Emergency managers and planners involved in mitigation and preparedness are playing vital roles in all aspects of managing the outbreak.

A few examples of actions that emergency managers are taking during the COVID-19 pandemic to help keep communities prepare and minimize impacts include:

- Communicating to the public about actions individuals can take to reduce the spread of coronavirus, including wearing masks and practicing social distancing.
- Helping to establish temporary facilities to distribute food and water to community members who may need assistance.
- Coordinating with public health and hospital systems to establish temporary testing sites, hospitals, and other facilities needed to treat patients infected with the virus.
- Providing emergency notifications about changes in rules and guidelines, including shelter-in-place regulations, travel restrictions, or other efforts to limit the spread of the virus and keep people safe.
- Modifying existing protocols for other hazards to adapt to public health concerns resulting from COVID, such as providing guidelines for temporary shelters intended for hurricanes, wildfires, or other hazards that accommodate social distancing.

5.2.9 Nuclear Accidents

Nuclear power plants use the heat generated from nuclear fission in a contained environment to convert water to steam, which powers generators to produce electricity. Nuclear power plants operate in most states in the country and produce roughly 20% of the nation's power. About 17 million Americans live within 10 miles of an operating nuclear power plant, and nearly 120 million Americans live within 50 miles of a nuclear power plant.

Although the construction and operation of these facilities are closely monitored and regulated by the U.S. Nuclear Regulatory Commission (NRC), accidents are possible. An accident may result in dangerous levels of radiation that could affect the health and safety of nearby residents. Exposure to radiation is caused by the release of radioactive materials from the plant into the environment, characterized by a plume (cloud-like formation) of radioactive gasses and particles. Wind speed, wind direction, precipitation, and the amount of radiation released from the plant are all factors in determining the area that could be affected. The major hazards to people in the vicinity of the plume are radiation exposure to the body from the cloud and particles deposited on the ground, and inhalation or ingestion of radioactive materials. State and local emergency management officials work together year round to coordinate emergency response plans and activities in the event of a radiation release.

5.2.10 Emergency Planning Zones

The electric utilities that are the owner-operators of nuclear power plants are required to develop, update, and practice emergency response plans to deal with a potential nuclear power plant incident. The plans define two "emergency planning zones." One zone covers an area within a 10-mile radius of the plant, where people could be harmed by direct radiation exposure. The second zone covers a broader area, usually up to a 50-mile radius from the plant, where radioactive materials could contaminate water supplies, food crops, and livestock.

Under federal rules, U.S. communities plan and practice for evacuation or other protective action by residents only within the 10-mile zone surrounding a nuclear power plant. However, because a major nuclear accident has not occurred in the United States, the reaction of residents in the 50-mile planning zone is unknown. It is possible that people living beyond the official 10-mile evacuation zone might be so frightened by the prospect of spreading radiation that they would flee on their own, clogging roads and delaying the escape of others. Emergency managers tasked with planning for nuclear accidents may need to take the potential for increased numbers of evacuees into account when developing evacuation routes and procedures.

THREE MILE ISLAND NUCLEAR REACTOR ACCIDENT

The accident at the Three Mile Island Unit 2 nuclear power plant near Middletown, Pennsylvania on March 28, 1979, was the most serious in U.S. commercial nuclear power plant operating history and, until the Chernobyl accident in the Soviet Union in 1986, was considered the worst civilian nuclear accident in the world. Although the incident resulted in no deaths or injuries to plant workers or members of the nearby community, the event did bring about sweeping changes involving emergency response planning, reactor operator training, human factors engineering, radiation protection, and many other areas of nuclear power plant operations. It also caused the U.S. NRC to tighten and heighten its regulatory oversight.

The sensibility of Americans to nuclear plant accidents was heightened by the meltdown at the Fukushima Dai-ichi nuclear complex in Japan, which was severely damaged by the massive tsunami triggered by an earthquake that occurred off the coast of Japan in 2011. Of the 65 commercial nuclear power plants operating in the United States, several are located in or near seismic zones, and several others are located in coastal areas that are prone to sea level rise, storm surge, and flooding. This proximity to known hazard areas requires emergency managers in these communities to use a rigorous approach to calculating the risk and potential impacts of a nuclear power plant accident. For a map and a list of power reactor sites in the United States, visit the NRC website (www.nrc.gov).

5.2.11 Hazmat Releases during Natural Hazard Events

Natural hazard events, including hurricanes, tornadoes, floods, and earthquakes, have often triggered technological hazards. Natural hazard events can rupture pipelines, spark fires, dislodge tanks and storage containers, and cause safety measures to malfunction. The occurrence of a technological hazard during a natural hazard event is often called a **secondary hazard**, because it occurs as a result of the primary natural event. Sometimes, the release of hazardous materials during a flood or other natural hazard causes more damage to the environment and surrounding community than the original event itself. One of the most striking examples of a secondary hazard caused by a precipitating natural event is the 2011 earthquake that struck Japan, causing a catastrophic tsunami with heights of up to 133 feet. The tsunami resulted in a considerable secondary hazard when a meltdown occurred in one of the reactors of the Fukushima Dai-ichi Nuclear Power Plant. Thousands of residents were evacuated because of the threat of radiation contamination. These evacuees were combined with the residents that survived the earthquake and tsunami to reach a total of several hundred thousand individuals and families seeking shelter from the multiple disasters.

SELF-CHECK

- Define **secondary hazard** and give an example of a secondary hazard that could occur.
- Explain how hazardous incidents can occur during transportation.
- Describe how emergency planning zones around nuclear power plants are determined.

5.3 TERRORISM

In the United States, the official definition of terrorism as stated in the U.S. Code of Federal Regulations is "...*the unlawful use of force and violence against persons or property to intimidate or coerce a government, the civilian population, or any segment thereof, in furtherance of political or social objectives.*"[2]

Terrorists often use threats to create fear among the public, to try to convince citizens that their government is powerless to prevent terrorism, and to get immediate publicity for their cause.

5.3.1 Elements of Terrorism

The term terrorism is interpreted in various ways depending on its context, but there are certain core elements that characterize most acts of terrorism:

- **Violence:** Terrorism generally involves violence and/or the threat of violence.
- **Target:** Terrorism usually entails the deliberate and specific selection of civilians as direct targets.
- **Objectives:** Terrorism usually is an attempt to provoke fear and intimidation in the main target audience, to attract wide publicity, and cause public shock and outrage.
- **Motives:** Terrorist activities may be intended to achieve political or religious goals; terrorists who act as mercenaries may also be motivated by person gain. Historical grievances, retaliation for past actions, and specific demands such as ransom or policy change may also be motivating factors.
- **Perpetrators:** War crimes and crimes against humanity are not usually included in the definition of terrorism. Likewise, overt government oppression of its own civilians (e.g., the 2013 chemical attacks against civilians in Syria) is not usually considered terrorism. However, state-sponsored terrorism can involve government support of terrorism carried out in another country.
- **Legitimacy:** Most definitions of terrorism require that the act be unlawful.

WHAT MAKES AN ATTACK TERRORISM?

Consider this example: An organized group enters a bank, kills the bank manager, blows up the vault, and escapes with millions of dollars. This would not be labeled as terrorism. But if the group did the same thing with the intent to cause a crisis in public confidence in the banking system and destabilize the economy, then the attack likely would be considered terrorism. In this case, the motive and long-term consequence are factors that distinguish between bank robbers who are seeking personal gain and bank robbers who are seeking to make a political statement and cause widespread and lingering impacts through their actions.

5.3.2 Types of Terrorism

The Federal Bureau of Investigation (FBI) characterizes terrorism as either domestic or international, depending upon the origin, base, and objectives of the terrorist actor or group.

- **Domestic terrorism** involves groups or individuals whose terrorist activities are directed at elements of our government or population without foreign direction.
- **International terrorism** involves groups or individuals whose terrorist activities are foreign-based and/or directed by countries or groups outside the United States or whose activities cross international boundaries.

The 1995 bombing of the Murrah Federal Building in Oklahoma City was an act of domestic terrorism, while the attacks of September 11, 2001 were international.

Within these broad categories, there are many different forms of terrorist activity. In the United States, most terrorist incidents have involved small extremist groups who use terrorism to carry out a specific agenda. There is often overlap between various motives and methods of these different types of terrorism, and some sorts of terrorism cannot be easily classified into any one group. The following list includes some of the different types of terrorism.

- **Nationalist:** A type of terrorism that involves actors trying to form an independent state in opposition to an occupying or imperial force. Examples: Lebanese, Palestinian, and Northern Ireland terrorist activities.
- **Religious:** The use of violence to further what the actors see as a divinely commanded purpose or objective. Examples: Christian, Jewish, Hindu, Islamic, and other world religion terrorist groups, often fanatical in nature.
- **Left-wing:** Terrorism growing from social movements on the left. Example: Symbionese Liberation Army of the 1970s.
- **Right-wing:** The use of terrorist tactics to eliminate threats to what is seen as traditional values or politically right-wing power structures. Examples: Neo-Nazi, white supremacist, anti-communist groups.
- **State:** Can include terrorist activities carried out, subsidized, or sanctioned by a national government or its proxy.
- **Racist:** Terrorism related to issues of race or ethnicity; may be carried out by racist, xenophobic, or fascist groups. Examples: Ku Klux Klan, Neo-Nazis, white supremacist groups.
- **Narco-terrorism:** Attempts by narcotics traffickers to influence or intimidate government policies, law enforcement, or the justice system.
- **Anarchist:** Terrorism intended to carry out the goal of anarchist groups or the elimination of all forms of government.
- **Political:** Terrorism used to influence sociopolitical events, issues, or policies.
- **Ecoterrorism:** Acts of sabotage, vandalism, property damage, or intimidation in the name of environmental interests; often target large corporations seen as exploiting or otherwise damaging natural resources. Examples: EarthFirst!, Animal Liberation Front, Earth Liberation Front.

5.3.3 Terrorism Tactics and Weapons

Terrorist attacks are conducted through a variety of means. The level of organization, technological expertise, and financial backing of the terrorist group often determines the type of technique used. The nature of the political, social, or religious issue that motivates the attack as well as the points of weakness in the terrorist's target also factor into the type of tactic employed. In the United States, the most frequent terrorist techniques have been shootings and the use of bombs, with shootings from right-wing extremist groups increasing in frequency over the past couple of decades.

The following tactics and weapons are among those that have been used to carry out acts of terrorism in the United States:

- Conventional bomb
- Improvised explosive device
- Biological agent
- Chemical agent
- Nuclear bomb
- Radiological agent
- Arson/incendiary attack
- Armed attack
- Cyberterrorism
- Agriterrorism
- Hijacking
- Car bomb
- Suicide bomb
- Kidnapping
- Assassination
- Sabotage

5.3.4 Biological and Chemical Weapons

- **Biological agents** are infectious organisms or toxins that are used to produce illness or death in people, livestock, and crops.
- **Chemical agents** are poisonous gases, liquids, or solids that have toxic effects on people, plants, or animals. Some chemical agents are odorless and tasteless, making them difficult to detect.

Biological agents can be dispersed as aerosols or airborne particles and can be used by terrorists to contaminate food or water supplies. Depending on the type of agent used, contamination can be spread via wind and/or water. Light-to-moderate winds will disburse biological agents, but high winds can break up aerosol clouds. Infection can also be spread through human or animal contact. Sunlight can destroy many, but not all, forms of bacteria and viruses.

Severity of injuries from chemical agents depends on the type and amount used, as well as the duration of exposure. Air temperature can affect the evaporation of chemical aerosols, and ground temperature can affect evaporation of liquids. Rainfall can dilute and disperse chemical agents but can also spread contamination. Wind can disperse vapors but can also cause the target area to be dynamic.

The effects of biological and chemical agents can be either instantaneous or delayed up to several hours or several days. Some biological agents can pose a threat for years depending upon conditions. Biological and chemical weapons have been used primarily to terrorize unprotected civilian population in other countries but have not been used on a large scale within the United States.

5.3.5 Cyber Threats and Cyberterrorism

As the internet has become an essential part of our lives, attacks to computer systems and networks have likewise become a major threat to individuals, businesses, governments, and our society at large. A cyber incident may involve the theft or modification of information or a system compromise with the potential to disrupt essential services.

The motives for cyberattacks can vary significantly, and many cyberattacks are not considered cyberterrorism. For example, many incidents are carried out for financial gain, such as stealing banking information. While such attacks can have significant impacts on individuals and businesses, they would not constitute cyberterrorism and are generally referred to as "cyber crimes." Others are indeed cyberterrorism in that they are intended for political or social purposes, such as attacks intended to sway political elections or spread misinformation to the public.

A cyber incident can impact a system's:

- Confidentiality: protecting a user's private information
- Integrity: ensure that data is protected and cannot be altered by unauthorized parties
- Availability: keeping services running and giving administration access to key network and controls.

The U.S. Department of Homeland Security (DHS) National Cybersecurity and Communications Integration Center developed the Cyber Incident Scoring System (NCISS) to evaluate risk severity and incident priority for cyberattacks. These range from minor priority incidents, medium priority, high priority, severe, or emergency, depending on the likelihood of affecting public health or safety, national security, economic security, foreign relations, civil liberties, or public confidence. Examples of incidents that would be categorized as "Emergency" cyberattacks are those that pose an imminent threat to the provision of wide-scale critical infrastructure, national government stability, or the lives of people in the United States.

Emergency managers are playing an increasingly important role in preventing cyberattacks and mitigating impacts from such attacks. This includes monitoring attacks and data breaches to understand trends and emerging strategies, educating businesses and the public about methods to reduce vulnerabilities of computer networks, and ensuring that critical infrastructure operators – such as electrical systems, water systems, and power plants – have protocols in place to prevent, detect, respond to, and recover from cyber threats.

5.3.6 Impacts of Terrorism

The effects of terrorism can vary significantly from injuries and loss of life to property damage and disruptions in services. Terrorists often seek visible targets where they can avoid detection before or after an attack, such as international airports, large cities, major international events, resorts, and high-profile landmarks.

Terrorist attacks are often carried out with the objective of crippling or destroying government functions and other fundamental elements of society. Targets with widespread impact include attacks on transportation infrastructure, communications networks, banking and financial sectors, the electrical power grid, the shipping industry, public water supplies, the food industry, and multiple government structures and services.

5.3.7 The Role of FEMA

When terrorism strikes, communities can receive assistance from state and federal agencies operating within the existing Integrated Emergency Management Systems (IEMS). FEMA is the lead federal agency for supporting state and local responses to the consequences of terrorist attacks.

FEMA's role in managing terrorism includes both antiterrorism and counterterrorism activities.

- **Antiterrorism** refers to defensive measures used to reduce the vulnerability of people and property to terrorist acts.
- **Counterterrorism** includes offensive measure taken to prevent, deter, and respond to terrorism.

The **Emergency Management Assistance Compact (EMAC)** is a congressionally ratified organization that provides form and structure to interstate mutual aid. Through EMAC, a disaster-impacted state can request and receive assistance from other member states quickly and efficiently.

SELF-CHECK

- Define **domestic terrorism, international terrorism, chemical agents, biological agents, antiterrorism**, and **counterterrorism**.
- Name six elements common to most acts of terrorism.
- List some of the different types of terrorism.
- Compare biological agents and chemical agents.

5.4 MASS SHOOTINGS

Mass shootings are incidents of gun violence, typically defined as involving the death of four or more people. While some mass shootings can be acts of terrorism that are intended to intimidate or coerce people toward political ends, a mass shooting is not, in itself, an act of terrorism.

The United States has had the most mass shootings of any country. In fact, a 2017 study estimated that 31% of public mass shootings occur in the United States, even though the country comprises only 5% of the world's population.[3] The disproportionate rate of these attacks in the United States is often contributed to higher accessibility and rates of gun ownership, rates of mental illness and lack of supportive treatment, and the proliferation of internet forums and communities that glorify shooters. In recent years, the frequency of mass shootings has been increasing in the United States, and some of the deadliest mass shooting attacks in the country's history have occurred in the past several years.

These shootings are typically carried out by a lone gunman who is not acting as part of an organization or identified group. The majority of perpetrators are white men. Mass shootings over the past few decades have occurred in numerous locations, but more than half of the cases involved school or workplace shootings; the remaining cases took place in other public locations including shopping malls, restaurants, and religious and government buildings.

5.4.1 Notable Mass Shooting Events

Mass shootings are a serious issue for law enforcement and emergency managers in large cities, small towns, and on educational campuses throughout the United States. Some of the most highly publicized mass shootings include the following:

- **Pittsburgh Synagogue Shooting**: A shooter opened fire during a morning service at the Tree of Life Synagogue in Pittsburg, Pennsylvania on October 27, 2018. The shooting was the deadliest attack on the Jewish community in the United States, killing 11 people and wounding 6. It was deemed to be domestic terrorism and carried out by a perpetrator who had expressed anti-Semitic beliefs.

- **Las Vegas Shooting:** On October 1, 2017, a 64-year-old man opened fire upon a crowd attending a music festival on the Las Vegas Strip in Nevada. From a 32nd floor room, the perpetrator fired more than 1000 rounds of ammunition at the crowd, killing 60 people and wounding 411, with an additional 867 injuries resulting from the panic that ensued during the attack. The incident was the deadliest mass shooting in modern U.S. history and helped bring about a ban by the U.S. Justice Department on bump stocks for weapons, which allow for shots to be fired in rapid succession.

- **Stoneman Douglas High School Shooting**: A gunman opened fire on February 14, 2018 at a high school in Parkland, Florida, killing 17 people and injuring 17 more. Following the shooting, students who had survived the attack developed an advocacy group to lobby for legislative reform on gun violence, which resulted in changed to Florida's gun laws and boycotts of the National Rifle Association.

- **Orlando Nightclub Shooting**: A total of 49 people were killed and more than 53 wounded in a mass shooting on June 12, 2016 at a gay nightclub in Orlando, Florida. The shooting was deemed a terrorist attack by FBI investigators, as the perpetrator claimed that the attack was in response to the American-led interventions in Iraq and Syria. The attack was also the deadliest incident in the history of violence against LGBT people in the United States.

- **Sandy Hook Elementary School Shooting**: On December 14, 2012, 20-year-old Adam Lanza fatally shot 20 children and 6 adult staff members in a mass murder at Sandy Hook Elementary School in Newtown, Connecticut. Before driving to the school, Lanza shot and killed his mother at their Newtown home. As first responders arrived, he committed suicide.

- **Aurora Theater Shooting**: On July 20, 2012, a mass shooting occurred in a movie theater in Aurora, Colorado, during a midnight screening of the film The Dark Knight Rises. A gunman, dressed in tactical clothing, set off tear gas grenades and shot into the audience with multiple firearms, killing 12 people and injuring 70 others. The sole suspect, James Eagan Holmes, was arrested outside the cinema minutes later.

- **Virginia Tech Shooting**: April 16, 2007, on the campus of in Blacksburg, Virginia, a student shot and killed 32 people and wounded 17 others in two separate attacks, approximately 2 hours apart, before committing suicide (another six people were injured escaping from classroom windows). The shooter had previously been diagnosed with a severe anxiety disorder.

- **Columbine School Shooting**: April 20, 1999, at Columbine High School in Columbine, Colorado. In addition to shootings, the attack involved a fire bomb to divert firefighters, propane tanks converted to bombs placed in the cafeteria, 99 explosive devices, and bombs rigged in cars. Two senior students, Eric Harris and Dylan Klebold, murdered a total of 12 students and one teacher. They injured 24 additional students, with three other people being injured while attempting to escape the school. The pair then committed suicide.

5.4.2 Lessons Learned

With each mass shooting event, emergency managers have learned more about ways to prepare and respond and to employ a variety of tactics to stop a shooting rampage in progress.

Among the lessons learned, communication alerts about an active shooter on the loose are key to survival of potential targets. For example, during the Virginia Tech shooting, students and others on campus used social media to send messages to one another during the two-hour ordeal. Following the Columbine event, there was increased attention to issues of high school cliques, subcultures and bullying, in addition to the influence of violent movies and video games in American society. That shooting resulted in an increased emphasis on school security as well as nationwide anti-bullying campaigns. The Sandy Hook shooting stressed the need for training and drills for students and staff to be prepared for all types of emergencies, including for young children.

While each event has unique characteristics, the large majority of mass shooting incidents are carried out by a lone gunman, often who was subsequently determined to be suffering from mental illness. This emphasizes the need for emergency management, law enforcement, and security forces to receive training informed by psychological experts in how to deal with people who are acting with intent to harm themselves and others and who may behave erratically.

SELF-CHECK

- Define **mass shooting.**
- Name two lessons learned in the aftermath of mass shooting events.

5.5 CIVIL UNREST

Civil unrest is a term used to describe a variety of events that can cause disorder and disruption to the normal functions of a community. Incidents of civil unrest can involve violence, looting, vandalism, sabotage, destruction of property, threats, and other forms of antisocial behavior. However, just as often, demonstrations of popular discontent are well-organized and carried out in a calm, lawful manner. Civil unrest can occur as the result of a planned event (for example, a parade or rally that unexpectedly changes character), or when witnesses or bystanders react or stage a counter-protest of their own. Civil unrest can also occur as a spontaneous reaction to an external catalyst, such as a wrongful death. Managing civil unrest involves a balancing act to ensure that actions taken by public authorities do not unreasonably restrict the ability of the public to organize protests, while also attempting to reduce the likelihood of violence, injury, and property damage. It is also important for emergency managers and law enforcement to consider how actions taken to quell civil unrest may incite further unrest as opposed to defusing tension.

PROTESTING THE WORLD TRADE ORGANIZATION

On November 30, 1999, a crowd of 40,000 took to the streets of Seattle, Washington to protest meetings of the World Trade Organization. Many of the protestors intended to conduct nonviolent methods of protest, but splinter groups engaged in property destruction and vandalism. Protestors chained themselves together, as police fired tear gas, rubber bullets, and pepper spray into the crowd. The mayor of Seattle imposed a curfew and created a 50-block "No-Protest Zone." The protests caused $2–3 million in property damage, city merchants lost approximately $9–18 million in sales, and further losses in the tourism and travel industries were reported for months following the incident.

5.5.1 Public Order Events on College and University Campuses

College and university campuses have long been a focal point for all forms of protests, demonstrations, and public order events. From the "Occupy Movement" to the "Black Lives Matter" movement, campuses can be a hotbed for activism. Campus emergency managers face a unique environment on a college campus. A large community of young students who are ready to publicly advocate for topical issues, an underlying philosophy of academic freedom, and the general atmosphere of tolerance and inclusiveness form the foundation for frequent demonstrations at many university campuses across the country.

Because of the different characteristics of colleges and universities, planning for security and incident response should be made based on a threat assessment of the campus. The primary challenge for emergency managers and law enforcement is to maintain control to protect life and safety of both protestors and bystanders, while at the same time respect and protect the constitutional rights of freedom of speech and assembly. For example, establishing a "Free Speech Zone" within the vicinity of a demonstration or protest can help diffuse tensions of counter protestors, agitators, or groups from outside the campus community. Similarly, working with protest organizers to facilitate marches, such as closing streets to traffic, can be an important element of reducing injury and helping to keep social movements from becoming violent.

NEED FOR RESTRAINT IN MANAGING CIVIL UNREST

An incident that is often cited as an example of over-reach on the part of law enforcement during a campus protest is the Kent State shooting that occurred on May 4, 1970. Also referred to as the Kent State Massacre, four students were killed and nine were injured by National Guardsmen who had been dispatched to the Kent State University campus in response to demonstrations carried out by students protesting the Cambodia incursion during the Vietnam War. Following the killings, unrest across the country escalated to the point that nearly 500 colleges were shut down or disrupted by intense and sometimes volatile protests.

5.5.2 Protests of Racial Injustice and Racially Motivated Violence

Historically, the term "race riot" has been used to describe a range of civil unrest spurred by protest movements fighting against racial injustice, both in the United States and abroad. Such events often involve tensions between racial or ethnic groups and law enforcement agents who are seen as unfairly targeting minorities. Racial profiling, police brutality, institutional racism, racially determined policies and politics, and inequitable economic systems are often common factors that drive civil unrest. Urban renewal and policies that local communities see as resulting in gentrification have also been cited as a contributing cause of unrest spurred by racial injustice.

Past incidents of race riots or similar civil unrest in the United States have included attacks on Irish Catholics and other immigrants in the nineteenth century, massacres of black people in the period following Reconstruction, and uprisings in African American communities such as the 1968 riots following the assassination of Martin Luther King, Jr. The Rodney King riot in Los Angeles was one of the largest incidents seen in the United States since the civil rights era of the 1960s. The LA riot lasted for four days in 1992 following the acquittal of white police officers who had been charged with police brutality that was caught on videotape.

Over the past several years, the "Black Lives Matter" movement and related protests in response to police brutality and racially motivated violence have resulted in civil unrest across much of the United States. Following the murder of George Floyd by a Minneapolis police officer on May 25, 2020, protests erupted across hundreds of cities across the country. While the vast majority of events were peaceful gatherings and marches, violent confrontations with police officers and law enforcement occurred in many cities, and incidents of looting, property damage, and destruction of police vehicles were reported. Multiple states called the National Guard to help manage unrest, and curfews were imposed in several major cities. While the movement is ongoing, the movement is resulting in important public conversations about the appropriate role of law enforcement, use of force among police departments, and racial impacts of policing on communities throughout the United States.

SELF-CHECK

- Define **civil unrest**.
- Cite two examples of civil unrest from U.S. history.
- Explain why emergency managers should not necessarily attempt to prevent civil unrest from occurring.

5.6 PUBLIC PERCEPTION OF HUMAN-MADE HAZARDS

One of the main differences in dealing with human-made disasters as opposed to natural disasters is that the majority of people have not had a personal experience with a human-made event. Although we are keenly aware of the increase in terrorist activities directed against the United States and have some knowledge of the number of industrial hazards located near population centers, the public's perception of the actual degree of risk that we face from terrorism and technological accidents varies widely.

There are many factors that affect how members of the public view the possibility and consequences of human-made hazards in their community. Knowledge of these factors is critical to a full understanding about human reaction to hazards; that knowledge is essential in the emergency manager's all-hazards approach to preparedness and mitigation in their communities.

5.6.1 Media Coverage

The media plays a vital role in shaping our attitude about and perception of terrorism as well as other human-made hazards. We live in an age of near-instant communication. We can mark some of the most dramatic events in our minds because we have seen them on television – sometimes during live coverage – and we are increasingly able to follow events as they occur through Twitter, Facebook, Instagram, and other forms of social media. The images that the media chooses to show the public, as well as the news coverage that accompanies those images, directly affect the way we think about human-made hazards. Often, the most startling and graphic images are those that sell the most news, and in a for-profit news industry, we may be subjected to the most graphic images of all. This is not to say that these are not newsworthy images, but we must remember that the public's knowledge is often limited to what the media choose to broadcast. For example, although many incidents of civil unrest are largely peaceful demonstrations, news outlets may disproportionately focus on violent or destructive acts, giving citizens a skewed perception of the level of risk associated with such events.

5.6.2 Individual Experience

A second element that factors into the public perception of risk involves an individual's experience with various hazard events. Relatively few people in the United States have actually lived through a human-made hazard event, either intentional or accidental. This is in huge contrast with natural hazard events, where millions of people have at one time or another personally experienced a flood, earthquake, severe winter storm, tornado, hurricane, or other type of natural hazard. Natural disasters in this country cause fewer deaths or serious injuries than in other parts of the world. But property damage from natural hazards is extremely common, and the costs of disasters from natural hazards have risen dramatically over the past few decades. In contrast, there are many fewer property owners who have been affected by a human-made hazard. Interestingly, this reality does not factor into the perception of risk that many people associate with human-made hazards.

5.6.3 A Range of Strong Responses

Because the United States has a relatively short history of human-made hazards, discussion on this subject may be characterized by elements of uncertainty and even fear. Planners and emergency managers who work with the public must realize that there could be strong personal responses as people try to grapple with the idea of the possibility of a terrorist attack or technological hazard. New issues may arise that do not come up when dealing with natural hazards, such as concerns over security, access to information, and civil liberties.

To gain public support for efforts to mitigate and prepare for human-made hazards, emergency managers and planners must be prepared to educate officials, citizens, and the private sector about the hazards that may affect the community and about the prevention and mitigation activities that can help address them. A realistic, comprehensive picture of hazard possibilities is essential, neither overstating or inflating the risk, nor underestimating or devaluing the possibilities.

SELF-CHECK

- Describe the role of the media in the public's perception of human-made disasters.
- Compare how public perception of risk may differ between a hurricane versus a terrorist attack.

SUMMARY

Emergency managers and planners must help communities prepare and reduce impacts of both accidental and intentional human-made threats. This chapter explains the ways in which natural hazards and human-made hazards differ. Hazardous materials are an integral part of life today, but our goal is to minimize the potential for technological disasters to detrimentally impact our communities through careful planning and advanced preparedness training and exercises. Antiterrorism and counterterrorism activities are at work to reduce the impact of terrorism on our country and in our communities, and efforts to prevent or reduce losses from other violent attacks such as mass shootings are an essential role for emergency managers. The chapter discusses acts of civil unrest, such as demonstrations and riots in the context of our emergency management system. Finally, the chapter examines the public's changing perception of human-made hazards and what can be done to proactively address and manage people's fears and concerns.

KEY TERMS

All-hazards approach: A method for dealing with both natural and human-made hazards.

Antiterrorism: Defensive measures used to reduce the vulnerability of people and property to terrorist acts.

Biological agent: Infectious organisms or toxins that are used to produce illness or death in people.

Chemical agent: Poisonous gases, liquids, or solids that have toxic effects on people, plants, or animals.

Civil unrest: Unexpected or planned events that can cause disorder and disruption to a community.

Counterterrorism: Offensive measures taken to prevent, deter, and respond to terrorism.

Domestic terrorism: Groups or individuals whose activities are directed at elements of the U.S. government or society without foreign direction.

Emergency Management Assistance Compact (EMAC): A congressionally ratified organization that provides form and structure to interstate mutual aid.

Hazardous materials: Chemical or toxic substances that pose a potential threat or risk to life or health.

International terrorism: Acts carried out by groups or individuals whose activities are foreign-based and/or directed by countries or groups outside the United States or whose activities cross international boundaries.

Mass Shooting: Shooting incident involving a lone gunman, or occasionally two gunmen, resulting in four or more deaths.

Safety Data Sheet (SDS): Provides useful information regarding acceptable levels of toxin exposure, including data regarding the properties of a particular substance, the chemical's risks, safety, and impacts on the environment; OSHA requires that MSDS be available to employees for potentially harmful substances handled in the workplace.

Secondary hazard: A technological hazard that occurs as the result of a primary natural event.

Technological hazard: Incident that occurs when hazardous materials are used, transported, or disposed of improperly and the materials are released into a community.

Terrorism: The unlawful use of force and violence against persons or property to intimidate or coerce a government, the civilian population, or any segment thereof, in furtherance of political or social objectives.

ASSESSING YOUR UNDERSTANDING

Summary Questions

1. The United States has experienced more natural hazards than human-made hazards. True or False?
2. Which of the following would be an intentional human-made hazard?
   a. Oil spill
   b. Train derailment
   c. Anthrax attack
   d. Fire
3. The all-hazards approach is a way for federal, state, and local agencies to deal with both human-made and natural hazards. True or False?
4. The Olympic bombing in Atlanta, Georgia, in 1996 was an act of international terrorism. True or False?

5. The protests in connection with Black Lives Matter movement would be classified as
   a. An accident
   b. Domestic terrorism
   c. A secondary hazard
   d. Civil unrest
6. Acts of terrorism combine violence, motives, and a target. True or False?
7. Contamination from biological agents can be spread by wind and water. True or False?
8. Antiterrorism involves offensive measures to prevent terrorism. True or False?
9. Civil unrest can take place in which of the following forms?
   a. Demonstration
   b. Rally
   c. Assembly
   d. All of the above
10. Dizziness and changes in skin color are possible symptoms of hazardous material exposure. True or False?
11. Which of the following is a technological hazard?
    a. Dry cleaner
    b. Overturned petroleum tanker truck
    c. Train crash
    d. Chlorinated swimming pool
12. The EPA provides standards for chemical use. True or False?
13. The probable cause for most transportation-related technological hazards is
    a. Weather
    b. Computer failure
    c. Human error
    d. Leaks
14. A technological hazard that is triggered as a result of a natural hazard is a
    a. Secondary hazard
    b. Train derailment
    c. Primary hazard
    d. Disaster
15. Emergency response plans in the event of a nuclear incident define two different emergency planning zones. True or False?
16. A plume is
    a. A measurement of radioactivity
    b. Nuclear energy produced by a nuclear power plant
    c. An emergency zone surrounding a nuclear power plant
    d. A cloud-like formation of radioactive gases and particles
17. More U.S. residents have experienced a human-made hazard than a natural hazard. True or False?
18. Human-made hazards are likely to produce a more emotional response than natural hazards. True or False?

Review Questions

1. List three examples of accidental human-made hazards.
2. Name three agencies that can be used as resources for information about human-made hazards.
3. Why is FEMA encouraging communities to adopt the all-hazards approach?

4. What are some of the criteria that are used to define an act of terrorism?
5. Recall the United States' official definition of terrorism.
6. Is it possible for an international terrorist attack to happen in the United States? Explain.
7. Give three examples of tactics used by terrorists.
8. Describe some of the underlying causes of civil unrest, including race riots.
9. Explain how medical facilities such as hospitals and research labs have contact with hazardous materials.
10. Identify five ways that hazardous materials can enter a community.
11. How do hazardous materials affect a home environment?
12. How has the 24-hour news cycle affected the public's perception of human-made hazards?

Applying This Chapter

1. Human-made hazards are not as predictable as some natural hazards. We can, however, judge some of the risk by the hazards of the past. What, if any, human-made hazards have occurred in your area?
2. How would the all-hazards approach be used differently in New York City vs. tornado-prone Indiana?
3. The media has covered certain measures that some larger cities have taken against terrorism (backpack searches on New York City subways, street closures in Washington, DC). Select a U.S. city and list any potential for terrorist activity and measures that have been taken to protect against the threat.
4. Imagine that a major public meeting has been scheduled about the proposed construction of a hazardous landfill in your community. You expect the meeting to be particularly contentious. What actions should the meeting organizers take to ensure a peaceful gathering?
5. Consider the household cleaners and other chemicals in your home. Give three examples of ways that an everyday product could have a hazardous effect on your home or your health.
6. In what ways has your life been affected by human-made hazards? Consider both the direct and indirect impacts.
7. What are some of the factors that influence the public's perception of the level of risk we face from human-made hazards? How can this public perception affect how emergency managers and other professionals carry out mitigation and preparedness activities?

You Try It

Risk Assessment

As the emergency manager in a mid-sized community, how would you go about determining your community's level of risk from human-made hazards as compared to the risk from natural hazards? What local elements would you assess to make your determination?

Transportation and Technological Hazards

Predict the risk of a technological hazard in your community based on any transportation routes (railroads, shipping channels, trucking routes, etc.) that may carry hazardous materials through or around the area.

Secondary Hazards Hit Home

Assess the likelihood that a natural hazard could trigger a secondary hazard in your community. Base your assessment on geographic, historical, and other data.

REFERENCES

1. Stephenson, J. 2009. *Chemical Regulation: Options for Enhancing the Effectiveness of the Toxic Substances Control Act.* Testimony Before the Subcommittee on Commerce, Trade, and Consumer Protection, Committee on Energy and commerce, House of Representatives.
2. *Code of Federal Regulations.* Title 28, Part 0.85.
3. Basu, T. 2015. *Why the U.S. Has 31% of the World's Mass Shootings.* New York, NY: Time Magazine.

Section II
Public and Private Roles in Disaster Management

This section introduces the institutional framework within which all mitigation and preparedness activities take place, focusing on the various levels of government that operate in our federal system. Chapter 6 discusses how the role of the federal government has changed over time and reviews the federal laws and programs that govern hazards management. Chapter 7 focuses on the authority that states have to manage hazards and the range of tools that states use to prepare for and mitigate against hazards. Chapter 8 reviews hazards management at the local level, including the techniques that local governments use to regulate private property and manage land use. Chapter 9 provides an overview of the ways in which the private sector and nonprofit organizations can reduce risks associated with hazards and help communities become more resilient.

Because of the federal system of government in the United States and the separation of powers within each level, intergovernmental relations are a significant factor in determining the manner in which public policy is formulated and public programs are carried out. The lack of centralization and high degree of pluralism in our country make for a patchwork system of governance that is not entirely uniform from one state to the next, or from one community to another. The hodgepodge nature of this system is particularly evident in the federal, state, and local programs and policies that govern hazardous areas and in turn affects how private landowners are permitted to use their property. Because there is no overarching, consistent policy for governing land use and development in hazard-prone areas within the United States, programs and policies administered by various agencies can often be redundant or sometimes even work at cross-purposes.

We explore throughout this section how our society has conflicting public policy goals with regard to the management of hazardous lands. On the one hand, we promote the economically beneficial use of private property. For instance, property located along the oceanfront may have significant value as residential or investment real estate, despite recurrent hurricanes, erosion, flooding, and other coastal hazards. Moreover, much of the land in the United States has already been developed in economically beneficial ways, and there is a reluctance to restrict or prohibit land uses in these developed areas, even if such regulation may prevent property damage from future hazards.

On the other hand, we also have a strong tradition of protecting public safety through government intervention. Unwise land use decisions can threaten property owners and become a drain on public resources, including government expenditures for emergency rescue and response, temporary housing, infrastructure repair, and disaster assistance payments. These tensions between private property rights, protection of public health and safety, and limits on government spending are caused and contribute to the patchwork system within which emergency managers carry out their duties and responsibilities with respect to reducing risks and preventing disasters.

To fully grasp strategies to reduce vulnerability to hazards and climate change within the United States, it is essential to understand how the various levels of governments, as well as private sector and non-governmental organizations, play unique but intertwined roles. The following chapters describe our hazards management framework, detailing the authorities, unique interests, and opportunities to make the nation more resilient.

6

The Role of the Federal Government in Disaster Management

What You'll Learn

- How the role of the federal government in emergency management has evolved over time
- Federal policies and programs to help communities prepare for and mitigate hazards
- The mission of the Federal Emergency Management Agency
- Federal programs that support adaptation to climate change
- The strengths and weaknesses of various federal mitigation policies

Goals and Outcomes

- Master the terminology and understand the perspective of federal mitigation and preparedness policies and programs
- Understand ways in which the federal government subsidizes hazard risk
- Consider ways to limit the federal burden of disaster assistance
- Evaluate the effectiveness of federal mitigation programs for reducing vulnerability

INTRODUCTION

Providing relief to people who have suffered the hardship and heartache of a catastrophic disaster is generally considered a worthwhile endeavor, even a moral obligation. This chapter summarizes how the federal government influences hazards management both through appropriations and directly through federal land holdings. The chapter then discusses how the federal government's involvement in emergency management has evolved over time. We then outline several federal programs that pertain directly to hazards management, as well as some other federal activities that are not focused on mitigation per se, but which nevertheless impact hazards management. The chapter concludes with a summary of federal climate change adaptation and resilience efforts that help individuals, communities, and businesses prepare for and mitigate climate-related risks.

6.1 FEDERAL GOVERNMENT INVOLVEMENT IN HAZARDS MANAGEMENT

The bulk of the federal government's domestic activities are accomplished through intergovernmental programs, particularly through appropriations of funding decided on by Congress and administered by federal agencies to state and local governments. The

DOI: 10.4324/9781003123897-6

federal government is also involved in hazards management as an owner of significant land holdings. This section explores the federal government's role in hazards management through the use of appropriations and actions taken on land owned by the federal government.

6.1.1 Federal Appropriations

Involvement of the national government in the affairs of states and local governments frequently occurs through appropriations of various kinds, many of which are directed toward public health and safety and homeland security programs. Federal agencies distribute billions of dollars each year in the form of grants, contracts, loans, and other types of aid. Some funds are given directly to local governments; other federal funds are administered by the state and then funneled to local communities. Federal grants and other aid packages are often used to secure the cooperation of state and local governments through the imposition of rules and criteria that apply to the use of the funds. The "strings" that are attached to appropriations from Washington, DC are a roundabout but effective way that the federal government has leverage over activities that would otherwise be entirely within the domain of state and local governments.

The federal government also appropriates vast amounts of funding to state and local governments for post-disaster assistance. Many of the largest grants and aid packages are directed toward post-storm rebuilding, as evidenced by the nearly $60 billion relief bill passed in the wake of Hurricane Sandy. Yet some critics claim that the nature of the congressional appropriations process for disaster assistance is one of the chief roadblocks to reducing future hazard losses, since it is often easier politically to provide relief funds through emergency supplemental appropriations than it is to reduce long-term risks through mitigation spending that must survive the ordinary budget process.

Most federal grants and other forms of aid are distributed on a cost-share basis, with the federal government providing the bulk of funds and state and local governments providing matching funds. For major development projects, such as those carried out by the U.S. Army Corps of Engineers, the current cost-share formula is typically 65% federal and 35% local. Cost shares that include a greater local contribution may provide a larger sense of local ownership in a project and thereby a greater level of accountability on the part of local communities.[1] However, with severely limited local government budgets in many communities, the cost-share model is often necessary to fund large infrastructure projects or capital improvements that reduce risk to hazards.

6.1.2 Managing Federal Property

Federal Lands

About 640 million acres, or 28%, of the 2.27 billion acres of land in the United States is owned by the federal government.[2] States with the largest percentage of federal landownership are located primarily in the west. In Nevada, for example, 80.1% of land is owned by the federal government, and 60.9% of land in Alaska is owned by the federal government.[2]

The Department of the Interior controls the majority of acreage owned by the federal government (68%) and has invested the most in land acquisition. The Department of Agriculture controls 28%; 24 agencies control the remaining 4%. Of the land, the federal government owns and leases within the United States, 30% is used for forest and wildlife, 22% is used for grazing, 16% is dedicated to parks and historic sites, 2% is used for military purposes, and the remaining 32% of federal land are used for other purposes.

FROM SMOKEY BEAR TO WOODSY OWL

The primary mission of the U.S. Forest Service is to manage the nation's 154 national forests and 20 national grasslands, which encompass 193 million acres. Part of this mission involves managing wildland fires, a process that has evolved over the last 100 years from a strategy of total suppression—putting out fires as quickly as possible—to an approach that recognizes the role of natural fire in the health of many ecosystems. The iconic symbols, Smokey Bear, first introduced in 1944 as the national symbol for the prevention of wildfires, and Woodsy Owl, the national symbol for the promotion of conservation practices since the 1970s, illustrate the changing focus of land management at the U.S. Forest Service over the decades.

Federal Buildings

The federal government also owns and leases thousands of buildings throughout the United States. Close to one-fifth of all the owned and leased federal buildings are used for housing (the second highest category behind government offices). Other predominant uses include post offices, service, storage, research and development, and institutional buildings.

HOMEGROWN TERRORISTS TARGET FEDERAL BUILDING

On April 19, 1995, a truck-bomb exploded outside the Alfred P. Murrah Federal Building in Oklahoma City, Oklahoma, killing 168 people and injuring hundreds more. Anti-government militants Timothy McVeigh and Terry Nichols planned and executed the blast. The men were members of a radical right-wing survivalist group with a penchant for guns. In the wake of the bombing, the U.S. Congress passed legislation designed to increase the protection around federal buildings to deter future terrorist attacks. In May 1995, the Murrah Building was demolished for safety reasons, and a national memorial and museum are now located at the site.

Federal Infrastructure

In addition to land and buildings, the federal government also owns and operates a large proportion of the country's civil infrastructure, including power development and distribution, flood control and navigation, utility systems, and roads and bridges. Approximately 17% of federally owned infrastructure (by cost) is for flood control and navigation, most of which is appropriated to the U.S. Army Corps of Engineers.

As a direct result of federal ownership of land, buildings, and infrastructure, the federal government has a significant amount of control over these assets. Areas that are used as timber and grazing lands are usually undeveloped, and relatively few structures (either private or government owned) are exposed to hazard impacts on these lands. Other federal lands, such as military bases owned and operated by the Department of Defense (DoD), are intensely used, and many of these are located in high-hazard areas such as the coastal zone. Many agencies have recognized that as stewards of public property, they have an obligation to protect federal investments, including making buildings and infrastructure more resilient in the face of both man-made and natural hazards. You can read about some of the hazard mitigation and climate change adaptation initiatives being implemented by various federal agencies later in this chapter.

6.1.3 Executive Order for Floodplain Management

In 1977, President Carter signed Executive Order (E.O.) 11988, "Floodplain Management," which required all federal agencies to take action to reduce the risk of flood loss, minimize the impact of floods on human safety, health and welfare, and restore and preserve the natural and beneficial values of floodplains whenever agencies construct buildings and infrastructure with federal funds or carry out federal programs.

On January 30, 2015, President Obama signed Executive Order 13690 (amending E.O 11988) and established a "Federal Flood Risk Management Standard." Under the Order, all roads, buildings, and other pieces of infrastructure paid for with federal money must be built in areas with less risk of flooding, based on the premise that climate change will make floods more common and much more destructive.

"These impacts are anticipated to increase over time due to the effects of climate change and other threats. Losses caused by flooding affect the environment, our economic prosperity, and public health and safety, each of which affects our national security," states the Order. "The Federal Government must take action, informed by the best-available and actionable science, to improve the Nation's preparedness and resilience against flooding."

Moving forward, the new standard mandates that all federal agencies and departments must "use data and methods informed by best-available, actionable climate science" and build either two feet above the 100-year flood elevation or to the 500-year flood elevation. All critical buildings, such as hospitals and evacuation centers, must be built at least three feet above the 100-year flood elevation.[3]

6.2 EVOLUTION OF EMERGENCY MANAGEMENT AT THE FEDERAL LEVEL

The role of the federal government in emergency management has evolved over the years from distant observer to immediate responder, principal financier of disaster costs, and, more recently, champion of hazard mitigation.[4] As a way of introducing the federal role in hazard mitigation and preparedness, this section discusses some of the notable changes in the federal approach to emergency management that have occurred from the 1800s to the present. This brief history might help explain some of the policies and programs that are in place today and provides background for some of the impediments to and opportunities for hazard mitigation and climate change adaptation facing emergency managers.

6.2.1 Early Federal Involvement: Limited and Ad Hoc

Under the U.S. Constitution, the function of protecting public health and safety rests primarily with the states. The role of the federal government is to step in and provide aid when state and local governments are overwhelmed or otherwise unable to provide the services that the citizenry needs. Over the years, however, this principle, while not eroding entirely, has come to mean that the federal government steps in on a regular basis, with more being expected of federal agencies and programs than ever before.

Between 1800 and 1950, there was a slow trickle of federal involvement in emergency management functions, but there was no national policy for responding to natural or human-caused disasters.[5] Catastrophes ravaged portions of the nation periodically, including notable disasters such as the following:

- New Madrid, Missouri, Earthquakes of 1811–1812
- Chicago Fire of 1873
- Johnstown, Pennsylvania, Dam Break in 1889

- Galveston Hurricane of 1900
- San Francisco Earthquake and Fire of 1906
- Miami Hurricane of 1926
- Lower Mississippi Flood of 1927
- New England Hurricane of 1938

Deaths from such disasters numbered in the hundreds to thousands. Costs in present-day figures ran into the billions of dollars. The response to these disasters was ad hoc, as organized by local groups and funded primarily by charities and some local and state monies. Any mitigation that took place was carried out by individual property owners or local governments in a piecemeal fashion; there was no concerted effort to push risk reduction at any level.[4]

The 1930s: The U.S. Army Corps of Engineers Becomes Active in Flood Control

The Flood Control Act of 1934 gave the U.S. Army Corps of Engineers increased authority to design and build flood control projects. This Act reflected a philosophy that humans could control nature and eliminate the risk of floods, setting the tone for the basic approach to mitigating the impacts of most natural hazards throughout the next several decades. The Corps' programs were very successful in the sense that hundreds of dams, levees, floodwalls, diversions, and other structural flood control projects were built across the country. Although the Corps' programs promoted economic development and population growth along the nation's rivers and coastlines, history has proven that this attempt at emergency management was sometimes shortsighted, costly, and had unintended consequences.

Emergency Management during the Cold War

The 1950s was a quiet time for large-scale natural hazards, although three significant hurricanes did occur: Hurricane Hazel, a Category 4, inflicted significant damage in Virginia and North Carolina in 1954; Hurricane Diane hit several mid-Atlantic and northeastern states in 1955; and Hurricane Audrey, the most damaging of the three storms, struck Louisiana and North Texas in 1957.

The newly passed Disaster Assistance Act of 1950 picked up the tab for some of the costs of these disasters, introducing Americans to the concept of federal disaster assistance, but the amounts compared to later distributions of aid were paltry at best.[4] The focus of the nation at this time was not on hazards posed by nature but on the potential for nuclear war and fallout. The era of the Cold War beginning in the 1950s meant that disaster management focused less on land use regulations to keep hazardous areas free of development and more on the threat of foreign invasion. The construction of bomb shelters in private homes and public buildings was widespread, which coincidentally provided protection from tornadoes and some other natural hazards, but only as a by-product of the more pressing need to combat the perceived threat of nuclear attack.

National Flood Insurance Act

In 1961, the Office of Emergency Preparedness was created to deal with natural disasters. As the 1960s progressed, the United States was struck by a series of major natural hazards: the Ash Wednesday Storm, a nor'easter that caused significant damage along the Atlantic Coast; the Prince William Sound earthquake, which set off a tsunami along the Pacific Coast; and Hurricanes Betsy and Camille, which killed and injured hundreds of people and caused millions of dollars in damage along the Atlantic and Gulf coasts.

The lack of insurance against such large-scale disasters prompted the passage of the National Flood Insurance Act of 1968, creating the National Flood Insurance Program (NFIP) that offered federally backed flood insurance for homeowners in flood hazard areas. The NFIP was unique in its day, as it called upon local governments to undertake community-based mitigation activities to lessen flood risk. We discuss the NFIP in greater detail later in this chapter.

Federal Disaster Activity in the 1970s: The Creation of FEMA

The federal Disaster Relief Acts of 1969 and 1970 further emphasized the role of the federal government as the primary source of disaster funding. By this time, more than 100 federal agencies bore some responsibility for managing risk and disasters. These agencies were scattered among the civil and defense departments—each operating on its own turf and with its own agenda—but none of these agencies focused primarily on mitigation as a viable way of reducing hazard risk.

In 1979, President Jimmy Carter created the Federal Emergency Management Agency (FEMA). Many of the responsibilities of other agencies were soon transferred to this agency. Integrating the diverse programs, operations, policies, and people into a cohesive operation was a mammoth task, fraught with political, philosophical, and logistical problems. At this point, mitigation was still not promoted or funded in any major way within FEMA itself. There were relatively few natural disasters during this period, so the disjointed nature of the agency, while inefficient and cumbersome, was not noticeable to any large degree.[5]

6.2.2 The 1980s and 1990s: An Explosion of Federal Aid

Abundant federal disaster assistance was made available through the passage of the Robert T. Stafford Disaster Relief and Emergency Assistance Act in 1988. During the 1980s and 1990s, federal expenditures for disaster relief expanded by leaps and bounds. More disasters, larger dollar losses, and an inconsistent method of defining what qualifies as a "disaster" contributed to spending in the millions, and even billions, each year.

The purpose of the Stafford Act was (and still is) to support state and local governments and their citizens when disasters overwhelm their capability to respond. A wide range of disaster assistance is available from FEMA under the Stafford Act. Such assistance generally falls into two categories:

1. *Individual and Family Assistance* (IA) grants provide funds to help meet the serious needs and necessary expenses of disaster victims that are not met through other means such as insurance, loans, or charities. Eligible costs include housing, personal property, medical and dental expenses, funerals, and transportation.
2. *Public Assistance* (PA) grants provide aid to help communities rebuild damaged facilities after a disaster. Grants cover eligible costs associated with the repair or replacement of facilities owned by state or local governments and some nonprofit organizations. Funds are used to restore water and wastewater services, establish emergency public transportation, and remove debris and other activities to return the community to pre-disaster conditions. While mitigation can be a component of rebuilding public facilities using PA funds, restoration rather than mitigation is the primary goal of the Public Assistance Program.

The Stafford Act also created the **Hazard Mitigation Grant Program (HMGP).** The purpose of the HMGP is to reduce the loss of life and property due to hazards by providing money for mitigation as part of the disaster assistance package that state and local governments receive following a disaster declaration. Mitigation projects utilizing HMGP funds are meant to be implemented during the window of opportunity that opens when communities are rebuilding after a disaster.

In addition to FEMA, other federal agencies also began to disburse greater disaster aid and loan packages during the 1980s and 1990s. The Small Business Administration, for example, issues low-interest loans to help community businesses reestablish their operations following a hazard event. The Department of Housing and Urban Development administers disaster-related Community Development Block Grants (CDBG) to local governments impacted by disasters as well as other programs such as the Public Housing Modernization Reserve for Disasters and Emergencies, the HOME Investment Partnership Program, and the Section 108 Loan Guarantee Program. The Farm Service Agency of the U.S. Department of Agriculture (USDA) provides numerous types of assistance to farmers following natural disasters, including loans, grants, technical assistance, and catastrophic risk crop insurance.

FEMA Struggles to Respond to Major Disasters

By the late 1980s, FEMA was up and running and the Stafford Act provided a process to disburse disaster assistance to impacted communities fairly quickly. However, a series of major disasters between 1989 and 1993 highlighted some of the deficiencies of FEMA's capability to deal with catastrophic disasters. In 1989, Hurricane Hugo pummeled North and South Carolina and the U.S. Virgin Islands. It was the worst hurricane in a decade, with over $15 billion in damages and 85 deaths. FEMA was perceived as slow to respond. Soon after Hugo, the Loma Prieta Earthquake rocked California, causing enormous property and infrastructure damage. In 1991, raging wildfires in Oakland, California, burned homes and businesses. In 1992, Hurricane Andrew struck with very costly consequences, devastating Florida and Louisiana. Hurricane Iniki soon followed, creating havoc in Hawaii.

In the eyes of many, FEMA and the entire emergency management system failed during these events. The public wanted, and by now expected, the government to be there to help in its time of need. This sentiment was highlighted by the famous "where are the cavalry?" plea to the federal government at a press conference by Dade County emergency management coordinator Kathleen Hale days after Hurricane Andrew. FEMA seemed incapable of carrying out the essential government function of disaster assistance.[5] The extent of the damages incurred during these disasters emphasized the need for reducing the risk of future disasters—in other words, mitigation seemed an obvious choice.

The Midwest Floods of 1993: A Test for FEMA

President Bill Clinton nominated James Lee Witt to be Director of FEMA, who initiated sweeping reforms inside and outside of the agency, including the creation of the Mitigation Directorate within FEMA. FEMA now placed emphasis on mitigation as a primary means of reducing vulnerability to future natural hazards. The need for a strong relationship between FEMA and state and local emergency managers was recognized as well, allowing for better coordination and communication before, during, and immediately following a hazard event.

Witt's reforms were soon tested during the Midwest Floods of 1993. Devastating flooding occurred in an area covering 525 counties in 9 states, and much of it was caused by the failure of dams and levees that had been built by the Army Corps of Engineers years earlier. It was now evident that reliance on engineered structures was a potentially dangerous approach to flood control, and the opportunity to change the focus of disaster recovery was realized. FEMA initiated a bold new approach to mitigation following the Midwest Floods, financing a large program to buy private homes and help relocate residents, the largest such program at that time. For the first time, large-scale removal of people and property from the floodplain was accepted as a long-lasting and cost-efficient method for avoiding future disasters. The Midwest buyouts were unique for a number of reasons, not the least of which was the massive scale of the projects. Entire neighborhoods and even entire towns were acquired with public funds and moved—buildings, facilities, people, pets, and all—and rebuilt on higher ground. You can read more about acquisition and relocation as a long-term mitigation strategy in Chapter 12.

When President Clinton elevated the Directorship of FEMA to cabinet-level status, the value and importance of emergency management and the federal role in disasters were recognized. In 1995, FEMA published the first National Mitigation Strategy, which declared mitigation to be the "cornerstone" of emergency management, with two primary goals: increasing public awareness of hazards and reducing loss of life and injuries.

PATTONSBURG BECOMES MORE SUSTAINABLE WITH FEDERAL MITIGATION FUNDING

Before the Great Flood of 1993, Pattonsburg was a classic Midwest farm community of 400, occupying a couple of dozen square blocks in the middle of Missouri's countryside. But Pattonsburg was also an unsustainable community. Located at the confluence of Big Creek and the Grant River (a tributary of the Missouri River), the village had been flooded 33 times. The Great Flood swept through Pattonsburg on July 6, 1993, exactly 84 years after the community's first major flood disaster on July 6, 1909. In a well-rehearsed ritual, the villagers cleaned up their homes and shops and moved back into the floodplain. Then the Great Flood came back a second time. On July 23, the Grant River sent another sickening surge of muck and debris back through the community. This latest flood was the last straw, bringing home the realization that Pattonsburg could not continue to survive in conflict with the river. In the fall of 1993, more than 90% of the residents voted in the favor of relocating their town and rebuilding it on higher ground. In the spring of 1994, Pattonsburg got the news that it would receive $12 million in federal disaster assistance. The new town was designed and built three miles away—outside of the floodplain—and incorporated additional sustainable methods into the rebuilding process, including codes for energy efficiency, solar access, and building orientation, plus guidelines for waste minimization and sustainable economic development.

6.2.3 Project Impact

In the years following the Great Midwest Floods, FEMA steadfastly increased its emphasis on hazard mitigation—breaking the cycle of destruction and rebuilding that had been the norm. FEMA encouraged disaster-resistant communities, whereby the community would promote sustainable economic development, protect and enhance its natural resources, and ensure a better quality of life for its citizens. Project Impact, a program initiated by FEMA in 1997 that encouraged the involvement of all sectors of the community in emergency management and mitigation activities, was an attempt to foster public-private partnerships for community-wide mitigation planning. Project Impact communities were designated in all 50 states, the Virgin Islands, and Puerto Rico.

While several worthwhile mitigation projects were undertaken with Project Impact funding, it has been criticized by some observers as having taken on a distinctly political quality with the emphasis on launching a corporate-style marketing campaign complete with logos on baseball caps and tote bags. Other analysts noted that Project Impact lacked the inclusion of all the relevant stakeholders who should have been involved for a community-based mitigation plan.[6] Despite these criticisms, Project Impact proved to be successful in some communities by increasing the awareness of mitigation, especially in the private sector among select businesses and industries. In any event, Project Impact funding was subsequently cut, and the initiative was replaced with the passage of the Disaster Mitigation Act (DMA) of 2000.

6.2.4 The Disaster Mitigation Act of 2000

On October 30, 2000, President Clinton signed into law of the **Disaster Mitigation Act (DMA)** of 2000 to amend the Robert T. Stafford Disaster Relief and Emergency Assistance Act of 1988. This legislation is aimed primarily at controlling and streamlining the administration of federal disaster relief and mitigation programs and places emphasis on pre-disaster mitigation planning to reduce the nation's disaster losses. In fact, the DMA requires state and local mitigation plans as a prerequisite for certain disaster assistance, in effect, making states and local governments work for their mitigation dollars.

6.2.5 The Threat of Terrorism Initiates Major Agency Reorganization

In the aftermath of the terrorist attacks against the United States on September 11, 2001, President George W. Bush decided 22 previously disparate domestic agencies needed to be coordinated into one department to protect the nation against threats of all kinds. The Department of Homeland Security (DHS) was created to serve this role. FEMA is now housed within DHS, where the agency carries out its long-standing role of disaster assistance and mitigation programming.

In the years following the creation of DHS, the primary focus of emergency management shifted to terrorism and security threats and away from natural hazards. State and local emergency management agencies received grants and loans to beef up security and anti-terrorism capabilities, in some cases at the expense of natural hazard mitigation programs. However, the recurrence of major domestic and international disasters, including the Indian Ocean Tsunami of December 26, 2004, the Pakistan Earthquake of 2005, and the hyperactive hurricane seasons of 2004–2005, were harsh reminders to politicians and the public that natural hazards remain very real threats to communities throughout the nation and the world.

6.2.6 Hurricane Katrina: Spurring Change within the Federal Government

The devastation of communities along the Gulf Coast following Hurricane Katrina in 2005 once again portrayed FEMA in an unfavorable light. A lack of coordination, a failure in communication, and a dearth of strong leadership created a string of mistakes and misdirection, culminating in catastrophe on a scale never before seen in this country. Granted, the hurricane itself was a major natural hazard, with winds, waves, and storm surge reaching near-record heights as the storm made landfall along the Gulf Coast. However, it was a lack of timely response and poor pre-disaster planning and preparedness that led to the wretched conditions that occurred in the aftermath of the storm.

Along with the hardship and heartache endured by thousands of Katrina survivors, another casualty of the disaster was the reputation of federal, state, and local government emergency management agencies and their employees. Much of the disaster was steeped in partisan political bickering, which stymied many of the genuine efforts of people dedicated to righting past wrongs and moving forward with recovery and reconstruction plans.

One outcome of Hurricane Katrina was the passage of the Post-Katrina Emergency Management Reform Act of 2006, or PKEMRA. The Act was aimed at correcting shortfalls highlighted by the response to Hurricane Katrina by reorganizing some components of FEMA and reshaping the agency's relationship to the DHS. In particular, the Act created new leadership positions within FEMA, assigned additional responsibilities to the agency, and gave the director of FEMA a direct line of access to the president during periods of disaster.[5]

6.2.7 Presidential Policy Directive 8: National Preparedness

Recognizing that preparedness is a shared responsibility, Presidential Policy Directive/PPD-8: National Preparedness was signed on March 30, 2011. At its core, PPD-8 requires the involvement of the whole community—not just the government—in a systematic effort to keep the nation safe from harm and resilient when struck by hazards, such as natural disasters, acts of terrorism, and pandemics. This policy directive is articulated through the National Preparedness Goal: "A secure and resilient nation with the capabilities required across the whole community to prevent, protect against, mitigate, respond to and recover from the threats and hazards that pose the greatest risk."[7]

A series of frameworks and plans related to reaching the goal has been developed, each of which corresponds to one of the five preparedness mission areas: Prevention, Protection, Mitigation, Response, and Recovery. Each framework includes core capabilities, or distinct critical elements needed to achieve the goal. For example, the National Mitigation Framework comprises seven core capabilities, including:

- Threats and Hazard Identification
- Risk and Disaster Resilience Assessment
- Planning
- Community Resilience
- Public Information and Warning
- Long-term Vulnerability Reduction
- Operational Coordination

The Frameworks follow a whole community approach to preparedness, which recognizes that everyone can contribute to and benefit from national preparedness efforts. This includes individuals and families, businesses, community and faith-based groups, nonprofit organizations, and all levels of government.

SELF-CHECK

- Explain the effect of the Flood Control Act of 1934 on the U.S. Army Corps of Engineers.
- Discuss the origins of the creation of the Department of Homeland Security.
- What is the National Preparedness Goal and how is it implemented?

6.3 FEDERAL HAZARD MITIGATION PROGRAMS

In the previous commentary about the evolution of federal involvement in emergency management, we briefly mentioned several programs that focus primarily on hazard mitigation. In this section, we discuss these programs in more detail, including:

- National Flood Insurance Program (NFIP)
- Community Rating System (CRS)

- Disaster Mitigation Act of 2000 (DMA)
- Hazard Mitigation Grant Program (HMGP)
- Building Resilient Infrastructure and Communities (BRIC) Program
- Flood Mitigation Assistance Program
- National Hurricane Program
- National Earthquake Hazard Reduction Program
- Community Development Block Grant
- Coastal Barrier Resources Act (CBRA)

We refer to these as explicit emergency management programs, because these programs are directly focused on emergency management and disaster mitigation. The majority of these programs are carried out by FEMA, with the exception of the CDBG and CBRA.

6.3.1 The Role of FEMA

We begin this discussion of federal mitigation and preparedness functions with a brief review of FEMA. We noted earlier in this chapter that FEMA was created in the late 1970s to act as the lead agency for many aspects of disaster management, and that mitigation as a recognized discipline became a major focus of the agency in the 1990s. We also mentioned that FEMA is now housed within the larger DHS, where it is one of many different component agencies responsible for protecting America from hazards of all kinds.

FEMA's official mission is to support our citizens and first responders to ensure that, as a nation, we work together to build, sustain, and improve our capability to prepare for, protect against, respond to, recover from, and mitigate all hazards. This involves fostering readiness for disasters at every level of the emergency management system. The Mitigation Division spearheads FEMA's efforts to reduce the loss of life and property and protect our nation's institutions from all types of hazards through a comprehensive, risk-based emergency management program of preparedness and preventive techniques. The Mitigation Division administers the nationwide risk-reduction programs and congressionally authorized efforts that are discussed in this section.

6.3.2 The National Flood Insurance Program

Objective observers may quibble about whether insurance alone fully qualifies as a mitigation tool, because it primarily transfers the financial risk of disasters from the property owner to the insurance company, as opposed to directly reducing risk. However, in the case of the NFIP, the availability of flood insurance is often viewed as a mitigation technique, because the insurance does not become available merely through the payment of premiums, but through community-wide efforts to reduce the risk of flooding.

Congress established the **National Flood Insurance Program (NFIP)** in 1968 through the National Flood Insurance Act to help control the growing cost of federal disaster relief. The NFIP began as a voluntary program for local communities who wished to provide the opportunity for residents to purchase federally backed flood insurance. In exchange, local governments were required to enact an **ordinance** to regulate development in their floodplains. The legislation was bolstered a few years later through the Flood Insurance Act of 1972, which required the purchase of flood insurance for all federally backed mortgages (Veterans Administration loans, for instance), as well as for all mortgages issued by lending institutions that are federally regulated or insured, which covers the majority of lenders in the United States.

The NFIP is intended to be a self-supporting program that requires no taxpayer funds to pay claims or operating expenses for the average historical loss year. Expenses are to be covered through premiums collected for flood insurance policies. The program has borrowing authority from the U.S. Treasury for times when losses are heavy. These loans are to be paid back with interest. The NFIP is the largest single-line writer of property insurance in the United States. As of 2017, the NFIP insured approximately 5 million homes.

Floodplain Management under the NFIP

Upon enrollment in the NFIP, local communities are required to adopt floodplain ordinances that meet criteria established by FEMA. The ordinances must include construction standards for all development in the floodplain areas of the community. These construction standards apply to both new development and reconstruction of homes and other buildings that suffer "substantial damage" during a flooding event, meaning the cost of repair or reconstruction after an event is more than 50% of the structure's value. NFIP's criteria require communities to issue permits for development in designated floodplains, all new structures located in the 100-year flood zone must be elevated above expected flood heights, drainageways and culverts must be properly sized and maintained, and all local water supply and sewage systems must be protected to minimize infiltration of floodwaters.

Flood Insurance Rate Maps (FIRMs)

In order to enforce local floodplain ordinances, communities must have accurate information about the location of floodplains in the jurisdiction. As part of the NFIP, FEMA develops Flood Insurance Rate Maps (FIRMs) for each participating community. FIRMs are paper or digital maps that represent the full range of flood risk in the community. Each FIRM indicates certain areas using special designations that help the community prepare their development regulations and ascertain where these regulations will apply. See Chapter 3 for a description of FIRMs.

Keeping FIRMs Current

There is much riding on a community's FIRMs. Development permits, ordinance provisions, and structural requirements such as elevation are determined by the location of property as shown on the local FIRMs. The maps also determine the various insurance rates for covered properties. No map is perfect, and floodplains change over time due to a number of factors, including development patterns and climate change. From time to time, FEMA, communities, or individuals may find it necessary for a FIRM to be updated, corrected, or changed. Conditions that may warrant a change in a local FIRM include the following:

- The occurrence of significant construction within the already identified floodplains on the FIRM.
- Significant development in upstream communities after the FIRM was published.
- The occurrence of flooding for which inundation patterns indicate that the FIRM boundaries are no longer accurate.
- The completion of a major flood control project within the community or upstream of the community.
- Changes in topography in or adjacent to existing mapped floodplains.

In 1997, FEMA developed the Map Modernization Program to update and digitize the entire U.S. floodplain map inventory. The completed multiyear effort to update and digitize the flood map inventory costs roughly $1 billion but is projected to prevent $45 billion in flood losses over the next 50 years. Unfortunately, that time frame means that many communities will still be using out-of-date flood maps when determining standards for future development in their floodplains. In many of these communities, changes in development, topography, and inundation patterns have occurred so rapidly that new construction of homes and businesses may be unwittingly allowed in areas of flood risk, even in communities that faithfully enforce their floodplain regulations.

STATE EFFORTS TO SPEED UP MAP MODERNIZATION

Some states have proceeded with their own flood Map Modernization Programs. For example, the state of North Carolina undertook a massive flood mapping project. Hurricane Floyd in 1999 revealed that flood hazard data and map were severely limited. At that time, approximately 75% of North Carolina Flood Insurance Rate Maps (FIRMs) were at least five years old, and approximately 55% of North Carolina's FIRMs were at least 10 years old. The flooding that occurred during and after Hurricane Floyd far exceeded the flood boundaries portrayed on the FIRMs. Many structures were flooded in locations that did not appear as flood hazard areas on the maps in existence at the time. Although FEMA had begun the process of updating FIRMs nationwide, the federal mapping budget was finite; on average, North Carolina would have received one updated flood study per county per year. In a state with 100 counties, the federal process was deemed inadequate to protect communities from future flood events, hence initiation of the state-level fast track to map modernization.

Borrowing from the Treasury to Stay Afloat

The NFIP has been criticized over the years because of flaws in its design and application. Foremost among these criticisms is the reality that the NFIP is not actuarially sound, meaning the program does not collect enough income from premiums to build reserves that can meet long-term future expected flood losses. This has occurred in part because Congress authorized subsidized insurance rates for some properties. Historically, FEMA was relatively successful in keeping the NFIP on a sound financial footing. In fact, the program was self-supporting from 1986 until 2005. However, following Hurricanes Katrina, Rita, and Wilma in 2005, FEMA paid more than $19 billion in claims, far exceeding the $2.2 billion in annual premiums and its $1.5 billion borrowing authority from the US Treasury. As a result, Congress has passed legislation over time to increase the NFIP borrowing authority, first to $3.5 billion, to more than $20 billion in 2006, and to more than $30 billion in 2013 following Hurricane Sandy.

These increases in borrowing have been necessary for the program to continue to pay claims. These figures suggest that the NFIP has heavily subsidized properties in high-risk areas in recent years, and the rising cost of disasters has made it difficult for the program to be self-supporting, as it was originally conceived.

The Problem of Repetitive Losses

Even the most ardent supporters of the NFIP admit that the program has historically not been run like a private insurance company—that is, with loss reduction as a primary goal. This problem is most evident with regard to the repetitive losses that occur on a regular basis, creating a significant drain on NFIP resources. **Repetitive Loss Properties (RLPs)** and Severe RLPs—those with multiple claims for flooding—represent a small proportion of the properties that are insured by the NFIP, but in an average loss year, they account for a much larger chunk of the NFIP flood claim dollars.

Most RLPs are older, less safe homes that were grandfathered into the NFIP when it first began. These properties were typically built before NFIP construction standards were created and prior to the issuance of FIRMs. In other words, many RLPs, known as Pre-FIRM structures, were built before local flood hazard risks were fully known and thus were not constructed to resist water damage. Most RLPs are residential structures, not vacation or investment properties, and many have been repaired multiple times. The sheer number and cumulative amount of these losses created the repetitive loss payout problem.

Through its repetitive loss provisions, the NFIP has had the unintended effect of helping people stay in areas that were repeatedly flooded when it might be in the property owners' and the communities' best long-term interests to mitigate the flood vulnerability of these properties or move elsewhere, to less flood-prone locations.

Attempts to Improve the NFIP

In recognition of the problems of repeated NFIP payouts with every flooding event, FEMA implemented a strategy to target severe RLPs for mitigation. The Flood Insurance Reform Act of 2004 established a pilot program requiring owners of RLPs to elevate, relocate, or demolish houses, with the NFIP bearing some of those costs. Funds from the Flood Mitigation Assistance (FMA) Program (discussed below) can also be used to help with these activities.

Additionally, to address concerns about the long-term viability of the NFIP and the program's ability to mitigate the impacts of flooding on communities, Congress passed the "Biggert-Waters Flood Insurance Reform Act of 2012." The Biggert-Waters Act reauthorized the NFIP for five years and required significant changes to the program. One of the most impactful of these changes was a restructuring of premium rates to make the NFIP more actuarially sound so that premiums more accurately reflect the current risk of floods to properties. The Act also required the phasing out of subsidies for second homes, business properties, and Severe Repetitive Loss Properties. The Act also required FEMA to create a repayment schedule to eliminate the debt within 10 years. These changes to the NFIP, particularly the requirement to charge premiums that align with the level of risk for a structure, have been touted as a critical step toward effective mitigation since the change removes existing incentives to develop in hazardous areas.

However, due to concerns about onerous insurance rate increases caused by the Biggert-Waters Act, Congress again took up the issue, passing the Homeowner Flood Insurance Affordability Act of 2014, repealing and modifying certain provisions of the Biggert-Waters Act. The primary change was to lower the rate increases on some policies and create a surcharge on other policyholders—such as owners of second homes. While the intention of the Homeowner Flood Insurance Affordability Act is to strive toward structuring the NFIP to be actuarially sound, it remains to be seen whether the limits on rate increases and reinstatement of certain subsidies will continue to incentivize unsafe development through the NFIP.

6.3.3 The Community Rating System

The Community Rating System (CRS) is administered by FEMA as part of the NFIP. The CRS provides flood insurance premium discounts for residents in communities who undertake floodplain mitigation activities above and beyond the minimum NFIP requirements. By rewarding sensible floodplain management with insurance savings for residents, the CRS program works toward the goals of reduced flood losses, accurate insurance ratings, and increased awareness of floods and flood insurance. As of October 2020, there were more than 1,700 communities spread throughout the United States, reducing insurance premiums for millions of policyholders. Communities receiving premium discounts through the CRS cover the full range of population—from small hamlets to large metropolitan areas, as well as different types of flood risk, including coastal and riverine.

CRS Classification

The reduction in insurance premiums is in the form of a CRS classification. There are 10 classes in the system, each providing an additional 5% premium rate reduction for properties in the community's mapped floodplain. A community's class is based on the number of credit points it receives for its floodplain management activities. Class 1 requires the most credit points and gives the greatest premium reduction. Class 10 receives no premium reduction. A community that does not apply for the CRS or does not obtain the minimum number of credit points is a Class 10 community.

ROSEVILLE, CA, GETS A TEN

Following damaging floods in Roseville, California in 1995, the community strengthened and broadened its floodplain management program and became the first community to receive the highest Community Rating System (CRS) rating. Because of their great Class 1 rating, residents within the 100-year floodplain can receive a 45% discount on their flood insurance premiums, while those outside the floodplain can receive a 10% discount. Not only did residents of Roseville receive the benefits of reduced flood insurance premiums, but also the town became energized to continue the successful mitigation activities that earned them the top CRS rating, and residents actively maintain the projects that continue to make their community safer. As of 2020, Roseville is the only Class 1 community in the country.

CRS Floodplain Management Activities

The CRS schedule identifies 18 creditable activities, organized under four categories, or "series." The schedule assigns credit points based upon the extent to which an activity advances the goals of the CRS. The following list explains the four series of the CRS schedule:

1. **Public Information Activities:** This series credits programs that advise residents about the local flood hazard, flood insurance, and ways to reduce flood damage. These activities also provide data needed by insurance agents for accurate flood insurance rating. Activities in the Public Information Series include elevation certificates, map information, outreach projects, hazard disclosure, flood protection information, and flood protection assistance.
2. **Mapping and Regulatory Activities:** This series credits programs that provide increased protection to new development, including additional flood data, open space preservation, higher regulatory standards, flood data maintenance, and stormwater management.
3. **Flood Protection Activities:** This series credits programs that reduce the flood risk to existing development, including floodplain management plans, acquisition and relocation, flood protection (retrofitting), and drainage system maintenance.
4. **Flood Preparedness Activities:** This series credits flood warning programs, levee safety, and dam safety.

The most possible credit points are awarded for acquisition and relocation projects to remove structures from the floodplain.

In 2011, the NFIP completed a comprehensive review of the CRS program. Based on the findings of this review, changes were made to drive new achievements in the following six core areas:

1. Reduce liabilities to the NFIP Fund
2. Improve disaster resiliency and sustainability of communities
3. Integrate a whole community approach to addressing emergency management
4. Promote natural and beneficial functions of floodplains
5. Increase understanding of risk
6. Strengthen adoption and enforcement of disaster-resistant building codes

6.3.4 Incentives for State and Local Mitigation Planning

The DMA of 2000 amends the Robert T. Stafford Disaster Relief and Emergency Assistance Act of 1988 and is intended to facilitate cooperation between state and local authorities, prompting them to work together. The DMA encourages and rewards local and state pre-disaster planning and promotes sustainability as a strategy for disaster resistance. The intention is for local and state governments to more accurately articulate needs for mitigation, resulting in faster allocation of funding and more effective risk-reduction projects.

Significant changes brought about through enactment of the DMA include the requirement that local governments create and adopt a mitigation plan in order to receive certain disaster assistance funds, including post-disaster project grants (bricks and mortar grants) under the HMGP as well as assistance for rebuilding public infrastructure following a major disaster.

The rules that accompany the DMA lay out a rigorous planning process that states, local governments, and Native American Tribes must follow. FEMA is in charge of reviewing all the state and local plans that are submitted to it for approval, and certain criteria must be met before a plan will meet FEMA's guidelines.

The plan must identify all the hazards that threaten a community and must also include a thorough risk analysis for each of those hazards. The plan lays out mitigation goals and objectives, as well as strategies and actions that will reduce the community's vulnerability to the hazards identified. The plan also must discuss the mechanism to implement the mitigation actions and a process to maintain, evaluate, and update the plan over time. These are not easy tasks to accomplish, and an effective mitigation plan requires many staff hours and community networking to meet FEMA standards. However, the benefits of developing and implementing a sound and well-thought-out mitigation plan are innumerable, and communities that make the effort are rewarded by far more than their eligibility to receive future federal mitigation money. Chapters 7 and 8 discuss the DMA as it pertains to state and local hazard mitigation planning and the consequences of not preparing a mitigation plan.

6.3.5 Hazard Mitigation Assistance Grant Programs

FEMA's Hazard Mitigation Assistance (HMA) grant programs provide funding for eligible mitigation activities that reduce disaster losses and protect life and property from future damages. Programs included in the 2013 HMA Unified Guidance include the HMGP, the Building Resilient Infrastructure and Communities (BRIC) Program, and Flood Mitigation Assistance (FMA) Program. The guidance consolidates the common requirements for all HMA programs and explains the unique elements of the programs in individual sections. Additionally, it provides information for federal, state, tribal, and local officials on how to apply for HMA funding for a proposed mitigation activity.

Hazard Mitigation Grant Program

The HMGP is the largest source of federal funding for state and local mitigation activities. HMGP funds are only available to communities after a disaster declaration has been made by the President, and the amount of mitigation funding is based on a percentage of the total disaster assistance package that is given, as calculated by damage loss estimates. As a result, the larger the disaster, the more mitigation funds are made available.

In recognition of the importance of planning, states that have an approved State Mitigation Plan in effect at the time of the declaration of a major disaster may receive additional HMGP funding. States, with local input, are responsible for identifying and selecting hazard mitigation projects.

Projects funded by the HMGP must be cost-effective, environmentally sound, conform to applicable environmental regulations, and substantially reduce the risk of future damage, hardship, loss, or suffering resulting from a major disaster. Types of projects for which HMGP funds can be used include the following:

- Construction activities that will result in the protection from hazards
- Retrofit of facilities, structures, and lifelines
- Acquisition/relocation of structures owned by willing sellers
- Elevation of flood-prone structures
- Development of state or local mitigation standards
- Development of comprehensive hazard mitigation programs
- Preparedness/response equipment and services
- Building code enforcement
- Public awareness campaigns

Building Resilient Infrastructure and Communities Program

The Disaster Recovery Reform Act of 2018 included a provision to have a more consistent means for funding pre-disaster mitigation. According to the legislation, approximately 6% of disaster grant expenses from the previous year should be set aside for proactive investments in community resilience. The program, called Building Resilient Infrastructure and Communities (BRIC), anticipates funding projects that demonstrate innovative approaches to partnerships, such as shared funding mechanisms between public and private sectors.

BRIC is a new FEMA program that replaces the former Pre-Disaster Mitigation Program as a source of federal grant money for states, local communities, tribes, and territories to undertake hazard mitigation projects that reduce risks from a range of hazards.

Flood Mitigation Assistance Program

The FMA Program expands FEMA's mitigation assistance to states, communities, and individuals by providing grants for cost-effective measures to reduce or eliminate the long-term risk of flood damage to the built environment and real property. The priority goal of the FMA is to reduce repetitive losses to the NFIP.

Unlike the HMGP, which is available only after a presidentially declared disaster, FMA funding is available to eligible communities every year. To be eligible for FMA grants, a community must be a participant in the NFIP and have jurisdiction over special flood hazard areas.

The FMA Program provides three types of grants: planning, project, and technical assistance. Planning grants allow states and communities to determine flood risks and identify actions to reduce these risks. Creation and approval of a flood mitigation plan is a prerequisite to receiving FMA project grants. The regulations do not mandate that FMA plans be limited to flood hazards, although funds will only be provided for the flood portion of a mitigation plan.

Once a community has a flood mitigation plan approved by FEMA, it is eligible for flood mitigation project grants from the FMA. Types of projects that are eligible for funding through the FMA include elevation, acquisition, and relocation projects; minor structural projects (flood retention ponds, floodproofing sewers, culvert modification, etc.); and beach nourishment activities.

6.3.6 The National Hurricane Program

The National Hurricane Program is a partnership between FEMA, the U.S. Army Corps of Engineers, and the National Oceanic and Atmospheric Administration (NOAA) National Hurricane Center to provide data, resources, and technical assistance for hurricane evacuation planning and response for state, local, tribal, and territorial governments. The program primarily supports evacuation studies and planning, including providing guidance about using evacuation modeling tools and decision-support tools to connect hurricane forecasts with government response. The program has also post-storm assessments that can, in part, be used to evaluate the effectiveness of mitigation measures and response activities.

6.3.7 National Earthquake Hazards Reduction Program

The National Earthquake Hazards Reduction Program (NEHRP) involves four agencies at the federal level: FEMA, the U.S. Geological Survey (USGS), the National Science Foundation (NSF), and the National Institute of Standards and Technology (NIST). The fundamental goal of the NEHRP is to reduce the impacts of earthquakes and subsequent loss of lives, property damage, and economic loss. To this end, the NEHRP provides financial and technical assistance to all levels of government and to the private sector to implement earthquake hazard mitigation measures. The NEHRP has fostered the development and implementation of seismic design and construction standards and techniques, promotion of loss estimation studies, and education and information dissemination of risk-reduction activities. Since the advent of the program, building codes in many states where seismic risk exists have been changed to include seismic resistance standards for new construction.

6.3.8 Community Development Block Grants

Administered by the U.S. Department of Housing and Urban Development, the CDBG program provides communities with resources to address a wide range of community development needs. CDBG funding can serve as a significant source of disaster recovery support for cities, counties, and states that have experienced a presidentially declared disaster. If the funds are applied in ways that prioritize safe and sustainable redevelopment, CDGB activities can also be an important mitigation tool.

In 2014, President Obama announced the National Disaster Resilience Competition, setting aside nearly $1 billion in funding available for communities that have experienced disasters in recent years to help them rebuild and increase resilience to future disasters. The funds, allocated through the CDBG program, encourage communities to enhance resilience by redeveloping in ways that incorporate hazard mitigation and by adopting policy changes to better plan for the impact of extreme weather and climate change.

In 2018, HUD created the CDBG Mitigation Program (CDBG-MIT), allocating nearly $16 billion for communities that had been impacted by recent major disasters to carry out strategic and high-impact activities to mitigate disaster risks and reduce future losses.

Grantees to the program are required to develop an Action Plan that builds off of the existing Hazard Mitigation Plan to identify targeted needs and investments that should be made using CDBG-MIT funding.

6.3.9 Coastal Barrier Resources Act (CBRA)

Congress passed the Coastal Barrier Resources Act (CBRA) in 1982 in an attempt to reduce costs to the federal government as a result of development in the extremely fragile environment of coastal barrier islands. Besides bearing the brunt of impacts from storms and severe erosion, most coastal barriers are made of unconsolidated sediments such as sand and gravel. This geological composition alone makes them highly unstable areas on which to build. CBRA prohibits spending federal money for growth-inducing infrastructure such as roads, bridges, wastewater systems, potable water supplies, and protective works, including seawalls and groins in areas that are within the Coastal Barrier Resources System (CBRS). The CBRS consists of 585 "units" of land that were undeveloped at the time the legislation was passed and were mapped according to criteria developed by the U.S. Fish and Wildlife Service. CBRA further stipulates that new development is ineligible for federal flood insurance in these areas.

A product of conservative political times, CBRA was intended to reduce threats to people and property as a cost-saving measure. It was widely recognized that federal programs such as flood insurance (through the NFIP) and infrastructure were encouraging building in areas that were prone to repeated natural hazards, including flooding, hurricanes, erosion, and coastal storms, and that the federal government would constantly be picking up the tab for damaged homes and businesses in a cycle of destruction and reconstruction. CBRA is a free-market approach to conservation. These areas can be developed, but federal taxpayers do not underwrite the investments.

Effectiveness of CBRA

It is important to recognize that the purpose of CBRA is merely to prevent federal funds from being spent on islands that are included in the System. The Act applies only to these specific mapped areas and does not restrict activities of the private sector or state or local governments within the CBRS.

Many local coastal communities wish to increase job opportunities and expand their tax base by encouraging development. Many states are also eager for these economic benefits and willing to invest in large infrastructure projects such as bridges and causeways to connect remote barrier islands to the mainland. Furthermore, some private developers are able to secure financial backing enabling them to construct their own infrastructure, such as roads, water, and sewer. In fact, some CBRA areas have been developed with high-value projects such as multistory condominiums in spite of the Act. However, studies have shown that, although local and state governments can step in to facilitate coastal development, areas that are not eligible for federal value-added programs are developed more slowly than other areas, and some barrier islands in CBRA have remained undeveloped.

SELF-CHECK

- Explain the mission of FEMA.
- Discuss how the **National Flood Insurance Program** works to mitigate flood hazards and the modifications resulting from the Biggert-Waters Act.
- List three sources of federal funding available for hazard mitigation projects.

6.4 FEDERAL PROGRAMS THAT INDIRECTLY MANAGE HAZARD IMPACTS

In this section, we will discuss a few federal programs that focus on protecting the quality and resources of the natural environment, including the Clean Water Act (CWA), the National Environmental Policy Act (NEPA), and the Coastal Zone Management Act (CZMA). We refer to these as "indirect" hazards management programs, because they do not focus on reducing hazard vulnerability per se but can result in risk reduction as a by-product of their main objective. We will also consider other federal activities that may make these and the explicit hazard management programs less effective, including capital improvement programs and taxation policies that foster development in hazardous areas later in the chapter.

6.4.1 Clean Water Act

The primary purpose of the federal CWA is to improve water quality in the United States by reducing pollutants discharged into bodies of water. The CWA consists of several pollution control programs primarily administered by the Environmental Protection Agency (EPA), including point source (pollution that is discharged from a specific definable source, such as a pipe), local stormwater management, and nonpoint source (pollutants that do not discharge from a specific source, such as agricultural runoff). In so far as water quality and flood mitigation are interconnected objectives, these CWA programs can help mitigate the impacts of flooding in local communities. In addition, Section 404 of the CWA contains provisions that help protect the nation's wetlands, which are sensitive environmental areas that can contribute to flood mitigation and storm surge damage reduction.

Section 404 of the Clean Water Act

Section 404 of the CWA requires a permit from the U.S. Army Corps of Engineers to discharge "dredge and fill materials" into the "waters of the United States." Through a complicated series of regulations and guidelines, the term *waters of the United States* covers many types of wetlands. The term *discharge of dredge and fill* can cover many kinds of development, because it is very difficult to build in a wetland without creating dry areas suitable for construction. As a consequence, in the process of protecting water quality, Section 404 limits development activity in wetlands, including coastal and many freshwater wetlands. The Corps will issue a permit only if it finds that there are no practicable alternative sites for the proposed activity. In addition to a permit, Section 404 requires that the impacts of the dredge and fill activity be offset through restoration projects or the creation of new wetlands elsewhere, a practice known as **compensatory wetland mitigation.**

The protection of the nation's wetlands is very significant for flood mitigation because, in their natural state, wetlands can absorb floodwaters, acting much like a sponge and provide storage for floodwaters, releasing the excess water slowly during dry periods. Coastal and estuarine wetlands also serve as natural barriers against storm surge, by dissipating the incoming energy generated by coastal storms.

404 Flaws

Without the protections afforded by Section 404, a substantial portion of the nation's wetlands would undoubtedly have been lost to development. However, there are some inherent limitations to the program as a conservation tool. First, 404 permit applies only to discharge of dredge and fill materials. It does not prohibit other methods of damaging or destroying wetlands, and many acres of wetlands across the country have disappeared without any "discharge of dredge and fill" taking place. Second, the Corps must issue a dredge and fill permit if the permittee demonstrates there is no practicable alternative site for the project. And finally, the definition of what qualifies as a wetland can be problematic. For instance, isolated wetlands (wetlands that are not adjacent to a navigable waterway) are not under the Corps of Engineers' permitting authority, leaving many wetland areas unprotected because they do not have a visible connection with another larger body of water.

LOSS OF WETLANDS LEFT NEW ORLEANS VULNERABLE

Wetlands along the southern coastlines of the United States serve as natural speed bumps to approaching hurricanes by starving them of warm ocean water and creating physical barriers to surging flood waters. However, in the last 100 years, the construction of levees and canals has starved floodplains of sediment and accompanying nutrients, turning thousands of square miles of wetland habitat into open water. These practices, combined with additional human and natural forces—including conversion of wetlands to agriculture and urban development, oil and gas pipeline canals, land subsidence, and hurricane storm surge—have served to weaken the natural protection provided by wetlands in last centuries. With a changing climate, sea level rise will likely cause further damage to wetlands, either by drowning these sensitive areas with ocean water and disrupting the delicate balance of fresh and salt water or through erosion.

Among the various forces that have played a role in the degradation of wetlands are activities of the U.S. Army Corps of Engineers itself, at times with devastating consequences. Louisiana's coastal wetlands provide an illustration. The state lost more than 70% of its substantial coastal wetlands between 1956 and 2000 and continues to lose more coastal wetland acreage each year,[8] leaving the region exposed to flooding and the full force of hurricane storm surge.

New Orleans' exposure to increased flood risk started half a century ago, 45 years ago, when the U.S. Army Corps of Engineers completed a 76-mile canal, the Mississippi River-Gulf Outlet (MRGO), from the Gulf to the city. The artificial shipping channel brought salt water into the wetlands, raising their salinity and killing off the lush, freshwater cypress swamps—including the 30,000-acre Central Wetlands, which is only 15 minutes from the city's French Quarter. Had they been in their more pristine, pre-MRGO state, the Central Wetlands, and other swamps may well have softened the 2005 storm surge from Hurricane Katrina that left adjoining communities like the Lower Ninth Ward under water for weeks. Since Hurricane Katrina, the Army Corps has dammed up the MRGO and is instituting a plan to restore natural features of the ecosystem, including the all-important diversion of fresh water back into the wetlands to resurrect their vital vegetation.

6.4.2 The Coastal Zone Management Act

When passing the CZMA in 1972, Congress declared that the coastal zone of the United States is of tremendous importance to the entire nation, not just to the individual coastal states, but also that the existing management programs (largely state programs) were not adequately managing the coast. The Act establishes a national policy "to preserve, protect, develop, and where possible, to restore or enhance, the resources of the Nation's coastal zone for this and succeeding generations." The CZMA is administered by the U.S. Department of Commerce, through the NOAA Office for Coastal Management and applies to the 35 states that border the Atlantic and Pacific Oceans, the Gulf Coast, and the Great Lakes.

The CZMA: A Flexible Program

To participate in the Coastal Zone Management Program, states must respond to all the requirements of the Act but are free to determine the substantive content of their own coastal programs. This flexible approach was established in recognition of the variability along the coast from state to state. For example, Maine, which is characterized by rocky beaches with numerous coves and bays, has a very different type of coastline than Georgia, which consists of sandy beaches and a string of barrier islands. And both of these coasts are very different from coastlines bordering the Great Lakes. This flexible approach recognizes, in addition to physical differences in the shoreline, many social, economic, and political differences exist from one state to the next.

CZMA Incentives for State Participation

Although participation is voluntary, the CZMA provides two strong incentives for states to formulate coastal programs. The first involves grants; grants under Section 305 assist states in preparing their Coastal Zone Management Programs, while Section 306 provides funding to administer approved programs. Grant allocations are based on the extent and nature of the state's shoreline and population. The second incentive to encourage states to participate in the Coastal Zone Management Program is the "consistency doctrine," found in Section 307 of the CZMA.

Under the consistency doctrine, actions of any federal agency in a state's coastal zone must be consistent with that state's coastal management policies, giving the state a degree of control over activities of the federal government. The consistency provision covers activities and projects carried out directly by a federal agency (for instance, highway construction by the U.S. Department of Transportation [DOT]), as well as activities and projects for which a federal permit or other form of approval is required (such as 404 permits issued by the U.S. Army Corps of Engineers). Examples of other federal actions that must be consistent with state coastal management programs include navigational and flood control projects, waste-water treatment facility funding, military activities, and federal fisheries management.

Hazard Mitigation through State Coastal Management Programs

In 1990, Congress amended the CZMA and added several additional activities for which states may use CZMA grant funds. These activities include measures to prevent or significantly reduce threats to life and property destruction by eliminating development and redevelopment in high-hazard areas, managing development in other hazard areas, and anticipating and managing the effects of sea level rise. With this amendment, Congress made explicit the need to mitigate the impacts of natural hazards as a part of state coastal management programs.

Some states have established policies and strategies under their coastal management programs that are effective in mitigating the impacts of natural hazards. These activities include the following:

- Shoreline management and retreat (e.g., creating setback rules, regulating shoreline development, shoreline stabilization)
- Regulating shore-hardening structures (e.g., prohibiting or restricting seawalls, revetments, groins, and other shore-hardening structures)
- Managing post-hazard reconstruction (e.g., regulating the repair and reconstruction of buildings damaged by a coastal hazard)
- Managing unbuildable lots (e.g., regulating construction on lots that should not be developed because of their proximity to hazard areas)

- Promulgating building codes and construction standards (e.g., regulating construction through rules, inspections, and enforcement)
- Protecting coastal wetlands
- Establishing policies to address sea level rise
- Implementing land acquisition programs (purchasing private lots in hazardous areas)
- Promoting local land use planning (encouraging or requiring local governments to include hazard mitigation in their land use plans)
- Developing special area management plans (creating plans that deal with coastal hazards in designated areas of the coastal zone)

6.4.3 The National Environmental Policy Act

The primary purpose of the NEPA is to require federal agencies to take environmental issues into consideration when making significant decisions. The Act requires federal agencies to prepare a detailed explanation of the environmental impact of agency decisions and inform other agencies and the public of that impact through various types of disclosure documents, including:

- Environmental Assessments (EA), which are prepared to assist the agency in deciding whether or not a more detailed study is required.
- Environmental Impact Studies (EIS), which are prepared when it is decided that an action is likely to cause a significant impact on the environment.
- Findings of No Significant Impact (FONSI), which are prepared if an EIS is not required.

NEPA: A "Toothless Ogre"?

NEPA requires *disclosure* of information regarding potential environmental impacts but lacks the regulatory muscle of other federal environmental statutes such as the Clean Air Act and the CWA. Because NEPA does not prevent an agency from implementing its decisions, regardless of the action's impact, some have characterized NEPA as a "toothless ogre." However, as a consciousness-raising device, NEPA does have the potential to require greater collaboration and transparency for activities that take place in environmentally sensitive areas, including the coastal zone, floodplains, and wetlands.[9] At a minimum, the requirements under NEPA can significantly slow down the progress of activities that could harm the environment, allowing citizens and affected local communities to respond.[10]

Recent Changes to NEPA

In 2014, the Council on Environmental Quality (CEQ) issued revised draft guidance for federal agencies to consider greenhouse gas emissions and the effects of climate change when they conduct reviews required by the NEPA. However, in 2020, the Trump Administration overhauled and weakened the program significantly. In an effort to speed up and remove barriers to construction of pipelines, power plants, freeways, and other major infrastructure projects, President Trump issued regulatory reinterpretations to significantly limit public review that is required by NEPA.

6.4.4 Cybersecurity: A New Federal Agency

The Cybersecurity and Infrastructure Security Agency (CISA) was created in 2018 as a standalone agency within the Department of Homeland Security to improve cybersecurity within all levels of government, as well as public and private sectors. The agency is intended to improve the government's cybersecurity protections against private and nation-state hackers. Local governments and other entities can take advantage of a range of services offered by CISA to mitigate the risk of cyberattacks, including trainings, exercises, and vulnerability scanning, to understand and correct potential weaknesses in computer networks.

As the name suggests, CISA is also charged with leading efforts to protect the nation's infrastructure, which includes a number of services offered to local and state governments, as well as owners and operators of infrastructure. These services include issuing guidance documents such as methods for securing hazardous chemicals to reduce the change of chemicals or explosives being weaponized, and leading trainings and workshops, such as "active shooter" workshops to help prevent and prepare for violence at people's workplaces and in schools.

SELF-CHECK

- Explain the importance of wetlands for flood mitigation.
- Discuss the purpose of the Coastal Zone Management Act (CZMA).
- Describe the limitations of National Environmental Policy Act (NEPA).

6.5 REDUCING RISK BY UNDERSTANDING AND ADAPTING TO CLIMATE CHANGE

As the impacts of climate change become better understood and more widely accepted, many federal agencies are developing new programs or modifying existing programs to reduce risks posed by climate change. As identified by the Intergovernmental Panel on Climate Change (IPCC), the phrase **climate change adaptation** refers to the process of adjusting to our climate and its effects in order to moderate harm or exploit beneficial opportunities. Many climate change adaptation programs work to reduce risks posed by natural hazards, ultimately achieving hazard mitigation and preparedness goals as well.

Myriad grant programs within federal agencies have also been expanded to include studies, plans, and projects that focus on climate change adaptation. For example, the National Coastal Wetlands Conservation Grant Program administered by the U.S. Fish and Wildlife Service provides financial assistance for acquisition, restoration, management, or enhancement of coastal wetlands, projects that may further climate change adaptation goals as well as hazard mitigation.

Other federal agencies with active climate change programs include the Centers for Disease Control (CDC), which carries out initiatives to help cities and states become "climate ready" in the face of possible disease outbreak and public health threats that can increase in frequency due to climate change. The Department of Interior (DOI) has developed an integrated strategy across the Department's agencies and bureaus to respond to the impacts of climate change on Indian tribes and on the public land, water, ocean, fish and wildlife, and cultural heritage resources that the DOI manages. In 2014, the DOT issued an updated Climate Adaptation Plan that lays out the potential impacts of climate change on the nation's transportation infrastructure. The plan specifies concrete steps the Department will take to fully integrate considerations of climate change and variability in DOT policies, programs, and operations to deal with issues such as rising sea level and changes in regional temperature that may affect our vast road and rail network.

In addition to the activities mentioned above, the following section highlights just a few of the many climate change adaption initiatives being implemented at the federal level.

6.5.1 U.S. Global Change Research Program

The federal government plays an extremely important role in coordinating scientific research and assessment to better understand the impact of climate change on the nation and the world. Established by Presidential Initiative in 1989, the U.S. Global Change Research Program (USGCRP) is a research program to help assess, predict, and respond to human-induced and natural processes of global change. A key outcome of this program is the National Climate Assessment, which summarizes the impacts of climate change on the United States. The Assessment has historically been updated every few years; however, the USGCRP intends to implement a "sustained assessment," which will ultimately facilitate continuous participation of scientists and stakeholders to update information in the National Climate Assessment as it becomes available.

The 2018 National Climate Assessment can be accessed at https://nca2018.globalchange.gov/.

6.5.2 Presidential Climate Action Plan

Through an Executive Order in 2009, President Obama convened the Interagency Climate Change Adaptation Task Force to develop a report with recommendations for how the federal government can strengthen policies and programs to better prepare the nation to adapt to the impacts of climate change. The Task Force represents more than 20 federal agencies, each of which is tasked with developing and annually updating a climate adaptation strategy.

On June 25, 2013, the White House released the Presidential Climate Action Plan to reduce carbon pollution, move the American economy toward clean energy sources, and begin to address the effects of climate change. The Plan acknowledges that, even if we take steps to reduce carbon pollution, we must also prepare for the inevitable impacts of climate change, such as increased flooding, prolonged periods of drought, and dangerous storm surge on top of higher sea levels.

The Presidential Climate Action Plan included the launch of the *Climate Data Initiative*, which provides access to federal climate-relevant data to stimulate innovation and private-sector entrepreneurship in support of climate change preparedness. The website (data.climate.gov) provides federal, state and local data, tools, and resources to conduct research, build applications, and design other value-added tools using government information.

Additionally, the Presidential Climate Action Plan committed the federal government to developing a Toolkit for Climate Resilience that centralizes access to data-driven resilience tools, services, and best practices. Released in November 2014, the *Climate Resilience Toolkit* (toolkit.climate.gov) provides scientific tools, information, and expertise to help people manage their climate-related risks and opportunities and improve their resilience to extreme events. While the Climate Data Initiative provides more raw data, the Climate Resilience Toolkit is designed to serve interested citizens, communities, businesses, resource managers, planners, and policy leaders at all levels of government.

An Executive Order by the President Trump Administration in 2018, aimed at encouraging energy and water efficiency standards for federal government buildings and operations, revoked the Obama-era policies that lead to the development of the Climate Action Plan.

6.5.3 Department of Defense Climate Change Adaptation Roadmap

The DoD has recognized climate change as an urgent threat to national security and made climate change an integral part of Pentagon planning. In October 2014, the Secretary of Defense released the Pentagon's Climate Change Adaptation Roadmap, a 16-page document that lays out the effects of extreme weather events and rising temperatures on military training, operations, acquisitions, and infrastructure. The Roadmap also details how the department will adapt to and mitigate climate change threats.

In the Department's 2010 Quadrennial Defense Review, the Secretary stated that the military could be called upon more often to support civil authorities and provide humanitarian assistance and disaster relief in the face of more frequent and more intense natural disasters. Our coastal installations are vulnerable to rising sea levels and increased flooding, while droughts, wildfires, and more extreme temperatures could threaten many of the department's training activities. Supply chains could be impacted, and DoD will need to ensure that critical equipment works under more extreme weather conditions. The Review points out that weather has always affected military operations, and as the climate changes, the way operations are executed may be altered or constrained.

6.5.4 Environmental Protection Agency Climate Change Adaptation Programs

The mission of the EPA is to protect human health and the environment. A major component of that mission is to address climate change, which the agency does through a variety of programs designed to help decision-makers better understand and address risks posed by a changing climate. EPA's regional adaptation programs provide information, tools, training, and technical support for climate-change preparedness and resilience throughout the country and make available the latest scientific data about climate change, its causes and impacts. Additionally, the EPA plays a major role in the regulation of wetlands under its authority to administer the CWA.

6.5.5 National Oceanic and Atmospheric Administration (NOAA)

NOAA's roots date back to 1807, when the Nation's first scientific agency, the Survey of the Coast, was established. Today, NOAA maintains a presence in every state, with the goal of building a "climate-smart nation" that is resilient to climate and weather extremes, and long-term changes. NOAA's objectives include the following:

- Reduce vulnerability to extreme climate and weather events
- Prepare for drought and long-term water resource challenges
- Protect and preserve coasts and coastal infrastructure
- Identify and manage risks to marine ecosystems and the services they provide
- Mitigate and adapt to climate impacts

NOAA meets these objectives by providing data and information on climate through a variety of programs and services, including:

- *The Office for Coastal Management* was established in 2014 when NOAA combined two offices: the Coastal Services Center and the Office of Ocean and Coastal Resource Management. A top priority for the Office is to unify efforts to make communities more resilient. The Office provides NOAA data and tools along with opportunities to work collaboratively within communities on issues that run the gamut from protecting endangered species to erosion to generating better building codes for storm-resistant buildings.
- *Digital Coast* is used to address timely coastal issues, including land use, coastal conservation, hazards, and climate change among others. The website includes tools, training, case studies, and information that help users incorporate climate data into coastal management decisions. For example, the *Digital Coast's Sea Level Rise Viewer* provides models illustrating potential marsh migration, and how tidal flooding will become more frequent with sea level rise.

- *NOAA National Weather Service (NWS) Climate Services*: The NWS Climate Prediction Center (CPC) has primary operational responsibility for short climate timescales (weeks, months, seasons). In support of the NWS preparedness and response mission, the CPC also has capabilities to provide climate information for the intermediate timescales (e.g., seasons, years, decades) at which preparedness and adaptation meet or overlap. This includes activities to link seasonal and decadal modeling and prediction (e.g., frequency and intensity of droughts and floods) and efforts to develop prediction techniques for regional climate information across timescales.
- *NOAA's Climate Program Office (CPO)* provides a climate research enterprise that focuses on the following:
  - Competitive grant programs that advance and extend our research capabilities
  - Partnerships with academia, businesses, and other agencies to develop and deliver targeted research and data products
  - Knowledge and information to improve public climate literacy and decision-making needed to maintain resilient economies and environmental services

6.5.6 USDA Regional Climate Hubs

In June 2013, the USDA announced the launch of seven Regional Hubs for Risk Adaptation and Mitigation to Climate Change. The Regional Climate Hubs deliver science-based, region-specific information and technologies to farmers, ranchers, and forest landowners to support climate resilience. These hubs work with universities and other partners to provide actionable information, as well as providing grants and technical support to agricultural water uses for more water-efficient practices in the face of drought and long-term climate change. The Hubs are also designed to partner with agricultural extension organizations to further disseminate information and best practices that enhance resilience to a changing climate.

The Regional Climate Hubs help translate climate change projections into potential impacts on the agricultural and forestry sector. In addition to helping farmers and foresters better anticipate climate impacts, the hubs provide information and tools to better manage risk, mitigate hazards, and ultimately become more climate resilient. For example, the Hubs draw on and downscale information published by programs such as the U.S. Drought Monitor to make climate data useful and actionable to farmers and others involved in agricultural land management.

SELF-CHECK

- What is the main product created by the U.S. Global Change Research Program?
- Explain why the Department of Defense has an interest in climate change adaptation.
- How does the Department of Agriculture facilitate adaptation among farmers in the United States?

SUMMARY

The federal government steps in to provide relief after every major disaster that happens in our country. In what ways do these disaster funds reduce the risk of future disasters, and when might they in fact contribute to the risk of future disasters? This chapter discussed how the federal government's involvement in emergency management has grown over the years. The FEMA and other federal programs play a direct role in the country's hazard management activities.

Other programs such as the CWA and CZMA play a more indirect role. The federal government has increasingly supported mitigation through investments in climate change adaptation and resilience efforts such as research, technical assistance, and grants to communities.

KEY TERMS

Disaster Mitigation Act (DMA) of 2000: Amends the Robert T. Stafford Disaster Relief and Emergency Assistance Act of 1988; streamlines the administration of federal disaster relief and mitigation programs; and places emphasis on pre-disaster mitigation planning to reduce the Nation's disaster losses.

Hazard Mitigation Grant Program (HMGP): Funding program administered by FEMA. The purpose of the HMGP is to reduce the loss of life and property caused by natural hazards by providing funding for mitigation to state and local governments following a disaster declaration.

National Flood Insurance Program (NFIP): Voluntary participatory program for local communities who wish to provide the opportunity for residents to purchase federally backed flood insurance. In exchange, local governments enact ordinances to regulate development in floodplains.

Ordinance: A piece of legislation enacted by a local government with the power of enforcement.

Repetitive loss properties (RLPs): Property with two or more National Flood Insurance Program claims over $1,000 each within a 10-year period.

Wetland mitigation: Compensatory mitigation refers to the restoration, establishment, enhancement, or preservation of wetlands to offset unavoidable adverse impacts of activities permitted under section 404 of the Clean Water Act.

ASSESS YOUR UNDERSTANDING

Summary Questions

1. Over the past several decades, federal involvement in emergency management has
   a. Increased
   b. Decreased
   c. Stayed the same
   d. Been insignificant
2. FEMA was created by President Carter to act as a lead agency for many aspects of emergency management. True or False?
3. The Small Business Administration's role in hazard management is to
   a. Provide technical assistance to farmers
   b. Reduce the loss of life and property
   c. Issue low-interest loans
   d. Administer community grants
4. FEMA took a Mitigation Directorate during the Clinton Administration. True or False?
5. Which federal agency was created after the terrorist attacks of September 11, 2001?
   a. FEMA
   b. Office of Emergency Preparedness
   c. Project Impact
   d. Department of Homeland Security
6. The National Flood Insurance Program is supported by federal taxes. True or False?
7. National Flood Insurance is available to anyone who can afford the high premiums. True or False?

8. A Flood Insurance Rate Map should be changed after a flood proves that the FIRM boundaries are no longer accurate. True or False?
9. The Community Rating System rewards
   a. Communities that have not experienced a flood in a given period
   b. Companies that provide insurance to their employees
   c. Communities that have undertaken extraordinary floodplain mitigation measures
   d. Homeowners who relocate structures
10. The Coastal Barrier Resources Act grants federal funds to aid the development of coastal areas. True or False?
11. The goal of Section 404 of the Clean Water Act is to protect wetlands from development. True or False?
12. The primary purpose of the National Environmental Policy Act is to
    a. Require federal agencies to acquire permits
    b. Create Special Area Management Plans
    c. Require federal agencies to consider environmental issues in the decision-making process
    d. Deter land development

Review Questions

1. Federal involvement in emergency management functions has increased in recent decades. Name five federal programs that directly relate to hazard mitigation or emergency management functions.
2. During the time of the Cold War, natural disasters were not a primary concern for U.S. citizens. Identify the act that introduced Americans to the concept of federal disaster assistance.
3. Explain what was unique about the National Flood Insurance Act of 1968.
4. Flood insurance is a major concern for many U.S. residents. Describe the purpose and major provisions of the National Flood Insurance Program (NFIP).
5. Those who make their living off the land can be particularly affected by natural disasters. In what way does the Farm Service Agency engage in disaster relief?
6. Hurricane Katrina opened a new chapter in the federal government's role in emergency management. Describe some of the reactions to FEMA's response to recent disasters.
7. Explain how a Flood Insurance Rate Map factors into flood mitigation.
8. Repeated losses cause a significant drain on the National Flood Insurance Program. Define Repetitive Loss Properties.
9. The Pre-Disaster Mitigation Program provides mitigation funding that is not dependent on a disaster. Give three examples of qualified mitigation projects under PDM.
10. Explain what an "indirect mitigation program" is, and name three such programs at the federal level.
11. Explain how the Coastal Zone Management Act provides a level of flexibility.
12. How do states benefit from the Coastal Zone Management Act?
13. What would be the benefit of raising National Flood Insurance premiums to reflect the true risks of living in flood-prone areas?

Applying This Chapter

1. Your small horse riding and stable business was hit hard by a tornado. You lost 3 of your 15 horses, and one-third of your buildings were damaged beyond repair. In addition, two of your three employees have had to quit and relocate as a result of losing their

homes in the storm. As the owner of this small business, which federal programs could you expect to get assistance from?

2. Nearly 20,000 communities participate in the National Flood Insurance Program. Your community, which hasn't had a major flood in more than three decades, is considering entering the program. Draft a proposal to your city council that describes the benefits of the program; be certain to include what, if any, steps your community will need to take to enter the program.

3. A developer has proposed to build a retail mall in a long-neglected area of your town. Most people in town support the move because it would bring business and interest to the area. A portion of the proposed site is believed to be wetlands, however. As the president of the local conservation group, how would you use the Clean Water Act to oppose the proposal? Alternatively, as the developer of the proposal, what would you do to satisfy requirements of the Clean Water Act and still get the job done?

4. Some critics have pointed to a major flaw in the Coastal Barrier Resources Act (CBRA) that manifests itself in the context of recovery from a natural hazards disaster. Based on the provisions in CBRA regarding the exemptions discussed in this chapter, does the Act open the door to expanded development of barrier islands using federal funds, despite the clear intent of Congress when it passed the legislation? Consider the following hypothetical scenario to help you formulate your answer:

> Suppose an 18-inch water line runs through a CBRA unit. The pipe connects development on one end of the unit to a water supply on the other end of the unit. Now suppose the pipe is damaged in a coastal storm. Does CBRA allow federal funds to be used to pay for the cost of replacing the 18-inch pipe? Can other funds, such as private financing or state and local government funds, be used to expand the pipe from 18 to 24 inches? What about the potential for more intense development that is made possible by the increased water capacity in the 24-inch pipe?

5. Assume you live in a hurricane-prone area of the United States. Many say that the federal government is subsidizing the privilege of living in a coastal community, and other taxpayers are unfairly being asked to support the subsidy with their taxes. How do you respond?

You Try It

Mitigation Powers

Imagine you have just been appointed "Mitigation Czar" by the President of the United States. What would you do to enhance the role of the federal government in reducing the country's vulnerability to natural hazards?

Flood-Wise Ways

Although your 100-year-old home is in the Maryland floodplain, it has only been flooded twice since the early 1900s. Unfortunately, that's no guarantee it won't happen again. Using the National Flood Insurance Program's website at www.floodsmart.gov, estimate how much your flood insurance premium would be for both your home and its contents (note: you're in zone A). Then, using the site, come up with things you can do—in addition to buying insurance—to minimize potential loss.

REFERENCES

1. Singer, P.A. 2006. *Hurricane season: A port in the storm. National Journal*, 38(21): 1422–1426; Czerwinski, testimony.
2. Congressional Research Service. 2020. Federal Land Ownership: Overview and Data. CRS Report: R42346.
3. Obama, B. 2015. *Executive Order 13690 – Establishing a Federal Flood Risk Management Standard and a Process for Further Soliciting and Considering Stakeholder Input.* The White House.
4. Platt, R.H. 1999. *Disasters and Democracy: the Politics of Extreme Natural Events.* Washington, DC: Island Press.
5. Haddow, G.D., J.A. Bullock, and D.P. Coppola. 2014. *Introduction to Emergency Management,* Fifth Edition. Burlington, MA: Butterworth-Heinemann.
6. The H. John Heinz III Center for Science, Economics and the Environment. 2002. *Human Links to Coastal Disasters.* Washington, DC: The Heinz Center.
7. Federal Emergency Management Agency. 2011. *Presidential Policy Directive-8: National Preparedness.* Washington, DC: The White House.
8. Flourney, A.C. and A. Fischman. 2013. Wetlands Regulation in an Era of Climate Change: Can Section 404 Meet the Challenge?. *George Washington Journal of Energy and Environmental Law,* Summer 2013, at 67. Available at: http://scholarship.law.ufl.edu/facultypub/368.
9. Beatley, T. et al. 2000. *An Introduction to Coastal Zone Management.* Washington DC: Island Press.
10. Kalo, J.J. 1990. *Coastal and Ocean Law.* Houston, TX: The John Marshall Publishing Co.

7

Mitigating Hazards at the State Level

What You'll Learn

- Differences in state approaches to hazards management and climate change adaptation
- Responsibilities of state emergency management offices
- Sources of funding for state mitigation programs
- The application of statewide building codes
- State regulation of hazard insurance
- Ideas for increasing the mitigation capabilities of states

Goals and Outcomes

- Discuss the role states play in local land use planning
- Describe state regulation in environmentally sensitive areas
- Understand the role of local enforcement of state building codes
- Identify some of the issues involved with insuring against catastrophic losses

INTRODUCTION

States use a variety of techniques to address hazards and reduce risk within communities under their jurisdiction. This chapter begins with an overview of the divergent approaches to hazards management and suggests some of the reasons for this diversity throughout the country. The chapter then discusses the authority, functions, and responsibilities of state emergency management offices and explores the significance of hazard mitigation planning at the state level, as well as the degree to which states are addressing climate change through adaptation planning. Next, the chapter considers how state mandates for local land use planning influence communities' approaches to hazards management. The chapter then examines some of the ways states directly intervene in land use decision-making, particularly in environmentally sensitive areas such as the coastal zone and wetlands. The chapter also takes a look at state building codes and insurance laws. The chapter concludes with a discussion of opportunities for states to increase the resiliency of their communities and the state as a whole.

DOI: 10.4324/9781003123897-7

7.1 OVERVIEW OF DIVERGENT APPROACHES TO HAZARDS MANAGEMENT

By virtue of the Tenth Amendment to the United States Constitution, all state governments have inherent power—called the **police power**—to enact reasonable legislation to protect the health, safety, and general welfare of the public. With no mandatory public policy regarding how to prepare for and mitigate against natural and human-made hazards, states have developed their own diverse methods of protecting public health and safety from the impacts of hazards. Some states take a direct approach, while other states are more hands off and delegate much of the responsibility to local governments or allow market forces to control land uses in hazard areas. Still others mandate specific action on the part of the local governments but allow implementation decisions to be made at the community level.

At least some of the divergence among states in their approach to hazards management and regulation of the built environment can be explained by differences in political climate and the degree of first-hand experience with natural hazards. Many policy makers in states like Florida, where hurricanes occur frequently and cause widespread and very visible damage, have accepted that natural hazards are inevitable. In these areas, state legislators have historically been willing to expend state resources and political capital to mitigate hurricane impacts. Other states have been lulled into complacency and have not intervened in the private development market. This is perhaps an appropriate response where natural hazards are few and far between and public expenditures for hazards management is less critical. However, some of these states may also be home to very strong building and development lobbies or other special interests, which sometimes can exert enough political pressure to counter state efforts to regulate development in hazard areas.

There is even more variation among the states in the way they are approaching climate change. A few front runner states, such as Maryland and California, have been aggressively tackling the issue for many years. Other states have been reticent to confront what is perceived as political quicksand and have not developed strong policies to adapt to climate change impacts.

A HAWAIIAN POLICY TOOL KIT

An example of the wide range of possible actions available to states can be found in a Policy Tool Kit that has been recommended to the State of Hawaii to address rising sea levels. The Tool Kit identifies and explains key land use policy tools for state and local government agencies and officials, such as incorporating scientifically-based projections for sea level rise in land use decision-making, locating coastal development where it is protected from hazards, and ensuring structures are resilient to flooding and other coastal hazards. Because sea level rise and climate change exacerbate existing coastal hazards, adopting forward-thinking policies ultimately will lessen future economic, social, and environmental impacts of rising sea levels along Hawaii's fragile coastlines.[1]

7.1.1 The Role of State Agencies in Hazards Management

In the rest of this chapter, we will discuss in more detail some of the various state approaches to hazards management, beginning with a brief exploration of the numerous state-level agencies that may play a role in reducing (or increasing) hazard risk. Table 7.1 lists a few

Table 7.1 State Agency Role in Hazards Management and Climate Change Adaptation.

State Agency	Programs and Policies
Office of the Governor	Promotes policies to increase hazard resilience and climate change adaptation; issues requests for federal assistance for large-scale disasters
State Planning Office	Formulates policy and creates a vision for the state for land use and development; capital improvement programs and budgets; plans for environmental protection, transportation, affordable housing, climate change, etc.
Division of Emergency Management	Oversees hazard mitigation planning and programs; administers disaster grants; conducts disaster preparedness training and exercises for local EM coordinators; manages the NFIP and floodplain regulations
Dept. of Transportation	Constructs and repairs damaged roads and bridges following hazard events; promulgates design standards for infrastructure to reduce risk of flooding; prepares roads for severe winter weather
Dept. of Insurance	Promulgates statewide building codes; regulates hazard insurance
Dept. of Natural Resources	Oversees regulation, management, and protection of state environmental assets, including water, air, and land
Division of Coastal Management	Issues development permits in the coastal zone; enforces setback/erosion regulations; identifies areas of environmental concern; maps and regulates coastal hazard areas including inlets, beaches, dunes, and erosion zones
Dam Safety Office	Issues permits, conducts inspections, and inventories dams
State Geologist	Identifies and maps seismic and landslide risk areas
Dept. of Agriculture	Assists farmers reduce their risk from flooding, hail, severe winter weather, tornados, livestock and plant disease, and terrorist attacks on food production
Division of Forestry	Oversees forest fire prevention and suppression; disease and pest control; promotes awareness of wildfire risk and mitigation options
Office of Water Resources	Regulates water supply and water quality; administers stormwater management permits; manages drought mitigation and response programs; monitors stream gauges
Dept. of Health and Human Services; Division of Aging	Administers programs to protect vulnerable populations during severe weather events
Division of Public Health	Prepares for threat of bioterrorism; oversees preventive measures for disease pandemics; develops plans for climate change impacts on human health (heat waves, drought, disease vectors, etc.)
Utilities Commission	Regulates public utilities; works with providers on contingency planning for power outages and restoration of service in hazard events
State Climate Office	Collects, analyzes, disseminates, and archives weather and climatic data; works with local weather offices and National Weather Service to forecast hazard events; provides scientific information on climate change to state and local policy makers

examples of agencies that are common to many states, along with their role in hazard mitigation and/or climate change adaptation. Many of these agencies do not include hazards management or climate change as a primary departmental mission, but they nevertheless implement policies, carry out programs, and enforce regulations that can have an effect on hazard resilience. This is particularly effective when agencies work together collaboratively to bring about reductions in vulnerability.

In Table 7.1, we will look more closely at a few of these state agencies, starting with the role of the state office of emergency management, before turning our focus to land use issues and various ways states control the built environment in hazard areas. We include in this discussion state departments of insurance, which are responsible for administering the state building code and for regulating hazard insurance, and also state departments of transportation, which, through the provision of infrastructure, can affect where development takes place.

SELF-CHECK

- Identify the Constitutional power that allows states to pass hazard mitigation regulations.
- List five common state agencies and the role they play in hazards management.

7.2 STATE EMERGENCY MANAGEMENT

State laws describe the responsibilities of the state government for emergencies and disasters, authorizing the Governor and state agencies to carry out plans and implement policies to respond to, recover from, prepare for, and mitigate disasters. In this pivotal position, the state serves as a key link between local communities and federal agencies and resources. One of the primary federal agencies that the states deal with is the Federal Emergency Management Agency (FEMA). Direct state interaction with FEMA is usually conducted through FEMA's 10 regional offices, with FEMA's national office providing overall policy guidance and oversight.

Each of the 50 states, US territories, and the District of Columbia maintains an office of emergency management. However, the organizational structure of state emergency management offices varies significantly from one state to the next. In some states, such as California, the Emergency Management Agency is housed in the Office of the Governor. In Tennessee, the Emergency Management Agency reports to the Adjutant General, while in Florida, the emergency management function is carried out in the Office of Community Affairs. In North Carolina, emergency management is in the Department of Public Safety. National Guard Adjutant Generals manage state emergency management offices in more than half of the states and territories. The remaining state emergency management offices are led by civilian employees.

State emergency management offices carry out a full range of emergency management functions. Some of the responsibilities that typically fall to state EMs include public awareness campaigns, emergency alert systems, family and business preparedness initiatives, hazardous materials management, chemical safety and reporting, nuclear power plant safety drills, severe weather preparedness, evacuation planning and coordination, and conducting extensive training and exercises for local EM coordinators. In addition, emergency management offices are largely in charge of the state's hazard mitigation policies, as coordinated by the State Hazard Mitigation Officer (SHMO).

7.2.1 The State Hazard Mitigation Officer

Each state and U.S. territory has a SHMO who serves as the primary contact between the federal government and the state in ongoing efforts to reduce risk to natural and human-made hazards. SHMOs are responsible for a multitude of tasks, not the least of which is to guide the state hazard mitigation planning process, as required under the Disaster Mitigation Act (DMA) of 2000 (more on state hazard mitigation planning below). In addition to serving as a coordinator among different levels of government, SHMOs are also in charge of implementing statewide laws and programs for mitigation and for providing staff and resources to assist local governments in their own planning efforts and in implementing local hazard mitigation activities.

Despite the daunting tasks that face SHMOs, many SHMOs throughout the country lack full staff support or adequate resources to perform their duties. However, a good working relationship between the state and the FEMA regional office often bolsters the SHMOs commitment to hazard mitigation. In addition, many SHMOs are supported in their coordinating efforts through interagency teams and committees at the state level, such as hazard mitigation advisory groups, task forces appointed by the governor, and similar working groups that can provide advice and assistance for mitigation initiatives.

7.2.2 Funding for State Hazard Mitigation and Preparedness Activities

Most states are heavily dependent on federal funding, especially from FEMA, to develop and implement mitigation programs. Significant support comes to the states in the form of grants such as the Hazard Mitigation Grant Program (HMGP), the mitigation portion of the Public Assistance (PA) program, the Flood Mitigation Assistance (FMA) program, and the Building Resilient Infrastructure and Communities (BRIC) program. Other federal agencies also provide disaster assistance in the form of grants and loans, including Community Development Block Grants from the US Department of Housing and Urban Development, the Small Business Administration, and assistance to farmers from the Department of Agriculture. Many of these federal disaster-related grants are administered by the states who then pass the funds to local communities.

Federal mitigation assistance programs can vastly augment the capacity of state agencies to carry out major mitigation initiatives at the state level and provide assistance to local governments for mitigation activities. States that experience repeated disasters—such as major flooding, damaging hurricanes, severe ice and winter storms, and destructive earthquakes—can receive significant levels of financial assistance from the federal government specifically for mitigation projects. However, much of this federal funding is only available after a disaster has been declared (with the exception of the FMA and BRIC programs, which are available on a recurring basis through a competitive grant process).

Because many states depend on disaster-based funding for much of their mitigation budget, a significant proportion of state emergency management positions that focus on hazard mitigation are time limited. In some states, there is only enough money to fund a single position on a full-time basis, usually the SHMO, along with a floodplain management coordinator to administer the National Flood Insurance Program (NFIP). A few states have no full-time staff devoted to natural hazard mitigation at all. The remaining staff positions that are necessary to carry out mitigation initiatives may fluctuate according to the level of disaster funding available at any given time. Although the occurrence of future hazards is inevitable, dependence on federal disaster assistance is an unstable and unpredictable source of funding for ongoing mitigation activities that support long-term reductions in vulnerability.

The good news, however, is that states are becoming increasingly adept at seeking additional ways to improve their mitigation capabilities and securing more permanent full-time positions to become less disaster dependent and more proactive before the next hazard event occurs.

7.2.3 Effectiveness of State Hazards Management

The effectiveness of the emergency management office to carry out specific functions varies widely from state to state. In general, policy-oriented offices (e.g., state planning) are suited to sustaining long-range activities such as hazard mitigation and recovery programs, while tactical and operations-oriented offices (e.g., state police) focus on managing preparedness and response. However, while the orientation and prominence of the office may dictate to some degree the ability of emergency managers to promote mitigation policies, a more important factor in the overall effectiveness of hazards management is the relationship with the governor's office and the willingness of the chief executive officer of the state to promote long-term resilience.

SELF-CHECK

- Explain the role of a state office of emergency management.
- Describe the duties of a state hazard mitigation officer (SHMO).
- List sources of funding for state level hazard mitigation programming.

7.3 HAZARD MITIGATION PLANNING AT THE STATE LEVEL

Hazard mitigation planning is an important aspect of a successful statewide mitigation program. Responsibility for plan development typically falls to the state emergency management office, although other state agencies may be involved as well. States and communities use the hazard mitigation planning process to set short- and long-range mitigation goals and objectives. Hazard mitigation planning is a collaborative process through which hazards affecting the state are identified, vulnerability to the hazards is assessed, and consensus is reached on how to minimize or eliminate the effects of those hazards on local communities and the state as a whole.

7.3.1 Mitigation Planning under the Disaster Mitigation Act of 2000

The **DMA of 2000** reinforces the importance of pre-disaster mitigation planning to reduce the nation's disaster losses and is aimed primarily at controlling and streamlining the administration of federal disaster relief and mitigation programs. States, Tribal governments, and local communities must have an approved mitigation plan in place to be eligible for post-disaster funds from several of the nonemergency assistance programs administered by FEMA.

Section 322 of the DMA specifically addresses mitigation planning at the state and local levels. The federal regulations that implement Section 322 are found in the Code of Federal Regulations (CFR) at 44 CFR Part 201, which lays out specific criteria that must be met and a planning process that must be followed by states seeking plan approval from FEMA. Many of the criteria that apply to state hazard mitigation plans are similar or identical to those required for local governments, including a risk assessment that consists of a hazard identification and profile, vulnerability assessment, and loss estimate; an evaluation of capabilities for mitigation; formulation of goal statements; and development of mitigation strategies and actions with identified sources of funding or potential funding. These specific criteria and the hazard mitigation planning process in general are described in detail in Chapter 12.

States are required to provide guidance and assistance to local communities in the development of local hazard mitigation plans that will meet DMA criteria. Services that some states provide to their local governments include training workshops and information sessions on risk assessment and hazard mitigation planning principles, planning assistance materials such as guidebooks and worksheets, and community outreach activities. Some states also provide data sets for their local governments, including information on demographics, soils, wetlands, hazard histories, updated floodplain maps, and other resources to help local communities prepare hazard mitigation plans.

Two Levels of State Plans: Standard and Enhanced

There are two levels of state hazard mitigation plans under the DMA, Standard and Enhanced. With an approved **Standard Plan**, states are eligible to receive 7.5% of the total disaster assistance amount granted from FEMA to be used solely for mitigation purposes. For example, if a state is eligible to receive $100 million in disaster assistance from FEMA, $7.5 million may be used for hazard mitigation purposes, such as buying out homes in floodplains or upgrading culverts beneath roads.

If a state's hazard mitigation plan is approved by FEMA as an **Enhanced Plan**, a state may qualify for a greater percentage of the total amount of disaster assistance to be used for mitigation projects. In addition to satisfying the requirements of the standard plan, the enhanced plan must demonstrate how the state will administer and implement its existing mitigation programs with a systematic and effective approach. The enhanced status acknowledges the extra effort a state has made to reduce losses, protect its resources, and create safer communities. As of 2020, states with Enhanced Mitigation Plans include California, Colorado, Florida, Georgia, Iowa, Kentucky, Missouri, Nevada, North Carolina, North Dakota, Ohio, South Dakota, Washington, and Wisconsin.

7.3.2 Consequences of Not Preparing a State Hazard Mitigation Plan

The consequences of not preparing and adopting a FEMA-approved hazard mitigation plan can be quite significant. If a state does not have an approved plan in place at the time a disaster strikes, FEMA is limited to providing only "emergency assistance." For example, under the PA Program, the only categories of assistance that are considered emergency are debris removal and immediate measures to protect human life and safety. The remaining PA project categories are considered permanent restorative work and will not be funded in that state. This means federal assistance will not be available to restore roads and bridges, water control facilities, public buildings, public utilities, and other facilities that are damaged in a hazard event. In addition, without an approved state hazard mitigation plan, states are not eligible for funding from the Individual and Family Grant (IFG) Program, HMGP, and Fire Suppression Assistance Program, each of which provides significant financial support to both communities and individuals and families impacted by disaster. States have taken this provision of the DMA very seriously, and all 50 states, the District of Columbia, and five territories (CNMI, Guam, American Samoa, Puerto Rico, and U.S. Virgin Islands) have adopted FEMA-approved State Hazard Mitigation Plans.

SELF-CHECK

- Explain the purpose behind the Disaster Mitigation Act of 2000.
- Identify two levels of state mitigation plans.
- Describe the consequences of not having a state hazard mitigation plan in place when a disaster occurs.

7.4 CLIMATE CHANGE ADAPTATION PLANNING AT THE STATE LEVEL

Many states have begun planning and implementing actions to reduce risks associated with climate change. One of the first steps that states can take is to develop a climate adaptation plan, which lays out climate-related risks that the state is likely to face and actions that can be taken to become more resilient to climate change. As of 2020, 17 states and the District of Columbia have completed adaptation plans, while several other states are in the process of developing plans.[2]

One notable example is the California Climate Adaptation Strategy. Initially developed in 2009 and updated in 2014 and 2018, the Strategy includes impacts, risks, and adaptation strategies to address the following categories: public health, biodiversity and habitat, ocean and coastal resources, water management, agriculture and forestry, and energy and transportation infrastructure. The state's climate change website (www.climatechange.ca.gov) includes links to their strategy and a range of other information and resources to facilitate climate change adaptation.

In many ways, climate adaptation planning is closely related to hazard mitigation planning, and states should ensure that these efforts are connected and mutually reinforcing. At present, there is no requirement for states to address climate change impacts in hazard mitigation plans, and many states have not yet taken steps to link adaptation and hazard mitigation planning.

7.5 STATE MANDATES FOR LOCAL LAND USE PLANNING

While state hazard mitigation plans can be very effective for reducing vulnerability through the promotion of various statewide mitigation programs and strategies, mitigation plans prepared under the Disaster Management Act typically do not focus directly on local land use decision-making. Yet, advocates of a holistic approach to hazard mitigation promote the value of using a land use-based approach, under the assumption that steering development away from hazard areas—such as floodplains and fire-prone areas—and toward more appropriate areas helps decrease our vulnerability to the impacts of future hazards. Land use regulation is most effective when carried out through a process of careful community-wide planning that takes into account the numerous factors involved in managing growth and development. At a large scale, this approach is most applicable for undeveloped land, although the land use planning approach can also be applied to land that is already developed as well.

The responsibility to create land use plans and the regulations necessary to carry them out falls primarily with local governments. Because planning is so essential for fair and comprehensive regulation of private property, some states have passed legislation requiring local governments to prepare comprehensive land use plans. Of these, a few states impose the planning mandate only on local governments in a certain region of the state, while the remaining communities are exempt from an explicit planning mandate. In North Carolina, for example, the 20 counties that make up the coastal zone must prepare local land use plans, while the remaining 80 counties in the state do not.

Some states that mandate local planning have made their policy objectives quite clear and have passed these on to the local governments with guidance as to how to achieve the state goals through the local land use planning process. Typically, states lay out criteria that the local communities must follow and specify the types of issues that the local land use plan must address. The states specify policy goals and objectives but, to varying degrees, leave the specific details of the content and implementation of plans to local governments. A few states have included natural hazards and problems posed by development in hazardous areas as topics that local governments must consider in their plans. California, Florida, Washington, Oregon, and a few other states have established planning mandates, with varying levels of incentives, to prod local governments into considering natural hazards as part of their comprehensive planning process.[3]

OREGON PLANNING SAVES MILLIONS

In 1996, FEMA estimated that Oregon had avoided about $10 million a year in flood losses because of strong land use planning that considered natural hazards. This was not accomplished by accident, but through the foresight of government officials over the course of more than two decades that required local plans to include inventories, policies, and ordinances for guiding development in designated hazard-prone areas. Using a comprehensive approach to planning has resulted in reducing losses from flooding, landslides, and earthquakes in communities throughout the state of Oregon.

SELF-CHECK

- Describe the role of local land use planning in hazard mitigation.
- Explain how state governments can influence local land use planning.

7.6 STATE REGULATION OF ENVIRONMENTALLY SENSITIVE AREAS

As we discussed in the preceding section, most states leave the bulk of land use decision-making to their local governments. Municipalities and counties usually have direct control over development and growth within their jurisdictions, with some states providing guidance and direction through statewide planning policies. Other states leave responsibility for land use regulation entirely in local hands. The one exception to this mostly hands-off approach is in environmentally sensitive areas, where many states play a direct role in controlling how these areas are used.

These so-called areas of particular concern are defined by states in a variety of ways. Most require that special areas have some sort of statewide significance. Areas of concern may be defined by their geographic boundaries, natural resource value, or by the function performed by a particular natural feature. Special areas include important riparian corridors, threatened and endangered species habitats, cultural and archeological resources, and unique scenic landscapes that the state assesses as in need of special management attention.

Areas that are especially vulnerable to natural hazards or which provide a natural mitigation function may also be designated as areas requiring state oversight. These include highly erodible coastlines, areas prone to flooding, inlet hazard zones, and other high-hazard areas. States regulate these areas in a variety of ways, such as issuing state-level permits for development, establishing setback requirements for construction, and restricting post-storm reconstruction among others.

NORTH CAROLINA AREAS OF ENVIRONMENTAL CONCERN

In North Carolina, Areas of Environmental Concern (AEC) are the foundation of the Coastal Resources Commission's permitting program for coastal development, as dictated by the NC Coastal Area Management Act (CAMA). An AEC is an area of natural importance. It may be easily destroyed by erosion or flooding, or it may have environmental, social, economic, or aesthetic qualities that make it valuable to the state. The North Carolina Coastal Resources Commission designates areas as AECs to protect them from uncontrolled development, which may cause irreversible damage to property, public health, or the environment. For example, the Ocean Hazard System AEC includes the band of narrow barrier islands that form the State's eastern border. The Ocean Hazard System is made up of oceanfront lands and the inlets that connect the ocean to the sounds, including ocean erodible areas, high-hazard flood areas, and inlet hazard areas.[4] All development in the Ocean Hazard System AEC must be located and designed to protect human lives and property from storms and erosion, prevent permanent structures from encroaching on public beaches, and reduce public costs (such as disaster relief aid) that can result from poorly located development.

7.6.1 Regulatory Setbacks

Most coastal states impose some sort of regulatory setback requirements on development that takes place along the shore. Although the specifics vary among the coastal states, in general, **setbacks** work by prohibiting or limiting the erection of structures within a specified distance from the ocean or Great Lakes. This method of "strategic retreat" can help reduce the risk to life and property from coastal hazards and prolong the life of the building. Setbacks also help protect public beaches, many of which are vital to state and local tourism industries. Because hurricanes and other coastal storms can cause more damage when development is poorly located, setbacks also help reduce the amount of tax money that is spent responding to disasters. Setbacks can also be an important tool for addressing sea level rise, by providing an added buffer between development and rising coastal waters.

Setbacks regulate construction in a zone that is a certain distance landward from the ocean or other environmental features such as streams or wetlands. Methods of determining the setback line include the first line of stable, natural vegetation; the mean high water line; local erosion rates; or various other marks. In most states, development must take place landward of this line and follow strict guidelines for construction.

The problem with many of the methods of measurement used by coastal states to establish construction setbacks is that the distances can be relatively arbitrary, generally ranging from about 40 to 100 feet. As understanding of beach and dune processes has increased, and as coastal engineering has become more sophisticated, delineation of setback lines has become highly technical. Setbacks based on seasonal fluctuations, vulnerability to storms and storm surges, and the threat of shoreline erosion are more scientifically valid, but they are also more difficult and costly for state regulators to implement and for landowners to understand.[5]

SETTING BACK FROM THE SHORELINE IN HAWAII

The State of Hawaii uses a setback that prohibits development in a zone 40 feet inland from the shoreline. The shoreline is defined as the debris or vegetation line that is visible on the shore. This line can fluctuate on a regular basis, which can lead to uncertainty on the part of property owners and state regulators. Recent recommendations for changes to the shoreline construction setback propose implementation of erosion-based setbacks that account for the life span of structures for each county in Hawaii and allow for adjustments based upon best-available sea level rise data.

7.6.2 Post-Storm Reconstruction

Many states have regulations in place to guide rebuilding and reconstruction after hurricanes and other hazard events. Usually a permit is required to rebuild structures that are "substantially damaged," typically defined as a structure for which the cost of restoration equals or exceeds 50% of the market value of the structure prior to the damage.[6] Following Hurricane Sandy, the New Jersey Department of Environmental Protection adopted emergency amendments to flood hazard area rules relating to post-storm reconstruction. Among the changes, the new rules require new or substantially damaged structures to build to the highest elevation level set by FEMA or the state. In addition, Flood Hazard Area Act rules require the lowest floor of each building in flood hazard areas to be constructed at least 1 foot above this elevation.

7.6.3 State Wetland Protection

Many states provide some degree of regulatory protection for wetlands. Wetlands are well known for their ability to protect water quality and are even called nature's kidneys because of their ability to filter impurities from surface water as it makes its way through the hydrologic system. Wetlands also perform an important function in the coastal zone and in inland riverine floodplains by storing and preventing rapid runoff of water, thus helping to maintain more constant water levels in streams, estuaries, and floodplains. Wetlands also protect against shoreline erosion. Wetland vegetation is often very dense, both above and below ground. The plant cover and root systems can absorb energy from floods and wave action. By dissipating the energy, binding the soil, and encouraging sediment deposition, wetlands stabilize shorelines along coastal streams, lakes, and sounds.

As discussed in Chapter 6, Section 404 of the federal Clean Water Act imposes restrictions on activities carried out in wetlands and requires permits from the U.S. Army Corps of Engineers for any deposition of dredge and fill material into wetlands. A few states have taken on the responsibility for administering the Section 404 program at the state level. In addition to the Section 404 regulations, some states have also imposed state-level restrictions on development in tidal or saltwater wetlands, prohibiting draining, ditching, or filling in wetland sites. A few states extend restrictions to nontidal or freshwater wetlands as well.

Some states also require **wetland mitigation**, which involves the off-site conservation of another wetland located away from the development activity or the creation of a new wetland to take the place of one that is impaired or destroyed. States sometimes impose fairly rigorous mitigation ratios, ranging from 2:1 to 7:1 (that is, the amount of created, restored, or enhanced wetland acreage required for each acre of natural wetland destroyed or damaged).[7] However, the science and practice of wetland restoration is still evolving, and preserving an existing wetland is likely to provide more environmental and flood control benefits than attempting to reconstruct the ecological complexity of a wetland.

SELF-CHECK

- Define **Areas of Environmental Concern, setback**, and **wetland mitigation**.
- Discuss situations in which states play a direct role in land use regulation.
- Describe methods of determining regulatory setbacks.
- Describe what happens when structures on the coast are damaged more than 50% during a hurricane or other coastal storm.

7.7 STATE PROVISION OF INFRASTRUCTURE

One of the most powerful tools states have to control land use in hazard areas is through the provision of infrastructure. Along with the federal government, and often in partnership with federal agencies, states provide a significant portion of our critical civil infrastructure nationwide. At the state level, much of this infrastructure is built and maintained through the state Departments of Transportation. A great deal of private investment, including investment in private property located in highly hazardous areas such as the coastal zone, is made financially feasible through state and federal dollars that fund or subsidize construction and maintenance of roads, bridges, water and sewer lines, and other facilities that foster development. State and federal funds are also used to repair public facilities after a storm causes severe damage. While this infrastructure is necessary to encourage and maintain economic growth, sometimes relatively little consideration is made for the increased vulnerability that results from development located in hazardous locations.

On the other hand, state policies that incorporate strong flood protection and other hazard risk reduction measures into state-built infrastructure can play a big role in reducing the need for costly rebuilding after a hazard event. States can also enact incentive programs to encourage local communities to design and build infrastructure that can withstand flooding and other hazard impacts.

FLOOD READY VERMONT

In August of 2011, the rains from Hurricane Irene caused massive flood damage along rivers throughout the state of Vermont. Realizing that flooding is a recurring problem in the state, policy makers asked, "How can we avoid blown out culverts, road washouts, and damaged buildings?" Through its Flood Ready Program, the state urges Vermont communities to plan ahead to ensure that they build and expand infrastructure with flood readiness in mind. Ideally, "flood ready" means built in a safe location, away from hazardous floodplain areas. For existing infrastructure already located in floodplains, it means making smart investments to minimize future damage when rivers rise.

The Vermont Agency of Transportation (VTrans) put together road and bridge standards to improve safety, reduce life cycle costs, and reduce environmental impacts. Communities that adopt standards that meet or exceed those laid out by VTrans can receive funding to improve their infrastructure before a flood occurs, and they can access more state funds to meet recovery costs if disaster does strike.

7.8 STATE BUILDING CODES

Thus far in this chapter, we have seen some of the ways that states play a role in how land is used in hazard areas. This section will focus on how states are involved in the construction of buildings, primarily through building codes that are enacted by the state legislature.

A **building code** is a collection of laws, regulations, ordinances, or other statutory requirements adopted by a government that controls the physical structure of buildings. The purpose of a building code is to establish the minimum acceptable standards of construction necessary for preserving the public health, safety, and welfare and protect the built environment. These minimum requirements are based on principles of engineering, on properties of materials, and on the inherent hazards of climate, geology, and use of a structure.[8] Among the natural hazards that are addressed through building codes include earthquake, wildfire, snowstorms, high winds, storm surge, flooding, and wave action. Building codes usually contain maps indicating various wind, flood, and seismic zones, where different levels of design standards apply depending upon the hazard risk. Building codes primarily regulate new or proposed construction. They have less application to existing structures, except when buildings are undergoing reconstruction, rehabilitation, or alteration, or if the occupancy category of the building is being changed.

Recent benefit/cost studies indicate that stronger minimum code provisions for natural hazard vulnerability reduction have positive benefit/cost ratios ranging from 3 to 16. In other words, for every $1 increase in construction costs, there is a long-term savings of $3–$16. This concept is similar to environmental and energy benefits when consumers invest in higher efficiency heating and cooling systems that are initially slightly more expensive but pay for themselves over the lifetime of the building or earlier. Investing in construction techniques that minimize damage to buildings from earthquake, flood, or high winds can sometimes pay off in a single hazard event!

7.8.1 Freeboard Requirements in State Building Codes

Many state building codes require structures to be built a certain number of feet above the 100-year floodplain to further reduce the likelihood of damage due to flooding. FEMA defines the term "**freeboard**" as a factor of safety, usually expressed in feet above a base flood level for the purposes of floodplain management. In Rhode Island, for example, the statewide building code requires that new or substantially improved structures incorporate 1 foot of freeboard, meaning structures must be built at least 1 foot above the 100-year flood level. In many areas, the amount of freeboard requires varies depending on the type of structure to take into account the relative risk of different types of buildings flooding. For example, a state building code may require hospitals, nursing homes, or facilities that store hazardous materials to include 3 feet of freeboard, while smaller structures like single-family homes may only require 1 or 2 feet of freeboard.

Freeboard can also help mitigate the impact of flooding due to sea level rise. For example, due to the combined forces of regional land subsidence and global climate change, parts of the coast in Maryland may experience 3–4 feet of sea level rise over the next century. Freeboard could help keep structures above floodwaters as storm surge elevations increase. For this reason, the Maryland Commission on Climate Change recommends 2 or more feet of freeboard for structures located in tidally influenced floodplains.

7.8.2 State Approaches to Building Codes

During the 1970s and earlier, relatively few states had statewide building codes. Where they did exist, codes were enacted and enforced by local governments. As a result, building standards varied widely from state to state, and even within a state there were different codes and levels of regulation in place. Since then, many states have retracted this complete delegation of power to the local government and have enacted a building code that applies across the state, with primary enforcement remaining at the local level. In many states, the building code is administered through the state department of insurance.

Many statewide codes are based on nationally recognized model codes, including the International Building Code (IBC) and the International Residential Code (IRC) developed by the International Code Council (ICC). States vary widely in the version of the model codes that have been officially adopted, and many states have made changes to the model codes. Some states allow local governments to deviate from the state code, while a few other states continue to have no statewide coverage. In some rural or semirural areas, there are no building codes in place, or codes that do not apply to single-family or two-family residential structures.

7.8.3 Building Code Updates and Enforcement

Regular updates are essential to ensure that building codes reflect changing conditions in terms of population, development, and hazard frequency and intensity. Building codes are also updated to incorporate the latest information on building techniques. However, in some states, updates to building codes may result in a weakening of minimum construction standards, citing, for example, "unfavorable economic conditions and lack of resources," changes may favor the building and development lobbies.

Even in places where a statewide code is in effect, the administration and enforcement of the building code generally rests with the local government. The local government is responsible for creating the organizational structure for the code enforcement process, designating those responsible for enforcement, and for providing the necessary resources for code administration.[8]

Enforcement of the building code typically occurs at several stages of the construction process. First, municipal or county employees must review all plans and proposals submitted by landowners, builders, and developers who propose to build any type of structure in the local jurisdiction. The plans must be consistent with the current building code to receive a building permit. If the plans do not meet code as proposed, the local plan review office may require that modifications, additions, or corrections be made, or the office may reject the proposal. If the plans meet code standards, a permit is issued and the building process can begin. During construction, the local government has a second opportunity to enforce the building code by carrying out on-site inspections of the building as it is being constructed. Any deviation from the plans or other activity that is not consistent with either the permit as issued or the code itself is grounds for a halt-work order from the local building inspector. Corrections must be made before construction is allowed to resume. At the end of the building process, the local building inspector must review the finished product, and only if all conditions have been met will a certificate of occupancy be issued.

It is clear from this discussion of building code enforcement that a heavy burden is placed on the local government to ensure that the code is being followed and that all construction taking place in the jurisdiction will meet code standards at every stage in the process. Plan review and site inspections are time-consuming and complex. Knowledgeable, well-trained building officials and inspectors are critical, and adequate resources are essential for local enforcement agents to carry out their duties. In addition, inspectors must not be overburdened with so many daily inspections that they are not able to give each structure a thorough review. This is especially critical in the aftermath of a disaster, when local building inspection offices are inundated with permit requests from homeowners and businesses who wish to restore damaged structures quickly.

LOUISIANA ADOPTS THE INTERNATIONAL BUILDING CODE TO BUILD BACK BETTER AND STRONGER AFTER HURRICANES KATRINA AND RITA

Louisiana Governor Kathleen Blanco signed a bill in December 2005 calling for the state to adopt the International Building Code (IBC), the International Residential Code (IRC), and other model codes developed by the International Code Council (ICC). The bill applied to structures that had to be rebuilt in the wake of Hurricanes Katrina and Rita and to all buildings constructed statewide starting in 2007. Under the legislation, the 11 parishes hit hardest by the hurricanes were required to put the new code into effect in 30 days, if those parishes already had inspectors, or 90 days if they had to hire inspectors. The bill also established a 19-member council to oversee enforcement of the codes by local governments.

7.8.4 State Support for Local Code Enforcement

Because the quality of enforcement depends so heavily on the caliber of the local building code officials, some states require testing and licensing of all building officials. Many of these states also provide training and qualification certification for local building inspectors. Of these, however, only a few states require that licensed inspectors receive continuing education to keep their expertise up-to-date with building code changes. Some states also require that general contractors for projects over a certain dollar value be licensed by a state board or commission. Other state licenses that may be required include electrical, mechanical, and plumbing contracting.

South Florida has long had a reputation of having a strong coastal building code. But when Hurricane Andrew blew into the state in 1992, the storm and its aftermath highlighted some serious flaws in then-current assumptions about building codes and construction standards.[9] Problems that were discovered in the South Florida building code following Hurricane Andrew included unlicensed contractors, understaffed inspection offices, ineffective building inspection processes, poorly trained building inspectors, inadequate design wind standards, inadequate standards for manufacturing and mobile homes, and egregious failure of building professionals to assume responsibility for safe construction. Ironically, many older structures fared better than newer buildings in the winds of Andrew.

SELF-CHECK

- Define **building code** and **freeboard**.
- List the natural hazards that can be addressed through building codes.
- Name two model building codes used in the United States.
- Cite which level of government is responsible for enforcing building codes.

7.9 STATE REGULATION OF HAZARD INSURANCE

In addition to managing environmentally sensitive areas and adopting building codes to set construction standards, states also play a critical role in regulating the availability and pricing of insurance products. Insurance is often categorized as a hazard mitigation tool because it can reduce the economic impact of a disaster by distributing the cost of the loss over multiple rate payers. Insurance companies can also promote hazard mitigation by enticing property owners to implement structural hazard mitigation measures in return for a reduction in premiums. The reduction reflects the additional protection provided to the property, for example, when the owner installs roofing shingles that are less prone to ignite during wildfires or elevates a building in a floodplain above the expected flood height. These added features can lessen the damage and, therefore, reduce the payout of insurance claims after a disaster, a win-win for both the property owner and the insurance company.

Although most forms of insurance are structured as voluntary, contractual private agreements, many states intervene and regulate the insurance industry. In the vast majority of states nationwide, state insurance laws require that premiums are not excessive, inadequate, or unfairly discriminatory. States monitor private insurance rates to ensure that they are adequately high to keep the company solvent, but not so excessive that the company earns exorbitant profits at the expense of customers. State regulation also ensures that coverage is not discriminatory among costumers—rates should ideally reflect differences in expected claims and expenses.

7.9.1 Insuring Catastrophic Losses

Insurance is generally available for some but not all natural disasters, varying from state to state and among carriers. Insurance coverage is nearly universally available for winter storms, volcanoes, tornadoes, lightning, and hail. These perils are covered under most standard property insurance contracts. Generally speaking, these events are sufficiently random and widespread to permit the private insurance mechanism to operate effectively.

However, the insurance industry encounters serious problems in providing insurance for properties located in areas subject to catastrophic losses, including hurricanes and earthquakes, when hundreds or even thousands of buildings can be damaged or destroyed in a single hazard event. Due to increasingly catastrophic wildfires along the West Coast, some private insurers have attempted to also drop wildfire coverage from standard property insurance policies in recent years. The problems fundamentally arise from the fact that many insurers do not have the resources to pay for a worst case event in those high-risk areas.[8]

This risk may also be compounded by climate change, since future losses may not mimic the range of past events. For this reason, flood damage from hurricanes is typically not included in most property insurance policies and must be purchased separately by homeowners under the NFIP in communities that participate in the program.[8]

The challenge of insuring property exposed to catastrophic natural disasters was exemplified by Hurricane Andrew in 1992. The massive amount of property damage resulting from the hurricane precipitated a major insurance crisis in South Florida, when more than $15 billion in insurance claims were paid. After Andrew, numerous small insurance companies went out of business, and many others stopped writing policies for South Florida. About 16,000 residents were left without homeowner's insurance following Andrew. Prior to Hurricane Andrew, estimates of the maximum insured loss from a hurricane in southern Florida were $10 billion, far below the actual cost of Andrew. Following the storm, these estimates increased to $50 billion, demonstrating the difficulty in predicting the scale of losses that insurance companies may be liable for when a large hurricane strikes an urban area.[10]

Insurers confronted by catastrophic loss situations have tried to deal with them in numerous ways, such as diversifying their portfolio of insured property to avoid overconcentration in a given state or region, purchasing reinsurance to spread out the risk more broadly and charging higher premiums in high-risk areas to cover catastrophic losses. Some companies have concluded that the resulting risk of insolvency is unacceptable and have attempted to withdraw entirely from those states. Others have stopped offering any new policies there until their risk exposure can be reduced.[8]

7.9.2 State Insurance Regulation

As state insurance regulators attempt to prevent premiums from being excessive, inadequate, or unfairly discriminatory, they are faced with the challenge of assuring an adequate supply of affordable insurance coverage at a time when many insurers are seeking to decrease their disaster exposure and increase their prices for the catastrophic component of that risk.

In theory, the job of state regulators is to protect the public from fraud and imprudent practices that threaten insurance companies' solvency and to ensure fair market practices. However, public policy is not forged in a political vacuum, and regulation increasingly has been influenced by voters' perceptions and preferences on how the cost of risk should be shared among different groups. In the process, insurers have largely lost the freedom to charge premiums based strictly on a structure's loss potential.[9]

States have created a variety of political mechanisms to regulate insurance. The primary mechanism is a state-mandated insurance pool, which offers subsidized coverage to high-risk properties, relying on additional fees imposed on all insurance contracts in the state to cover the losses of a major disaster.[10] Since 1968, various forms of wind, beach, and/or coastal insurance pools have been established in every Atlantic Coast state south of Virginia and in every Gulf Coast state. California also maintains an insurance pool for earthquakes. Since the insurance pools typically do not charge a premium high enough to cover the catastrophic loss potential of the properties involved, they subsidize people living in high-hazard areas and impose the excess cost on people residing elsewhere. Moreover, these state pools do not eliminate the problem of catastrophic losses. Private insurers in those states remain liable, on a market share basis, for the net losses generated by the state pools. Thus, any increase in voluntary business carries with it an increase in the insurer's share of the adverse results of the pool. This creates a disincentive for existing insurers to remain in those states or for new companies to establish operations there.[8]

Another regulatory tool that states employ is a guaranty fund. Rather than subsidizing individual high-risk properties, a guaranty fund is designed to pay claims on the policies of insolvent insurance companies. Through this mechanism, states raise revenue that can be used to help private insurance companies with benefit payments in the event of a catastrophic disaster. Guaranty funds have been criticized because of the possibility that they may reduce the incentive for consumers to choose insurance companies that are financially sound.[10]

There are several arguments used to justify state programs that subsidize insurance coverage to high-risk areas. One argument centers on equity: some low-income homeowners reside in high-hazard areas, and the government has an obligation to support these homeowners afford insurance. Another argument is economic in nature: certain development in high-risk areas such as coastal beaches provides economic benefits that may outweigh and justify insurance subsidies.[11]

Despite these arguments in favor of state subsidies or supports for the insurance market, there are also significant risks that these programs may ultimately lead to greater disaster losses. The design of state insurance programs requires that we ask who should pay for catastrophe risks, and how these programs are likely to alter the costs of developments and, ultimately, the exposure to natural hazards.

SELF-CHECK

- Name some natural hazards for which insurance is generally available.
- Discuss why hurricane and earthquake risks are more difficult to insure.
- Explain one benefit and one drawback of state insurance pools.

7.10 INCREASING STATE MITIGATION CAPABILITIES

Most states are steadfastly increasing their capability for hazard mitigation and have progressed far beyond the days when the concept of mitigation was foreign to many state agencies. These states continue to implement programs, carry out policies, and formulate new strategies to increase resiliency. Outreach and education programs carried out at the state level have further educated the public about the threats of flooding, wildfires, hurricanes, earthquakes, coastal erosion, and other hazards, although residents often remain unaware of the specific risks their community or neighborhood faces.

7.10.1 Developing Partnerships with Multiple Stakeholders

Despite multiple instances of successful collaboration to mitigate hazards, many states need to broaden their base of support for hazard mitigation planning and policy implementation. States should be sure that all relevant stakeholders are represented and contribute to the state's mitigation planning process. Although most state mitigation plans are developed by the state emergency management agency or its equivalent, many other state departments should have a place at the table during the planning process. For example, state departments of instruction (to ensure safe school construction and placement), the department of tourism (to address policies that protect visitors), departments of insurance (where building code policy is often established), state infrastructure and transportation departments (to deal with issues of development in hazardous locations), and many other state departments and agencies can and should contribute to the overall resilience of the state.

The need to broaden participation in state mitigation policy formation spills over into the private sector and nonprofit communities as well. Several states are improving their efforts to engage in mutually beneficial partnerships with a wider range of stakeholders. Major employers, universities, corporations, and businesses all have a stake in enhancing resilience and can bring a new approach to hazard mitigation and climate change adaptation. Nonprofit conservation organizations such as state-level nature conservancies, land trusts, and the Sierra Club may readily support mitigation efforts that coincide with their goals of natural resource protection. Habitat for Humanity and other housing advocacy groups can contribute to state efforts to provide housing that is both affordable and located out of dangerous areas such as floodplains. Charitable groups such as faith-based organizations, the Salvation Army, as well as the American Red Cross and its state-level chapters can also play a larger role in implementing hazard mitigation policy, especially during the critical post-disaster period when they are directly engaged in disaster management.

7.10.2 Expanding Hazard Mitigation Coverage

Some states take a single-hazard approach to their mitigation planning and tend to focus on the hazard with the greatest public attention, while other states are placing greater emphasis on an all-hazards approach. Hazard identification and risk assessments in many states are now incorporating some of the less visible or pronounced hazards that may exist in their state, such as infectious disease, contamination of groundwater, insect infestation, and bio-terrorism, to name a few. The COVID-19 pandemic underlined the need for state emergency management apparatuses to prepare for a wider range of hazard and threats, including those that are less frequent but have the potential for debilitating consequences.

The disaster assistance that has been provided to the states from the federal government has contributed significantly to their ability to respond to, prepare for, and recover from multiple disasters. But more importantly, many states are learning from their experiences and putting that knowledge to good use. Each disaster brings more knowledge about how to restore power quickly to utility customers, remove people and structures from hazardous areas, revive impacted businesses, gather perishable data quickly and efficiently, coordinate interagency efforts, engage the private and nonprofit sectors, and, more importantly, how to help people put their lives back together. Despite these lessons learned, many states must capitalize more fully on that fleeting window of opportunity that occurs following a disaster. During the next hazard event, the states need to mobilize their mitigation forces faster and wider than ever before, implementing the many strategies and actions that have been put in place to further reduce vulnerability to future hazard events.

SELF-CHECK

- Discuss the role of interagency coordination
- Explain the responsibilities of the private sector and nonprofit communities in increasing participation in mitigation efforts.

SUMMARY

How states approach disaster prevention varies greatly, depending on past hazard experience, resources that are available, and political commitment to reducing vulnerability. This chapter explored the authority and responsibility of state emergency management agencies and the role of mitigation planning at the state level. We also looked at the influence of state mandates on local government land use planning for addressing hazard issues at the community level. The chapter also discussed how some states directly intervene in land use decision-making, particularly in environmentally sensitive areas. The chapter examined state building codes and state insurance laws, with an eye to understanding how different states approach regulation of construction in hazard areas and insuring against hazard losses. The chapter concluded by outline some opportunities for states to augment their capability to mitigate the impacts of hazards and increase the resilience of their communities.

KEY TERMS

Areas of Environmental Concern: Land designated for added state protection; defined by geographic boundaries, habitats, or natural resources.

Building code: A collection of laws, regulations, ordinances, or other statutory requirements adopted by a government that controls the physical structure of buildings.

Freeboard: Elevating a building's lowest floor above predicted flood elevations, generally by an additional height of 1–3 feet above the minimum height requirement set by the National Flood Insurance Program.

Setback: Regulation that prohibits or limits the erection of structures within a specified distance from the **ocean or other hazard area**.

Wetland mitigation: The off-site preservation of another wetland located away from a development activity, or the creation of a new wetland to take the place of one that is impaired or destroyed.

ASSESS YOUR UNDERSTANDING

Summary Questions

1. States follow federal regulations for land use planning and mitigation. True or False?
2. Local governments are not authorized to regulate land use and development. True or False?
3. What influence does a state have on local land use planning?
    a. No influence
    b. Total control
    c. Varying influence
    d. Advisory capacity only
4. Each state maintains a regional FEMA office. True or False?
5. Funding for state emergency management offices is the sole responsibility of the states. True or False?
6. The Pre-Disaster Mitigation Program is one of the federally funded programs available to states to develop and implement mitigation efforts. True or False?
7. Hazard mitigation planning assesses vulnerability to hazards. True or False?
8. Section 322 of the Disaster Mitigation Act of 2000 requires that
    a. State, local, and tribal governments submit a mitigation plan for natural hazards
    b. States submit proof of Clean Water Act compliance
    c. Local governments apply for federal funding
    d. Local and state governments comply with federal building codes
9. A building code sets minimum acceptable standards of construction. True or False?
10. Which of the following is responsible for the enforcement of building codes?
    a. Local government
    b. Regional agencies
    c. State management offices
    d. Federal officials
11. The federal government provides support to local code enforcement by requiring licenses for all building officials. True or False?
12. Homeowners insurance does not typically cover which of the following natural hazards?
    a. Tsunami
    b. Earthquake
    c. Flood
    d. Tornado
13. A state-mandated insurance pool eliminates the problem of catastrophic losses from natural hazards. True or False?
14. The practice of direct state regulation occurs most frequently in
    a. Areas of repeat insurance claims
    b. Environmentally sensitive areas
    c. Earthquake zones
    d. Urban areas
15. A setback is used to harden the coastline to prevent erosion. True or False?
16. Which of the following are not used to establish setback distances for coastal construction?
    a. The roadbed located closest to the body of water
    b. First line of natural vegetation
    c. Local erosion rate
    d. Mean high water mark

17. Owners of storm-damaged properties are not guaranteed the right to rebuild. True or False?
18. Areas of Particular Concern are determined by:
    a. Local government
    b. Regional agencies
    c. State government
    d. Federal agencies

Review Questions

1. Though states are responsible for some degree of regulation, local governments have the highest degree of control over land uses. Explain how.
2. Land use plans have been touted as a valuable mitigation tool. Explain why.
3. Give examples of states that have taken the initiative to establish responsible planning mandates that address the issue of development in hazard areas.
4. State governments serve as a key link between federal agencies and local communities. Describe the flow of interaction between the three levels.
5. Describe the role of a State Hazard Mitigation Officer and list some SHMO responsibilities.
6. Much of the funding for state emergency management offices comes from FEMA; list the types of grant programs that provide support to states.
7. Describe the role of hazard mitigation planning, an important aspect of a successful mitigation program.
8. The Disaster Mitigation Act of 2000 is an important element of state planning. Explain the goal of the DMA.
9. State hazard mitigation plans are serious business for the federal government. Describe the consequences of not preparing a plan.
10. A building code is used by a government to control the physical nature of buildings. List four components of a building code.
11. Give examples of natural hazards that can be addressed through building codes.
12. Explain how strict building codes can be cost-effective in the long run.
13. The insurance industry faces great challenges in regard to areas subject to catastrophic losses. How are insurers coping?
14. What is the purpose of a state-mandated insurance pool?
15. Coastal areas are particularly vulnerable to the impacts of natural hazards. List three ways which states can regulate the coast.
16. Setbacks are a critical tool for protecting vulnerable coastal areas from development. Describe how setback lines are determined.
17. Many states provide some degree of protection for wetlands. Define wetland mitigation.

Applying This Chapter

1. As a developer looking to build a small housing development of homes in a former agricultural area, you are faced with the prospect of upgrading the infrastructure to accommodate the new homes. All that currently exists on the property is a narrow country road, well water, and public electric lines. Outline the infrastructure projects that would be required to go further with the plan.
2. What types of local land use planning would be required for a previously underdeveloped tract of lakeside property in Wisconsin? What support would be available from the state and federal government?

3. As a public information officer in a small Texas town that experienced a minor wildfire last year, outline various emergency management systems that support your community. Name the State Hazard Mitigation Officer and determine the location of his/her office.

4. The first step in risk assessment is to identify hazards; the second is to profile hazard events. Using these two steps, compare the risk assessment of New Orleans to San Francisco.

5. As an insurer in tornado-torn Indiana, a recent dramatic increase in insurance claims has forced you to raise premiums. Draft a letter to your clients justifying your reasons.

6. Consider the different types of land areas in your state. Which would be classified as Areas of Particular Concern, and what protection should they be given?

7. If you were a state official in Colorado, how would you apply in all-hazards approach to your mitigation planning?

You Try It

Plan for the Worst

List the types of natural hazards that might occur in your state. Predict the worst case scenario. What state-level mitigation efforts would be appropriate to protect communities statewide?

Disasters in Your State

Using the "Billion Dollar Weather/Climate Disasters" website (http://www.ncdc.noaa.gov/billions) from the National Ocean and Atmospheric Administration, has your state experienced any disasters in recent history that have exceeded $1 billion in damages? If so, what efforts has the state taken to reduce the impacts of similar events in the future?

Road Rules

Using information from your state's office of emergency management website, assess the types of hazards, both natural and human-made that your state informs its residents about. Were you aware of all the threats? Using the site or other government resources, can you determine your evacuation route in the event of a natural hazard or disaster?

REFERENCES

1. Codiga, D. and K. Wager. 2011. *Sea-Level Rise and Coastal Land Use in Hawai'i: A Policy Tool Kit for State and Local Governments.* Honolulu, HI: Center for Island Climate Adaptation and Policy, University of Hawai'i Sea Grant College Program. Available at http://seagrant.soest.hawaii.edu/publications.

2. Georgetown Climate Center. *Climate Adaptation Progress Tracker.* Georgetown Climate Center. https://www.georgetownclimate.org/adaptation/plans.html (accessed 10.21.20).

3. Burby, R.J. and L.C. Dalton. 1994. Plans can matter! The role of land use plans and state planning mandates in limiting development of hazardous areas. *Public Administration Review* 54(3): 229–238.

4. *North Carolina Administrative Code.* Title 15A, Part 7H, Section 0306.

5. Christie, D.R. and R.G. Hildreth. 1999. *Coastal and Ocean Management Law.* 2nd ed. St. Paul, NM: West Group.

6. *Code of Federal Regulations.* Title 44, Part 59.1.

7. Beatley, T., D.J. Brower, and A.K. Schwab. 2000. *An Introduction to Coastal Zone Management*. Washington, DC: Island Press.

8. Mileti, D.S. 1999. *Disasters by Design: A Reassessment of Natural Hazards in the United States*. Washington, DC: Joseph Henry Press.

9. Godschalk, D.R., T. Beatley, P. Berke, D.J. Brower, and E.J. Kaiser. 1999. *Natural Hazard Mitigation: Recasting Disaster Policy and Planning*. Washington, DC: Island Press.

10. Sutter, D. 2007. *Ensuring Disaster: State Insurance Regulation, Coastal Development, and Hurricanes*. Mercatus Center, George Mason University.

11. Kousky, C. 2010. *Managing the Risks of Natural Catastrophes: The Role and Functioning of State Insurance Programs*. Resources for the Future. DP: 10-30.

8

Local Government Powers
Building Resilience from the Ground Up

What You'll Learn

- The duty of local governments to protect public health and safety
- Powers and limitations of local governments
- Types of local governments in the United States
- Hazard mitigation tools that lie within local government authority
- How the characteristics of growth can influence local vulnerability to hazards
- What local governments can do to adapt to climate change

Goals and Outcomes

- Recognize the land use policies and tools of local governments that can be used to increase community resilience
- Identify the most effective way to promote hazard mitigation and climate change adaptation policies within the structure of a local government
- Evaluate the degree to which principles of resiliency and sustainability are implemented in a community

INTRODUCTION

This chapter offers a broad understanding of the types of powers that local governments can wield to manage hazards and threats within their jurisdiction. The chapter opens with a discussion of why local government is often the most appropriate level to deal with the impacts of hazards and climate change. We then introduce the topic of local policy with a discussion of the sources of local government authority, including a description of the powers that some states have delegated to their local governments. These powers include acquisition, taxation, spending, education, and planning. The chapter then describes some of the basic forms of local government that are prevalent in the United States to provide an idea of the organizational structure where local hazard mitigation and climate change adaptation policies are developed and carried out. Within the boundaries set by state and federal constitutions and legislation, the authority to manage hazards and adapt to climate change is often limited only by the creativity and willingness of the local decision-makers to be proactive. The chapter concludes with a discussion about the political willpower required to create a resilient community.

 DOI: 10.4324/9781003123897-8

8.1 WHY FOCUS ON LOCAL GOVERNMENT?

When we think of large-scale disasters, we might have images of a massive government response taking place that includes officials from the Federal Emergency Management Agency in their blue windbreakers, reservists in fatigues, and Red Cross volunteers in their red vests hauling ice, setting up emergency shelters, and conducting search and rescue operations. We may picture active state agencies, too—for example, we may envision the Governor ordering an evacuation, calling up the National Guard, and requesting a disaster declaration from the President. But the reality is that the local community takes on the lion's share of all of these activities, and state and federal governments only step in alongside local governments when communities become overwhelmed by natural disasters, acts of terrorism, or other emergencies that are of a magnitude that exceeds the capacity of the local government to cope. After all, it is at the local level that disasters are felt most directly and acutely—it is where streets are blocked by flooding, buildings are damaged by earthquake, and homes are destroyed by wildfire. And it is primarily at the local level where responsibility to take action to prepare and mitigate the impacts of disasters lies.

Local governments are also at the heart of adapting to climate change. When we think about the causes and consequences of climate change, it can seem like a vast global issue, one that is so daunting that people give up in despair thinking there is nothing to be done. We may want to rely solely on international organizations such as the Intergovernmental Panel on Climate Change, or national agencies such as the Environmental Protection Agency (EPA) to explain and prepare for climate change. Yet the phrase "Think Globally—Act Locally" is more than a cliché. All levels of government, the private sector, and ordinary citizens can take action to reduce the degree of climate change and its effects of communities. In fact, local governments are particularly well positioned to promote adaptation and reduce risk through land use planning, infrastructure improvements, building codes, floodplain management, energy conservation and more. Local governments have the authority and a variety of tools to address many of these issues and are in the best position to take meaningful action.

8.1.1 Characteristics of a Resilient Community

Communities can be impacted by any number of calamities. The shutdown of a mill or factory can result in massive unemployment. The contamination of a river or lake can make water supplies undrinkable. Unchecked growth can bring about urban sprawl, leading to air pollution, traffic congestion, and inefficient use of land and public resources. A lack of equal access to quality education, affordable housing, health care, and job opportunities can lead to crippling poverty and foster social unrest. Sustainable communities are those that face these issues head on and take proactive measures to combat the economic, environmental, and social problems that come their way.

In its most widely used definition, **sustainable development** is development that "meets the needs of the present without compromising the ability of future generations to meet their own needs."[1] Sustainable development implies that those who are living on the Earth now will not lessen the opportunities of future generations but will strive to pass on a natural, economic, and social environment that ensures a high quality of life for all to come. Sustainability envisions a wise use of resources and a fair chance for all community members to live meaningful, productive lives both now and in the future. Sustainability also calls for seeing beyond our own borders and realizing that we are all interconnected in a complex system of natural processes.

But sustainability policies are largely futile if a community is exposed to natural and human-made hazards and does nothing to reduce vulnerability. Earthquakes, hurricanes, ice storms, tornadoes, floods, wildfires, technological disasters, and other types of hazard events can be economically devastating, ecologically damaging, and socially disruptive. The occurrence of a natural or human-made hazard highlights existing vulnerabilities and can exacerbate the problems a community was experiencing before the disaster hit. With the approach of a changing climate, these preexisting conditions become even more apparent. As we experience increased storm intensity, higher temperatures, more frequent droughts, sea level rise, and other climate-related changes, local communities will feel the brunt first— from issues of public health to heightened demands placed on local facilities and services. A truly sustainable community must also be a **hazard-resilient** community, one that considers disaster prevention and climate adaptation along with issues of environmental stewardship, quality of life, economic vitality, and a fair legacy for future generations, with a sensibility of the changes yet to come. Local communities are in a unique position to promote resiliency as they strive to become more sustainable.

8.1.2 A Duty to Act

There are many ways to increase resilience that are available to local communities both large and small, ways that fall well within the power of local governments to pursue. Local policy to cultivate resilience indicates a community's commitment to reducing damage from high-risk hazards and provides the authority and guidance for mapping, regulation, planning, spending, and other local hazard mitigation and preparedness activities. These tools are increasingly being used by proactive local governments to adapt to specific impacts of climate change that are anticipated or are already being felt by people in communities nationwide.

Disaster prevention is more than a soapbox issue for politicians and community leaders— it is also an affirmative duty of local governments to protect the health and safety of community residents. Development decisions that do not take into account known risk factors such as flooding, earthquakes, sinkholes, high winds, storm surge, erosion, chemical spills, toxic wastes, and other natural or human-made hazards could place people and property in danger. In light of climate change, this means taking steps to protect citizens from the risk of more intense hurricanes, the risk of higher temperatures, the loss of property from sea level rise, and much more. It is in the best interests of the community at large to ensure that residents and property owners are fully aware of the inherent risks of building in hazard locations and for the authority of the local government to be directed toward mitigating those risks.

Not only are local governments under a duty to protect the health and welfare of their residents, actions to reduce risk may also be spurred by the prospect of legal liability. When individuals experience damage from flooding or erosion, for example, they might file a lawsuit against the government claiming that the government has caused the damage, contributed to it, or failed to prevent or provide adequate warnings of the hazard. Such lawsuits are expensive for the public sector not only because court-ordered damage awards are growing, but also because of large attorney and expert witness fees.[2]

8.2 LOCAL AUTHORITY: EXERCISING THE POLICE POWER

We have touched on the fact that local governments have the authority, and even the duty, to protect their citizens from risk of harm. But where does this power come from? Under the Tenth Amendment to the U.S. Constitution, every state government has authority to protect public health and safety through what is known as the state's **police power**. The states, in turn, delegate some of these powers to local governments. According to a principle known as **Dillon's Rule**, local governments cannot act without the proper delegation of authority.

The derivative authority granted to local governments under Dillon's Rule varies from state to state; however, most local governments are given a fair amount of autonomy to enforce their police power, particularly with regard to public safety functions such as emergency management. Typically, localities are authorized (and in some states are required) to adopt basic land use management measures, for example, comprehensive plans and zoning ordinances, some of which may be used to address hazards and adapt to climate change.

Home Rule: In **Home Rule states**, general police power is delegated by the state legislature to local governments to enact laws and to adopt and enforce regulations that are necessary for it to govern. In these states, the local governments have predominant power over local matters within their jurisdiction. In states that do not follow the Home Rule principle, local governments are only allowed to exercise powers that have been expressly granted to them in the state constitution or by other state laws. However, even in non-Home Rule states, the authority to regulate for disaster prevention and climate change adaptation is quite broad.

Extraterritorial Jurisdiction: The authority granted to local governments to regulate behavior and land use is limited to the area within the boundaries of that local government. However, most states establish **extraterritorial jurisdiction** as a way to give municipalities control over development just outside the town or city limits and over areas that eventually could be annexed. The extraterritorial jurisdiction typically extends 1 mile beyond city limits. In some states, with approval of the county governing board, a city may extend its extraterritorial land use planning jurisdiction to 3 miles. Extraterritorial jurisdiction can be an effective way for municipalities to broaden the geographic reach of their control over land uses in ways that help reduce hazard vulnerability. This is particularly effective to mitigate hazard risks that are widely distributed and cross-political boundaries, such as flooding.

8.2.1 Limits on the Police Power

While local governments generally have broad authority to regulate development within their jurisdiction, including regulation that controls development in hazard areas, there are defined limits on how far the police power can go in restricting the actions of private citizens. There is always a balancing act between protecting the general public from hazard risks and restricting the rights of private property owners to use their land as they wish. Of course, no private property owner is allowed unfettered use of their land. For example, under the ancient legal doctrine of "nuisance," courts generally maintain that people can use their own property so long as it does not injure another's property. In particular, this has been extended to mean that no landowner (public or private) has the right to use their land in a way that substantially increases flood or erosion damages on their neighbor's property.

In addition to abiding under the law of nuisance, private property owners are also subject to zoning, building codes, taxation, environmental laws, and a whole host of regulations and restrictions. But both federal and state constitutions assert that land use controls such as zoning cannot be exercised *arbitrarily* or *capriciously*, that restrictions on use cannot be *unreasonable*, and all regulations must be applied *uniformly* upon all landowners in similar circumstances. These and other rules are found in **Equal Protection** and **Due Process** clauses of state and federal constitutions. Additionally, the government cannot restrict the use of private property to such a degree that the property is effectively "confiscated," as we will discuss in more detail below.

Regulatory Takings

We have noted that state and federal constitutions place limits on the power of local governments to restrict the use of private property. In addition to the rules of equal protection and due process, if a court determines that a government has gone *too far* in regulating private property, then the government must pay the owner **just compensation**, which is usually determined as the fair market value of the property. This principle is found in the **Takings Clause** of the Fifth Amendment of the U.S. Constitution and applies to all levels of government. States have parallel requirements in their own constitutions.

Before we go further, a little background about the takings rule may provide some helpful context. At the heart of the matter is the legal authority of **eminent domain**, one of the most potent government powers. Eminent domain, or *condemnation*, refers to the power of the government to "take" (condemn) private land for public purpose. Eminent domain is commonly used by local and state governments to obtain rights-of-way for highway construction and to acquire property to build public facilities such as schools and government facilities. These are instances where the public purpose is well accepted and recognized as within the authority of local governments.

Physical occupation of private property requires payment of just compensation under the Fifth Amendment Takings Clause. However, the takings rule also applies when the government "takes" an owner's land by severely restricting its use. Although it is the duty of the landowner to obey all applicable laws and regulations in the jurisdiction where the property is located, occasionally, those regulations may amount to a "taking."

The state courts and the U.S. Supreme Court have developed a range of legal tests to determine when a regulation reaches the point that it has gone too far. The following list summarizes some of the key components and limits related to takings:

- The physical occupation of private land by the government is almost always a taking.
- All land use regulations must serve a valid public purpose.
- There must be a rational connection between the regulation and the purpose.
- Even a temporary loss of use that does not have a valid purpose and a rational connection is a taking.
- A regulation that deprives the owner of all economically beneficial use of the property is a taking.

Many cases involve a balancing of factors, including the character of the government action, the economic impact of the action, and whether the regulation interferes with the owner's expectations.

8.3 CONFLICTING AND COMPLEMENTARY INTERESTS AT THE LOCAL LEVEL

Under their police power, local governments typically have authority to manage many features of growth and development within their jurisdiction and implement a wide range of mitigation, preparedness, and climate change adaptation programs. Later in this chapter we will provide some examples of the types of actions local governments can take to increase resilience. However, authority to act does not necessarily ease the decision-making process. Regulation of private property can be contentious, and a full range of conflicting issues may arise when local authorities attempt to restrict land use or implement risk reduction measures, many of which may take years to become fully effective. Local politicians are often pressured to meet the immediate needs of their constituents, and the short election cycle of most local governments may make some elected officials hesitant to put forth risk reduction strategies that could be construed as a limit to growth, costly to taxpayers, or reducing the value of an individual's land. Yet, when viewed in the context of the overall wellbeing, safety, stability, and sustainability of the community, some of these competing interests may actually be complementary, rather than at odds.

8.3.1 Economic Pressures on Local Governments

On the one hand, local governments must govern land use for the public good. We have already discussed the fact that protecting public health and safety is a paramount duty of local government. Regulations targeted toward reducing damage to property and protecting residents are essential to carry out this duty. On the other hand, local governments are also responsible for providing a full range of services to their citizens, including education, police and fire protection, water and sewer facilities, health care and social services, public transit, parks and recreation, libraries, recycling and refuse disposal, and other critical needs of the community. State and federal governments provide some funding for these services, but much of the financial burden falls on the local government, and the pressure to provide quality services is an ongoing struggle for many communities; this pressure can be especially acute during a regional or national economic downturn.

Property taxes represent a significant source of revenue for local governments. In general, developed property is more valuable, and therefore, more lucrative in terms of local taxes, as it can be taxed at a higher rate. In many communities, there is a strong incentive to allow growth and development to occur to increase the local tax base, giving governments more money to spend on programs and services. In their eagerness to attract new growth to the area, local jurisdictions may overlook the hazards that pose a risk to the built environment and may allow or even encourage development in vulnerable locations. Furthermore, many communities, particularly those located in highly desirable areas such as the coast, are already intensely developed, adding to the tensions and conflicting interests at the local level. Avoiding hazardous land uses is much more difficult when investments have been made and construction has already taken place.

Although these local concerns are significant factors in the creation of policies and regulations that concern land uses in high-hazard areas, many communities have come to realize that the interests of protecting public health and safety and promoting responsible development are not mutually exclusive. In fact, a safe, resilient community that is proactive and thoughtful about reducing risk and exposure to natural hazards can ultimately *attract* rather than repel future growth and development in safe locations, where it can contribute to the long-term economic health of the area. We will read about some of the specific techniques that local governments can use to manage development in the next section of this chapter.

SELF-CHECK

- What is the police power and how is it passed on to local governments?
- What are some of the limits on a local government's authority to regulate?
- Discuss the conflicting goals that many local governments face when managing land use to reduce hazard vulnerability.

8.4 LOCAL GOVERNMENT POWERS TO MANAGE GROWTH AND DEVELOPMENT

Public controls on private property are not a recent innovation. Land use laws existed in various forms in England long before the United States existed and even extend back into the ancient Roman past. The earliest code of Roman law, the Twelve Tables (451–540 B.C.), required setbacks for structures from parcel boundaries and regulated the distances between trees and lot lines. From the time the concept of private ownership arose in our legal tradition, property has literally been subject to the "law of the land."

What the law of the land means for the average landowner has changed over time. Early on, judge-made law, such as the law of nuisance, was sufficient to handle land use conflicts. In its simplest form, under the nuisance law, a property owner who uses his or her property in such a way that it causes annoyance, inconvenience, or danger to the public or to another property owner can be ordered by a court of law to put an end to the "nuisance." But as our society became more complex and populous, and as increasing demands were placed on limited natural resources, there was a need for more extensive public land use controls. Today, these land use controls are adopted by state and local governments under the police power to manage the characteristics of growth.

8.4.1 Rates

In this section, we will examine some of the fundamental powers that local governments possess under their basic police power authority. These powers can be remembered using the acronym RATES: **R**egulation, **A**cquisition, **T**axation, **E**ducation, and **S**pending. We will also discuss *planning* as a very powerful tool that can help create a cohesive framework for all other local powers (see Table 8.1).

Table 8.1 Local Government Powers to Control Land Use and Development.

Regulation	Local governments have the power to control land use through regulations such as zoning, subdivision ordinances, and floodplain regulations. Regulation also includes building codes and standards to make structures more hazard resilient.
Acquisition	Local governments are authorized to acquire and hold property for public benefit and use. Removing at-risk property from the private market can be a useful mitigation tool.
Taxation, Fees, and Special Assessments	Taxes, impact fees, and special assessments can be an important source of revenue for governments to help pay for mitigation activities. In addition, the power of taxation can have a profound impact on the pattern of development in local communities. Special tax districts, for example, can be used to discourage intensive development in coastal hazard-prone areas.
Education	Public awareness and understanding of hazards that face the community are essential for effective hazard management activities. Education and information dissemination are important functions of local governments to protect the health and safety of the community.
Spending	Spending is a fundamental power of local government. Local governments can choose to pay for public facilities that are placed in nonhazardous areas and are built to withstand known hazard impacts. Local governments can also influence private development by withholding spending for public infrastructure and capital improvements in known hazard areas.
Planning	Local governments are authorized to make and carry out plans through the establishment of goals, policies, and procedures for a social or economic purpose. Planning provides a context for all other local government activities, ensuring that policies and actions are carried out according to a conscientious, organized, and rational process.

We will discuss each of these powers, as well as the planning function of local governments in the following sections of this chapter. Many of the activities discussed here are also found in Chapter 12 that describes hazard mitigation and climate change techniques in detail. The focus of this chapter, however, is on the authority of local governments to take action to protect the community.

8.4.2 Managing Growth in Hazard Areas

The powers available to local governments that fall under "RATES" can be used—separately or in tandem—to manage the characteristics of growth in a community. This management authority can be used by local governments to deter development in identified hazard areas and steer growth into desirable locations within the jurisdiction. Growth management tools can also be used to impose conditions or make changes in proposed development plans so that new construction is sited and built to standards that do not increase exposure to hazards.

Local land use management tools and techniques influence one or more of the following characteristics of growth:

- **Quantity:** The total amount of development, such as the number of buildings, facilities, and structures; the amount of acreage developed; and the percentage of total land area that is developed.
- **Quality:** Soundness of construction in terms of safety, energy efficiency, hazard resilience, aesthetics, etc.
- **Type:** The class of development. Major types include residential, commercial, government/religious/nonprofit, industrial, and open space. Subtypes can include single family/multifamily residential, light/heavy industrial, or strip/mall commercial.
- **Location:** The area within the local jurisdiction where development of various types is allowed.
- **Density:** Intensity of development in terms of distance between structures, lot size, building height, and number of people and structures per acre.
- **Timing and Rate:** When and how fast growth will be allowed. Control of the timing and rate of growth is critical to ensure adequate public facilities (e.g., water and sewer, public schools) and infrastructure (e.g., road capacity) are in place to meet new levels of demand.
- **Cost:** Expenses borne by the public as a result of development, for example:
  - *economic costs:* water, sewer, schools, emergency and local services, and infrastructure
  - *distribution costs:* issues of who will pay, property taxation and assessments, and efficiency of public services
  - *environmental costs:* water quality degradation, water resource depletion, increased stormwater flows, loss of open space, damage to habitats, clear cutting, changes in topography, waste management, landfill capacity, traffic congestion, air pollution, or noise pollution
  - *social costs:* stratification of incomes or class, deterioration of city centers, urban sprawl, overburdened services, or segregation by race or ethnicity

All of these characteristics of growth determine the level of vulnerability in a community. When undertaken thoughtfully, growth management can be used to control development in hazard-prone areas of the local jurisdiction. As a general rule, local governments have used growth management techniques more frequently to control factors, such as pollution, traffic congestion, aesthetics, and make sure that adequate public services are available to serve new development, rather than for hazard mitigation purposes directly.

However, communities throughout the country are coming to realize that many of the impacts of climate change can be lessened by sound land use practices that factor in *future* as well as current conditions, both in terms of population growth and changing levels of precipitation and flood patterns, increased drought, more severe heat waves, more frequent and intense hurricanes, and rising sea level. These factors should be part of all siting and design decisions for new development.

GUIDING GROWTH TO MEET NEW DEMANDS ON WATER SUPPLIES

Expansion into rural areas of Medina County, Ohio placed new demands on county water supplies. Some homebuilders initially wanted to develop large plots that would require filling in existing wetlands and natural floodplains. The building plans also required firefighting services to truck in large amounts of water in the event of an incident. A broad-based coalition that included the local government, county floodplain manager, planning commission, homebuilders association, and emergency manager came together to spearhead a process to promote development in the county while protecting water supplies and preserving wetlands and ponds. The partnership achieved a building standard that allowed builders to develop their desired housing design but also required them to build ponds and wetlands within each housing subdivision in an effort to sustain water supplies and allow for improved fire protection and floodplain management. The zoning and land use mitigation efforts promoted and protected the health, safety, and welfare of the residents by making the community less susceptible to flood and fire damage.[3]

8.4.3 Using the Power of Regulation

Regulatory powers granted by the state to local governments are the most basic way that a local government can control growth and development within its jurisdiction. Local governments regulate private property to protect the natural environment, encourage economic development, and protect the public's health and safety. Some of the most common types of regulatory powers available to local governments include:

- Zoning ordinances
- Subdivision regulations
- Building codes
- Flood damage prevention ordinances

Before zoning became widespread, the police power was used by local governments for relatively simple controls, such as fire safety, or for making sure incompatible uses did not encroach on neighboring property (such as prohibiting a brickyard in a residential neighborhood). Once zoning came into judicial favor, it allowed governments to protect certain uses in certain districts, or *zones*.

Exercise of the Police Power through Zoning

Zoning is the traditional and nearly ubiquitous tool used by local governments to control future uses of land within its jurisdiction. At its core, zoning continues the basic protections of **nuisance law**, the ancient legal doctrine still in effect that prohibits property owners from using their land in ways that interfere with the rights of adjoining property owners or inflict injury on the general public.

While nuisance law provides long-standing protection against general harms, it is retroactive in practice and cumbersome to enforce. Zoning, on the other hand, is a more direct and proactive method of governing land uses and allows the local government to impose more specific restrictions on property owners than were available under the law of nuisance. Furthermore, zoning's true beauty is that it enables the government to *predetermine* uses that will be permitted in particular locations, *before* development occurs.

Zoning regulates the permissible uses of property in a jurisdiction by dividing the community into different districts (or zones). **Zoning maps** identify the location of various districts. An accompanying **zoning ordinance** or **code** defines the type and intensity of uses that are allowed within each district. The code is enforced through the permitting process for new development. In some cases, landowners must apply for and receive a zoning permit from the local government before beginning construction of a new building. In other cases, only certain types of new developments require zoning approval. Zoning districts are labeled according to the dominant use that will be permitted in that zone. Some communities have more elaborate systems of zoning than others, but the most basic zoning districts include Residential, Commercial, Industrial, Government, Open Space/Conservation, and Religious/Nonprofit.

The local zoning ordinance specifies standards that must be met in each zone, such as lot size, building height, floor area or footprint, setbacks (minimum/maximum distance of structures from property lines as well as the amount of space between structures), required parking spaces, density of residents, and so forth. For hazard mitigation purposes, local zoning maps may be accompanied by regulations that restrict inappropriate uses in designated hazard areas or incentives to provide additional development rights if buildings are constructed to mitigate risk. This presupposes that the locality has mapped the locations of likely hazards (for example, flooding) and has incorporated this spatial information into the zoning process (Figure 8.1).

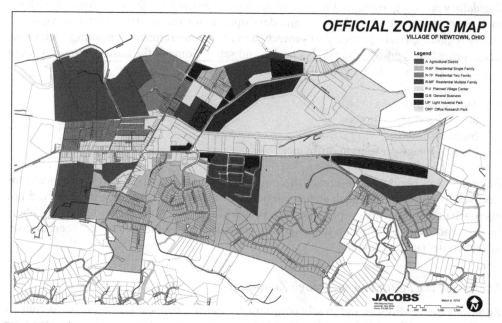

Figure 8.1 The zoning map of Newtown, Ohio is typical of many small towns and cities, designating areas for different uses and densities, such as agriculture, business, residential, and industrial.

Nonconforming Uses

Most zoning codes allow for prior uses to continue as nonconforming uses after changes in the code are made. As these buildings are replaced or destroyed, the former use becomes illegal. Over time, this process reduces the number of buildings that are out of conformance with a city's zoning code. Communities can also require that nonconforming structures be replaced within a certain time period under a process known as **amortization**. For example, a community may require a homeowner to relocate his or her beachfront home outside the beach erosion zone by a specified date. The length of time over which amortization takes place must approximate the expected depreciation of the building or it could be challenged as an unconstitutional taking.

Overlay Zones

Some local zoning ordinances include overlay zones, which apply conditions to development in addition to, or in place of, the standard zoning ordinance for a certain area. Overlay zones can be effective in high hazard areas. For example, floodplain overlay districts have been used to regulate development in mapped flood areas. Overlays have also been used in coastal high hazard areas such as beachfront, storm surge, and highly erodible areas.

Overlay zones can be triggered by a certain specific event, such as a hurricane that causes substantial damage. Until the event occurs, the overlay zone remains "transparent" and has no effect on the property located in the overlay zone. Recovery overlay zones can include temporary regulations that restrict reconstruction in an area impacted by a disaster until a thorough damage assessment has been made or require any new development in the zone to include hazard mitigation techniques.

Bonus and Incentive Zoning

Bonus and/or incentive zoning is the practice of allowing developers to exceed the limits of current regulations, such as building height, floor area, or density, in return for certain concessions. This technique is generally used in metropolitan areas, where land is scarcer, and the market benefit to the developer is more easily realized. When used as a hazard mitigation tool, communities offer bonuses to developers who avoid building in hazard-prone areas or who incorporate mitigation into their building designs, for example, elevating homes above the expected flood height, or using fire-retardant roofing materials. In return, the developer is allowed to build more intensely than is normally allowed on other portions of the property or elsewhere in nonhazardous areas within the community. Bonus and incentive zoning have been used to encourage developers to provide on-site mitigation facilities, such as dune walkovers and sand fencing to reduce beach erosion, and retention ponds to reduce flood risk.

Strengths of Using Zoning for Hazard Mitigation

There are notable strengths associated with zoning when used for mitigation purposes. Zoning can be used to keep inappropriate development out of hazard-prone areas by **down-zoning**, or decreasing density. Down-zoning can be accomplished by increasing minimum lot size or reducing the number of dwelling units permitted per acre. By reducing density, fewer people and buildings are located in high hazard areas. This, in turn, helps protect the local tax base, matches the population with the capacity of local emergency shelters, lowers the amount of time needed to evacuate the population before a hazard strikes, and can prevent large, hard-to-relocate structures from being built in high-hazard zones like beach erosion areas. Safer areas can be zoned for higher-intensity uses including small-lot residential structures, apartments, and commercial businesses.

While zoning can be used to keep intensive uses out of hazardous areas, it can also designate hazardous areas for more appropriate low-intensity uses including parks, open space, greenways, resource conservation, wildlife habitat, agriculture, or beach access that benefit the entire community and add to local aesthetic and environmental quality. Zoning can help preserve natural areas that mitigate against hazards such as wetlands, floodplains, and dunes. Zoning can also prohibit the storage or handling of hazardous chemicals or other dangerous materials in floodplains, seismic zones, and other hazard areas.

Weaknesses of Zoning for Hazard Mitigation and Climate Change Adaptation

There are also some limitations to using zoning for hazard mitigation and climate change adaptation purposes. Zoning primarily applies to new structures and vacant land rather than existing buildings and property that is already developed (except through nonconforming use provisions, which often take decades to become effective). As a result, zoning is a poor way to make current development more hazard resilient. Zoning is also a spatial control and primarily suited to hazards that are spatially defined or clearly mapped (e.g., flooding, but not tornadoes). Furthermore, zoning can be subject to legal and political challenges: downzoning that decreases density may also increase the cost of providing public services, including mass transit, water and sewer lines, waste collection, and fire protection, all of which tend to become more expensive and less efficient when spread out over large land areas. Less dense areas may also mean less tax revenues for the local government. Additionally, zoning regulations are subject to a fluctuating political climate; as new leaders assume local elected and appointed positions, decision-making can change to suit the current administrative agenda. Lastly, zoning is limited in its ability to adapt to climate change because most zoning maps are drawn based on the *current* understanding of hazard risks (if the maps incorporate hazard risk at all). For example, shoreline erosion areas shown on zoning maps often underestimate flood heights or storm surge levels that may occur in the future because of more intense rainfalls, more frequent coastal storms, and sea level rise.

These weaknesses of using zoning for hazard mitigation and climate change adaptation usually preclude a blanket prohibition of development in hazard areas; however, they do not preclude the careful and precise application of the zoning ordinance to meet specific hazard problems, now and in the future.

Subdivision Ordinances

Subdivision ordinances govern the partition of land for development or sale. In addition to controlling the configuration of parcels and lot layout, subdivision ordinances set standards for developer-built infrastructure, such as roads and storm drains. The local government must approve the subdivision plat (map) prior to the division and sale of the land into individual lots. It is at the point of subdivision review that many communities impose conditions on the developer in exchange for plat approval. Local governments often charge exactions and fees to help pay for the demands that new construction will place on local facilities and services, such as schools, water and sewer, fire and police protection, and garbage pickup. Developers may also be required to pay for impacts on the community and the environment, such as traffic congestion, air and water pollution, excess noise, stormwater runoff, and similar burdens that result from increased development in a community. Many local governments also require dedication of land to build needed public facilities as a condition of subdivision approval.

Subdivision regulations can be used for mitigation and climate change adaptation purposes in several ways and are most commonly applied to prohibit the subdivision of land subject to flooding, wildfire, or erosion. When hazard zones can be identified on a parcel map, communities may require minimum distances between those zones and the site of construction. For instance, coastal communities may require the configuration of deep lots on the oceanfront. These lots allow homes to be relocated further inland on the same parcel if erosion, sea level rise, or coastal storms threaten the structure.

Subdivision Buffers for Flood Hazards

If the subdivision layout does not keep entire lots out of the flood-prone area of a parcel, buffers can help minimize the amount of development exposed to flooding. A **buffer** is typically a setback of a specific distance, such as 25 or 100 feet, from a channel, floodway, wetland, or other water feature. In that area, no cutting of vegetation, clearing of ground cover, or alteration of natural features is allowed, but the rest of the lot can be graded and built on. In the state of Maryland, for example, a 25-foot buffer is required next to all wetlands and a 100-foot buffer is required for "wetlands of special state concern." Subdivision ordinances may also allow developers to cluster homes in greater densities away from hazard-prone sites and require dedication of unbuildable lots to green space or parkland for use by all the residents.

Subdivision regulations can also require that infrastructure meets standards that address known hazard risks. For example, the installation of adequate drainage and stormwater management facilities, as well as limits on impervious surfaces, can be required in flood-prone and landslide-prone areas. To reduce fire risk, subdivision ordinances may require wide building spacing, installation of firebreaks, drought-resistant or indigenous vegetation and landscaping, on-site water storage, multiple access points, and streets built wide enough to accommodate fire trucks and emergency vehicles.

Building Codes

Building codes are laws, ordinances, or regulations that set forth standards and requirements for structural integrity, design, and construction materials used in commercial and residential structures. In most states, the building code is established by the state legislature, but permits and enforcement are the responsibility of the local government (see Chapter 7 for discussion of state building codes). The issuance of a building permit is a *ministerial function* of the local government, so that if building plans meet code requirements, a building permit must be issued; there is no discretion allowed in this decision. If the plans do not meet code, however, the local government can reject the proposal or require revisions before granting approval. Local building inspectors conduct site reviews during the construction process to ensure that construction complies with the approved plans. Studies have found that regulations can be effective when supplemented with economic incentives. Local communities can help build public support for strict enforcement of building codes by initiating publicity campaigns with this objective in mind and alerting citizens about ways to strengthen structures beyond code requirements.

HURRICANE SANDY LEADS NEW YORK CITY TO STRENGTHEN BUILDING CODE

In response to damage wrought by Hurricane Sandy, Mayor Michael Bloomberg convened a Building Resiliency Task Force to study potential changes in the New York City building code to help reinforce existing structures and more effectively floodproof new projects. The resulting rules increase the required minimum floodproofing elevation so that substantially damaged buildings and other new construction must be built to withstand greater flood risk. The regulations are variable depending on the use—so buildings like hospitals, schools, or facilities with hazardous materials must be constructed at higher elevations than other structures like single-family homes. The measures are also intended to help New Yorkers limit the cost of future flood insurance premiums by better protecting properties in flood-prone areas from risk and damage. In addition to the changes in the building code, the Department of City Planning modified the Zoning Resolution to provide more flexibility in height limits so that buildings can more easily comply with the updated Building Code.

Post-Disaster Building Moratoria

Some communities have enacted moratoria to deal with the construction in the post-storm environment. A **moratorium** is a short-term suspension of the right to develop, usually accomplished by a refusal of the local government to issue a building permit. Moratoria are only effective if they are ready to be activated by a predetermined trigger, such as a hurricane, earthquake, or flood, and are an official part of the local regulatory code prior to the event. Moratoria give local officials more time to assess damage and set priorities for response, planning, and mitigation efforts. They are often used to prevent property owners from rebuilding damaged structures before a complete damage assessment can be made or an acquisition program can go into effect. Moratoria can also allow officials to expand high-hazard designated areas to reflect the actual damages from a hazard event.

Flood Damage Prevention Ordinance

Structures built in the floodplain are subject to damage from rising water. In addition to increasing the number of properties at risk, development in the floodplain reduces the flood storage capacity of these areas, resulting in greater flood heights. Local floodplain regulations can keep people from locating in the most dangerous areas and require safe building designs for other flood-prone areas.

Local flood damage prevention codes prohibit or establish conditions for development in high-risk areas. Conditions can include a variety of requirements, including setbacks, flood-proofing, and elevation. In some communities, these conditions are imposed in addition to or in place of other zoning, subdivision, building codes, or other local regulations.

Many local flood prevention ordinances are enacted according to minimum standards issued by the National Flood Insurance Program (NFIP), a program administered by the Federal Emergency Management Agency (FEMA) that provides the opportunity for residents in participating communities to purchase federally backed flood insurance. Development in the floodplain is regulated based on Flood Insurance Rate Maps (FIRMs) published by FEMA that show the boundaries of the 100-year flood zone (known as Special Flood Hazard Areas), as well as other types of flood areas in the jurisdiction.

There are several critical issues involved in local floodplain management. A significant problem in many communities involves inaccurate flood maps that do not reflect actual flood risks in the jurisdiction, often because new development has changed stormwater flows, which can increase flood levels dramatically. Gradual shifts in the likelihood and severity of hazards due to climate change, such as increased precipitation, earlier snowmelt, and sea level rise can also contribute to inaccurate flood maps.

Floodplain management programs can be foiled if development pressures in a community are strong, and there is insufficient leadership to honor mitigation goals. This is especially problematic in communities with a lack of suitable building sites located outside the flood-plain. Flood hazard risk reduction has often focused narrowly on the protection of structures in the floodplain rather than the preservation of the floodplain's natural functions. Restoration and conservation programs that protect wetlands and floodplains can help alleviate these limitations.

Since floodplains rarely fall within a single jurisdiction, floodplain management is often best addressed through multi-jurisdictional collaboration or regional governing bodies. A river basin-wide approach to flood management can be more effective than local regulatory programs enacted by individual communities. Collaborative agreements acknowledge that development in one community can affect neighboring communities both upstream and down. However, such multi-jurisdictional management agreements can be difficult to achieve, especially if left solely to local initiative.

8.4.4 Using the Power of Acquisition

The types of land use regulations discussed above allow a local government to control development within the jurisdiction without changing title or ownership patterns in the community. However, regulation of private property is not the only method available to local governments for controlling growth; the authority to acquire property through purchase or condemnation is a very important government power. Public land ownership and conscientious management of public lands provides direct control over the use of property. This control can be used to implement hazard mitigation and climate adaptation policies that keep development out of hazard areas.

Willing Sellers, Willing Buyers

At times, a local government must use its power of eminent domain to condemn property for certain community needs, such as schools and roads. Eminent domain is less frequently used, however, to acquire land for hazard mitigation purposes (and may never be used if federal funds are involved). More common is government purchase of land from a willing seller. Through an acquisition program, the local government offers to buy a home or business that the owner voluntarily agrees to sell. Often, when property owners have experienced multiple hazards over the years, such as repetitive flooding, they are more than willing to participate in a local **buyout program**. Acquisition programs for hazard mitigation are most successful when the program is fully explained to the property owner, the purchase price reflects market value, and an affordable housing alternative is available. After the sale, the local government assumes title to the property, demolishes any structures on it, and the former owner can use proceeds from the sale to move to another, safer location. Some acquisition programs include **relocation** rather than demolition, when the owner's house is moved to an alternative lot out of the hazard area.

Through a buyout program, the local government becomes the new owner of the formerly hazardous property. The local government must be able to maintain the property in perpetuity (forever) so that it will never again be used in a way that poses a risk to people or structures. For some impoverished communities or those located in rural areas, being responsible for maintaining the property can be burdensome. However, local governments can transfer title to other government agencies (the state or county, for example), or the local government can deed the property to a nonprofit agency, such as a conservation land trust or environmental protection organization. This option has allowed some communities to benefit from removal of people and buildings from hazard areas without the burden of continual property maintenance.

Multiple Goals of Acquisition

Public acquisition serves to effectively "disaster-proof" a particular piece of property. The property is removed from the private market, and the possibility of inappropriate development is reduced. Although acquisition is typically one of the most expensive mitigation tactics, in the long run, it may be less expensive to acquire and demolish a building than to repeatedly use public disaster recovery and insurance money to subsidize its reconstruction.

In addition to reducing the public cost of recovery and reconstruction, acquisition can be a tool for accomplishing other community goals, such as increasing floodplain storage capacity; preserving wetlands, maritime forests, estuaries, and other natural habitats; protecting aquifer recharge zones and riparian buffers; and providing open space, beach access, and parks and recreation areas.

Types of Land Interests Acquired

Land ownership is often described as a "bundle or rights," or interests, of which the right to develop is only one. A local government may acquire the entire bundle of rights to a piece of hazard-prone property, or it may acquire a lesser interest such as an easement or right-of-use.

Fee Simple Acquisition of Land and Damaged Structures

When a single owner has all the rights associated with a parcel of land, that owner is said to hold the land in **fee simple**. Acquiring property in fee simple provides a local government with the greatest level of control over the use and disposition of a parcel.

Fee simple purchase is usually the most expensive method of land acquisition. Acquiring land that is not yet developed may be significantly less expensive to purchase than developed parcels and has the added advantage of preventing damage to structures before a hazard event occurs. Conversely, after a disaster, high-density, repetitive loss properties may drop in price and become a better long-term investment for mitigation purposes.

Acquisition of Easements

As an alternative to fee simple acquisition, a local government may acquire a lesser interest in hazard-prone property, such as an **easement**. The owner of an easement has one or more of the rights in a property, leaving the rest of the rights in the hands of the landowner. Easements either grant an *affirmative right* to use the property, such as a right of access, or can *restrict* the landowner's right to use the property in a particular way. Local governments can prevent development in hazard areas by purchasing a negative easement that prevents building on the land.

Easements that prevent development may be nearly as expensive to acquire as fee simple rights. Many governments also prefer to own land in fee simple because easements must be policed, and the terms of the easement must be enforced, often at considerable expense. Many governments offer to lower the tax burden for properties that cannot be developed due to an easement. However, the local government could see its property tax revenues decrease with each donated easement. For these reasons, easements have not frequently been used for hazard mitigation purposes.

Purchase of Development Rights (PDR)

Purchase of a property's development rights is similar to acquiring a negative easement against development. Local governments can use this technique as an alternative to fee simple purchase or easements when the only purpose is to prevent building on the land. The purchase of development rights (PDR) may not be significantly less expensive than fee simple acquisition, but by owning development rights, the government assumes a very high level of control over property without being responsible for its maintenance. PDR is particularly suited to land in forestry or farming, where the current use is compatible with hazard mitigation goals. In this case, PDR can prevent the land from changing into a higher-risk use, while allowing the landowner to benefit from harvesting crops or timber.

Transfer of Development Rights (TDR)

Like PDR, Transfer of Development Rights (TDR) programs treat development as a commodity separate from the land itself. The local government first awards the property owner in the "sending area" a set of development rights based on the value or acreage of land. The sending area contains land the local government seeks to protect. The government then establishes a "receiving area" for the development rights. The receiving area is located some distance from the sending area and is a more preferable site for development. Landowners in the sending area are typically prohibited from developing their land, but they can realize the value of their property by selling their development rights to developers in the receiving areas. Developers who acquire development rights can build to higher densities than would otherwise be permitted in the receiving zone.

TDR is a complex system, which often makes it difficult for local governments to implement and for landowners to understand and accept. However, by designating high hazard areas as "sending zones," and more appropriate, safer areas of the community as "receiving zones," the local government can effectively shift the location of development without reducing the overall property value of the jurisdiction. Of course, to be successful, suitable receiving zones must be available outside of the hazard area, but since a large area of the community can be designated (not just specific individual parcels), TDR provides some flexibility to developers who put the purchased development rights to use.

Neighborhood-Wide Acquisition

Hazard loss reduction is less pronounced and mitigation less effective when isolated parcels are purchased, creating a patchwork effect. Such a checkerboard pattern of purchases is also more costly and difficult for the local government to manage and maintain. Relatively few large-scale acquisition projects undertaken with federal funds to date have been conducted in the context of a comprehensive management program to avoid a disorderly land use pattern; instead, local governments have generally acquired an inventory of scattered empty lots. However, some communities are beginning to proactively address this issue by prioritizing groups of structures or neighborhoods for acquisition projects, rather than focusing only on specific sites. For example, in 2012, Charlotte-Mecklenburg Storm Water Services developed an Orphan Property Floodplain Acquisition Plan to complement the ongoing Flood Risk Assessment and Reduction Plan. The Plans put more emphasis on acquiring groups of properties, referred to as "Project Areas," rather than individual properties for mitigation purposes.

8.4.5 Using the Power of Taxation and Fees

Like other government powers, the local government's authority to raise revenue is dictated by state law. Taxes, especially property taxes, have traditionally been the largest single source of revenue for most local governments, sometimes providing more than half of all receipts. Local governments are also granted the power to charge user or administrative fees, make special assessments, issue bonds, and receive grants-in-aid. It is important to note that the power to levy taxes, assessments, and fees extends beyond merely the collection of revenue and can have a profound impact on the pattern of development in the community.

By assessing certain areas of the community with differential tax rates or assessments, the local government can influence the affordability of development. The community can thereby steer development to desirable, safe areas, while providing disincentives for developers to build on lands identified as hazardous or environmentally sensitive. Tax abatements may also be used by local governments to encourage property owners and developers to integrate mitigation measures into new construction and to retrofit existing buildings. Incentives have been applied to promote storm proofing, flood proofing, wind strengthening, and seismic retrofitting. This is similar to programs that use taxation as an incentive for property owners to carry out energy conservation, historic preservation, and other activities of value to the community.

Real Property Taxes

Real property taxes are based on the assessed value of property, including the value of the land along with any improvements, such as structures. **Differential assessment** is a technique for reducing the tax burden on land facing development pressure by recognizing that undeveloped properties require fewer public services. This technique can moderate the pressure to develop land at its best use by reducing the tax rate applied to land so that payments are equal to the cost of essential services. Tax assessments may also reduce the assessed value of land to a percentage of urban land, or assess the land based on its income-producing capacity, as opposed to its market value.

Preferential taxation has been used to preserve land that is valuable to the community in ways other than monetary, such as farmland, forestland, historic properties, and wildlife habitat. Although preferential taxation has not been used extensively for mitigation purposes per se, local governments can apply differential assessments to reduce the development pressure on hazard-prone lands such as floodplains. This is especially effective where hazard areas overlap other sensitive lands such as wildlife habitat or aquifer recharge areas, effectively linking multiple community goals.

Special Assessments and Fees

Many local governments levy special assessments against property owners who receive a direct benefit from a public improvement. This technique shifts the financial burden from the general public to those who gain the most. Local governments often levy special assessments for public improvements such as streets, sidewalks, water and sewer systems, storm sewer and drainage systems, and watershed improvement projects.

There are a number of ways to apply this technique for mitigation purposes, from one-time assessments that raise revenue for a specific improvement to long-term assessments that fund ongoing projects. Special assessments for hazard mitigation can include:

- Construction of structural projects, such as seawalls, retention basins, dikes, and berms
- Establishing a regional floodplain management organization
- Creation of a special storm services district, where funds go toward mitigation, disaster recovery, and response activities in that district, including replacement of damaged infrastructure
- Maintaining stormwater management systems
- Implementing beach erosion programs
- Floodproofing water, sewer, or other public service systems

These charges may or may not have the effect of discouraging development in the assessment district. However, they do transfer some of the cost of living or doing business in environmentally sensitive or hazard-prone areas to those who choose to do so.

PAYING FOR HARD SURFACES

In Charlotte-Mecklenburg County, NC, a stormwater fee program pays for local efforts to reduce flood risks, improve drainage, and reduce water pollution. The cost of the program is funded completely by a user fee. In contrast to property taxes, which are calculated based on the value of property, the tiered stormwater fee system is based on (1) how much each property contributes to stormwater runoff and (2) the cost of providing stormwater services. The rate structure is based on the size of each property's impervious area (hard surfaces). During a rain storm, a house or commercial property with more impervious surface will send more rainwater into the storm system. Impervious areas include parking lots, sidewalks, driveways, rooftops, patios, tennis/basketball courts, swimming pool aprons, and any other area that does not allow rainwater to soak into the ground (see Photo 8.1). The size of a parcel's impervious surface is determined by aerial photos taken during the winter and early spring when leaves have fallen off the trees. Computer software is used to draw around the edges of the hard surfaces shown on the photo to calculate the impervious square footage for each parcel.

In addition to maintaining the county and city's vast system of pipes, catch basins, grates, and culverts, the stormwater fee also pays for maintaining and improving named creeks, mapping flood risks and regulating floodplain development, and monitoring and improving water quality in creeks and lakes.

Photo 8.1 Many techniques can be used to reduce impermeable surfaces that increase stormwater runoff, including rain gardens, vegetated swales, and green roofs. These permeable pavers can be used for low-intensity parking while also allowing rainwater to filter into the soil. (Public Domain.)

Impact Fees

Impact fees require new developments to share in the financial burden that their arrival imposes on a community. **Impact fees** are typically one-time up-front charges (although some jurisdictions allow payments over time) against new development to pay for off-site improvements, including schools, sewer and water treatment plants, fire stations, community centers, and other local facilities. The fees can be set up to allow new development to buy into existing services with excess capacity.

Impact fees are typically based on ratios that show what services the average new resident will require. While there are several methods for analyzing impacts, most consider only a single project in isolation. An alternative method is to carry out a **cumulative impact assessment**, which looks at the total effect of all development in a particular environment. For example, this approach can be used to estimate the combined effects of several potential developments on the flood storage capacity of the watershed. The fee in this case would go toward mitigating increased flood heights, perhaps by creating flood storage elsewhere in the floodplain.

8.4.6 Using the Power of Spending

To provide the services that their residents need, local governments have the authority to spend public funds for public purpose. There are basically two types of expenditures that local governments make on a regular basis. We will discuss both *operational budgets* and *capital improvement spending* in this section.

Most local government spending involves a considerable amount of discretion. Ideally, spending decisions are made within a broader policy context, so that spending authority is used to accomplish broader development goals for the community. It is also important to note that local governments have the power to withhold spending when it is in the best interest of the public at large. This authority to make or reserve expenditures can be a powerful tool for communities to mitigate the impacts of some types of hazards and adapt to climate change.

Annual Operating Budgets

Each year, local governments set an operating budget to pay for ongoing services, such as waste collection, fire and police protection, drainage maintenance, and the like. These types of expenditures are usually covered in the **annual operating budget** of the municipality. The operating budget is not generally used to pay for large, one-time mitigation projects, but there is ample opportunity within a municipality or county's operating budget to insert risk reduction and climate change adaptation strategies into day to day activities. Some of these strategies involve no extra money at all, just a rethinking of how and where local funds are spent to perform routine tasks. For example, regular trimming of tree limbs over power lines can help reduce a community's risk of outages during high winds and ice storms. Keeping enough money in the operational budget is crucial to maintaining these programs.

Spending for Capital Improvements

The second type of local expenditure involves major one-time capital improvement projects. The definition of a **capital improvement** differs from community to community. The common meaning includes new or expanded physical facilities that are relatively large in size, expensive, and permanent, such as streets and bridges, schools, public libraries, water and sewer lines, water treatment plants, parks and recreational facilities, and government offices.

In smaller communities, some expenditures, such as the purchase of a fire engine, may also be considered a capital expenditure.

Capital Improvement Programs and Budgets

Most communities make plans in advance to help guide decisions about how, when, and where public spending for major projects will occur. A **capital improvements program (CIP)** is a multiyear schedule of public physical improvements. The scheduling is based on projections of available fiscal resources and the choice of specific improvements to be constructed for a period of five to six years into the future. The **capital improvements budget** usually refers to facilities that are programmed to come on line during the next fiscal year.

An important distinction between the capital improvements budget and the CIP is that the one-year budget may become a part of the legally adopted annual operating budget. In contrast, the longer-term program does not necessarily have legal significance, nor does it necessarily commit a local government to a particular expenditure in a particular year. It merely serves as a planning tool to guide future decisions about upcoming expenditures.

Standards for Government Buildings and Facilities

When local governments build new structures and facilities or renovate old ones, they have the opportunity to build them according to hazard-resistant standards. These standards can be incorporated directly into local capital improvement policies, along with features that call for sustainable building practices such as the use of natural lighting, water reclamation systems, and efficient heating and cooling systems that use renewable energy sources. At a minimum, public buildings should conform to the standards set for private development. Ideally, government structures should be built to even higher standards if the risk of loss is significant.

The decision of where to locate public facilities is also critical. By locating public facilities outside of hazardous areas, local governments can reduce the costs of repair and replacement following a disaster. Locating **lifeline services** such as fire, police, hospitals, emergency operations centers, and rescue stations outside of hazard areas is especially important to ensure that the response capability of the local government is not impaired during a disaster. Building public facilities to high standards and in nonhazardous areas also makes the local government a good leader in mitigation and sustainable building practice, setting the example for private property owners.

Influencing Private Development through Public Spending Decisions

In addition to being directly involved in the siting and construction standards of public buildings, ideally capital improvement programs can be used to influence private development. Public spending decisions have long been considered a growth management tool, since growth and development tend to follow the availability of public services. In particular, highways and water and sewer utilities have been called "growth shapers." The conscientious withholding of public spending can also impact patterns of development in the community. By establishing certain areas where the local government will *not* extend essential services, such as water and sewer systems, growth may be limited in those areas. Local governments can use policies about where (and where not) to provide public infrastructure to discourage development in identified hazard areas.

Withholding public spending to discourage private development is less feasible in areas that have already reached build-out, or where private developers are able to front the cost of the infrastructure necessary to support new construction. In localities where soils and other topographical conditions can support on-site sewer (septic tanks) and potable water (wells), the refusal to extend public infrastructure has little influence as a hazard management tool. Public health laws may restrict the use of septic systems or private wells in some areas, but often these laws are not based on hazard risks (although some local and state laws do restrict septic tanks and wells in areas subject to frequent flooding because of the risk of contamination).

Effectiveness of Capital Improvement Programs for Hazard Mitigation

A key component of a resilient community is the location of public infrastructure. This is particularly true following a disaster. The placement of roads, water, sewer, schools, libraries, and other public facilities is crucial during the rebuilding phase to guide the overall community development patterns. Following a hazard event, where and how capital improvements are built and rebuilt can dramatically shape future vulnerability of the community. Some communities have made use of the window of opportunity following a disaster to revamp their public investment policies. For example, Nags Head, North Carolina, implemented a policy not to expend public funds to repair any private road that is damaged or destroyed as a result of a severe storm, except in conjunction with the repair of the town's water system.

Despite the theoretical potential, in practice capital improvement programs are not widely used for hazard mitigation. Furthermore, jurisdictions often ignore their own capital improvement programs. Studies have shown similar ineffectualness for policies that locate public facilities to discourage development. Such policies tend not to alter the basic spatial pattern of private development in hazard areas.[4] Moreover, restricting public services is usually unpopular with property owners who require the infrastructure to develop their land. Local governments may feel obligated to limit the geographic scope of the program to make it more politically acceptable. Local governments may also count on receiving federal support to rebuild public facilities in the event of a disaster and therefore have little incentive to spend their own funds on protecting them. Generally, these policies are much more effective when linked with complementary land use regulations and tax policies.

Not All Spending Decisions Are Made Locally

Although local governments are responsible for providing much of the infrastructure and many of the facilities that support community development, a significant number of spending decisions are not within the control of local governments. Federal and state agencies, as well as many regional entities, often enact legislation or carry out programs and policies that trump local government authority. For example, most major highway projects are funded with federal and/or state funds, with little local influence on road capacity, location, or even maintenance and repair.

Water resource development in many parts of the country is also controlled by state and regional agencies, with relatively little local input. Some federal land management programs, such as beach nourishment undertaken by the U.S. Army Corps of Engineers, provide additional stimulation for growth in vulnerable coastal areas. State law can also dictate that local governments provide necessary infrastructure to developed land within their jurisdiction. These adequate facilities laws can make it difficult for local governments to control growth by withholding spending.

8.4.7 Using the Power of Education

Among the powers held by local governments is the authority, and perhaps even the duty, to provide public access to reliable data and accurate information about the community. An informed and educated citizenry is an integral part of managing hazards at the local level. It is arguably equally important to educate the public about the effects of climate change, which in many areas is a less immediate concern, but one which will have long-lasting implications for the resiliency of the community. Local residents often assume that current building codes, zoning regulations, subdivision review, and permitting processes will adequately protect them and their property from the impacts of hazards, but this is not always the case. Making the public aware of the hazards it faces is the first step toward making the community safer, and overcoming a lack of awareness should be an integral part of any local mitigation or adaptation program.[5]

Learning about Natural Hazards

Many local governments have carried out programs to alert residents to natural hazards— both the dangers as well as the opportunities to lessen hazard risks. Other communities have focused on educating visitors about fragile ecosystems, sensitive natural areas, endangered wildlife and plant species, or other natural wonders that need to be protected and conserved. In addition to residents and tourists, local target audiences for education and awareness include a wide range of community members, such as lenders and insurance agents; builders, architects, and realtors; and local elected and appointed officials and public staff, including the governing board, building inspectors and zoning officials, and emergency first responders.

It is not uncommon that the prevailing perception of risk in a community is skewed, even in areas where natural hazards have occurred in the past. Information regarding hazard frequency is often misunderstood. For example, the common understanding of the 100-year floodplain is that this area will only be flooded once in a century. Residents also often fail to grasp the extent of past hazard events, such as flood heights. The understanding and acceptance of climate change also varies widely, and many citizens may have unclear or incorrect information about the expected impacts on a community's vulnerability. Such misperceptions highlight the need for publicizing accurate information.

There are several different methods that local communities can use to promote community awareness, including real estate disclosure, community awareness campaigns, hazard maps, and disaster warnings. These are discussed in more detail in Chapter 12.

8.4.8 Local Government Planning

Local government planning provides a cohesive framework for managing all aspects of growth and development in the community. Most large and mid-sized municipalities and county governments in the United States carry out some sort of planning function. In some states, local planning is mandated, and all regulations and ordinances must be consistent with the plan. Even in states that do not mandate local comprehensive planning, communities may be required to prepare plans to be eligible for certain funding programs. These include federal programs such as the Community Development Block Grant (CDBG) — administered by the U.S. Department of Housing and Urban Development (HUD); grants under the Clean Water Act from the EPA; and grants provided under the Disaster Mitigation Act administered by FEMA. These federal programs establish planning criteria that must be met in return for local access to grant funds.

There is a wide variety of plan types, some of which are narrow in scope and deal with only one particular topic (such as transportation plans, or beach management plans), while other local plans are broader and combine multiple objectives. Some local plans are free-standing documents, others are included as part of a wider community management program. Some communities have officially adopted all their plans and view them as regulatory devices, while other communities merely use plans as policy guidance without the force of law. The degree to which plans are actually implemented and the level of their effectiveness for influencing land uses also varies widely.

Among the types of plans that local governments commonly use are hazard mitigation plans, post-disaster recovery plans, land use plans, comprehensive plans, floodplain management plans, capital improvement plans, emergency operations plans (EOPs), transportation plans, economic development plans, parks and recreation plans, and open space management plans, to name but a few. Many communities have come to realize the value of incorporating principles of hazard resiliency in their current planning efforts. Still others have begun to consider climate change impacts and have crafted adaptation action plans to deal with growing implications of climate change.

Land Use and Comprehensive Plans

In many jurisdictions, a land use plan serves as the basis for much of the regulation of property use. A comprehensive plan also addresses economic development, environmental, transportation, and social concerns. City and county planners study the physical characteristics of the land. Where are the steep slopes? Where are the waterways—rivers, streams, and lakes? They map existing streets, rail lines, water lines, sewers, schools, parks, fire stations, and other facilities that can support development. They also note current uses of the land. Where are the factories, the warehouses, the stores and offices, the residential neighborhoods? Ideally, the comprehensive plan also surveys the hazard locations in the community: what areas are subject to flooding? Where are wildfires more likely to occur?

On the basis of their studies, planners prepare maps showing how various areas might be developed to make use of existing public facilities and to avoid mixing incompatible land uses such as industrial processing plants and residential housing. The maps may also indicate where new water lines and sewers might be built most easily. These maps are then presented to the public for comment. After the public has reviewed the maps, the planners prepare a detailed set of maps showing current and possible future uses of the land. The local governing board might review and vote on this final set of maps itself or delegate planning authority to an appointed planning board. The approved maps and supporting narrative become the official land use plan for the community, called a Comprehensive Plan.

Local officials can use land use plans to guide their decisions about where to locate new public facilities. Some governments use them only for these nonregulatory purposes. A land use plan also establishes a basis for regulation of property uses. However, the plan itself does not set up a system of regulation. Zoning and subdivision ordinances are systems of regulation based on a land use plan.

The main advantage of land use or comprehensive plans as a hazard mitigation tool is that they guide other measures, such as capital improvement programs, zoning ordinances, and subdivision ordinances. Comprehensive planning requires local governments to collect and analyze information about land's suitability for development. This process helps policymakers and local residents understand the limitations to development in hazard-prone areas. In turn, land uses can be tailored to the hazard risk, typically by reserving dangerous areas for less intensive, hazard-compatible uses such as parks, golf courses, backyards, wildlife refuges, or natural features.

Hazard Mitigation Planning

Planning is the key to transforming mitigation from a reactive process to a proactive one. Hazard mitigation planning is the comprehensive and orderly process of determining how to reduce or eliminate the loss of life and property damage resulting from natural and human-made causes. However, in the past, many communities have undertaken mitigation actions with good intentions but with little advance planning. In some cases, decisions have been made on the fly in the wake of a disaster. In other cases, decisions may have been made in advance but without careful consideration of all options, effects, or contributing factors. Chapter 12 discusses hazard mitigation planning in detail.

The primary purpose of hazard mitigation planning is to identify community policies, actions, and tools for implementation over the long term that will result in a reduction of risk and potential for future losses community wide. Under the Disaster Mitigation Act of 2000 (DMA), local and state governments are required to prepare hazard mitigation plans to receive federal mitigation funds in the future. As a result, many more communities are now preparing mitigation plans than ever before, and it is an exciting time for those in the planning and emergency management fields as they find ways to work together to bring these plans to life (the Disaster Mitigation Act is discussed in more detail in Chapter 6). Effective planning forges partnerships that will bring together the skills, expertise, and experience of a broad range of groups to achieve a common vision for the community and can also ensure that the most appropriate and equitable mitigation projects will be undertaken. Hazard mitigation planning is most successful when it increases public and political support for mitigation programs, results in actions that also support other important community goals and objectives, and influences the community's decision-making to include hazard reduction considerations.[5]

Emergency Operations Plans

All counties and many municipalities (depending upon size) develop and adopt an **EOP**, which predetermines actions to be taken by government agencies and private organizations in response to an emergency or disaster event. EOPs typically describe the local government's capability to respond to emergencies and establish the responsibilities and procedures for response. To keep plans up to date, local governments conduct exercises based on actual risk scenarios. Issues that emerge from post-disaster scenarios often draw attention to pre-disaster activities that can be undertaken now to prevent future losses. FEMA makes available post-disaster mitigation and recovery exercises for flood, earthquake, and hurricane disaster scenarios, as do many state emergency management agencies.

Climate Change Adaptation Plans

One of the most effective adaptation tools used by local governments is the power to plan communities. Through land use planning, local governments can increase resiliency to major climate shifts and ensure that our communities are equipped with built-in mechanisms to face and mitigate such changes.[6] Traditionally, local plans have drawn on past experience to direct decisions for both present and future growth. But with the advent of climate change and the need to plan for adaptation, a dramatically different approach to community development planning is called for.

Climate adaptation planning requires decision-making to account for changes that are projected to take place in the future. Furthermore, climate change differs both in scale and in type from past challenges faced by communities and, as such, will compel local governments to explore new concepts and new planning tools and approaches. For instance, because the rate of change along some coastlines is rapidly increasing due to heightened intensity of storm activity and sea level rise, coastal local governments may be unable to rely on traditional methods for identifying the safest locations for transportation, housing, commerce, industry, recreation, and essential public facilities. Methods such as erosion studies based on erosion rates of the last 30 years, or flood maps that have not incorporated potential sea level rise onto flood zones, are quickly becoming outdated. In other regions of the country, where changes in water availability due to climate change-induced higher temperatures are occurring, communities are experiencing higher frequency of drought and wildfire. These local governments will need to consider future water demands that exceed current resource supplies to come up with ways to plan for new conditions involving less water.

Planning for a range of strategies and actions can help local governments reduce the negative impacts of climate change and maximize any positive impacts. What make climate adaptation planning strategies so appealing are their numerous co-benefits: saving money, decreasing energy use, increasing community livability, enhancing public health, and creating more robust and just communities.[6]

A critical component of emerging adaptation plans is the consistent use of metrics, baselines, and assessments. These tools can help local governments understand their climate change vulnerabilities; identifying metrics allows for an effective measurement of climate change impacts relevant to the local community; and establishing baselines for each metric helps communities track ecological, economic, and social changes: "Collecting the evidence" is the first step to effectively creating an adaptation plan and creating a foundation for delivering adaptation actions. Finally, assessing changes in the selected metrics will require communities to put the data to work by comparing opportunities, threats, and assets.[6]

For example, the City of Chula Vista, California recognized rising temperatures as a relevant climate changing condition and proposed 11 adaptation strategies to address this condition. The City identified potential metrics that could be tracked and reported on an ongoing basis to quantify their performance in preparing for changing conditions. Some of those metrics included:

- Actual temperature reductions
- Total square footage of "cool" paved surfaces
- Number of wildfire education materials distributed
- Percent increase in community awareness from outreach and education
- Number of surveys performed to monitor shifts in local species range and diversity
- Number of habitat restoration areas where climate change impacts were incorporated into designs

The adaptation plan drafted by the City of Lewes, Delaware provides another good example of how communities can benefit from the use of metrics, baselines, and assessments. The City identified key metrics, established baselines, and then honed in on two key vulnerabilities through an assessment process. Those vulnerabilities – saltwater intrusion into the aquifer and property damage from increased flooding—were then given priority in seeking methods to adapt to these changing conditions. This process provided a basis upon which Lewes could measure indicators of local importance (thereby keeping adaptation planning relevant to the community) and fashion response plans in the most effective way.

These examples illustrate the range of climate adaptation planning that is taking place in communities large and small. Using metrics and assessments to gauge progress toward resiliency, along with moving beyond exclusive reliance on historical patterns and trends is helping local governments to retool their planning processes. This approach of integrating new science and new technological and policy opportunities is pushing communities to be truly prepared for climate change.

SELF-CHECK

- Define **building codes, zoning maps, cumulative impact assessment, capital improvement,** and **lifeline services.**
- Name the five basic local government powers.
- List at least two regulatory powers of local governments.
- Name two ways local governments are changing their planning processes to develop climate change adaptation plans.

8.5 LOCAL GOVERNMENT STRUCTURE

So far in this chapter we have reviewed the authority of local governments under the police power to make communities more resilient to the impacts of natural hazards and adapt to climate change. To understand how these powers are executed during the day-to-day business of the community, we must be aware of how local governments are organized and the political machinery that is necessary to implement mitigation strategies.

The type of organization dictates where emergency management and planning fit into the local government structure. This can have direct bearing on the ease to which hazard mitigation, preparedness, and climate change adaptation can be integrated into the policies and programs of the community. For example, in communities where the manager wields significant authority, the manager can direct department heads to consider hazard risk reduction as part of their regular duties. This can be as simple as ensuring the public works director understands the importance of keeping storm drains cleared as part of routine stormwater management system maintenance so as to avoid flooding during minor or major precipitation events. In any case, no matter which type of local government is in place, it is critical to have a champion, or visionary figure, who is willing to take a stand on issues that may be politically contentious—such as climate change adaptation or land use regulation—that can determine the future resiliency of the community.

8.5.1 Definition of Local Government

For purposes of federal disaster assistance and mitigation planning under Disaster Management Act, FEMA defines a *local government* as

> any county, municipality, city, town, township, public authority, school district, special district, intrastate district, council of governments…regional or interstate government entity, or agency or instrumentality of a local government; any Indian tribe or authorized tribal organization, or Alaska Native village or organization; and any rural community, unincorporated town or village, or other public entity.[7]

In the following sections of this chapter, we will describe how units of government are typically established, the processes by which decisions are made, and how policy is formulated and adopted at the local level. As you read this material, consider how resiliency and risk reduction might be implemented in each type of government structure.

8.5.2 Types of Local Government

There are roughly five basic types of local government in the United States, which can be grouped into general-purpose and single-purpose governments. **General-purpose local**

governments perform a wide range of government functions and include counties, parishes, municipalities, towns and townships. **Single-purpose local governments** such as school districts and special districts have a specific purpose and perform one function.

Counties

All states, except Connecticut and Rhode Island, are divided into counties (in Alaska these subunits of government are called boroughs and in Louisiana they are called parishes). Counties can be urban or rural. They can combine municipalities within them or can have no incorporated communities within their borders.

Counties were originally created to act as an administrative unit of the state and to perform activities of statewide concern at the local level. Today counties often have more policy- and decision-making responsibility. Basic county functions include property assessment, revenue collection (taxation), law enforcement, jails, elections, land records, road maintenance, and emergency services. Counties may also provide additional services, including health care, social services, pollution control, mass transit, and industrial and economic development.

Organization of County Governments

There are three main types of county governments in the United States:

1. A **County Board** is made up of "Supervisors" or "Commissioners." This is the most common type of county government in the United States, where the board is elected by voters in the county. The board serves as the central policy-maker, approves the county budget, and appoints other officials. In some counties, the board shares power with other elected officials, including the sheriff, public safety officer, county prosecutor or district attorney, county tax assessor, coroner, and the county clerk or clerk of court.
2. In the **County Council-Elected Executive** form of local government, the board and all executive officers are elected by the county voters. In these counties, the board performs legislative (rule-making) functions, adopts the budget, sets policy, and performs financial audits. The executive officer performs executive functions such as preparing the budget, implementing policy, and appointing department heads.
3. In the **County Council-Administrator** form of local government, the board is more hands off in the day-to-day running of the government. In these counties, the board performs legislative functions such as setting policy and adopting the budget, while a professional administrator hired by the Board manages government affairs.

Municipalities

Municipalities are incorporated units of government, formed by the state through charter or other means. Throughout the United States, municipalities are variously referred to as cities, towns, hamlets, villages, or boroughs. These are the most frequently used terms to describe urban areas that, in general, are more densely populated than unincorporated areas (areas outside municipal boundaries). In some states, various terms have no special legal meaning, while in others, different status is afforded to each type. In all states, municipalities are authorized to make decisions for the community and to implement policies and programs that fall within their delegated powers and responsibilities. Like counties, municipalities are general-purpose units of government. Unlike counties, they generally have greater decision-making authority and discretion, especially in home-rule states.

Organization of Municipalities

There are three main types of municipal government: (1) mayor-council, (2) city commission, and (3) council-manager.

1. *Mayor-council* is the older and most common type of local government in both the smallest and largest of cities. There are two varieties, depending upon the strength of the mayor:
   a. In the *strong mayor-council*, the mayor is elected by the voters and is the source of executive leadership. The mayor prepares the budget, hires and fires top-level city officials, performs daily administrative duties, and has veto power over the council.
   b. In the *weak mayor-council*, power and authority are fragmented. The council is the source of executive power, while the mayor is considered an executive figurehead ("ribbon cutter"). The council appoints city officials, develops the budget, and elects the mayor.
2. In the *city commission* plan, the legislative and executive functions are merged. Each commissioner, who is a politician, tends to be an advocate for his or her department (usually by asking for a larger share of the city budget). The commissioners generally make policy and lead major departments. One commissioner serves as mayor, presiding over commission meetings.
3. The *council-city manager* form of municipal government predominates in cities of 10,000–50,000, especially in suburban communities and cities of the Sunbelt. In theory, the politics and policy-making functions of government are separated from the administration and execution of policies. The City Manager serves at the pleasure of the council, appoints and removes department heads, oversees delivery of services, prepares the budget, and makes policy recommendations to the council. In many communities, the manager is quite powerful and can play an activist role in local affairs. Because of the heightened level of professionalism and degree of coordination between departments that this organizational structure involves, local governments conducted under the council-manager plan are more likely to infuse mitigation into all local government operations, from keeping new school buildings away from the dangers of landslides, to designating stream banks as recreational greenways, to constructing safe rooms in all government buildings.

Local Government Departments

Most local governments carry out the day-to-day business of running a municipality or county through local government employees located in individual government departments. The number, size, and organizational complexity of various departments depend on the size, relative wealth, and geographic location of the community itself, but there are a few basic types of departmental functions that are typical nationwide. For instance, most local governments have an administrator or manager's office, as well as a budget and financial office. Local governments may have their own building code enforcement and inspections departments or may share such functions among several smaller municipalities in a single county. These offices are often combined with planning and zoning, as well as floodplain management. Local governments must have an attorney on staff, and counties are required to have an emergency management or preparedness department or agency, as well as fire protection, public safety, medical emergency agencies, and hazardous materials management. Most counties and municipalities also have departments that deal with day-to-day services, such as mass transit, housing, and sanitation and public works. Increasingly, municipalities have offices that deal specifically with sustainable development, resiliency, and climate change adaptation.

Towns and Townships

Towns and townships are general-purpose units of local government, distinct from counties and municipalities. In some states, towns and townships have broad powers, acting like other general-purpose units of government. Examples of this type of township can be found in New England, New Jersey, Pennsylvania, Michigan, New York, and Wisconsin.

In other states, towns and townships have more limited authority. These tend to be more rural in nature, offering limited services such as roads and law enforcement. These townships are found in Illinois, Indiana, Kansas, Minnesota, Missouri, Nebraska, North Dakota, Ohio, and South Dakota.

Special Districts

Special districts are single-purpose local governments that are authorized to perform one function or to meet the service needs of one particular area. Special districts are created to address specific issues in the community such as fire protection, sewage and water management, mosquito control, drainage and flood control, soil and water conservation, school districts, mass transit, and even redevelopment and disaster recovery.

Special district officials may be elected or appointed by another government, such as the county. Budgets and staff of special districts range from very large to minimal. Examples of powerful special districts include the Port Authority of New Jersey, the Chicago Transit Authority, and the Los Angeles County Sanitation District.

Service districts can extend services beyond the borders of a general-purpose local government and can tackle regional problems that transcend political jurisdictions. For example, a flood control district can deal with flooding of a river that runs through several counties. Service districts are often used to provide services that are inefficient to provide on an individual basis, based on economies of scale. For example, electric power can often be provided more efficiently to several counties than one single county's population. Regional utilities may also be better equipped to handle power outages and other emergencies.

8.5.3 Regional Governance

In many respects, local governments act as freestanding, autonomous units, each with its own power base, its own basic governmental structure, and its own decision-making and policy-formulation processes. Yet while a strong identity and unique character are essential to a community's sense of place, many of the challenges that face communities are broader in scope and best addressed with a regional approach. Natural hazards clearly fall into this category of issues that communities must deal with, because many types of hazards do not strike solely within clearly defined political boundaries and their impacts can be experienced over a wide geographic area. This is particularly true of flooding, which can be exacerbated by communities living in the same watershed or river basin. A parochial view is not uncommon among local governments, and cooperative, joint-venture activities are not entered into lightly. Nevertheless, finding solutions to hazard-related problems in a collaborative way can often be more effective than individual local governments working alone.

Regional agencies are often based on ecosystem boundaries, such as a river basin or watershed. Other regional governments consist of multi-jurisdictional collaborations, such as councils of government (COGs) that operate within a state, or multistate compacts and alliances. There are many different approaches to implementing regional or ecosystem management. In some areas, management has been undertaken by a regulatory agency. This may take the form of a free-standing body spanning local or state borders, or it may operate within a state government, either as a separate entity or as a division of an existing department or agency. Such regulatory agencies are usually created by the legislatures of the state(s) and may be given both regulatory and enforcement powers.

Other regional management bodies are more administrative in nature and may perform coordinating functions or act as advisory boards to state and/or local governments. Many states have legislation that enables localities to voluntarily form councils or federations to study regional resources and problems and to promote cooperative arrangements and coordinated action among their member governments.

The success of regional organizations in tackling concrete problems such as development in hazard areas has been spotty at best. Some observers have argued that fragmentation among levels of government within a federal system is a fact of life that cannot be changed. The function of regional entities in governing land use in areas prone to natural hazards is likely to remain limited to broad-brush planning, intergovernmental coordination, and capacity-building functions of providing information, education, and technical assistance to local governments. Special purpose regional organizations have been more successful when they have been granted authority to directly implement or compel implementation of their plans and policies.

Multi-Jurisdictional Planning

In its administration of the DMA, FEMA encourages communities to cooperate with one another when preparing their mandatory local hazard mitigation plans.[5] Planning on a broader scale can bring additional resources, such as staff, funding, technical ability, and experience to the effort, and can help mitigate hazards that originate outside of a community's jurisdictional boundaries. For example, a multi-jurisdictional planning area may include several towns located along the same fault line, the main hazard of which is earthquake, or communities that lie within the same watershed. Multi-jurisdictional plans may also be created by communities that are contiguous to one another (for example, a tri-county plan), or by a county government and the municipalities and townships within it.

Councils of Government (COGs)

In some regions of the country, local governments band together to form COGs. The voluntary organizations of county and municipal governments provide services that are handled on a regional basis rather than by individual local governments. Some COGs are fairly small, consisting of a pair of local governments working together, while other COG-like structures are much larger. In Washington, DC, for example, the local COG in essence covers three states, while a quad-state partnership exists in the eastern panhandle of West Virginia.

Typical services provided by COGs include programs for senior citizens, land use planning, economic development, environmental protection, and other types of collaborative efforts. Member governments pay dues to support the work of the regional council and appoint representatives to discuss problems they share and to work out ways to deal with issues of mutual concern. Frequently, areas of a state that are least advantaged and that have fewer resources (often rural counties) rely on COGs to help administer federal and state programs, write grants, and provide assistance with plan writing and other local functions. Although some COGs have successfully addressed hazard risks that span the region, in general, COGs have not typically been used to deal with natural hazards or climate change impacts on a larger than local scale. More commonly, COGs have provided assistance to local communities to carry out federal disaster recovery programs and develop local hazard mitigation plans.

Mutual Aid Agreements

Legislation in some states allows municipalities and counties to enter into interlocal agreements to cooperatively perform any function that can be carried out as an individual local government. Many of these mutual aid agreements enable local governments to work together to provide emergency services. The agreements establish a means through which signatories can offer and receive assistance in times of disaster. Mutual aid agreements address logistics, deployment, compensation, and liability issues and can also assist in faster reimbursement of federal disaster aid. The preestablished policies and procedures of a mutual aid agreement make intragovernmental cooperation more expansive and efficient, serving to protect property, minimize costs, and save lives.

SELF-CHECK

- Define **general-purpose local governments** and **single-purpose local governments**.
- Discuss the role of the city or county manager.
- List three issues that might be addressed in a mutual aid agreement.
- Describe two types of local collaborative activities.

8.6 MAKING IT HAPPEN: POLITICAL WILL

We have seen throughout this chapter that local governments have a range of powers that allow them to control growth and development in ways that can decrease the risk of natural hazards, adapt to climate change, and establish policies to increase the overall resiliency. In all cases, no matter which type of local government is in place, what the local hazards are, or what level of resources is available, it is critical to have a champion, or visionary figure or organization who is willing to take a stand on issues that may be politically contentious, such as climate change adaptation or land use regulation. In other words, the capacity of the community to tackle these challenges depends on a certain level of political willpower. The immediate and mid-range fiscal benefits of intense growth must be weighed carefully against the long-term costs associated with that growth, including increased vulnerability when development occurs in hazardous locations or when new homes, buildings, and public facilities are built on the cheap, without incorporating high standards to withstand high winds, floods, wildfire, storm surge, or earthquake. These are issues that require foresight and long-range thinking and should be addressed holistically, even in a political climate that might sway with each election cycle. The local champion—whether it be the manager, mayor, citizen advocate, local business leader, or community activist—is the one who will step up to the plate to make sure that climate change is considered and hazard risk is minimized with each public development decision that is made.

SUMMARY

Local governments represent only one of the many layers of management in hazardous areas, but they are arguably the most critical for creating resilient communities. It is at the local level that land use patterns are determined and most development issues are decided. It is also at the local level where hazards are experienced and losses are suffered most directly, and where local knowledge can help inform various approaches to minimize those losses. This chapter discussed the powers delegated to local governments by the states, powers that can be used to reduce hazard risk. These powers include regulation, acquisition, taxation, education, spending, and planning. The chapter also described some of the legislative and constitutional limitations on these powers and presented the types of local government structure most prevalent in the United States. We also explored the ways that local governments relate to one another within the state or across regions. The chapter summed up the key to successful long-term risk reduction by observing the need for a local leader who will champion the cause of community resiliency, even when it may be politically unpopular to do so.

KEY TERMS

Acquisition: The government authority to acquire property, including privately owned property, through purchase or condemnation. Public land ownership and conscientious management of public lands provides direct control over the use of property. This control can be used to implement hazard mitigation and climate adaptation policies that keep development out of hazard areas.

Amortization: Process that requires nonconforming structures to come into compliance with local zoning regulations or be removed from the property within a certain time period.

Annual operating budget: The amount of money a local government sets aside each year to pay for ongoing services, such as police and fire, trash and recycling pickup, and maintenance of roads and parks.

Buffer: A setback of a specific distance, such as 25 or 100 feet, from a channel, floodway, wetland, or other water feature. In that area, no cutting, clearing of ground cover, or alteration of natural features is allowed.

Building codes: Laws, ordinances, or regulations that set forth standards and requirements for structural integrity, design, and construction materials used in commercial and residential structures.

Buyout program: Public acquisition of privately held property located in hazardous areas.

Capital improvement: New or expanded physical facilities that are relatively large in size, expensive, and permanent.

Capital improvements budget: Schedule of public facilities to be constructed in the current or next fiscal year.

Capital improvement program (CIP): A multiyear schedule for public physical improvements.

Cumulative impact assessment: An evaluation that looks at the total effect of all development in a particular environment.

Differential assessment: A technique for reducing the tax burden on land facing development pressure by recognizing that undeveloped properties require fewer public services.

Down-zoning: Provisions in the zoning code used to keep inappropriate development out of hazard-prone areas; can be accomplished by increasing minimum lot size or reducing the number of dwelling units permitted per acre.

Due process: Constitutional provision that the rights of private citizens must be protected during all legal proceedings.

Easement: A type of property ownership that grants an affirmative right to use a particular piece of property, such as a right of access; may also restrict the landowner's right to use the property in a particular way.

Emergency operations plan (EOP): Establishes responsibilities, actions, and chain of command for responding to emergencies at the state or local level.

Eminent domain: Also known as *condemnation*, The power of the government to "take" (condemn) private land for public purpose.

Equal protection clause: Constitutional requirement that laws must be applied uniformly upon all persons in similar circumstances.

Fee simple: When a single owner has all the rights associated with a parcel of land.

General-purpose local government: Type of local government that performs a wide-range of functions; examples: counties, municipalities, and towns and townships.

Impact fee: A one-time, up-front charge against new development to pay for off-site improvements, including schools, fire stations, community centers, and other local facilities.

Just compensation: The constitutional requirement that property owners are paid fair market value for private property that is confiscated by the government.

Lifeline services: Services provided by local governments that are essential to protect human life and safety, such as fire, police, emergency medical services, and search and rescue operations. Also applies to critical municipal or county services such as hospitals, power generation, telecommunications, transportation, and water and sewer.

Moratorium: A short-term suspension of the right to develop, usually accomplished by a refusal of the local government to issue building permits during a defined period, such as following a major disaster.

Police power: The basic authority of governments to make laws and regulations for the benefit of the public. The Tenth Amendment to the U.S. Constitution confers the police power to states, which in turn delegate the power to their political subdivisions, allowing local governments to enact measures that preserve and protect the public's safety, health, and welfare.

Relocation: Removal of privately owned structures from hazardous areas and relocating them to nonhazardous sites; most often used in combination with acquisition.

Single-purpose local government: Type of local government that has a specific purpose and performs one function; example: school district.

Subdivision ordinance: Local regulations that govern the partition of land for development or sale. In addition to controlling the configuration of parcels, subdivision ordinances set standards for developer built infrastructure, including drainage and flood control.

Sustainable development: Growth that meets current needs without compromising the ability of future generations to meet their needs. Sustainable communities require a high level of resiliency to hazards.

Takings clause: Provision of the 5th Amendment to the U.S. Constitution that applies when the government takes an owner's property by physical occupation or by severely restricting the owner's use of the property. Requires the government to pay the owner just compensation for the taking.

Zoning: The traditional tool available to local governments to control land use; zoning maps divide the jurisdiction into zones where various regulations apply as described in the zoning ordinance.

Zoning map: Divides the area under local government control into zones where various development regulations apply.

ASSESS YOUR UNDERSTANDING

Summary Questions

1. Sustainable communities are those that reduce opportunities of future generations to meet their own needs. True or False?
2. A sustainable community should also be a
   a. Federally subsidized community
   b. Local government
   c. Resilient community
   d. Hazardous area
3. Keeping people and property out of hazardous areas is one of the main goals of mitigation. True or False?

4. Development of environmentally fragile areas decreases a community's resiliency. True or False?
5. A building code is an example of a local government's taxation powers. True or False?
6. Which of the following is an example of a local government's regulatory powers?
   a. Impact fees
   b. Planning
   c. Floodplain ordinances
   d. Special assessments
7. A zoning ordinance defines the types and intensity of uses allowed within a designated zone. True or False?
8. Moratoria are used by communities to
   a. Prevent rebuilding of damaged structures
   b. Update hazard maps
   c. Reassess zoning districts
   d. All of the above
9. Eminent domain gives the government the right to
   a. Enforce the law
   b. Impose taxation
   c. Change zoning
   d. Condemn property
10. Local governments require developers to provide infrastructure in subdivisions according to the highest profit margin. True or False?
11. New developments share in the financial burden that they impose on a community through
   a. Property taxes
   b. User fees
   c. Capital improvements
   d. Impact fees
12. A regulation that deprives an owner of all economically beneficial use of the property is an unconstitutional
   a. act of mitigation
   b. Management act
   c. Taking
   d. Land trust
13. A special district is an example of a single-purpose government. True or False?
14. Emergency management is the sole responsibility of county governments. True or False?
15. Which of the following is the most common type of local city government?
   a. Mayor-council
   b. City commission
   c. Council-manager
   d. Mayor-manager
16. Special districts can tackle regional problems that transcend political jurisdictions. True or False?

Review Questions

1. Consider a community that has been affected by a natural hazard. In what ways are hazard mitigation and preparedness linked to the sustainability of a local community?
2. A sustainable community must be hazard resilient. What are four other issues that a sustainable community must consider?

3. How does suburban sprawl affect a community's sustainability and vulnerability to hazards?

4. When is the pressure to rebuild after a disaster most intense, and why?

5. How can local government powers be used to manage a community's growth to mitigate the impacts of natural hazards or adapt to climate change?

6. How is acquisition a long-term solution to the problem of repeatedly paying for rebuilding?

7. Give reasons why easements should and should not be used for hazard mitigation purposes.

8. Explain the relationship between eminent domain and acquisition.

9. A disaster warning system is a critical part of a community's hazard planning process. What are the inherent weaknesses in disaster warning systems?

10. What are the five types of local government structures in the United States? Which are general-purpose and which are single purpose?

11. Counties were originally created as an administrative unit of the state. Name the two states that are not divided into counties.

12. Special districts are single-purpose governments created to meet service needs in a particular area. List five types of special districts.

13. A community that seeks hazard resilience must be willing to invest in the capability for developing and carrying out mitigation programs and policies. List five government activities that demonstrate this principle.

Applying This Chapter

1. Keeping in mind the considerations of a sustainable community, assess the sustainability of where you live. Is there a particular unsustainable land use that has increased the vulnerability of your community to hazards?

2. In what ways could a local government use zoning to try to manage the impacts of growth associated with the arrival of a large communications company that plans to build an industrial park in the area? In particular, consider ways that address traffic concerns, pollution, and housing issues.

3. How might special assessments discourage development in areas vulnerable to hazards? Identify a type of special assessment at work in your area.

4. If you were the emergency manager in a mid-sized municipality, what would be some of the advantages to having a council-manager type of local government for pushing a hazard mitigation agenda through the local policy-making process?

5. Explain ways that local governments manage the risk of human-induced hazards versus natural hazards.

You Try It

Hazard Maps and You

To determine how best to protect a community from disaster, it is necessary to first identify the local hazard risks. Hazard maps can dramatically illustrate where areas of development overlap with areas of hazards such as floods, landslides, earthquakes, and hurricanes. Using the internet or other resources, find hazard maps of your area, determine the distance between your home and the hazard(s), and assess your risk of experiencing a disaster event.

Power to the People

States empower local governments to control the use of land. How are the four regulatory powers of zoning ordinances, subdivision regulations, building codes, and flood damage prevention ordinances at work in your community?

Community Resiliency

What are some of the principles of resilience and sustainability that you would need to employ when crafting a hazard mitigation program for your local community? Which activities are in place in the community's capability for developing mitigation policies?

REFERENCES

1. United Nations World Commission on Environment and Development. 1987. *Our Common Future* (p. 43). Oxford, United Kingdom: Oxford University Press.
2. Kusler, J.A. 2004. *No Adverse Impact: Floodplain Management and the Courts*. Madison, WI: Association of State Floodplain Managers.
3. Woodruff, S.C. et al. 2013. *Adapting to Climate Change: A Handbook for Local Governments in North Carolina*. Chapel Hill, NC: Coastal Hazards Center at the University of North Carolina at Chapel Hill. Available online at: coastalhazardscenter.org/adapt.
4. Olshansky, R.B. and J.D. Kartez. 1998. Managing Land Use to Build Resilience. In. *Cooperating With Nature: Confronting Natural Hazards with Land Use Planning for Sustainable Communities*. Edited by Raymond J. Burby. Washington, DC: Joseph Henry Press.
5. FEMA. 2013. *Local Mitigation Planning Handbook*. Publication 302-094-1. FEMA.
6. Hirokawa, K.H. and J.D. Rosenbloom. *Land Use Planning in a Climate Change Context*. Research Paper Legal Studies Research Paper Series, Research Paper No. 12-33. Drake University.
7. *Code of Federal Regulations*. Title 44, Part 201.2.

9

Community Resilience and the Private Sector

What You'll Learn

- The role of private landownership in creating resilient communities
- Economic impacts of disasters on a community
- Mitigation actions a business can use to protect assets, inventories, and human resources
- The role of developers and investors in reducing risk
- Strategies for businesses and communities to work together to mitigate the impact of hazards

Goals and Outcomes

- Consider the connection between private sector development decisions and local vulnerability
- Understand the process of business continuity planning to mitigate hazard impacts
- Apply the principles of a risk assessment to make informed investment decisions
- Distinguish among types of insurance that are available to businesses for hazard perils
- Learn how to protect a company's assets, employees, and business viability in the face of hazards
- Evaluate incentives for businesses to enhance community resilience

INTRODUCTION

A resilient economy is an essential element of a resilient community. Economic resilience calls for wise use of privately owned real estate, as well as for a strong business sector that can withstand the impacts of natural hazards and climate change. Communities that have built resilience into the local economy before a disaster strikes are more likely to experience fewer disruptions in productivity and are better able to maintain a stable tax base, a vibrant marketplace, and a higher quality of life for community members. This chapter discusses the decision-making process of private landowners and real estate investors, and how choices they make regarding the location and use of property can impact community vulnerability. The chapter also describes how public sector actions can influence decisions made by the private sector. The chapter then explores ways that local businesses, particularly small businesses, can protect their assets, their employees, and their businesses' viability in the face of natural hazards and climate change. The chapter concludes by discussing ways in which the

DOI: 10.4324/9781003123897-9

private sector can participate in community mitigation programs and lead efforts to promote hazard resilience and adaptation to climate change.

9.1 RESILIENT ECONOMIES, RESILIENT COMMUNITIES

At the heart of a hazard-resilient community is a resilient economy. Residents need a reliable source of decent jobs and affordable housing options. Businesses need an accommodating venue for commerce and trade and a steady workforce. The local government needs a stable source of revenue in order to build and maintain infrastructure and provide services and amenities to community members. All of these elements of a vibrant economy depend on a steady flow of capital investment from both the public and private sectors. At no time are these issues more critical than during the period of recovery and reconstruction following a disaster. After a hazard event, it is essential for the recovery of the community that the economy remains stable or quickly returns to stability after a short period of readjustment. Communities that have built resiliency into the local economy *before* a disaster strikes will be in a much better position to return to stability after a hazard event. Resilient communities are able to maintain or quickly restore economic vitality following a disaster.

9.1.1 Private Landownership

A local community's overall resilience depends upon the ability of its economy to withstand the impacts of a wide range of hazards and the speed with which the economy can bounce back when a disaster occurs. This is accomplished by placing people and property in hazard-safe locations and integrating mitigation building techniques into the construction process, such as installing wind-resistant roofing and elevating flood-prone structures. The local government plays a major role in determining what types of structures are permitted within its jurisdiction and where they are allowed to be built; however, the private sector is the main driving force behind a community's patterns of land use. Choices that property owners make about how to use their land and protect their property have a profound effect on community's vulnerability.

A major controlling factor in a community's economic staying power lies in the patterns of land use that predominate in the area. Because the built environment is such a critical determinant of vulnerability, the first section of this chapter deals with the issue of landownership, particularly private landownership in hazardous areas.

9.1.2 Community Resilience Depends on Business Resilience

Creating a disaster-resilient community depends not only on locational and structural decisions made by private property owners but also decisions regarding the types of economic activity that are most appropriate for the area in terms of hazard exposure. A truly sustainable local economy is diversified and less easily disrupted by internal or external events, including natural disasters. For instance, a coastal town that depends solely on tourism as its economic mainstay is more likely to suffer dire long-term consequences after a major hurricane than a community with a more diversified economy. Economies that include a mix of industries are much more stable. Making the private sector more resistant to disasters through mitigation and diversification provides fiscal assurance to the local government by making the local tax base more secure, residents safer, and businesses more competitive.[1]

Although many factors play into whether the local economy will survive following a disaster, much of the economic resilience of a community depends on the individual businesses and industries located there, how well they are able to prevent large-scale damages, and how quickly they are able to resume operations. A resilient economy is one where productivity is only minimally disrupted by a hazard event. Disasters can have the effect of accelerating economic trends that were present in the community before the disaster hit. For example, if a downtown is experiencing a slow decline, a disaster might fast-forward the negative trend, compounding the difficulties of sanitation, public safety, transportation, and general deterioration.[2] On the other hand, a disaster can also provide an opportunity for a community to make positive changes and focus new energy on revitalizing areas of blight or neglect.

BUSINESSES EMBRACE SUSTAINABLE REDEVELOPMENT IN GREENSBURG, KANSAS

When an EF 5 tornado swept through the small town of Greensburg, Kansas on May 4, 2007, the damage was so extensive that many residents wondered if the community would ever rebuild. About 95% of the structures in the town of 1,600 residents were destroyed, and the few remaining structures were considerably damaged. In the weeks and months that followed, residents held meetings beneath FEMA tents to discuss the recovery effort. Though various and sometimes conflicting visions were debated, the community gradually resolved to rebuild a sustainable town, constructing energy-efficient buildings and utilizing 100% renewable energy.[3]

The business community played a vital role in embracing sustainability and even found opportunities to capitalize on sustainable redevelopment as a way to strengthen the local economy. The Bucklin Tractor and Implement (BTI), the local John Deere supplier, not only constructed a new LEED-platinum dealership powered by a wind turbine but eventually opened a new company—BTI Wind Energy—which supplies small turbines for farms and small businesses.[4]

Business Protection through Mitigation and Preparedness

In addition to an exploration of the role played by private landowners in hazardous land management, this chapter also gives a broad overview of how hazards can impact individual businesses, as well as a brief introduction to some of the steps that business and industry can take to protect their inventory, income stream, employees, and other assets to become more resilient. This is important not only for the individual businesses that choose to take the mitigation and preparedness steps necessary to protect their livelihoods but also for the local economy as a whole. A healthy, viable economy is highly dependent upon healthy, viable businesses that are resilient to the impacts of hazards and that work to lessen, rather than contribute to, a community's overall level of vulnerability.

SELF-CHECK

- Describe the foundations of a resilient economy.
- Explain why a resilient economy is integral to community resilience.
- Discuss how a local economy could become more sustainable after recovering from a disaster.

9.2 PRIVATE LANDOWNERSHIP IN THE UNITED STATES

Private landowners have rights and privileges with regard to their property, such as the right to cut the timber; divert the surface water; graze livestock; mine ore, coal, and mineral deposits; and otherwise extract the land's natural resources. The rights and privileges of property ownership also include the right to develop and build upon the land as well as to sell it and profit from the sale. These rights of ownership are not absolute. Owners of private property also have duties and responsibilities. Owners must conform to all applicable public laws, regulations, and ordinances, even when such regulations interfere with the landowner's wishes as to the use of the property. Nevertheless, within the boundaries established by federal, state, and local laws, there is wide latitude for putting one's property to uses that meet investment-backed expectation. Sometimes, however, these uses are not in the best interests of the community at large.

9.2.1 Location, Location, Location

It is often quipped that the three most important factors of determining the value of real estate are "location, location, location." This is equally true for determining a property's vulnerability to many kinds of natural hazards. The experience of past hazard events in this country has made it clear that patterns of land use are one of the primary determinants of a community's level of vulnerability to natural hazards. When growth and development take place in the floodplain, along the coastline, in areas of seismic risk, near the urban-wildland interface, and other hazardous areas, there is a greater likelihood that property will be damaged and that death and injury may occur as the result of a flood, hurricane, wildfire, or earthquake. When we consider this probability, it is important to realize that the majority of land in the United States is held by private landholders and investors. This includes land owned by individual homeowners, small businesses, and large corporations. In addition to the raw and developed land in private ownership, nearly 85% of the nation's infrastructure is also controlled by the private sector.[5]

9.2.2 The Role of Developers and Investors

One of the most important rights of landownership is the right to put the land to economically beneficial use, which often includes development. While many owners use their property to locate a business, build their primary residence, or construct a vacation home for their own families, a great deal of real estate is purchased, held, built upon, leased, and sold as a money-making venture. This is particularly true in the coastal zone, which is an especially hazardous area, subject to high rates of erosion, hurricanes and storms, inlet migration, and other coastal hazards. As such, we will use the coastal zone as an example during the following discussion about the ways that many property investment decisions are made. However, the same considerations apply in the development decisions of other types of hazardous lands as well, such as floodplains, wildfire areas, and seismic risk zones.

To understand how coastal lands are developed, and the degree to which natural hazards may or may not be considered during the development process, we must understand the interests of developers and investors. Generally speaking, the private sector operates with regard to expected profits. Development occurs where and when the investor will likely receive an acceptable return on the investment. Some development projects are relatively small in scale—a single building, for instance—while other developments involve hundreds of units complete with supporting facilities and infrastructure. Whatever the scale of the particular project, commercial developers analyze markets and trends and build where they expect there is sufficient demand for their product with a minimum risk.

Factors in Development Decisions

There are a few common factors that investors take into consideration before making a major investment decision:

- **Demand:** In economics, demand is the desire for a commodity together with the ability to pay for it. Scarcity increases the desire for a particular product, such as beachfront property in highly developed coastal areas. When demand is high, the private sector will try to meet that demand.

- **Risk:** As a general rule, investors are risk averse. The degree of risk that is acceptable depends upon the likelihood and magnitude of the potential profit. Developers consider many aspects of the region, community, and site, as well as the general market and economy, when deciding what and where to build. Natural hazards are sometimes, but not always, one of the factors considered along with other characteristics of a site when deciding upon the feasibility of a particular project.

- **Regulation:** The regulatory requirements that apply in a particular location play a major role in investment decision-making. Some of the land use regulations imposed by state and local governments dictate the height, square footage, setback distances, and occupational capacity of buildings constructed in the coastal zone. Zoning and subdivision ordinances, building codes, fire regulations, environmental protection laws, and other types of regulatory mandates can increase the cost of construction many times over. These constraints are factored into the profitability of an investment project.

- **Infrastructure:** The availability of infrastructure also plays a major role in development decisions, including where to build and at what density. Development cannot take place without adequate water, sewer, roads, and public services to support it. All but the very largest development companies are dependent to some degree upon public infrastructure in order to build. Much infrastructure is provided by local governments, often subsidized by state and federal funds. The extension of infrastructure into hazardous areas can encourage inappropriate development. Likewise, the refusal to extend municipal services and infrastructure to hazardous lands may help prevent or delay intense development.

- **Time value of money:** Investors also consider the time value of money when deciding on the viability of a proposed project. Returns on investment that can be realized quickly maximize the profitability of a development project. If a structure is in imminent danger of damage or collapse from storms, rapid erosion, or other coastal hazards before rents or sales can recoup the cost of construction, developers may determine that potential gains are not worth the risk. Part of this calculation depends on what types of mitigation techniques are available to safeguard the property from the impacts of future hazards. The relative ease or difficulty in obtaining government permits to build can also influence investment decisions. Delays in the permitting process add substantially to development costs.

Hazards Awareness in Investment Decision-Making

As these development decision factors indicate, investors always consider the level of risk involved in a proposed project or venture. In order to incorporate natural hazards into this calculation of risk, investors must first be aware of the hazards that could potentially impact their properties. Furthermore, the risk must be articulated in ways the investors can understand and appreciate—how will it affect the bottom line? A thorough hazard identification and risk assessment that includes the probability of various hazard events, their expected magnitude and intensity, as well as the severity of potential impacts should be carried out for all projects proposed in vulnerable locations. In the case of projects with heavy up-front capital expenditures (such as a multistory high-rise structure located directly on the beach-front), studies of hazard risk factors are essential.

Despite the obvious need for a complete understanding of risk, investors and developers do not always perform a thorough assessment of potential hazards. Some investors, especially those from out of state who are not familiar with the geography and climate of the local environment, may be unaware of the degree of risk posed by natural hazards. Other investors may rely too heavily on state and local government hazard assessments, which may not be at a scale that is directly relevant to the building site in question. Developers may also rely on the agency in charge of issuing building permits to gauge whether a site is safe for property investment. If a permit is issued, the reasoning goes, the area must be free of hazards. Unfortunately, this assumption is not always correct. There remains a high degree of personal and corporate responsibility for thoroughly investigating all of the risks associated with the use of private property.

RESPONDING TO COASTAL CHANGE: GOING WITH THE FLOW

A fundamental challenge with living (and investing) in the coastal zone is that all of our static, immobile construction (buildings, roads, bridges, and utility supply lines) is placed in a dynamic zone. The shoreline, inlets, dune fields, overwash terraces, marshes, and maritime forests shift over time in response to ongoing changes in the coastal environment. Sometimes, these changes happen very slowly over decades or centuries, and other times, they happen very quickly. Changes in the levels of the sea and the land, changes in storm frequency and wave regime, change in the patterns of currents, change in the offshore topography, and change in sand supply—change is the rule, especially for barrier islands. Awareness of these dynamic factors is essential to living within this ever-changing environment.[6] The price for not paying attention to the natural processes along the coast is property damage, costly rebuilding, loss of investment, and risk to human life.

Incorporating Hazard Mitigation into Investment Decisions

The understanding of hazard risk must be further translated in terms of trade-offs—how should capital resources be allocated to protect the investment? The more hazards can be linked to the financial viability of a project, the more weight they will be given in the developer's decision process. In some cases, site-specific risks can be mitigated if adequate funds are expended.[7] For example, structures located along the oceanfront can be elevated above the expected flood height to reduce the risk of flooding and damage from storm surge. However, modifying a structure of a site to correct hazardous conditions often adds considerably to the engineering and construction costs of the project. A developer will avoid costs considered unnecessary in order to increase the financial attractiveness of a project. In egregious cases, shortcuts to cut costs can lead to unsafe buildings that are unable to withstand the impacts of known hazards.

9.2.3 Public Sector Actions Influence Private Sector Decisions

Although private property owners have many choices and opportunities to realize profit and make financial gains from investment property in the coastal zone and other hazardous locations, the private sector is not granted free reign to exercise its property rights. While developers may avoid unnecessary costs when making financial projections for a development project, regulations and policies set by all levels of government can partially determine the relative weight that hazard exposure plays in those development decisions. For example, many coastal states have setback regulations that determine how far back from the shoreline a structure must be built. Larger structures are usually required to be built further back from the oceanfront than smaller, one-family units. A developer/investor must have enough space on the lot to build the size structure that will realize a profit. Some states also prohibit shoreline hardening structures like groins and bulkheads that damage fragile coastal ecosystems and transfer erosion risks to other locations along the shore. Building codes and construction regulations also play into the determination of profitability. Stringent building standards typically increase the cost of construction but provide added security to the building against hazard impacts.

These types of trade-offs can result in wiser investment decisions where a developer may still realize a profit, but projects that are unsustainable or considered inappropriate will not receive the regulatory green light. While the imposition of regulatory requirements does not supersede the requirement of personal responsibility in land use decision-making, actions by the public sector can help prevent some of the more foolish (or dangerous) property investment choices.

Local communities benefit immensely from the value that is added to the tax base when private property is put to its best use. At the same time, it is in the best interest of both the public and the private sectors that coastal lands, as well as other lands of intense natural beauty, environmental significance, and culture and societal value, are used in a way that is sustainable over the long term.

SELF-CHECK

- Describe three factors considered during development investment decisions.
- List two public sector actions that can influence private sector building and investment decisions.
- Explain how hazard awareness can result in sound investment decisions.

9.3 ECONOMIC RESILIENCY: PROTECTING BUSINESS FROM HAZARDS

So far in this chapter, we have been discussing the private sector in terms of landownership and investment in privately held real estate. But the vulnerability of a community depends upon more than the decisions that landowners make regarding the use of their property. We know when a disaster strikes that individual families are affected, property is damaged, roads are blocked, power outages occur, and local government services such as drinking water and sewer treatment are disrupted. But one of the longest lasting and most pervasive effects of a hazard event often involves the local economy. The roots of a community's economic troubles can be traced to the way hazards impact local businesses. The economic fallout resulting from the COVID-19 pandemic is a clear indication of the vulnerability of communities when local businesses and the jobs and services they provide are upended by a disaster.

9.3.1 Economic Impacts of Natural Hazards

Staggering economic losses can be suffered following natural hazards of all types. Consider the following financial losses to businesses due to some of the nation's largest hurricanes over the last few decades. For example, Hurricane Andrew, which devastated much of southern Florida in 1993, seriously affected 8,000 businesses and more than 100,000 jobs in Dade County alone. The area's $500 million-per-year tourist industry was disrupted for several years; agriculture experienced $1 billion in damages with a permanent income loss of $250 million, and storm-affected areas suffered daily lost outputs of $22 million. Flooding from Hurricane Dennis and Floyd in eastern North Carolina in 1999 affected about 60,000 businesses, resulting in more than $955 million in business losses. The average repair cost for physical damage was about $40,000 per business, with an average revenue loss of nearly $80,000.[8] As a result of Hurricane Katrina in 2005, the majority of businesses in the affected Gulf Coast region have suffered a significant decline in net income, while others have simply ceased to exist. Property damage, destroyed assets, lost revenues, and other financial losses are estimated in the billions of dollars. The economic repercussions of Hurricanes Katrina, Wilma, and Rita were felt in the Gulf region and throughout the country for years. Hurricane Sandy caused more than $250,000 in damages to more than 19,000 small businesses in New Jersey alone, and approximately $950 million in losses to travel and tourism that reduced employment by over 11,000 workers.[9] Economic impacts of disasters can often persist long after buildings and infrastructure are repaired, and some industries never fully recover to their pre-disaster productivity. These figures demonstrate business losses due to hurricanes. Many other types of hazards have also caused economic devastation, including wildfire, tornadoes, riverine flooding, and earthquakes.

A Temporary Boost

Ironically, in some cases, a major disaster can actually boost a local economy, at least in the short term. As disaster assistance funding and insurance payments pour into the community for reconstruction and recovery, a building boom often results. Construction jobs, and the services needed to support the construction activity, can often bring in more income to a community than previously existed. New York state government estimated that construction costs to repair and replace buildings and infrastructure damaged by Hurricane Sandy would amount to approximately $42 billion. This influx in new spending was expected to generate 352,000 new jobs, including about 299,000 jobs in the relatively high-wage construction industry.[9] However, many of these jobs are temporary and are often filled by workers from outside the affected area. Some communities prioritize licensing for contractors from the local area to help inject additional money into the local economy.

LOCAL HIRING IN MISSISSIPPI TO SPUR ECONOMIC RECOVERY

In the aftermath of Hurricane Katrina and the BP Oil Spill, community leaders in coastal Mississippi were concerned that federal recovery funds were not being used to hire local residents. In response, the Mississippi Jobs First bill was signed into law in 2012, which prioritizes hiring local residents for recovery jobs in Mississippi.[10] Minor Sinclair of Oxfam America explained that the bill is an "innovative approach that looks beyond the damaged buildings in a disaster to focus on the heart of the problem...we can replace the things that we lose but we need to revitalize a whole economy and the life of a community. This bill puts people back to work, which is vital to putting life back into the area."[11] Under the new law, contractors for public works projects that receive federal disaster funds are required to describe the types of jobs available, skills required, and wages paid, and how the contractor will attempt to recruit disadvantaged, low-wage, and unemployed applicants. The Mississippi Department of Employment Security can then use the information provided by the contractor to identify and train local workers to meet these needs.

Businesses associated with preparedness and recovery activities, such as building materials suppliers, roofers, and appliance and furniture store, are also likely to have increased levels of business in the recovery period following a disaster. Some of these industries may experience a significant rise in profits. Large building supply outlets, such as The Home Depot, routinely warehouse plywood, generators, and other materials needed for disaster response and recovery. They can send supplies quickly to a targeted region, extend store hours, and otherwise respond to the increased demand, often experiencing record sales in both retail and wholesale markets.[12]

Similarly, FedEx has developed a reputation for using its tremendous transportation and logistics network to aid in disaster preparedness and response. Each year, FedEx sets aside space for more than 4 million pounds of disaster-related charitable shipping and has formed innovative partnerships with FEMA, the American Red Cross, Salvation Army, and other public and nonprofit organizations. However, in recent years, FedEx and other private sector companies, large and small, are beginning to understand that the vitality of their business depends on the resilience of communities. Businesses are therefore making greater efforts to invest in preparedness, community resilience, and long-term recovery to ensure that communities are able to get back on their feet quickly following a disaster.

As the physical reconstruction phase winds down, economic activity can flatten out to a more normal pace, and the structure of the local economy begins to regain its pre-disaster balance. It is at this juncture that local communities and the businesses that operate in them have an opportunity to rebuild an economic structure that is less vulnerable to future disruptions from natural disasters.[1] Much of this work involves strengthening the businesses that make up the community's economic sector.

9.3.2 Keeping Small Businesses Afloat

Communities depend upon their business and industries for their very existence. The local business sector provides jobs and tax revenue and stimulates commerce, trade, and other economic activity. Aside from the temporary boost that occurs from selected business operations during the recovery phase of a disaster, the ripple effect of a disaster can permeate all other sectors of community life. Destroyed businesses have multiplier effects on community difficulties, as residents lose jobs, property values decline, and tax receipts diminish.[12] When a business protects itself from natural disasters, it is also protecting one of its community's most valuable assets.

Small Business is Big Business

Of all employers in the United States, more than 99% are small businesses, which employ nearly half of the U.S. workforce.[13] All businesses and industries are subject to hazards, but small ones (generally defined as those employing less than 50 people) are especially susceptible, with some 30% not surviving when stricken by a natural disaster.[12] The percentage of small business failures can be even higher in some disasters. For instance, it is estimated that about 50% of the smaller or newer businesses in North Carolina did not recover following Hurricane Floyd, a storm that caused massive flooding throughout the eastern third of the state. Of the larger, more well-established businesses in the state, approximately four out of six recovered. In general, many small local businesses are lost after a major event.

In addition to direct impacts that can damage property and destroy company assets and inventories, small businesses typically suffer a host of burdens associated with their relative size and place in the local economy when a disaster strikes. For example, small businesses typically rely on a local customer base, much of which can be eroded when residents and surrounding businesses can no longer patronize the company.[13] Small businesses also suffer disproportionately from a shortage of employees when community residents are displaced, in addition to experiencing cash flow problems, lack of capital, and a loss of suppliers.

Many small companies fail primarily because of a lack of knowledge and resources to develop property and business protection plans. Many small business owners do not fully understand how the local economy is structured nor do they comprehend the ways in which the economy may change because of a hazard event. Small companies may exhaust personal and business sources of capital in an attempt to revive and may fail to adjust their business plans to meet the changing post-disaster economy.[2] All these factors point to the need for businesses to prepare a business protection plan well in advance of a hazard event.

SELF-CHECK

- List several economic impacts of disasters on businesses.
- Describe how some communities experience a temporary economic boost following a disaster.
- Explain why small businesses take a harder hit from disasters than large corporations.

9.4 BUSINESS RISK ASSESSMENT AND IMPACT ANALYSIS

Businesses that are aware of the hazards that face them and take action before disaster strikes can often prevent many of the losses and damages associated with natural and human-made hazards. There are many different approaches to business protection planning, but all preventative measures begin with an assessment of risk and an analysis of the potential impacts of hazards on business viability.

9.4.1 Types of Business Protection Plans

Various terms are used to describe the types of planning activities that many companies carry out in order to protect business. **Contingency planning**, for example, is the process of developing advanced arrangements and procedures that enable an organization to respond to a disaster so that critical business functions resume within a defined time frame, the amount of loss is minimized, and the stricken facilities are repaired or replaced as soon as possible. **Business continuity planning** is another commonly used term to describe this process, as is **Continuity of Operations Planning**. These plans are usually directed toward maintaining the business's viability when one or more functions are impaired or disrupted. Many of these plans focus on data and digital records protection, retrieval, and restoration.

Some businesses have very specific plans for dealing with situations particular to that industry or activity, such as a **Spill Prevention Control and Countermeasures (SPCC)** plan, or similar procedures for handling hazardous waste or dangerous substances. Many businesses maintain a **safety and health plan** designed for workplace safety and employee health. Many of these planning activities are undertaken in response to regulations issued by state and federal agencies, including the Occupational Safety and Health Administration (OSHA) and the Environmental Protection Agency (EPA).

Fewer businesses, however, have a comprehensive emergency plan that covers all the types of hazards, including natural hazards and human-made hazards, and all the components of the business, including physical assets as well as operations. Many of the various stand-alone plans that businesses may have in place can be consolidated into a comprehensive emergency management program or process, but it is essential that mitigation and preparedness be a part of that system. If a business already has an emergency plan, mitigation for natural and human-made hazards can often be incorporated into the existing plan.

A comprehensive disaster preparedness and mitigation plan for a business involves three main elements:

1. **Property protection**: Safeguarding physical facilities and their contents (e.g., equipment, inventories, raw materials, digital files) from known hazards
2. **Contingency planning**: Anticipating all the emergencies that could occur and creating plans accordingly to minimize disruptions
3. **Insurance**: Determining adequate coverage and purchasing the right kinds of insurance to help defray immediate and long-term costs if a disaster does occur

To become more disaster resilient, a business must first identify and understand what hazards it faces and what is at risk from those hazards. A business risk assessment helps answer these questions.

9.4.2 Business Risk Assessment

Thousands of communities throughout the nation experience social and economic disruption from natural and human-made hazards every year. Every year thousands of businesses also experience emergencies internal to their operations, such as a frozen pipe that bursts over a long holiday weekend and floods the facility. Hazardous materials and dangerous chemicals can be unintentionally released, causing plant closures and downtime while containment and decontamination measures are carried out. For example, in 2013, an explosion in a fertilizer plant in West, Texas, killed 15 people and wounded another 226, in a tragic and preventable event in a county that did not have an emergency response plan or a fire code. These scenarios clearly demonstrate the vulnerability of businesses located in every region to all sorts of hazards. For these reasons, a business mitigation and preparedness program begins with a thorough risk assessment that factors in the types of hazards that might occur, the vulnerability of the business to those hazards, and the losses that might result if the hazard event does happen.

Elements of a Business Risk Assessment

Central to preparing a business for the potential consequences of natural and technological hazards is an understanding of risk. Chapter 10 covers the steps involved in a risk assessment in greater detail, but the process is outlined here as it pertains to businesses. There are three basic levels of hazard assessment that businesses should carry out for a complete understanding of their risks:

1. **Hazard identification** defines the magnitudes (intensities) and associated probabilities (likelihood) of hazards that may pose threats to the business and community.
2. **Vulnerability assessment** characterizes the exposed populations and property, and the extent of injury and damage that may result from a hazard event of a given intensity in a given area.
3. **Business impact analysis** considers issues associated with an entire range of hazard intensities and probabilities, from the fairly common, low-intensity event (e.g., minor flooding from groundwater seepage) to the relatively rare, catastrophic event (e.g., a magnitude 6.8 earthquake). Risk analysis captures the full range of potential casualty and damage experiences and provides the basis for a business impact analysis and strategy to minimize losses.[14]

9.4.3 Hazard Identification

The first step in a business risk assessment is to identify and list the full range of potential hazards that can impact the company. For business planning purposes, a hazard is any unplanned event that can cause death or significant injuries to employees, customers, or the public; or that can shut down a business, disrupt operations, cause physical or environmental damage; or can threaten the company's financial standing or public image.[15] These include emergencies that can occur within a facility, emergencies that can occur in the community, and emergencies that occur with a business supply chain. Hazards include the full range of natural hazards that face the community where the business is located, including earthquakes, hurricanes, drought, and other natural events. In addition to the natural hazards that can potentially affect a business are numerous types of technological events, including nuclear facility accidents, terrorism, hazardous material incidents, and cyber-risks. Each of these types of events must be addressed within the context of the impact it has on the company and the community. What might constitute a nuisance to a large industrial facility could be a disaster to a small business.[15]

Gathering Hazard Information

There are numerous ways a business can gather information about the hazards that are present in the community and that may affect its facility. Some factors to consider include the following:

- **Historical:** What types of emergencies have occurred in the community, at this facility, and at other facilities in the area?
- **Geographic:** What can happen as a result of the facility's location? Factors to consider include proximity to floodplains, coastal areas, seismic faults, forested areas, dams, and so forth. Proximity to potential human-made hazards, such as facilities that produce, store, use, or transport hazardous materials, or proximity to major transportation routes and airports is also pertinent.
- **Technological:** What could result from a process or system failure? Possibilities include fire, explosion, hazardous materials incidents, safety system failures, telecommunications failures, power failures, or heating/cooling system failures.
- **Human error:** What emergencies can be caused by employee error? Are employees trained to work safely? Do they know what to do in an emergency? Human error is the single largest cause of workplace emergencies and can result from poor training, poor maintenance, carelessness, or fatigue.

There is a wide variety of sources businesses can rely on for information about hazards, including local and state emergency offices; federal, state, and local regulatory agencies; local planning, zoning, building, and public works departments; fire, police, and emergency medical services; electric and telecommunications utilities; local emergency planning committees (LEPCs); the American Red Cross; National Weather Service; and neighboring businesses. If the community where the business is located has a current local hazard mitigation plan in place, the company can also refer to that plan during its hazard identification, as well as to the state hazard mitigation plan.

9.4.4 Vulnerability Assessment

Armed with information about the natural and technological hazards that could conceivably impact the business, a company is in a position to assess its vulnerability to these hazards. During the vulnerability assessment, a business determines the probability and potential impact of each hazard. In other words, a prediction is made about what will happen to the business if any of the hazards identified were to actually occur. The location of the business relative to the probability of natural hazard events is one of the primary determinants of vulnerability (e.g., businesses located on the coast are more vulnerable to hurricanes and storm surge). Business vulnerability is also a function of the community's overall vulnerability, including the infrastructure and local services that the business depends upon for daily operations.

Vulnerability may change as the business grows (or shrinks), new buildings are constructed, more inventory and customers are acquired, and greater value is accumulated. For this reason, it is important to assess future vulnerability to hazards based on likely trends and changes, as well as present vulnerability based on current conditions.

A business can gauge its vulnerability using a ranking system such as low, moderate, or high for each hazard based on frequency, as determined by historical records and expected future trends, the relative strength of typical hazard events, and the direct and indirect impacts that can be expected from each type of hazard.

- **Direct impacts** include physical damage to structures, such as buildings and other facilities. Direct impacts also include losses to inventories, equipment, and other physical assets.
- **Indirect impacts** result from the closure of roads or obstruction of transportation networks; loss of utilities, such as water, sewage, electric power; and disruption of telecommunications.

9.4.5 Business Impact Analysis

Once a business has a general idea of its vulnerability to certain identified hazards based on location, probabilities, and intensities, the analysis must turn toward the specific impacts these hazards will have on that particular business. This is done by conducting a **business impact analysis**, which involves calculating the types of damages and losses that can be expected during any one of the identified hazard events and relating them to the characteristics of the business itself. This in turn will determine the types of actions that must be taken to reduce vulnerability.

The conditions that make a business operate smoothly and profitably vary from company to company. For example, the protection of inventory and business records may be most critical to a retailer or a business in the service sector (e.g., finance, insurance, real estate, restaurant, hotel). A small manufacturing plant may have equipment or machinery that is essential for the success of the business. For farmers, it may be the protection of crops that have been harvested and stored, livestock and poultry, or critical farm equipment. The purpose of a business impact analysis is to identify the parts of the business that need to be up and running as soon as possible in the aftermath of a disaster as well as those that the business must keep intact to remain viable.

The factors that determine the impact a hazard will have on a business include the following:

- **Services or products provided**: Whether the product or service can be deferred is an important consideration in assessing the financial impact of a disaster on a business. For example, if a burger stand cannot sell hamburgers for one week because the kitchen is closed for repairs due to damage from an earthquake, the owner cannot make up for the lost income from the missed sales. The same applies to a bed and breakfast, where every day without a patron represents lost revenue. However, in the case of a store that sells appliances, the customer can defer his purchase if the store is closed, which does not necessarily result in lost income for the business (assuming the inventory has been adequately safeguarded).

- **Site dependence**: Whether a business is at a fixed site or whether business functions can be temporarily moved to a safer location has an important bearing on preparedness and risk reduction strategies. If the business is unable to relocate in the event of an emergency, it is more important to consider mitigation actions to protect or strengthen the building and its contents. A manufacturing plant or a restaurant, for example, cannot easily transfer operations to another locale, while an investment firm or travel agency may be more flexible and can temporarily work out of alternative office space.

- **Dependence on information technology**: In the case of customer service and similar industries, business continuity is very dependent on the functionality of information technology and the protection of critical data and files. These businesses will focus on securing continual access to their vital records in order to minimize disruption from hazards.[14]

Operational problems due to disasters are not always connected to property damage or impacts on the business itself. External impacts include disruptions to the flow of supplies and in the ability to ship goods or deliver services to customers and clients. Therefore, the business impact assessment will also consider losses that can occur upstream from the business as well as those downstream. This is particularly true during the aftermath of large-scale disasters that have a regional impact involving multiple communities.

Upstream and Downstream Losses

Even if a business escapes a disaster unharmed and its employees are not directly impacted, there is still a risk that the business will suffer significant losses. When some local businesses fail, there is a chain reaction because of the negative impact on the local economy and the interrelationships among various members of the economic sector. These can be broken down into two types of losses: upstream and downstream. Upstream losses are those the business will suffer when one or more of its suppliers are affected by the disaster and cannot deliver the goods or services the business needs. Many businesses depend on regular, sometimes daily deliveries, such as produce to a restaurant or machine parts to a manufacturer. If the supplier's operation is damaged by the disaster and it cannot keep up its pre-disaster schedule, this upstream loss will affect other companies, even those that are undamaged. Downstream losses occur when a key customer and/or the lives of residents in the community are affected by the disaster. For example, if residents in the area are cleaning up debris and repairing their homes after a major flood, a local theater may experience a dramatic loss of customers and will not be in a position to accept deliveries from upstream suppliers.[16]

The resilience of the regional transportation system is also an important factor when projecting potential up- and downstream losses. If goods are shipped to and from a business by surface transport or air, damage to local or regional road systems, rail lines, and airports can severely impact a business's ability to obtain needed supplies or deliver its product to market. For example, if an assembly plant relies on the delivery of parts by truck, but the highway between the supplier and the manufacturer is damaged by flood or earthquake, the plant and the supplier will both suffer losses.

SELF-CHECK

- What is a business protection plan?
- What are four factors to consider when gathering hazard information for a business?
- What are the elements of a business risk assessment?

9.5 PREPARING A PLAN TO MINIMIZE LOSSES

Upon completion of a thorough hazard risk assessment and business impact analysis, a business will be able to create a mitigation and preparedness plan to bolster resiliency. The plan will list mitigation strategies and actions that the business intends to carry out and incorporate into the company's larger business plan. There are three major components to an effective business protection plan: property protection, business continuity, and insurance.

9.5.1 Business Property Protection

A business strategy to protect company property from hazard losses covers the building(s) and other structures, the building interior, as well as exterior components and surroundings. The building's physical conditions and how well it can survive a natural or technological hazard can determine whether the company is able to keep the business open following an incident.[16] Though building owners typically have more control over their property than renters, business tenants have many of the same concerns, as the issues remain the same whether the occupants own the building or rent space in it.

An ideal time for structural improvements that make company property more hazard resistant is during a major addition or renovation. Replacement windows and doors, materials for a new roof, and other items can improve structural integrity and overall building safety and might also have other positive benefits, such as increased energy efficiency or ease of maintenance. Whether the company is planning to remodel or build an entirely new facility, the plans must conform to state and local building code requirements. These codes reflect the lessons experts have learned from past disasters and incorporate engineering and structural specifications to strengthen buildings against known hazard impacts. Older buildings may need to be inspected by a professional engineer to check whether they are up to code. If a business is located in a particularly hazardous area (along the oceanfront, for example), constructing or retrofitting a structure to exceed minimum code requirements can often provide additional protection. Although these added improvements may increase the cost of construction, it is often a wise investment that enables the company to reopen its doors to customers or clients quickly after a hazard event.

Examples of physical retrofitting measures that businesses may consider include the following:

- Upgrading facilities to withstand the shaking of an earthquake or high winds
- Elevating buildings above expected flood heights
- Constructing tornado safe rooms
- Installing fire-resistant roofing materials
- Installing storm shutters for all exterior windows and doors

Businesses located in special flood hazard areas may wish to consider floodproofing, a term that covers a variety of techniques that provide some protection to certain types of buildings. Although the National Flood Insurance Program (NFIP) does not allow new residential buildings to be floodproofed, nonresidential buildings, such as commercial space or manufacturing facilities, can be retrofitted or floodproofed. There are two approaches to floodproofing:

- **Dry floodproofing** involves strengthening walls to withstand hydrostatic and dynamic forces, including debris impacts. Openings, including doors, windows, and vents, are sealed or filled with special closures to block entry of floodwater. In some instances, walls can be coated with waterproofing compounds or plastic sheeting.

- **Wet floodproofing** intentionally allows floodwater to enter certain enclosed areas to reduce the damaging pressures that can collapse walls and foundations. Flooring and wall materials must be resistant to flood damage, and the contents of floodable areas should be removed when flood warnings are issued. The NFIP regulations typically only allow wet floodproofing measures for certain spaces within new buildings, such as minor storage or parking. However, such measures can be used to reduce damage to existing buildings.

There are also nonstructural mitigation measures for protecting business property from hazards, such as:

- Move valuable, including equipment, from lower floors to upper floors above flood level
- Elevate or relocate the main breaker, fuse box, heating, ventilation and air conditioning system, etc. above anticipated flood levels
- Install sewer backflow valves
- Anchor fuel tanks and gas-fired, hot water heaters
- Secure light fixtures and other items that could fall or shake loose in an earthquake
- Move heavy or breakable objects to low shelves
- Attach cabinets and files to low walls or bolt them together
- Install automatic sprinkler systems
- Install fire-resistant landscaping around the exterior of the business
- Insulate water piping to prevent frozen or burst pipes

These and similar strategies can help reduce the likelihood that a business will fail because of physical damage to the structure during an anticipated hazard event. Many property protection measures can serve double duty, enhancing safety for one or more hazards. Securing roof shingles, for example, helps protect a building from high winds due to hurricanes, as well as from tornadoes and thunderstorms.

9.5.2 Business Contingency Planning

Even the best-designed and well-maintained buildings can be damaged, forcing a business closure. Even if a building sustains no damage, a major hurricane, earthquake, flood, or other catastrophic events can close roads, cause power outages, or create other problems that force a business to shut down. This is why every business needs a continuity plan to get up and running as quickly as possible in case disaster strikes. Based on the business impact assessment performed earlier, each company will need to create a plan that specifically speaks to its particular risk and minimizes downtime.

Minimizing Upstream Business Disruptions

The ability of many businesses to resume operations following a disaster relies on the ability of suppliers to deliver what the business needs and make the delivery on time. To ensure that critical suppliers of services and materials will be available when needed and encourage the continuity of the supply chain, there are several things a business can do, such as:

- Diversify the pool of principal suppliers, making sure they are not all located in the same geographical areas.
- Request or require that all critical suppliers have a business continuity plan of their own.

- Encourage a mutual aid agreement between the main supplier and similar companies.
- Maintain a list of backup vendors that can provide the business with materials, supplies, and services in case the primary ones are disabled.

These and other measures can keep the business going, even when a widespread hazard cripples much of the community. By planning in advance, a business won't be left scrambling in the aftermath of a disaster in an attempt to resume operations with contacts that are unfamiliar.

Protecting Data and Vital Records

Certain records are essential to perform critical business functions. Without access to data and information, business operations can come to a standstill. Some business records are required for legal or contractual reasons, others are required by regulatory or oversight agencies. Certain vital records may also be necessary to support recovery efforts following a disaster and make insurance claims. A company's vital records might include the following:

- Employee data/payroll/financial records
- Strategic plans/research data
- Product lists and specifications
- Formulas/trade secrets
- Supplier contacts/inventory lists
- Customer/client/patient/student records
- Building plans/blueprints/engineering drawings
- Property lease/insurance records

Any number of hazards can cause data to become lost, corrupted, or damaged, and a crucial element of a business contingency plan must include provisions to protect data and vital records. The majority of businesses today are dependent on computers and computer networking systems. Online security is a critical consideration for these businesses, and maintaining connections during power failures and other disruptions caused by natural hazards must be addressed in the pre-disaster phase.

The most important records should be backed up on one of more forms of media (printed copies, electronic, removable storage devices, cloud-based servers, etc.). Some companies and universities contract for a "hot site" or "mirror site" at a host institution or facility in a different state where important backup information is stored. Contracting with a mobile information technology service is another option, but this assumes the downed business will have transportation access as well as a source of power. Procedures for protecting and accessing vital records may include the following:

- Label vital records
- Back up computer systems
- Make copies of records
- Increase security of computer facilities
- Arrange for evacuation of records to backup facilities
- Backup systems handled by service bureaus
- Arrange for backup power

The services of a data center and disaster recovery facilities can be helpful in securing vital records, as data is backed up on a regular basis and can be made available if normal business operations are interrupted.

9.5.3 Preparing a Business Relocation Plan

In areas of the country that experience repetitive floods and other disasters on a fairly regular basis, it is important to identify alternate sites for business relocation following a disaster. Moving to a safer location can save money, prevent lost revenues, and break the cycle of destruction and rebuilding that occurs when businesses are located in hazardous areas. The three main elements of a business relocation plan include the following: (1) land use planning and site selection; (2) building standards and design; and (3) temporary business location.[14]

Land Use Planning and Site Selection

In the long term, the most direct and cost-effective strategy to minimize or prevent damages and losses from natural hazards is to guide development away from hazard-prone areas when other development locations are available. Local governments, working with private businesses and organizations such as the local chamber of commerce, can use a combination of planning and regulatory tools, ordinances, and interagency cooperative agreements to reduce the number of people and value of property at risk from hazards. This involves planning for the construction of new businesses that might enter the community in the future, as well as selecting sites where current businesses may move before or after a hazard has caused severe damage.

In selecting a location for new businesses or business relocations, there are several factors to consider, including (1) access to customers, (2) access to suppliers, (3) access to employees, (4) cost to lease or purchase office/retail/manufacturing space, (5) access to key services electrical, water, telecommunications, and (6) the vulnerability of the property and building to natural and technological hazards, including flooding, landslides, earthquakes, fires, and hazardous materials spills.[14]

Temporary Business Locations

When business owners are displaced from their buildings as the result of a disaster, income is disrupted and the solvency of the business becomes a critical issue. An important section of a business relocation plan is the identification of viable alternative business locations that can accommodate—at least temporarily—the displaced business. Before a disaster strikes, businesses should select an alternative site from which to operate during recovery. Some businesses have established mutual aid agreements with similar businesses or made pre-arrangements to rent available space at another location if base operations are unusable or inaccessible. Some businesses may have other facilities or branch offices that can be used to resume operations.

Considerations to be made during the business recovery location plan include the following:

- Select a site that is not on the same electric power grid.
- Factor in the ability of vendors/suppliers or rental companies to quickly transport critical items such as computers, inventory, and equipment to the recovery location.
- Pre-arrange for an industrial cleanup or emergency repair service and/or a security service to protect damaged facilities.
- Review the lease of the primary location space to determine who is responsible for what in the case of damage from a natural disaster.
- Explore rental options to replace damaged equipment, machinery, vehicles, and other assets during the time they are being repaired or replaced.

9.5.4 Protecting Employees and Their Families

The traditional approach to business protection focuses on planning for continuity of operations, strengthening buildings and facilities against hazard impacts, and carrying out non-structural mitigation measures. Unfortunately, businesses often have overlooked the impacts of disasters on their employees, yet employees are the company's most important asset. "A business can be as secure as Fort Knox, but if employees cannot make it to work, the bottom line will be affected."[12] Businesses should always consider ways to help employees prepare themselves and their families for emergencies. This will increase their personal safety and help the facility get backup and running quickly and effectively. Those who are prepared at home will be better able to carry out their responsibilities at work.[15]

There are many tactics for making employees safer on the job as well as enhancing their ability to withstand a disaster in their own homes so they can return to work as soon as the facility is open for business. Types of activities in an employee assistance plan may include the following:

- Disseminate hazard information to all employees
- Allow employees time off to implement home protection measures
- Pre-arrange alternate forms of transportation for employees, such as a carpool or pickup service, including four-wheel drive, if necessary
- Provide or assist with emergency housing for displaced employees
- Address immediate needs of employees, including short-term financial aid
- Pre-arrange for child and elder care at the primary or alternate site
- Offer flexible work schedules/reduced hours
- Arrange for crisis counseling
- Provide information on property insurance for employee homes and belongings

Another important consideration involves employee compensation. Payroll continuity following a disaster is key to maintaining the loyalty of employees and supporting community members who may be struggling to get back on their feet. Examples of companywide policies that can help employees handle disaster-related problems at home and meet their personal financial obligations include direct deposit of paychecks for all employees, cash advances, overtime pay during disaster, and payment of one week's salary (or other amount) even if the business is not operational. Many companies choose to set up an Employee Assistance Program (EAP), which is typically a third-party organization that contracts with a business to provide a variety of support programs for employees. For example, some EAPs collect donations from employees or fundraisers that can then be used to support employees in times of need.

Businesses should also make it a priority to ensure the safety of all employees during a hazard event at company facilities. Many companies establish policies to convene all employees at least once a year to review emergency plans, practice evacuation drills, and provide CPR, first aid, and other emergency training. It is also essential that employees have direct access to emergency phone numbers, such as fire department, police department, ambulance service, and the local emergency management agency. Installing weather radios to listen for tornado, hurricane, ice, thunderstorm, and other severe weather warnings issued by the media and the National Weather Service can alert employees to impending events. Onsite sheltering measures to protect employees, including space for their families, during a hazard event can also create a safer and more secure workplace.

9.5.5 Business Protection through Insurance

Most companies discover that they are not properly insured only after they have suffered a loss. Lack of appropriate insurance can be financially devastating. On the other hand, the proper amount and kind of insurance can allow a business to resume operations, make up for lost revenues, repair damaged property, replace equipment and materials, and otherwise recover from a disaster. There are three main types of insurance protection for businesses: (1) property insurance for all structures, equipment, and vehicles; (2) business interruption insurance to cover lost income during downtime; and (3) extra expense insurance, which compensates the business for additional expenses that are incurred due to a disaster. Despite the availability and wisdom of purchasing insurance to cover base assets and operations of a business, a surprising number of small businesses fail to take this basic step to protect their investment.

Checking the Policy

Of the small businesses that do carry insurance, many are not fully aware of the details of their insurance policies. Businesses should always include a discussion with insurance advisors as part of a thorough hazard mitigation and preparedness effort. For instance, most policies do not cover flood or earthquake damage; these hazards may require separate policies for coverage. The insurance should be tailored to the individual business and take into consideration not only property damage but also the loss of revenue and extra expenses that occur when business is halted by a disaster.

Like many aspects of a viable business plan, the devil is in the detail when it comes to insurance. Issues that should be addressed in the pre-disaster stage include a wide range of topics addressing property valuation and an extent of coverage. Sample questions a business may wish to pose include the following:

- How will property be valued?
- What perils or causes of loss does the policy cover?
- What does the policy require the business to do in the event of a loss?
- To what extent is the business covered for loss due to interruption of power?
- Is coverage provided for both on- and off-premise power interruption?
- Is the business covered for lost income in the event of business interruption?
- Is there enough coverage?
- For how long is coverage provided?
- How long is the coverage for lost income if the business is closed by the order of a civil authority (for example, a mandatory evacuation order)?
- To what extent is the business covered for reduced income if customers do not come back once the business reopens?
- Does the policy cover the cost of required upgrades to meet current building codes if a structure is in need of repair following a disaster?
- Will mitigation and preparedness measures result in a decrease in premium rates?[16]

These and other questions can help a business specify the type of coverage it chooses to carry, as well as other options that may be available through additional insurance products.

Property Insurance

Typically, general property insurance policies exclude coverage for flood or earthquake damage. These hazards are usually covered through additional policies to supplement the fire insurance that many businesses routinely carry. If a business is located in the flood zone of a community that participates in the NFIP, the company may be able to purchase a federally backed flood insurance policy, though they are rarely required to purchase flood insurance like residential properties.

Commercial insurance policies through the NFIP are typically limited to $250,000 in coverage for the building and an additional $250,000 for the building contents. While this may seem like a lot of money, many commercial buildings and businesses far exceed this value, and NFIP policies may not sufficiently insure the business for potential losses. For this reason, businesses may choose to purchase private insurance that kicks in for losses above the NFIP limit.

Business Interruption Insurance

Business interruption insurance can help even when businesses sustain significant losses during a hazard event. Just a short duration without customers, suppliers, and other critical operations can create a huge gap in revenue and net income. Furthermore, businesses typically experience a lag in revenues even after reopening following a disaster. Customers may seek alternative sources to fill their needs and may not readily resume relations with previous service providers. Business interruption insurance can help fill some of these gaps until the company is up and running again.

Business interruption insurance compensates for income lost if the company must vacate the premises due to disaster-related damage. Business interruption insurance also covers the profits that would have been earned, based on financial records, had the disaster not occurred. The policy covers recurring operating expenses—such as utilities—even though business activities have come to a temporary halt. The price of the policy is generally related to the risk of a fire or other disaster damaging the premises.[14]

Extra Expense Insurance

As income shrinks following a disaster, expenses—both previous ongoing business expenses and new expenses due to the disaster—will rise. Extra expense insurance reimburses a company for expenditures made over and above the normal operating expenses to avoid a shutdown during recovery and reconstruction following a qualifying disaster. Extra expense insurance is generally calculated by estimating projected revenues and expenses, calculating anticipated income, and then determining the potential losses from a temporary closure.[16] Extra expense insurance will usually only be paid if the extra expenses help to decrease business interruption costs. In some instances, extra expense insurance alone may provide sufficient coverage, without the purchase of business interruption insurance.[14]

SELF-CHECK

- Describe upstream and downstream losses.
- List four business mitigation strategies to lessen the impact of natural hazards.
- Explain the purpose of property insurance, business interruption insurance, and extra expense insurance.

9.6 PRIVATE SECTOR PARTICIPATION IN COMMUNITY MITIGATION EFFORTS

Business continuity planning, property protection, and insurance can help a company safeguard its assets against hazard impacts, but these measures alone cannot guarantee the post-disaster viability of the business. Any pre-disaster planning must be carried out within the context of the larger community, or a business will find it very difficult to survive a temporary closure. It is in the best interests of businesses to engage in mitigation practices that not only provide a direct benefit to an individual company by minimizing potential downtime but also make the community as a whole more resilient to hazards. By looking beyond its own plant, factory, retail, or office space and broadening its mitigation efforts, private sector business owners can also secure a workforce that is able to return to their jobs; facilitate the reactivation of utilities, roadways, and government services; and help commerce resume quickly following a disaster.

Public-private partnerships are increasingly being developed to help address disaster preparedness and mitigation. A wide range of public-private partnership models is emerging around the country to channel business sector involvement in the adoption of local hazard mitigation and preparedness as well as climate change adaptation practices.[14] These partnerships are likely to lead to more viable solutions than would be developed by any one group working independently.[12]

STRENGTHENING PREPAREDNESS THROUGH PUBLIC-PRIVATE PARTNERSHIPS

The City of Newport News, Virginia, developed a public-private partnership in March 2012 to build relationships and improve coordination across multiple stakeholders to increase resiliency throughout the city. The City of Newport News houses several large companies, including Newport News Shipbuilding, Huntington Ingalls Industries, and Canon Virginia. To better connect these private sector partners to the emergency management structure, a Private Sector Liaison position was created within the Division of Emergency Management to involve private sector partners in trainings and exercises, improve communication and information sharing, and enhance situational awareness during disaster events. In addition to the Private Sector Liaison position, the staff at the Newport News Emergency Operations Center have opened the doors to key private sector partners during both day-to-day and incident operations to improve understanding throughout the community of public sector emergency plans, procedures, contacts, and resources.

Mitigation partnerships bring together the leadership and expertise of business, state and local governments, utilities, research and academia, nonprofit groups, and other community organizations to develop integrated strategies to reduce exposure to hazards and make postdisaster recovery easier. Partnership activities can include awareness and education activities, integration of business and community vulnerability assessment programs for identifying community-wide hazards and risks, a team approach to disaster response and recovery, and sponsorship of community-based programs that address hazard mitigation and sustainability.

One of the most important actions the business sector can take to bolster community resiliency is to support the building code—a strong and well-enforced building code actually costs businesses less in the long run. Even though initial outlays for new construction may be higher to incorporate the latest disaster-resistant materials and construction techniques, these standards are generally designed to ensure safety at certain specific impact levels, such as wind speed or seismic ground shaking.

9.6.1 Using Incentives to Promote Community Resilience

Sometimes being a good corporate citizen is not sufficient motivation for private businesses to become involved in hazard mitigation and preparedness initiatives at the community level. There are a variety of incentives that communities can use to encourage the private sector to become engaged. Some incentives are offered by the local government, such as lowered tax rates or tax discounts for property that is built or retrofitted to withstand hazard impacts (e.g., hurricane shutters to prevent wind damage, elevation to protect against flooding, seismic retrofit to strengthen a building against earthquake shaking). Other types of incentives can be offered by the building supply and home improvement industry, such as rebates or discounts on purchases of mitigation-related materials and supplies. In return, the retailer, wholesaler, or distributor receives increased sales, good public relations, and recognition in the community as a partner in mitigation efforts. The lending and insurance industries can also play a part in stimulating mitigation actions by home and business owners through premium discounts and lowered loan rates. In return, both the lender and the insurance provider benefit from the increased safety of the secured property.

When properly applied, incentives can be a powerful lever to engage individual businesses and homeowners in a community-based risk reduction initiative. Combinations of incentives can also be used to reward risk reduction efforts. Sample incentives are displayed in Table 9.1.[17]

There are some impediments to adoption of incentives as an integral feature of a local mitigation strategy. Incentives can be complex, cumbersome to administer, and, in the short term, can have negligible impacts on reducing risk. In the long-term, however, incentives, when applied as a package and in combination with accurate hazard assessment and risk analysis information, can motivate homeowners, business, and communities to take action to protect their property from the effects of natural hazards.[17]

PROPERTY PROTECTION REBATES

The Village of South Holland, Illinois, has a rebate program to help property owners fund retrofitting projects to protect against surface and subsurface flooding. If a project is approved, installed, and inspected, the village will reimburse the owner 50% of the cost up to $5,000. As of 2019, more than 1,170 floodproofing and sewer backup protection projects have been completed under this program. Perhaps not surprisingly, contractors have become some of the best agents to publicize this program.

Table 9.1 Incentives for Community-Based Risk Reduction Initiatives.

Incentive	Provisions
Tax	• Reduction in local government taxes for property protection measures undertaken by homeowners and business owners. • Waiver of sales tax on building materials to retrofit structures.
Insurance	• Differentiated premiums in hazard areas based on mitigation measures. • Waiver of deductible on natural hazard losses for strengthened buildings. • Reduced premiums/waived deductibles for strengthened public facilities. • Building code enforcement grading system to allow property owner premium discounts on new construction built at or above code.
Retailer, manufacturer, or wholesaler pricing	• Manufacturer's rebates on products used for mitigation. • Discounts or rebates at point of sale (e.g., The Home Depot). • Project-specific discounts or rebates.
Financial	• Building fee waivers/reductions for structures built with mitigation features. • Discounted construction loans/lower rates for retrofitted structures.

9.6.2 Private Insurance Participation in Community Mitigation

The bulk of this chapter has addressed the link between the decisions private landowners and businesses make and the resulting vulnerability of communities and emphasized the need to encourage private sector decision-makers to mitigate and prepare for the impacts of hazards in order to protect the economic base of communities. However, it is increasingly clear that some private sector industries have a particularly central role and interest in encouraging mitigation and preparedness. The insurance industry exemplifies this unique role and serves as a fundamental risk manager, developing tools to understand risk and mechanisms to spread risk across society to lessen the individual impact of disasters. For example, the insurance industry played a leading role historically in transitioning cities to be significantly less vulnerable to extensive fires that wreaked havoc in many major urban areas a century ago. Today, many insurance companies— and the reinsurance companies that purchase insurance policies and further distribute risk—are taking an active role to partner with the public sector and nonprofit organizations to devise new ways to better communicate risk to individual landholders and municipalities, incentivize mitigation and preparedness, and ultimately reduce the vulnerability of insured properties.

As disaster losses continue to increase in the United States, insurers are faced with the challenge of providing affordable coverage to properties facing growing vulnerability— which is especially pronounced with climate change making the level of risk more uncertain. Additionally, regulators often limit the degree or pace at which insurers can raise rates. As a result, several prominent insurance companies are acknowledging that for many properties to remain insurable, investments in physical resilience are needed.

NEW YORK CITY DEVELOPS A "CATASTROPHE BOND" TO INSURE SUBWAY

Hurricane Sandy caused nearly $19 billion in damages to New York City and brought much of the city's transportation system to a halt. During the recovery process, the city soon realized that obtaining insurance for its subway system was prohibitively expensive, especially in the face of rising sea levels and the likelihood of more extreme flooding events in future years. The Metropolitan Transportation Authority (MTA) took an innovative step to work with a global catastrophe modeling company to develop a catastrophe bond.

The bond is triggered if the water level during a storm reaches 8.5 feet above the normal water level at a NOAA Water Level Station in New York's Battery Park; when flooding is above this critical level, the MTA is able to use the proceeds from the bond sales to repair and rebuild facilities. Since the bond will not cover damages due to flooding below this level, the MTA has an incentive to enhance resilience to smaller storms that do not meet the bond threshold. Through this innovative financing mechanism, New York City is able to reduce its insurance premiums while simultaneously investing in mitigation of its subway system. Issued in July 2013, this was the first catastrophe bond ever issued to protect solely against storm surge.[18]

SELF-CHECK

- Why is it important for a business to be engaged in community-wide mitigation planning and programs?
- List four incentives for community-based risk reduction and describe their provisions.
- Discuss why insurance companies have a unique interest in promoting community resilience.

SUMMARY

Economic resilience is a vital part of creating a disaster-resilient community. This chapter has described the planning process a business can follow to become more resilient to disasters and identified a number of mitigation actions a business might take to reduce its vulnerability to natural hazards. This chapter provided a list of factors to consider during private land investment and development decision-making and described how these decisions relate to a community's economic resiliency. This chapter also outlined several types of business protection plans and described the purpose and process of conducting a business impact analysis. It is important for a community and its businesses to work together to mitigate the impacts of hazards. The chapter explored this connection, as well as the processes by which a business can mitigate the impacts of hazards on its own facilities and operations, thereby improving the resilience of the whole community.

KEY TERMS

Business continuity planning or Continuity of Operations Planning (COOP): Plans directed toward maintaining a business's viability when one or more functions are impaired or disrupted. Since the advent of computerized business operations, many of these plans focus on data protection, retrieval, and restoration.

Business impact analysis: A calculation of the types of damages and losses that can be expected during an identified hazard event; the damages are related to the characteristics of the business. The business impact analysis assists in determining the types of actions that must be taken to reduce vulnerability.

Contingency planning: The process of developing advance arrangements and procedures that enable an organization to respond to a disaster so that critical business functions resume within a defined time frame, the amount of loss is minimized, and the stricken facilities are repaired or replaced as soon as possible.

Demand: The desire for a commodity together with the ability to pay for it. Scarcity increases the desire for a particular product—for example, beachfront property in highly developed coastal areas.

Direct impact: Includes physical damage to structures, such as buildings and other facilities. Direct impacts also include losses to inventories, equipment, and other physical assets.

Dry floodproofing: A structural mitigation technique that strengthens walls to withstand hydrostatic and dynamic forces, including debris impacts. Openings, including doors, windows, and vents, are sealed or filled with special closures to block entry of floodwater. In some instances, walls can be coated with waterproofing compounds or plastic sheeting.

Hazard identification: A step of the business risk assessment that defines the magnitudes (intensities) and associated probabilities (likelihood) of hazards that may pose threats to the business and community.

Indirect impacts: Result from the closure of roads and disassembly of transportation networks; loss of utilities, such as water, sewerage, and electric power; and disruptions to telecommunications.

Infrastructure: Facilities and systems that support development, such as water, sewer, and roads.

Land use regulation: Legislation that controls property uses, including zoning and subdivision ordinances, building codes, fire codes, environmental protection laws, and other types of mandates that dictate where and how growth and development take place.

Risk: The potential losses associated with a hazard, defined in terms of expected probability and frequency, exposure, and consequences.

Risk assessment: A process or method for evaluating a risk associated with a specific hazard and defined in terms of probability and frequency of occurrence, magnitude and severity, exposure, and consequences.

Safety and health plan: Plan for ensuring workplace safety and protecting employee health.

Spill Prevention Control and Countermeasures (SPCC): Plans and procedures for dealing with hazardous waste or dangerous substances.

Time value of money: One of the basic concepts of finance, the time value of money is based on the premise that faster returns on investment maximize profitability.

Vulnerability assessment: A step in the business risk assessment that characterizes exposed populations and property and the extent of injury and damage that may result from a hazard event of a given intensity in a given area.

Wet floodproofing: Structural mitigation measure that intentionally allows floodwater to enter certain enclosed areas to reduce the damaging pressures that can collapse walls and foundations.

ASSESS YOUR UNDERSTANDING

Summary Questions

1. A resilient community needs a resilient economy in order to contribute to geo-global stability. True or False?
2. Landownership in the United States means that an owner can do anything she wants on her land. True or False?
3. A diverse economy is advantageous for a community because it offers jobs to people of diverse ethnic backgrounds. True or False?
4. Community infrastructure planning can be used to steer development away from hazardous areas. True or False?
5. Investors are required to take natural hazards into consideration when deciding when and where to build. True or False?
6. Established businesses are usually not affected by natural hazards because they are insured. True or False?
7. Small businesses typically open sooner than larger stores or chains simply because they are smaller and easier to clean up. True or False?
8. A COOP is a
   a. Residence for poultry
   b. A term of endearment for a person named Cooper
   c. A continuity of operations plan
   d. A community optional operations plan
9. As part of a business risk assessment, a business should
   a. Identify the hazards that can impact the business
   b. Withdraw all of its funds from the neighborhood bank
   c. Fire the CFO
   d. None of the above
10. A risk assessment should inform the business about
    a. The extent to which the business is vulnerable to a particular hazard
    b. The time and date of the next natural hazard
    c. Alternative methods of preventing natural hazards
    d. All of the above
11. Upstream losses refer to the damage that is caused by the development in the river basin that results in increased flowage in the community. True or False?

12. Building codes
    a. Regulate the methods and materials used in construction
    b. Prevent unauthorized entrance to a building during a natural hazard
    c. Are rarely used because they are difficult to administer
    d. Decrease the cost of construction
13. Local mitigation plans may play an important part in mitigating the impact of natural hazards on business operations
    a. By discouraging development from locating in hazardous areas
    b. By encouraging a business to relocate to the community following a disaster
    c. By extending infrastructure only to areas that are hazardous for development
    d. All of the above
14. Insurance should be tailored to the particular business and should take into consideration (indicate all applicable)
    a. Property damage
    b. Loss of revenues
    c. Extra expenses resulting from the disaster
    d. Vacation plans

Review Questions

1. What is a resilient economy?
2. What two things does landownership consist of?
3. Can a community completely control the viability of a local economy?
4. What is a factor following a disaster that may have long-term impacts on resilience?
5. What does community resiliency have to do with economics?
6. Describe why business protection plans are important.
7. Name three elements that a comprehensive disaster preparedness and mitigation plan should contain.
8. Why is hazard awareness important for businesses?
9. Describe the positive and negative aspects of hazard insurance as a mitigation action for businesses.
10. How can a local jurisdiction's mitigation plan contribute to economic resilience?

Applying This Chapter

1. Imagine that you have just inherited a business from a somewhat foggy relative in a community you are not familiar with. What steps would you take to make your newly acquired business resilient to natural hazards?
2. Still focusing on the inherited business: what are some of the mitigation actions that you might consider?
3. In this same situation, what factors would you consider in choosing an insurance policy?
4. After moving to this community, how would you rely on the community to make you less vulnerable to the next natural hazard event? How would you contribute to the community's hazard mitigation efforts as a member of the business sector?
5. Imagine that you are a local economic development director and have been invited to give a speech to the local chamber of commerce on "Building a Resilient Community." Outline such a speech.
6. Imagine that you are a city manager. What sort of policies, programs, and projects would you promulgate to insure that the business community in your jurisdiction was moving toward resilience?

You Try It

READY ... Set ... Go!

Natural hazards are a part of the natural environment and will be with us forever. There are indications that disasters resulting from the impact of natural hazards on the built environment are increasing in frequency and magnitude. This means, of course, that businesses may be impacted more heavily than in the past. Think of possible careers that this generates. Explore the Internet to find possibilities in business administration, management, continuity planning, insurance, and so forth.

Mock Interview

Contact a local business owner and discuss with them their business contingency plans for natural hazards in your community. What are they doing to be prepared? Are they taking any mitigation measures? Are they concerned about disaster striking their business? What types of insurance do they have? What help from the community do they desire?

Turning Lemons into Lemonade!

As a kid, did you ever run your own lemonade stand? If you were to start your own business today (whether it be selling lemonade or otherwise), what from this chapter would you incorporate into your business location, design, and policies?

REFERENCES

1. Schwab, J., et al. 1998. *Planning for Post-Disaster Recovery and Reconstruction.* Chicago, IL: American Planning Association Planning Advisory Service. Report No. 483/484.
2. Eadie, C. 2001. *Building Economic Vitality into Disaster Recovery in Holistic Disaster Recovery: Ideas for Building Local Sustainability after a Natural Disaster.* Boulder, CO: Natural Hazards Research and Applications Information Center, University of Colorado.
3. National Renewable Energy Laboratory, U.S. Department of Energy. *Greensburg, Kansas: A Better, Greener Place to Live.* Revised October 2009.
4. Quinn, P. 2013. *After Devastating Tornado, Town is Reborn "Green."* USA TODAY Green Living Magazine. April 25, 2013.
5. Johnson, L., L.D. Samant, and S. Frew. 2005. *Planning for the Unexpected: Land-Use Development and Risk.* Chicago, IL: American Planner Association.
6. Lennon, G., W.J. Neal, D.M. Bush, O.H. Pilkey, M. Stutz, and J. Bullock. 1996. *Living with the South Carolina Coast.* Durham, NC: Duke University Press, p. 41.
7. French, S.P. 2002. Incorporating resilience in private sector project planning and review. In *Building Disaster Resilient Communities Instructor Guide,* edited by R.J. Burby. Emmitsburg, MD: Federal Emergency Management Agency, Emergency Management Institute.
8. Delia, A.A. 2001. Population and economic changes in eastern North Carolina before and after Hurricane Floyd. In *Facing Our Future: Hurricane Floyd and Recovery in the Coastal Plain,* edited by J.R. Maiolo, et al. Wilmington, NC: Coastal Carolina Press.
9. Henry, D.K., S. Cookie-Hull, J. Savukinas, F. Yu, N. Elo, B. Van Arnum. 2013. *Economic Impact of Hurricane Sandy: Potential Economic Activity Lost and Gained in New Jersey and New York.* U.S. Department of Commerce, Economics and Statistics Administration.
10. Grossman-Cohen, B. May 1, 2012. *Mississippi "Jobs First" Legislation Breaks New Ground in Providing Jobs for Local People.* http://www.oxfamamerica.org/press/mississippi-jobs-first-legislation-breaks-new-ground-in-providing-jobs-for-local-people/.
11. Sturgis, S. May 3, 2012. *New Mississippi Law Boosts Local Hiring in Disaster's Wake.* The Institute for Southern Studies. http://www.southernstudies.org/2012/05/new-mississippi-law-boosts-local-hiring-in-disasters-wake.html.
12. The H. John Heinz III Center for Science, Economics and the Environment. 2002. *Human Links to Coastal Disasters.* Washington, DC: The Heinz Center.

13. https://www.sba.gov/sites/default/files/advocacy/2018-Small-Business-Profiles-US.pdf U.S. Small Business Administration Office of Advocacy. 2018. United State Small Business Profile. Washington, DC.
14. NC Division of Emergency Management, 2001. *Managing Your Business to Minimize Disruption: A Guide for Small Business in North Carolina*. Raleigh, NC: NCEM.
15. Federal Emergency Management Agency. October 1993. *Emergency Management Guide for Business and Industry. A Step-by-Step Approach to Emergency Planning, Response and Recovery for Companies of All Sizes*. Publication 141. FEMA.
16. Institute for Business and Home Safety. 2005. *Open for Business: A Disaster Planning Toolkit for the Small to Mid-Sized Business Owner*.
17. North Carolina Division of Emergency Management, May 2003. *Keeping Natural Hazards from Becoming Disasters: A Mitigation Planning Guidebook for Local Governments*. North Carolina Department of Public Safety.
18. Metropolitan Transportation Authority. July 2013. *Metropolitan Transportation Authority Secures $200 Million of Insurance Protection for Future Sandy-Like Storms*. MTA Press Releases.http://www.mta.info/press-release/mta-headquarters/mta-secures-200-million-insurance-protection-future-sandy-storms.

Section III
Developing Preparedness and Mitigation Plans

Chapter 10 Risk Assessment

Chapter 11 Preparedness Activities

Chapter 12 Hazard Mitigation
Planning

Now that we have learned about the range of hazards facing communities in the United States and the disaster management framework that has evolved to address these hazards, we are ready to explore the approach for assessing risk and developing preparedness, mitigation, and climate change adaptation programs to enhance resilience. This chapter delves into the process of understanding the unique hazard profile of a community and assessing risk based on the physical, economic, and social characteristics of the area. Chapter 11 focuses on the role of preparedness, including major activities undertaken by government, businesses, volunteer organizations, and families and individuals. Chapter 12 describes hazard mitigation activities, emphasizing opportunities to reduce vulnerability by influencing land use decisions. In this chapter, we also lay out the foundation of the process that communities use to develop a comprehensive hazard mitigation plan. Cumulatively, this section provides the building blocks to set priorities and work collaboratively with a wide range of community members and organizations to effectively plan for and become more resilient to hazards and the impacts of climate change.

Communities, states, and businesses across the United States are increasingly assessing how risk is changing as climate change influences the distribution, variability, and intensity of many extreme weather events. For example, we can no longer rely on historic averages of rainfall to appropriately size stormwater infrastructure. Effectively managing hazards requires us to use the best available science about how our climate and communities are likely to change. These chapters discuss methods, tools, and sources of data to incorporate information about our changing climate with preparedness and mitigation planning in an attempt to address both current and future risk.

Being prepared for the impacts of natural and human-made hazards is an ongoing process rather than a one-time solution. Resilient communities are those that incorporate relevant weather and climate science into nearly every aspect of decision-making—from siting and design of roadways to irrigation techniques employed in agriculture. The following chapters describe the process to instill a foundation of preparedness and mitigation that allows communities to absorb and bounce back from the impacts of hazards.

10

Risk Assessment
Identifying Hazards and Assessing Vulnerability

What You'll Learn

- The purpose of a risk assessment
- The steps of the risk assessment process
- Sources of data to carry out a risk assessment
- Types of data collection and mapping

Goals and Outcomes

- Select tools to inventory community assets and conduct a hazard risk assessment
- Assess vulnerability using hazard maps
- Identify community practices and trends that may alter vulnerability
- Evaluate hazard risk assessment strategies used by communities

INTRODUCTION

Communities that are resilient to the impact of natural hazards are not built by chance. The decisions we make about how and where to build determine how successful we are at avoiding disasters. This chapter explains how a risk assessment informs us about the hazards we face, so that we can choose the most appropriate hazard mitigation, preparedness, and climate change adaptation strategies in an effort to become more resilient. A risk assessment consists of several different elements, or steps. To conduct a thorough risk assessment, the community must first identify the hazards that could affect that particular jurisdiction. There must then be a determination of how likely these hazards are, as well as their potential intensity and severity. The community must also assess its level of vulnerability to the hazards identified. Assessing vulnerability includes identifying the people and property that could suffer harm, estimating losses in dollar figures, and predicting who or what could be affected in the future. Increasingly, communities are also assessing the added level of risk from climate change, calculating the degree to which natural hazards may be changing in the future. The final step in the risk assessment involves assembling and analyzing the relevant data and information in order to form conclusions as to whether the level of risk the community faces is considered acceptable or unacceptable. Each step in the risk assessment process provides additional information to build a sound fact base upon which the community can develop strategies and policies. When completed, a careful risk assessment allows the

DOI: 10.4324/9781003123897-10

community to target hazard mitigation, preparedness, and climate change adaptation efforts where they are most needed.

10.1 THE PURPOSE OF A RISK ASSESSMENT

Risk assessment is the process of defining which hazards could impact a community and describing how these hazards could affect people and property. A risk assessment is often performed as part of a comprehensive hazard mitigation planning process, which uses data obtained during the risk assessment as part of a solid fact base that can help direct and justify mitigation policies and strategies. States, local governments, and Native American tribes are required under the Disaster Mitigation Act (DMA) of 2000 to prepare an all-hazards mitigation plan to be eligible for certain federal disaster assistance and mitigation funding. The risk assessment is one of the required steps in preparing such a plan.

This chapter describes how a typical risk assessment is carried out and how the information may be put to use for reducing community vulnerability to hazards. We primarily focus on mitigation plans prepared at the local level here. While there are a few different steps for state-level plans, in general, the process is similar for all risk assessments. Many of the steps described in this chapter are based on the risk assessment procedure as outlined by the Federal Emergency Management Agency (FEMA) in guidance materials designed to help communities prepare hazard mitigation plans as required by the DMA.

SELF-CHECK

- Define **risk assessment**.
- Discuss the purpose of a hazard risk assessment.

10.2 STEPS IN THE RISK ASSESSMENT PROCESS

Each local community is unique, and no two towns or counties would carry out an identical risk assessment. However, there are certain steps common to all hazard risk assessments:

1. Identify hazards
2. Profile hazard events
3. Inventory assets and populations
4. Estimate losses
5. Describe land uses and development trends
6. Form conclusions and determine acceptable risk

The steps of the risk assessment process are applicable to all sorts of hazards. There are some unique aspects of the hazard profiling, asset inventory, and loss estimation steps for human-made hazards, but in general, a similar process to assess risk is used whether the community is dealing with natural hazards, terrorism and other intentional threats, or technological hazards such as hazardous material accidents.

10.2.1 Tools for Conducting a Risk Assessment

Some of the information gathered during the risk assessment process is best displayed on maps, which illustrate the geographic area that could be affected by various hazards. This is true for hazards like flooding, storm surge, and landslides that are more prevalent in certain locations. This can also be true for human-made disasters, such as locations surrounding chemical or industrial facilities, or areas that could be potential targets of terrorist attacks. Other hazards, such as cyberattacks or blizzards, may not be helpfully described with spatial mapping, since these are not tied to a specific geography.

There are many methods for creating hazard assessment maps to illustrate local hazard-prone areas and locate important community features. **HAZUS** (Hazards U.S.) is a computer modeling system that can also be helpful in creating maps and gathering and analyzing data for many of the steps in the risk assessment process. HAZUS was originally developed by FEMA to estimate losses from earthquakes. The latest version, HAZUS-MH (Multi-Hazard), is used to estimate losses from earthquake, hurricanes, and flooding. The software also contains useful information for preparing inventories and mapping community features vulnerable to other hazards as well.

Geographic information systems (GIS) is a category of software that can be used with varying degrees of skill and training and at varying levels of sophistication, from basic mapping to sophisticated analysis. In essence, GIS capitalizes on the fact that everything on earth has a unique location (a specific address) in space, allowing the user to create layers of spatial data and superimpose them on one another. For example, maps that show where residential structures are located in a community can be overlaid with flood maps, thus illustrating the relationship between the two layers. The GIS software captures this spatial information, helping us visualize correlations, analyze relationships, and identify patterns over time and space. This information can then be leveraged to formulate conclusions and make decisions about local land use conditions. The most commonly used GIS software is ESRI ArcGIS, a private company that provides software and data for public and private sector use. ArcGIS serves as the software on which HAZUS and many other GIS applications run.

For analyzing risk associated with hazards that are less connected with spatial data, a number of other tools exist that emergency managers and planners can draw from. For example, an assessment tool used to determine vulnerability of potential targets to terrorism is the CARVER Matrix. Developed by the U.S. Army Special Forces during the Vietnam war, the matrix involves assessing each potential "target" on a scale of 1–10 across six different factors. After going through the exercise, the results are used to determine sites or assets that should be prioritized for mitigation. The elements of analysis for the CARVER Matrix are described below:

- Criticality: Is the asset a choke point or single point of failure for a larger system?
- Accessibility: How easy is it to access the asset or system?
- Recuperability: How much time and effort would be required to recover from an adverse event?
- Vulnerability: How effective is the current security system relative to potential capacity of those trying to cause damage?
- Effect (on the population): What is the scope and magnitude of adverse consequences resulting from a malicious action?
- Recognizability: To what extent would malicious actors recognize the asset or system as a critical or valuable target?

10.2.2 Data Quality: Using the "Best Available"

It is important to remember during the data gathering stage that the quality of the information source directly affects the quality of the assessment and its results. However, raw data that is not entirely accurate or complete should not prevent a community from carrying out a useful risk assessment. FEMA requires that local and state governments use the "best available data," a phrase that reflects the fact that a community will never have access to perfect information. Plan developers should always make note of the source of the data used, its date, and any other metadata (data about data) that could indicate potential errors, gaps, inaccuracies, or other imperfections. The end results of any data analysis, including (or especially) an assessment of hazard risk, should always be viewed with a critical eye that acknowledges possible flaws. This is true of all natural hazards, including data that deal with climate change, which is typically generated at a much larger scale—such as an entire state or region—rather than at a finer grained community level.

USING THE KNOWLEDGE OF INDIGENOUS POPULATIONS TO ASSESS CLIMATE CHANGE RISKS[1]

Often on the forefront of impacts, indigenous tribes in the United States are frequently cited for their vulnerability to climate change. The Swinomish tribe in Washington State is combining traditional environmental knowledge with modern-day science—including maps of locally specific relative sea level rise scenarios—to assess their risks to climate impacts. In 2007, the Swinomish became the first tribal nation to pass a climate change proclamation, spurred on by a first-hand experience of changing conditions on tribal land. The catalyst for the Swinomish tribe came in 2006, when a strong surge from a winter storm pushed logs across a road and into the yards of a number of homes. The tribe considered what the future would look like with a few more feet of sea level rise and decided that tribal economic development projects that were being planned at the time should not be located in low-lying areas that would be under water in the next 100 years.

Tribes often have good insight into how conditions change over time. They've lived in places hundreds and sometimes thousands of years and have seen extremes and learned how to live in those places. Because of their intimate connection to the environment, many tribes are seeing the changes that are happening.

"Very few people have lived in a place long enough within a community to know what's normal and what isn't normal, what's changed and what hasn't changed." The tribes retain generations of individual and community knowledge that goes back before humankind started rearranging rivers and reshaping landscapes.

To read the Swinomish climate change proclamation and action plan, go to www.swinomish-nsn.gov/climate_change/climate_main.html.

10.2.3 Creating a Base Map

Hazard mapping begins with a base map, upon which hazard-specific information can be superimposed. A **base map** shows the basic topography, physical elements, and infrastructure of the community. A good base map for hazard assessment purposes will include political boundaries, such as city limits, extraterritorial jurisdiction, and ownership patterns (i.e., public and private land); roads, bridges, and rail lines; water features, including rivers, streams, and watershed; and other natural features such as wetlands and beaches; and steep slopes. The base map should also indicate where development is currently located, as well as the location of infrastructure, such as water and sewer lines, that is scheduled to be laid in the future. The majority of these features can be found on local and state highway maps, local land use and zoning maps, in capital improvement plans, and aerial photography.

SELF-CHECK

- List the steps in the risk assessment process.
- Describe **HAZUS** and **GIS**.

10.3 RISK ASSESSMENT STEP ONE: IDENTIFYING HAZARDS

Once a base map is established, the risk assessment can begin in earnest. The first step in the risk assessment process asks the question: "What kinds of hazards can affect the community?" **Hazard identification** involves listing all the hazards that might occur in the local region and providing a description of each one. Some hazards occur quite infrequently, while others are regularly recurring events in a community. Even very large hazard events may occur in rapid succession. For example, during the 2004 hurricane season, Florida experienced four major hurricanes within the span of a few weeks. The hurricane season of 2005 saw a similar rapid sequence of huge coastal storms, including Hurricanes Katrina, Rita, and Wilma. Hazard identification involves researching all potential hazards and including them in a list of possible events.

Some hazards may be chronic (regularly occurring but not causing extensive damage each time). These repetitive occurrences can lead to a cumulative impact over time, such as flooding or landslides that can result from numerous rainfalls of average amount. Other hazards may be less regular but can have more catastrophic impacts when they do occur, such as large hurricanes and earthquakes. The risk assessment should address both chronic and episodic hazards.

10.3.1 Finding the Information

There is a wide variety of information sources for hazard identification. Research into the community's past can indicate the types of hazards that typically occur in the local area. Newspapers, weather reports, past disaster declarations, and other historical records from community archives can contain a treasure trove of information. Interviews of long-time residents can also be a good source of information about the types of hazards that have struck the community in the past.

Collecting old accounts of hazard events will provide an overview of the major hazards in the area, but contacts should be widened in order to obtain information about all the possible hazards, not just the "big ones" that community members easily recall or that made major headlines at the time. Local plans and documents that are publicly available often contain information about hazards, even though hazards might not be the focus of these documents. For example, transportation, environmental, or public works reports could have references to local hazard possibilities. Local comprehensive plans, land use plans, and building codes and regulations often contain information about hazards as well. Personnel in local departments may also be able to provide information about hazards that are likely in the area. Police, fire, rescue, and emergency management workers who deal with emergencies on a regular basis are also familiar with hazard possibilities.

The search for information about potential hazards should be expanded beyond local sources. Some hazards are more common in large regions of the country or throughout the state, and these regional hazard possibilities should be included in the hazard identification as well. For example, communities located in "tornado alley" in the Midwest will likely experience more tornadoes in any given year than other parts of the United States. The assumption is simply based on the fact that tornadoes have often impacted that area in the past. State and federal agencies have data banks and other records of hazards on a county or regional level. Many government agencies maintain hazard-specific websites, including state emergency management offices, the National Oceanic and Atmospheric Administration (NOAA), FEMA, the U.S. Geological Survey (USGS), the National Hurricane Center, and the National Weather Service.

The list below includes examples of sources that states or communities may turn to as they document past events. In addition, individuals preparing a risk assessment may choose to look for local sources of information, such as local historians and librarians, recent emergency management offices, and long-standing businesses and residents in the community.

- NOAA Storm Events Database: Documents occurrences of storms and other significant weather phenomena, including details about dates, intensity, loss of life, property damage, and crop data. https://www.ncdc.noaa.gov/stormevents/
- Data.gov: Managed by a consortium of federal agencies, data.gov includes more than 100,000 GIS datasets available for download. https://www.ncdc.noaa.gov/stormevents/
- National Avalanche Center: Includes a searchable database to learn about historical events. https://avalanche.org/
- Earthquake Catalog: The USGS maintains a searchable database of historical earthquake events, which can be customized based on the magnitude, date, and location. https://earthquake.usgs.gov/earthquakes/search/
- Dam Incident Database: The Association of State Dam Safety Officials maintains a searchable database of dam failures that communities can use to produce reports of events in or near their location. https://damsafety.org/incidents
- Snowstorm Database: Available on data.gov, this database includes more than 500 snowstorms dating back to 1900, documenting storms with heavy snowfall extending across a large area. https://catalog.data.gov/dataset/snowstorm-database

10.3.2 Finding Information on Human-Made Hazards

Terrorist attacks and technological disasters occur infrequently enough in the United States that there may be a few relevant records that can help determine what human-made hazards could affect a local community. The Department of Homeland Security (DHS), the Federal Bureau of Investigation (FBI), and the U.S. Department of State issue annual reports on terrorism activity domestically and around the world. State emergency agencies and environmental resource departments, as well as the U.S. Environmental Protection Agency (EPA), are sources of data on hazardous material incidents. Also, in many communities, plans are in place to respond to numerous types of technological hazards, and these plans—and the people who develop them—may be valuable sources of information about human-induced risks. Such plans include emergency operations plans, chemical stockpile contingency plans, Toxic Release Inventory reports, community right-to-know reports, local emergency planning committee files, and other types of emergency and notification documents.

A few resources that communities may use to identify and describe past events are listed below:

- Chemical Safety Board: Responsible for investigating industrial chemical accidents, the CSB website contains reports on current and completed investigations. https://www.csb.gov/

- Toxic Release Inventory: The Toxic Release Inventory Program contains a database of chemical releases and waste management activities reported to the EPA, including the location, type of release, and type of chemical(s). https://epa.gov/tri/
- Annual Uniform Crime Report: The FBI provides crime statistics from more than 18,000 law enforcement agencies. The Crime Data Explorer allows users to search the database, download the data, and create visualizations: https://crime-data-explorer.app.cloud.gov/

NYC UNVEILS HAZARD HISTORY & CONSEQUENCE TOOL

As part of their 2019 Hazard Mitigation Plan, New York City has undertaken a new approach for their hazard identification and vulnerability assessment. The Hazard History & Consequence Tool (https://nychazardhistory.com/) compiles a tremendous amount of information about not only past hazard events but also ways these events impacted the functioning of the city. For example, the database includes information about school closures and attendance, delays on the subway, changes in Department of Sanitation pickups, and other metrics alongside data about historical hazards, allowing the agency and the public to better understand the nature of past events. Going back in time hundreds of years, the tool allows for custom searches by the threat or weather event, time period, or location.

SELF-CHECK

- Define **hazard identification**.
- List sources of information for identifying potential natural hazard events.
- List sources of information for identifying potential human-made hazard events.

10.4 RISK ASSESSMENT STEP TWO: PROFILING HAZARDS

A hazard profile asks the question: "What is the potential impact of the identified hazards on the community?" The **hazard profile** helps determine how each hazard will affect the community, how often each hazard may occur, and where the hazards might take place. It is important to ascertain whether the hazards the community has identified are cyclical, seasonal, or whether they can happen at any time. It is also important to know the location and geographic extent of each hazard type. Certain portions of the community will be affected on a regular basis in identifiable areas, such as floodplains surrounding streams and rivers. Other types of hazards, such as earthquakes or snowstorms, will affect the entire community. Hazards of various intensities will also affect the community in different ways. For example, a tornado that ranks 4 or 5 on the Enhanced Fujita scale would probably cause more damage than a class 1 or 2 tornado. This is important information for the hazard profile. The effects of climate change on natural hazards add a layer of complexity to a hazard profile, but this complexity should not stop communities from addressing the potential impacts of climate change on the hazards the community already faces.

10.4.1 Creating a Hazard History

A good way to begin the hazard profile is to provide information on past occurrences of each hazard. These hazard histories can provide a snapshot of specific events from which we can make some general assumptions about future hazard events based on patterns and trends. A community that has experienced a tornado in the past might assume that another could occur. On the other hand, the fact that a community has experienced an average of three tornadoes each year for the last 30 years does not mean that a tornado will hit any particular point in the locality in the following year. It is clear that there are limitations to using historical data to estimate events that are likely to occur in the future. Nevertheless, a hazard history can provide a good sense of what lies within the range of possibilities. Sources of information of past occurrences are often the same as the sources used to create the hazard identification list in the previous step, such as archived news accounts, weather records, and interviews with local residents and community officials. The hazard history developed during the profile step elaborates on the list and paints a more complete picture of how historical events have affected the community.

"KNOW YOUR LINE: BE FLOOD AWARE"

The "Know Your Line: Be Flood Aware" High Water Mark initiative, created by FEMA and seven other Federal agencies, helps communities remind residents of major local floods and encourage residents to prepare for the next one. Participating communities post high water mark signs in prominent places, hold a special launch event to unveil the signs, and conduct ongoing education to build local awareness of flood risk and motivate people to take action.

The local hazard history should contain a description of all the elements of a past hazard event, as well as how long the hazard lasted, how severe the event was, and what damage resulted. Some hazards are single-force events, while other types of hazards are made up of multiple elements—such as a hurricane—which can involve the combined threats of high winds, storm surge, and flooding, as well as secondary impacts such as chemical spills. Each of these hazard characteristics should be described in detail for each event mentioned in the hazard history.

10.4.2 Identifying the Extent of Each Hazard

The hazard profile must assess the extent of each potential hazard listed during the identification step, which involves identifying the magnitude and intensity. The estimates of hazard extent should be based on local historical evidence and regional data. The potential extent of a hazard may be described using relative terms or the profile may refer to standardized intensity scales. Reliable hazard rating scales include the Saffir-Simpson scale that categorizes hurricanes, the Enhanced Fujita rating scale for tornadoes, and the Modified Mercalli scale that ranks earthquakes (see descriptions of these rating scales in Chapters 3 and 4). Flood severity is often measured in terms of water depth and velocity. For wildfires, severity can be expressed as fire line intensity (a measure of the rate at which a fire releases heat, or the unit length of the fire line), the rate of fire spread (feet/second), and flame length. For other types of hazards with no formal rating scale, severity may be indicated through general terms, such as mild, moderate, or severe.

Table 10.1 Hazard Impact Levels and Effects on Communities.

Level	% Area Affected	Impact
Catastrophic	More than 50%	Multiple deaths Complete shutdown of facilities for 30 days or more More than 50% of property severely damaged
Critical	25%–50%	Multiple severe injuries Complete shutdown of critical facilities for at least 2 weeks More than 25% of property severely damaged.
Limited	10%–25%	Some injuries Complete shutdown of critical facilities for more than 1 week More than 10% of property severely damaged.
Negligible	Less than 10%	Minor injuries Minimal quality-of-life impact Shutdown of critical facilities and services for 24 hours or less Less than 10% of property severely damaged

The extent of a hazard event also includes a measure of its potential impact, which is a combination of the magnitude of the event, how large an area within the community is affected, and the amount of human activity. Table 10.1 illustrates one way to describe the various impacts that a hazard might have on a community.

10.4.3 Determining the Probability of Each Hazard

Some hazards are more likely to occur in a particular community than others. An estimate of **probability**, or likelihood of occurrence, is not an actual prediction. Instead, probability is based on regional data and local historical evidence to indicate the frequency of occurrence in the past and likelihood of occurrence in the future. Table 10.2 shows one method for communicating probability, based on frequency of occurrence.

Table 10.2 Likelihood of a Hazard Based on Frequency of Occurrence.

Likelihood	Frequency of Occurrence
Highly likely	Near 100% probability in the next year
Likely	Between 10% and 100% probability in the next 10 years, or at least one chance in the next 10 years
Possible	Between 1% and 10% probability in the next year, or at least one chance in the next 100 years
Unlikely	Less than 1% probability in the next year, or less than one chance in the next 100 years

Standardized information is available to help determine the probability of some types of hazards within a range of frequencies or **recurrence intervals**. For instance, the probability of a flood is based on a statistical chance of a particular size flood (expressed in cubic feet/second of water flow) occurring in any given year. The annual flood is usually considered the single greatest event expected to occur on an annual basis. The flood that has a 1% probability (1 in 100) of being equaled or exceeded in any year is referred to as the 100-year flood. This term is simply a convenient way to express probability. It should not be interpreted to mean a flood will happen exactly once every century, nor does it imply that if a 100-year flood occurs, there is a little risk of another "100-year flood" occurring in the near future. In fact, multiple 100-year floods can happen in rapid succession in any community that is at risk of flooding.

10.4.4 Identifying the Location of Each Hazard

The hazard profile must identify the location—the geographic area—that will be affected by each potential hazard. Some types of hazards occur in fairly predictable areas. For instance, floodplains and steep slopes (where landslides can occur) can be identified and described geographically. Other types of hazards are not site-specific and cannot be geographically defined so readily, such as tornadoes, ice storms, and severe winds. For these types of hazards, the entire community is considered exposed.

The most effective means of identifying the location of potential hazards (for those hazards that can be geographically defined) is to create or obtain a map that shows the hazard boundaries. Many types of hazards are mapped by state and federal agencies and made available to local communities. For instance, Flood Insurance Rate Maps (FIRMs) are provided by FEMA to communities participating in the National Flood Insurance Program (NFIP). Other commonly mapped hazards include earthquakes, coastal erosion, storm surge inundation areas, wind speed zones, tsunamis, landslides, and wildfires. The U.S. Nuclear Regulatory Commission (NRC), which regulates all nuclear power facilities in the country, can provide information about Nuclear Planning Zones (NPZ) that are safety and evacuation zones delineated around all nuclear power plants.

10.4.5 Profiling Climate Change Impacts

As we discussed in earlier chapters, changes in climate conditions are leading to shifts in the frequency, duration, intensity, variability, and/or location of many natural hazard events. Risk assessments may be most effective if they consider how hazards are likely to change over time. For example, the Lewes, Delaware Hazard Mitigation Plan includes the following statement that describes the potential impacts of climate change on winter storm events:

> Currently there are two climate change impacts that are likely to affect winter storms in Lewes. First, it is believed that precipitation in the winter will become more episodic with it falling in more extreme events. These extremes could exacerbate current winter storms making the overall effects of the storms worse. Additionally, the increase in average temperature will likely cause a reduction in the amount of precipitation falling as snow or ice as that precipitation will likely fall as rain instead. When snow and ice are reduced and the increased episodic precipitation is rain, Lewes could see an increase in inland flooding during winter storm events.

CLIMATE CHANGE RESOURCES TO INFORM RISK ASSESSMENTS

Climate.gov—NOAA launched Climate.gov to serve as a single point-of-entry for NOAA's climate information, data, products, and services. This climate portal provides information about the impacts of climate on nearly every aspect of our lives from agriculture to energy to transportation (climate.gov).

Climate.data.gov: —Launched as a pilot phase in 2014, the climate.data.gov website contains a wide range of federal datasets related to climate change. The site contains data and resources related to coastal flooding, food resilience, water and ecosystem vulnerability, human health, and energy infrastructure.

Digital Coast: —The Digital Coast website was created to provide tools, trainings, stories from the field, and information that allow users to incorporate updated climate data into coastal management decisions. This includes a Sea Level Rise and Coastal Flooding Impacts Viewer to allow communities to visualize inundation zones on top of other community data so that managers can see what is at risk. Additionally, the Digital Coast's Social Vulnerability Index (SOVI) measures the social vulnerability of U.S. counties to environmental hazards (csc.noaa.gov/digitalcoast).

U.S. Global Change Research Program: The U.S. Global Change Research Program coordinates and integrates Federal research on changes in the global environment and their implications for society. The Program produces regular assessments of global change, including anticipated regional shifts in climate within the United States and anticipated impacts (globalchange.gov).

10.4.6 Profiling Human-Made Hazards

A variety of resources available from FEMA, OSHA, and other federal and state agencies provides information about event profiles for both intentional and technological hazards. These profiles include information about the characteristics of human-made hazards, such as:

- **Application Mode:** Describes the human act or unintended event that causes the hazard (e.g., detonation of an explosive device, rupture of a chemical storage container).
- **Duration:** The length of time the hazard is present on the target (e.g., the duration of a tornado may be just minutes, but a chemical warfare agent such as mustard gas can persist for days or weeks under the right conditions).
- **Dynamic/State Characteristics:** Describes the tendency of the hazard's effects to either expand, contract, or remain confined (for example, a cloud of chlorine gas leaking from a storage tank can change location by drifting with the wind and can diminish in danger by dissipating over time).
- **Mitigating Conditions:** Characteristics of the target and its physical environment that can reduce the effects of a hazard (e.g., earthen berms can provide protection from bombs, exposure to sunlight can reduce the effectiveness of some biological agents).
- **Exacerbating Conditions:** Characteristics that can enhance or magnify the effects of the hazard (e.g., depressions or low areas can trap heavy vapors; obstacles in the street such as parked cars or mail boxes can provide concealment opportunities for explosive devices).

These hazard profiles can provide useful information for assessing the various risks associated with human-made hazards. In addition to details about the various agents' characteristics, information about the ways in which they can impact the built environment and human populations can help inform decisions about actions that can reduce or eliminate the resulting damage.

10.4.7 Completing Steps One and Two

At the conclusion of the hazard identification and profile steps, the planning team will have created a map indicating the areas impacted by each hazard type or a report containing information regarding the characteristics of hazard events affecting the community. In some cases, such as those involving flooding, both types of information will be available. The importance of hazard mapping becomes clear during the next step of the risk assessment process, when we inventory community assets and populations.

SELF-CHECK

- Review ways of determining the probability of a hazard.
- Explain what factors determine the extent of a potential hazard.
- List some characteristics of human-made hazards that are important to include in a hazard profile.

10.5 RISK ASSESSMENT STEP THREE: INVENTORYING VULNERABLE ASSETS AND POPULATIONS

Steps one and two of the risk assessment process determine whether a community might experience various types and intensities of hazards, what level of impact those hazards might have, and where within the community those hazards are likely to occur. Step three helps answer the question: "What will be affected by the hazard event?"

During this step, the planning team will determine the number of people and amount of existing assets that are at risk from the identified hazards. **Assets** are all those features of a community that have value, including buildings, facilities (such as wastewater treatment plants), infrastructure (roads, bridges, etc.), historic and cultural landmarks, and other important local resources. Combined with steps four and five, the community will also be able to estimate losses to assets and determine whether the locality is encouraging or allowing additional development to take place in locations that have been identified as unsafe. The planning team may also identify places where hazard mitigation actions are already being implemented, for example, homes that have been elevated above expected flood heights. In other words, by building on the information gathered during the previous steps, and by following the subsequent steps, the community can gauge its level of **vulnerability** to hazards, both now and in the future. As always during the risk assessment process, it is important to remain focused on the ultimate goal—creating and implementing mitigation and preparedness measures that will reduce vulnerability.

10.5.1 Tasks in Step Three

To create a complete inventory of assets and populations, we gather and analyze information in two stages or tasks and compile the information into a spreadsheet, chart, GIS map, or other types of reports.

- **Task One:** Identify assets throughout the community. This community-wide perspective is useful because some types of hazards can affect the entire area, such as earthquakes, ice storms, and tornadoes. It is also useful for indicating the types of land uses that are prevalent in non-hazardous areas of the community so that, if possible, the community can steer future growth and development to these safer areas.
- **Task Two:** Determine what proportion of total community assets are located in known hazard areas. This task indicates what percentage of community assets is vulnerable to hazards as compared to the rest of the community.

10.5.2 Sources of Information

Sources of information to carry out the asset inventory vary from community to community. Some communities have elaborate data management and GIS capabilities. These communities may also wish to use HAZUS to assist in inventorying assets and populations. Other communities may rely more on local property tax records, subdivision plats, aerial photography, and U.S. Census data. Some communities' emergency 911 systems, especially those that are contained in a GIS format, can also provide valuable information about the location of populations and assets.

10.5.3 Task One: Inventorying Assets and Populations in the Community

The first task in the inventory step involves creating a list and description of assets located throughout the community, identifying each one on a map, and tallying up the total amount of assets. Particularly important to identify are the community's **critical facilities** that are necessary for the health and safety of the population, especially following a hazard event. These include hospitals and clinics, police, fire and emergency operations stations, and evacuation centers. **Lifeline utilities** and other infrastructure should also be listed, including water and sewer systems, communications lines, energy services, as well as major transportation routes. **Essential facilities** that aid in recovery following a disaster should also be included, such as government and civic buildings, major employers, banks, schools, day-care centers, and certain commercial establishments such as grocery stores, hardware stores, and gas stations. Hazardous materials facilities that manufacture, store, or process industrial/hazardous materials, such as corrosives, explosives, flammable materials, radioactive materials, and toxins should also be identified. Data from HAZUS, tax records, aerial photography, or local planning documents are useful for gathering this information and displaying it on a map.

Estimating the Value of Each Asset in the Community

GIS, HAZUS, public documents, or tax records can be used to estimate the total value of the buildings and facilities inside each hazard area. The approximate replacement value for each type of building, accessible through local tax assessment records (for privately owned buildings) and government records (for public buildings and facilities), indicates the cost of rebuilding these structures if they are damaged severely or destroyed by a hazard event. Insurance replacement value is also a good indication of asset value for risk assessment inventory purposes, although these figures may be more difficult to obtain for privately owned structures.

Table 10.3 Vulnerable Population Groups (King County, WA Hazard Mitigation Plan).

Jurisdiction	Non-English Speaking (%)	Disabled (%)	Over Age 65 (%)	Poverty (%)	K-12 Students (%)	Homes Over 40 Years Old (%)
King County	5.4	16.1	10.7	6.4	16.6	33.5
Washington State	14.0	17.7	11.2	10.6	19.1	29.4

Sources: U.S. Census Bureau, Profile of Selected Social Characteristics: 2000, and Profile of Housing Characteristics, 2000 (Washington State figures); 2007 Census Bureau; 2008 King County Annual Growth Report.

Counting the Number of People in the Community

People are your highest priority when inventorying assets. The risk assessment should identify areas of population density as well as the location and number of people with unique vulnerabilities. Whether it's due to age, disability, poverty, language, mobility, or other barriers, socially vulnerable populations often face greater challenges preparing for, coping with, and recovering from disasters. These populations may also demand a relatively larger deployment of resources such as first responders immediately before, during, and after a disaster.

Table 10.3 shows an example taken from the Hazard Mitigation Plan in King County, Washington, where the risk assessment includes a description of vulnerable population groups within the county and the state.

In addition, itinerant populations might also be at greater risk from hazard events. Itinerant populations include students, second homeowners, migrant farmworkers, tourists, and visitors for special events such as sporting events and festivals where large numbers of people are concentrated. Visiting populations may be less familiar with the local environment and ill-prepared to evacuate or protect themselves.

10.5.4 Task Two: Calculating the Proportion of Assets Located in Hazard Areas

Task two of the asset inventory involves calculating the proportion of assets and their values that are located in hazard areas as compared to the community total. This task is carried out by dividing the number or value in each hazard area by the total number or value in the community as a whole. For example, if 20 residential structures are located in the community and 10 of those are located in the 100-year floodplain, 50% of local residential structures are located in the flood hazard area. This is valuable information for gauging overall vulnerability.

By presenting information about the percentage of the building stock (and the community tax base) that is susceptible to hazard damages, we can see "by the numbers" how vulnerable the community is. These figures can serve as a real eye-opener to local officials and citizens, encouraging them to financially and politically support proactive mitigation and preparedness efforts.

10.5.5 Inventorying Assets for Intentional Human-Made Hazards

Conducting a risk assessment for intentional human-made hazards involves an asset-specific approach to identify the structures and facilities that may be potential targets of a terrorist attack or other threats. Each asset is then assessed individually for its particular vulnerabilities. Critical infrastructure and systems that should be inventoried during this step include those of which the incapacity or destruction would have a debilitating effect on the defense or economic security of the community, state, region, or nation. These critical infrastructure categories include the following:

- Food supplies, storage, and distribution systems
- Water and wastewater
- Public health (hospitals, medical clinics, etc.)
- Emergency services
- Defense industries
- Telecommunications
- Energy (oil, gas, electric power lines, nuclear reactors)
- Transportation (airports, roads, railroads, etc.)
- Banking and finance
- Chemicals and hazardous materials
- Postal and shipping

The vulnerabilities of these assets can be identified through two basic approaches: inherent and tactical vulnerabilities.

- **Inherent vulnerability:** The way a building or facility is used, how visible it is, how accessible it is, how many people are located there, and other factors determine that asset's level of inherent vulnerability. For example, a football stadium and large concert arena are settings where thousands of people gather and where it is relatively easy to gain entry. A terrorist may find such a target attractive because many people could be hurt during an attack. An assessment of such inherent vulnerabilities must be conducted for each asset to determine its weaknesses.
- **Tactical vulnerability:** The way a building is designed, built, landscaped, and engineered determines its tactical vulnerability. For example, if an HVAC system is designed so that it is not easily accessible and has security cameras aimed at it, a terrorist may be less likely to attempt to use the system as a weapon to release poisonous gas. A tactical vulnerability assessment should be completed for each asset that has been identified as at risk from intentional hazards to determine how well it is protected from attack.

10.5.6 Mapping Assets and Populations

The next step in the vulnerability assessment involves creating map overlays. Hazard maps created during step two of the risk assessment process can be overlaid on the community's base map to visualize the number and value of buildings and the populations that could be impacted in these areas. Overlay maps that show community features and the ways that hazards can affect these features can be produced through the use of GIS.

SELF-CHECK

- What are tasks required to inventory vulnerable assets populations?
- Define **assets**, **vulnerability**, **inherent vulnerability**, and **tactical vulnerability**.
- Describe several types of information that you might want to gather during an inventory of hazard areas.

10.6 RISK ASSESSMENT STEP FOUR: ESTIMATING POTENTIAL LOSSES

The fourth step in the risk assessment process answers: "What could the community lose in a hazard event?" So far, the risk assessment has determined that one or more hazards may affect the community (step one), profiled hazard events (step two), and inventoried the assets and populations that could be damaged by a hazard event (step three). In this step, the community estimates losses using dollar amounts that indicate how the community could be impacted economically by the various hazards that threaten it. HAZUS, the loss estimation software produced by FEMA, has been useful to many communities when carrying out this step.

A **loss estimate** assesses the level of damage that could happen to each individual asset in the inventory from each type of hazard. This involves calculating the losses that could occur to each structure, based on the building's replacement value in various hazard scenarios. For example, 3 feet of floodwater in a building causes more damage than 6 inches. The replacement cost of the building's contents is also added to the calculation. A very detailed loss estimate adds to this the costs incurred when the use and function of each structure is disrupted, for example, if the service provided in that structure must be carried out in an alternative location. When added together, these figures provide an estimated total asset loss for the community.

> ### LOSS ESTIMATE CALCULATION
>
> **Structural Loss + Content Loss + Use and Function Loss = Total Loss**

The loss estimation step of the risk assessment provides one more piece of information illustrating the community's level of vulnerability. The ultimate goal is to reduce vulnerability; knowing exactly what is at stake can help develop and target the most appropriate hazard mitigation strategies for achieving that goal.

10.6.1 Calculating Human Losses

The costs from a flood, earthquake, or other types of hazards that are captured during the loss estimate are financial in nature. The human losses are much more difficult to calculate. Software products from various state and federal sources can provide credible estimates of the number of people that may be hurt or killed in different types of buildings under different hazard conditions. For the risk assessment, it is important to note that the likelihood of people being injured or killed depends upon such factors as warning time, the quality and age of the structures, local response capabilities, and the characteristics of the hazard itself. For some hazards, such as flooding, deaths or injuries are relatively rare in our country and most often occur when people fail to heed evacuation warnings or when they drive through floodwaters. For other hazards, such as heat waves, injury and loss of life can be widespread. In any event, it is extremely problematic to place a dollar value on human lives; rather, the planning process should incorporate every opportunity to reduce the risk of human injuries and casualties to the greatest extent possible for all sorts of hazards.

SILENT KILLER: HEAT WAVE

Heat is the most deadly weather in the developed world. Every year, there are about 700 deaths in the United States due to heat-related illness, more than from floods, lightening and tornadoes combined. In the 1980s, 2 severe heat waves killed up to 20,000 people in the United States. In 1999, a drought and heat wave in the eastern part of the country claimed 502 lives, making it the deadliest weather event of the 1990s. During a heat wave that struck Western Europe in 2003, over 35,000 people were killed by heat-related conditions. For comparison, the death toll of Hurricane Katrina was 1836.[2]

SELF-CHECK

- Explain the loss estimate equation.
- Discuss factors involved in estimating potential loss of life from hazards.

10.7 RISK ASSESSMENT STEP FIVE: DESCRIBING FUTURE LAND USE AND DEVELOPMENT TRENDS

So far, during the risk assessment process, we have been focusing on the impact a hazard event could have on a community as it exists right now. But communities are constantly changing. As towns and cities grow, their level of vulnerability changes. We might assume that, in general, more assets and people mean greater vulnerability, and in many cases, this is true. Yet we do not have to accept this assumption. Communities can choose to grow and develop in such a way that their vulnerability to hazards does *not* increase. This does not mean that the hazards will disappear, but it does mean that a community will be conscious of its direction of growth and will make decisions so that new development is not located in places of danger or is built to better withstand the impacts of hazards. Step five in the risk assessment process evaluates the community's future vulnerability by asking the question: "What people and property will be at risk from hazards in the future if we continue to grow and develop as we are right now?"

Although there is no sure way to foretell a community's future, trends in population and land use indicate future directions in growth. The community's attitude toward new growth is also indicative of future growth trends. These attitudes are articulated through the local ordinances and regulations that control land use in the jurisdiction. During the risk assessment, we predict where future development might occur so that if development is being allowed in hazard risk areas, mitigation strategies can be formed to help foster change in the regulatory system.

10.7.1 Describing Undeveloped Areas

A good place to start when assessing a community's potential future vulnerability is to describe all the areas within the county or town limits that are currently undeveloped. Local land use maps, tax data, aerial photography, and even a "windshield tour" of the community can identify empty parcels. For each undeveloped area, the risk assessment includes a description of the dominant form of land cover, such as forest, desert, wetland, farmland, and parkland.

In addition to describing the current state of undeveloped areas, the risk assessment also describes potential future conditions by considering the types of development that are likely over the course of the next several decades in these undeveloped areas. Most local governments have policies, plans, and regulations that deal with future land uses that dictate what types of new development are allowed. For example, a local comprehensive plan often spells out how and where a community wants to grow over the next 10 or 20 years. Local zoning ordinances and subdivision regulations are usually more specific and describe how many and what type of buildings are allowed in certain areas of the community. These rules and policies provide information about what could be built where, *if* the rules remain unchanged and if developers and landowners take full advantage of those rules. It is useful to involve the local planner or zoning administrator in this step to get the best information about trends and policies regarding future development. See Chapter 8 for a more detailed discussion of local regulations and land use policies, and how they can be used to reduce future vulnerability.

10.7.2 Describing Scheduled-Infrastructure Areas

In addition to looking at the community's land use plans and zoning regulations to determine the type and location of development that is permissible, the risk assessment should also include a review of local infrastructure plans that show where and when public services will be extended into undeveloped areas, including roads, water lines, sewer lines, schools, and other community facilities. The decision to build large public infrastructure projects is most commonly implemented through a capital improvement plan, a plan that schedules where and when a local government will build its public assets during the next 5–10 years. Some communities use their master or comprehensive plan to describe the overall land use pattern for the community over the next decade.

If You Build It, They Will Come

Scheduled infrastructure is a good predictor of future development because once these services are provided, development will usually soon follow. These items are necessary to support new neighborhoods, shopping centers, factories, office complexes, and other sorts of construction, and they are typically very expensive to build and maintain. Most large-scale development projects rely on hookups to public water and sewer, as well as other public facilities, to be viable investments for the developer and builder.

In smaller communities that may not have enacted land use regulations or a formal capital improvement plan, planners and emergency managers can rely on their own judgment about how and where the community is growing and whether there is potential for development to take place in areas that are currently undeveloped. Insight derived from local residents, business owners, elected officials, and local staff can help inform these conjectures about future land use trends. Is the locality considered a bedroom community for a growing city nearby? Are large employers likely to be attracted to the area? Is a major interstate or connector road going to be constructed to which the community will have access? Has the state or local government created tax incentives or other economic development programs to lure business and industry to the area? These and other questions help predict—at least in a general way—the future development potential, and thereby future vulnerability, of the community.

10.7.3 Determining Where Undeveloped Areas Intersect with Hazardous Areas

Knowing which areas of the community are undeveloped and which of these areas may be developed in the future provides a basis for determining whether developable portions of the community are located in known hazard areas. This step involves comparing the hazard area descriptions created during step two of the risk assessment process with the descriptions of undeveloped land and scheduled-infrastructure areas created during this step. An overlay of hazard maps onto the community base map is helpful for visualizing this step.

If the overlays indicate that undeveloped lands intersect with hazardous areas, more specific information about this potential for future vulnerability is necessary. An overlay of the hazard map with the community's zoning map, for instance, can indicate the types of development that are allowed in hazard areas. If it appears that development will be allowed that could put more people and property in harm's way, the community may choose to change the rules before a disaster happens.

SELF-CHECK

- Explain why it is important to include anticipated future development in a risk assessment.
- What do capital improvement programs tell you about development trends?

10.8 RISK ASSESSMENT STEP SIX: FORMING CONCLUSIONS (DETERMINING "ACCEPTABLE RISK")

The risk assessment process can provide a wealth of information about the community's level of vulnerability to a wide range of potential hazards. Much of this information will be in the form of charts, spreadsheets, tables, and reports full of figures and projections, as well as maps that illustrate the locations of community assets in relation to known hazard areas. But the value of this information lies in the conclusions that are formulated—conclusions that are based on the data collected and the analysis conducted.

10.8.1 Each Community Must Decide for Itself

Each community must look at the risk assessment in its entirety and decide whether the sum of all the various bits of information put together equal a risk scenario that is either acceptable or unacceptable. In other words, are the problems presented during the risk assessment so great that the community would agree to do something about it? If so, then the level of risk will be considered unacceptable, and the community should then take the necessary steps through hazard mitigation and preparedness to reduce those risks. On the other hand, it might be discovered that only an insignificant portion of the community is actually vulnerable to known hazards, and the community might decide to forgo spending the necessary money, time, and energy in trying to solve its relatively minor hazard problems. The risk assessment may also show that the community already has some mitigation strategies in place; these will factor into the conclusions as well, perhaps strengthening public resolve to continue risk reduction further. Either way, it is important that the conclusions formed at the end of the risk assessment process are directly tied to the information that was gathered and analyzed.

The conclusions drawn from the risk assessment are not set in stone. Over time, the community's level of vulnerability may change. For example, a rapid rise in population may call for revisions of the asset and population inventories to make sure incoming residents aren't placed in an area of risk. On the other hand, overall vulnerability may decline, as mitigation strategies are implemented and risk is reduced. The risk assessment process is not meant to be static, and as local conditions change, the risk assessment will need to be updated and modified to reflect those changing conditions.

10.8.2 Creating a Hazard Mitigation Plan Based on the Risk Assessment

If a community decides that its level of risk is unacceptable, the risk assessment can provide a factual basis for creating targeted mitigation strategies. This is often effectively accomplished by developing a mitigation plan, a policy document that lays out goals, objectives, and actions intended to reduce the vulnerabilities highlighted during the risk assessment process. The risk assessment and loss estimations are just one element of a complete hazard mitigation plan, but it is the plan itself that will put measures in action to reduce vulnerability. Through a mitigation plan, we can use the information obtained during the risk assessment to protect existing buildings and retrofit older buildings against hazard impacts. Where land is not yet developed, we can guide future development and keep people and property out of areas we know are hazardous.

10.8.3 Dealing with Uncertainty

Throughout this chapter, we have tried to emphasize that a risk assessment is not a silver bullet—it cannot predict with certainty that any particular hazard will impact any particular community; this level of uncertainty is especially true when we try to assess how a changing climate will change what we know about hazards. So how do we deal with all this uncertainty? One way is to use the information gleaned from the risk assessment to develop risk reduction policies that will leave us with "no regrets." In other words, we implement actions that are good for the community regardless of the precise degree of risk involved. These actions often involve multiple participants and fulfill more than one local goal in a win-win for the entire community.

SELF-CHECK

- List ways to incorporate the results of the risk assessment into actions that will reduce vulnerabilities.
- Discuss factors that influence a community's decision to act on a risk assessment.
- Explain how a risk assessment can be used to steer development away from hazardous areas.

10.9 HAZARD CITY

Now that we have described the necessary steps to carry out a thorough risk assessment to serve as part of the foundation for mitigation and preparedness activities, we are ready to begin applying these concepts. In this section, we use a fictitious community named Hazard City to illustrate the risk assessment process. As you read this section, imagine yourself as the emergency manager or planner of this community, so you can visualize going through the steps as both a concerned citizen and a professional tasked to improve your community's resiliency to hazards. Read the Hazard City case study below and pause to consider the bulleted questions interspersed in the section. It is our hope that the exaggerated conditions we present will spark ideas about options the community might take, and that you will have a bit of fun while you tackle some serious issues.

10.9.1 Welcome to Hazard City, United States

Hazard City, nestled in the Mountain-Coastal Territory of Atlantic State, is home to 10,000 residents. It's an area of incredible natural beauty, with steep-sloped mountains covered with pine forests and a broad, quiet river with gently sloping banks. Nearly 80 years ago, an earthen dam was built across the Lazy River to create a man-made lake, which serves as the source of drinking water for the town. The crown jewel in Hazard City is its wide sand beach that flanks the coast of the Atlantic Ocean, accessible only by a narrow causeway from the mainland. Every summer, hundreds of visitors converge on the oceanfront to attend a 3-day music festival.

Hazard City is undergoing tremendous population growth. The investment in public and private infrastructure has been in the millions of dollars for the past 5 straight years. New schools and shopping centers are being built, and roads, water, and sewer lines are being planned for areas not yet developed. The wetlands located near the river are considered particularly desirable for new growth and are slated to be drained and filled soon, although a local conservation group, however, has identified an endangered species of frog that lives only in the particular habitat provided by the marsh. A chemical plant located on the riverbank at the end of a railroad spur has just hired 200 workers, and new subdivisions are springing up to accommodate families moving into the area. Investors are considering building a large hotel on prime beachfront real estate to attract more tourists. Developers, the mayor, and the town's tax assessor are ecstatic.

Over the years, however, natural hazards such as a cluster of hurricanes in the 1990s, devastating tornadoes in 2009, 2011, and 2014, as well as annual, intense forest fires have impacted local residents, businesses, and the tourism industry. Flooding threatens Hazard City every year, as the river swells its banks with melted snow from the mountains. In 2018, back-to-back snowstorms shut the city down for nearly a week. Power was out for 2 weeks in some neighborhoods, and roads were impassable for days. Occasionally, mild earthquakes can be felt in the area, although no damage from quakes has been recorded since 1910, when a grain elevator just outside of town was toppled. Periodic landslides have closed some of the mountain roads with rock and debris.

Historically, drought has not been a problem in Hazard City. However, in 3 of the last 5 years, there was significantly less snowfall in the mountains that the region normally gets, leading to lower water levels in the Hazard City reservoir. Some local environmental groups and the water utility are requesting a study about the potential effects of climate change on the municipal water supply.

By far, the single most devastating natural hazard to hit Hazard City in recent memory was Hurricane Zelda in 2013. The scars of Zelda, a powerful Category 3 storm, can still be seen throughout the city. Although the town had survived hurricanes before, the storm surge and flooding seemed particularly high during Zelda. Even the "old timers" who had lived in Hazard City all their lives could not recall waves so high or flooding that reached so far inland. In some neighborhoods, many of the damaged homes have not been fully repaired, where roofs and siding were ripped off by high winds and entire buildings were uprooted. A majority of the town's small businesses have never reopened. The coastal areas took the brunt of the storm, and numerous oceanfront lots have yet to be redeveloped, while some lots were eroded so severely that very little shorefront remains. However, the homes that were located a few rows back from the oceanfront that had been elevated on stilts above the flood level of the last storm received relatively minor damage.

The Hazard City town council has just appointed a team to develop a hazard mitigation plan that meets FEMA requirements, so that the town will be eligible for federal disaster assistance—including funds for hazard mitigation projects—when the next disaster strikes. The team, lead jointly by the planning director and the director of emergency management, is about to embark on the risk assessment phase of the mitigation planning process.

Step One: Hazard Identification

- What natural hazards does Hazard City face?
- What human-made hazards does Hazard City face?
- Are there any hazards or secondary impacts not specifically mentioned in the description that could affect Hazard City?

The types of hazards that would be listed in the hazard identification step of the community's risk assessment include hurricane (with storm surge and erosion), riverine flooding, tornado, forest fire, severe winter storms, earthquake, and landslide. The hazard identification may also include a potential dam break and chemical spill, as well as sea level rise. Of course, in reality, additional sources of information to complete the hazard identification step for Hazard City would be available, including government websites for the region, interviews with residents, a review of local documents and plans, reports of municipal employees, and old weather reports and archives. In fact, information overload is often experienced when planners and emergency managers begin gathering information about local hazards. It can be difficult to determine when to stop the data gathering stage and move on to the next step in the planning process.

Step Two: Hazard Profile

- What potential impact might we expect from each of the hazards identified for Hazard City?
- How likely is each of the hazards identified?
- Are there certain hazards that affect only part of the City?
- What climate change impacts should be noted in the risk assessment?

As we mentioned earlier in the chapter, a great place to start with a hazard profile is to explore and document the community's hazard history. Instead of merely noting each event, details that give us information about the extent, severity, and location of the hazard are particularly helpful. For example, instead of merely mentioning that Hurricane Zelda occurred in 2014, the hazard history for Hazard City should indicate the critical features of Zelda, including wind speeds, depth of flooding, height of storm surge, as well as a description of property damages and the number of deaths and injuries. A complete hazard history would also indicate longer lasting impacts of a past hazard event, such as whether businesses closed, either permanently or temporarily, whether people were displaced and moved away, whether specific populations within the community were disproportionately affected, and other pertinent facts about how the event affected the local economy, social networks, and the built environment.

Although no single natural hazard event can be attributed to climate change, a discussion of how trends in hazard occurrence are changing could be a helpful part of a comprehensive hazard profile. For example, the fact that Hurricane Zelda's storm surge, flood levels, and erosion were record-breaking may be indication that conditions are starting to change with regard to sea level rise and the severity of future storms.

The emergency manager of Hazard City has obtained many hazard maps from state and federal agencies, including the town's FIRM, storm surge inundation maps, erosion rate maps, topographical maps (for steep slope and landslide areas), seismic zone maps, wildfire maps, and a dam inundation map that shows flood potential downstream in the event of a dam break. The community has also chosen to illustrate potential sea level rise along the shoreline, using several scenarios that show a range of projections. By layering all these maps onto the base map, the Hazard City planning team can create a map that defines the boundaries of all the city's potential hazards.

Since Hazard City takes an all-hazards approach to emergency management, the planning team should include the potential risk from technological hazards in its risk assessment. The existence of a chemical plant on the riverbank could pose such a hazard risk, for instance, if hazardous materials spilled into the river, or an accident occurred during transportation. However, for security purposes, identifying the specific location and contents of the chemical plant may not be advisable. For extremely volatile industries, states often have secure-access maps, which can only be viewed by authorized personnel. In these communities, decision-makers must balance the citizens' right to know about the hazards in their neighborhood with security concerns.

Step Three: Asset and Population Inventory

Table 10.4 indicates the proportion of Hazard City assets and population that are located in the town's flood hazard area. We can see from the last row in the chart that 40% of Hazard City's structures and 42% of the town's property values are located in flood areas. We can also see that 42% of the town's population lives and works in the flood hazard area. This chart tells us that a very significant percentage of the town's total property value and many of its people are in danger from flooding.

Note that counting the number of people that live in the residential structures and adding them to the number of people in the other types of buildings results in some double counting. The planning team should keep this weakness in mind when assessing population numbers at risk. A more sophisticated analysis calculates the number of people in a given location over a 24-hour period. Such an analysis might show, for example, that the majority of the population of Hazard City is at school, shopping, or at work during the daytime hours, but they are predominantly located in residential structures at night. This is important information for preparedness efforts such as emergency warnings. For example, more deaths are reported from tornadoes that strike at night, when people are asleep and are not tuned into television or radio announcements to seek shelter. Conversely, winter storms and blizzards can be most dangerous that occur during the day because more people tend to be on the roads trying to drive home.

- What additional information would be useful to know about assets in Hazard City that would help us understand the level of risk?
- Are there certain populations that we may want to know more information about at this stage of the risk assessment?

Table 10.4 Hazard City Asset and Population Inventory: Flood Hazard Area.

Type of Structure	Number of Structures			Value of Structures			Number of People		
	Total No. in City	No. in Hazard Area	% in Hazard Area	Total $ in City	$ in Hazard Area	% in Hazard Area	Total No. in City	No. in Hazard Area	% in Hazard Area
Residential	2500	100	40	250,000,000	100,000,000	40	10,000	4000	40
Commercial	10	8	80	10,000,000	7,000,000	70	570	345	61
Industrial	1	1	1	2,000,000	2,000,000	100	200	200	200
Government	7	5	71	7,055,000	2,555,000	36	570	170	30
Education	4	2	50	6,000,000	3,000,000	50	3000	1500	50
Utilities	4	4	100	4,750,000	4,750,000	100	30	30	100
Religious/Nonprofit	3	1	33	3,450,000	1,500,000	43	351	10	0.03
Total	2529	1021	40	283,255,000	120,805,000	42	14,721	6255	42

Step Four: Loss Estimate

Now that we have a better sense of the hazards facing Hazard City, as well as the assets and populations that may be exposed to these hazards, it is time to begin estimating potential losses that could occur from various scenarios. For hazards that only occur in some locations, such as flooding that may occur from a hurricane's storm surge, we may choose to add the value of property located within a certain distance and elevation from the shoreline. For a snowstorm, in addition to damages to structures and infrastructure, we may look at the average length of time it takes the city to clear snow and restore power sufficiently for businesses to reopen. Loss estimate software, such as the FEMA-developed HAZUS, can be invaluable at this stage of the risk assessment.

Step Five: Future Land Use and Development

- How much development should we expect in Hazard City over the coming years, and where will it be located?
- How will changes in the way land is used in Hazard City influence vulnerability to hazards? Is this more pronounced for specific hazards?

In addition to understanding how the overall population is changing, it is important to think about where development is occurring. This information is essential to understand how future houses, businesses and people in Hazard City may be susceptible to floods, winter storms, water shortages, dam breaks, and other known perils. This information is also critical in understanding how this development may actually change the hazard profile. For example, might anticipated development in Hazard City that requires filling a wetland increase the risk of flooding? If the population doubles over the next decade or two, will the reservoir have sufficient capacity to provide drinking water to the future population? What if we factor in the impact of climate change on the winter snowpack that drains toward Hazard City during the spring?

The goal of an assessment of land use and development patterns in the risk assessment is not necessarily to slow development but rather to provide information that allows more thoughtful management of development to avoid unnecessary risk. As we move into the final stage of the risk assessment and draw conclusions from all of the information we gather, we may want to think about how economic, political, and social factors are influencing development patterns? Is Hazard City subsidizing or encouraging development in a certain area through taxes or regulatory policies? Do citizens have sufficient information about hazards when making decisions about investments in new properties?

Step Six: Forming Conclusions

We have now pulled together myriad maps, charts, spreadsheets, projections, and other forms of information that paint a picture of the level of risk that Hazard City faces now and into the future. But how do we make sense of all of this information? What is the most important, requiring action to prepare for hazards or strategies to mitigate risk?

In addition to summarizing key information gathered in the risk assessment, we must determine the acceptable level of risk. Based on the likelihood and severity of an event similar to Hurricane Zelda, should we take action to reduce the level of risk in Hazard City? Are we preparing too much for some types of events and not enough for others? Are some neighborhoods or population groups disproportionately at risk? While there are no set conclusions that a community should draw from their risk assessment, it is essential that they be tied to data and information gathered and grounded in the values and aspirations of the community.

SUMMARY

This chapter explains how a risk assessment informs us about the hazards we face, so that we can choose the most appropriate mitigation and preparedness strategies in the effort to become more resilient. To begin, a community must identify all the hazards that might occur, information that is largely based on events of the past, as well as other local and regional data. In the second step of the risk assessment process, the community creates a profile of the hazards that includes the areas that may be affected, the possible impacts, and the probability of recurrence. The third step involves an inventory of those assets and populations that are vulnerable to hazards. In the fourth step, the community estimates what could be lost in a hazard event, using dollar figures, as well as projected numbers of deaths and injuries. The community uses the fifth step of the process to anticipate future vulnerability by describing growth and development trends. The chapter concludes with a discussion of the sixth step, outlining ways that communities can arrive at conclusions about the acceptable level of risk based on risk assessment findings.

KEY TERMS

Asset: Any human-made or natural feature that has value, including, but not limited to, people, buildings, infrastructure, critical facilities, and environmental, cultural, and recreational features.

Base map: Graphic that shows the basic topography, physical elements, critical facilities, and infrastructure of a community; can be used to superimpose hazard-specific information for an illustration of vulnerability.

Critical facilities: Facilities critical to the health and welfare of the population, especially following hazard events. Critical facilities include, but are not limited to, evacuation shelters, police and fire stations, hospitals, lifeline infrastructure such as water and sewer treatment facilities, power generation stations, and communication and transportation networks.

Essential facilities: Facilities important for a full recovery of a community following a hazard event. These include the following: government buildings, major employers, banks, schools, and certain commercial establishments such as grocery stores, pharmacies, hardware and building supply stores, and gas stations.

Geographic information systems (GIS): A computer software application that relates physical features on the earth to a database to be used for mapping and analysis.

Hazard identification: The process of identifying hazards that threaten an area.

Hazard profile: A description of the physical characteristics of hazards and a determination of various descriptors, including magnitude, duration, frequency, probability, and extent.

HAZUS: A risk assessment tool used to estimate hazard losses. HAZUS contains a database of economic, census, building stock, transportation facilities, local geology, and other information.

Inherent vulnerability: Factors such as the way a building or facility is used, how visible it is, how accessible it is, how many people are located there, and other factors that determine the asset's level of susceptibility, often in reference to intentional man-made hazards.

Lifeline utilities: Services that are essential to a community's health and well-being, such as potable water, wastewater treatment, power systems, and communication networks.

Loss estimate: A calculation in dollar amounts of the potential damage to structures and contents, interruption of services, and displacement of residents and businesses caused by a hazard.

Magnitude: A measure of the strength of a hazard event, or how much energy is released. The magnitude (also referred to as severity) of a given hazard event is usually determined using technical measures.

Probability: A statistical measure of the likelihood that a hazard event will occur.

Recurrence interval: The time period between hazard events of a similar size in a given location. It is based on the probability that the given event will be equaled or exceeded in any given year.

Risk assessment: The process or methodology used to evaluate risk. Risk assessment typically includes five preliminary steps: (1) identify hazards; (2) profile hazard events; (3) inventory assets and populations; (4) estimate losses; (5) determine future development and population trends. A sixth step, (6) determine acceptable level of risk, is often included in a risk assessment to decide whether further action is warranted.

Tactical vulnerability: Factors such as the way a building is designed, built, landscaped, and engineered that determine the asset's susceptibility to hazard impacts, often in reference to intentional man-made hazards.

Vulnerability: The extent to which people will experience harm and property will be damaged as the result of a hazard. Present vulnerability involves who and what is at risk now; future vulnerability indicates who and what may be at risk in the future under projected development and population trends.

ASSESS YOUR UNDERSTANDING

Summary Questions

1. The purpose of a risk assessment is to determine what would happen if a hazard event occurred in a community. True or False?
2. Repetitive occurrences of chronic hazards do not lead to a cumulative impact over time. True or False?
3. The risk assessment process for a hurricane greatly differs from that used for hazardous material accidents. True or False?
4. A base map is used
   a. To periodically update HAZUS maps
   b. To view hazard-specific information against basic topography
   c. To illustrate zoning districts in a community
   d. To depict floodplains
5. Hazard identification involves creating a hazard history. True or False?
6. Research into a community's past hazard events should include major events as well as those that are less significant. True or False?
7. A hazard profile identifies the severity of a potential hazard, in some cases, using terms such as mild, moderate, or severe. True or False?
8. A hazard's potential impact is
   a. Equal to its probability
   b. Greater than its severity
   c. A combination of frequency of occurrence and magnitude of event
   d. A combination of magnitude of event, area affected, and amount of human activity

9. The 100-year flood is one that has
   a. Near 100% probability in the next year
   b. A 1% chance of occurring in a given year
   c. At least one chance in the next 10 years
   d. Less than one chance in the next 100 years
10. An evacuation center is one example of a community asset. True or False?
11. Tactical vulnerability is partly determined by how a facility or building is used. True or False?
12. Potential losses from a man-made hazards area are typically divided into three groups: people, assets, and functions. True or False?
13. Methods to estimate losses from natural hazards work equally well with hazards of a terrorist or technological nature. True or False?
14. Over the years, a community's vulnerability
    a. Remains the same
    b. Decreases
    c. Increases
    d. Varies
15. An evaluation of a community's undeveloped areas and their potential for growth helps determine a community's potential future vulnerability. True or False?
16. A geographic information system is
    a. A type of computer software product
    b. A tool for creating digital overlays of geographic features
    c. A tool for creating printed maps
    d. All of the above

Review Questions

1. How does a risk assessment factor into mitigation efforts?
2. What are the six steps of the risk assessment process?
3. Which steps in the risk assessment process help you determine the community's level of vulnerability?
4. List several components of a good base map.
5. Describe three examples of where to find information about past hazard events.
6. What sources can be used to find information about man-made hazards?
7. What sources are available to find out about regional climate change impacts?
8. Which types of hazards are commonly mapped?
9. What are the limitations of using historical information to estimate what will happen in the future?
10. List three examples of community assets.
11. The extent of a hazard is identified in the second step of the risk assessment process. Which scale could be used to describe the potential severity of a tornado?
12. Step three of a risk assessment, inventorying vulnerable assets and populations, involves three tasks. Describe each of the three tasks.
13. As part of the inventory process, you must estimate the value of each community asset. Explain how.
14. Two approaches can be used to identify the vulnerability of an asset. Define tactical vulnerability and give an example.
15. What is the name of the risk assessment program used for analyzing potential losses from floods, earthquakes, and hurricane winds?

16. What is scheduled infrastructure, and what does it indicate for the future?
17. What is a hazard mitigation plan?
18. Explain hazard probability for flooding and what a 100-year floodplain means.

Applying This Chapter

1. What elements of your community's risk assessment process would you choose to display on maps? Why? What are some of the sources you would use to create your maps?
2. As a planner in Biloxi, Mississippi, you have been charged with carrying out the city's risk assessment. What role does the risk assessment play in creating the city's mitigation strategies? Identify the natural hazards that affect your community; determine if any are chronic hazards.
3. In the past 8 years, two trains have derailed on the rail line that runs through your community. One was significant, involving a hazardous material and two deaths. Create a hazard profile for this hazard. How does this profile differ from one for a natural hazard?
4. How would you go about determining the level of vulnerability to natural hazards for Lewes, Delaware? What resources, internet or otherwise, would you go to for the information you needed for the three tasks required for this step?
5. Using the formula provided in the text for calculating estimated total losses, determine the total loss that would result from a hazard event impacting your home or residence. Would that loss vary depending on the hazard? If so, indicate why?
6. As a planner, what would you do if you discovered an undeveloped area of your community was vulnerable to landslides? You've already read about plans to build a bigger road and bring water and power to this potentially hazardous area.
7. Imagine you live a rural farming community in Ohio. Why is a future project to install water and sewer lines in an area an indicator of future development? What does this tell you about the future vulnerability of this area?

You Try It

Measure the Cost of Flooding in Your Home

All it takes is a few inches of water to cause major damage to your home and its contents. An interactive tool provided by FloodSmart.gov (a resource of the National Flood Insurance Program) shows you what a flood in your home could cost, inch by inch. When the waters "rise," the dollar figures mount, as carpets, appliances, electrical outlets, personal belongings, furniture, and other household goods get soaked. The educational site even includes the cost of cleaning. To check out the tool yourself, visit https://www.floodsmart.gov/flood-insurance-cost/calculator.

Describing the Future

Part of assessing a community's vulnerability is determining what's at stake for loss in the future. Describe areas of your town or county, which are undeveloped, including their current state as well as their potential future condition. Use resources such as the Internet, aerial maps, tax maps, and local land maps. Whenever possible, indicate who owns the property.

Hazard History 101

Choose what you think is the most significant natural hazard that threatens your community. Complete a hazard profile, determining the hazard's extent, probability, and location.

Risk Assessment

Consider the hazard-prone areas of your community where people live or work. Predict the feasibility of a mitigation plan based on your community and local political attitudes toward growth and mitigation.

REFERENCES

1. NOAA. 2014. Lessons in Resilience: How Indigenous Tribes Are Helping Lead the Way on Climate Change. *Coastal Services* 2(17): 11–14.
2. Woodruff, S.C. et al. (2013). *Adapting to Climate Change: A Handbook for local governments in North Carolina*. Chapel Hill, NC: Coastal Hazards Center at the University of North Carolina at Chapel Hill. Available online at: coastalhazardscenter.org/adapt.

11

Preparedness Activities
Planning to Be Ready When Disaster Hits

What You'll Learn

- The role of preparedness as part of the emergency management cycle
- Responsibilities of government authorities, businesses, and individuals in preparedness
- Key preparedness programs in the United States
- Hazard-specific examples of preparedness exercises

Goals and Outcomes

- Evaluate the effectiveness of preparedness at all levels
- Identify key preparedness players and understand how their actions should be coordinated
- Create informed disaster plans, whether contributing to a local emergency operations plan or a family disaster plan

INTRODUCTION

This chapter outlines the differences and similarities between hazard mitigation and preparedness and discusses the role of preparedness in the disaster management cycle, including the need to incorporate climate change information into preparedness programs. We also give a brief overview of how preparedness helps ensure an efficient response to a disaster, including an introduction to the National Response Plan and the Presidential Policy Directive 8, which guides national preparedness. The chapter then describes various preparedness activities undertaken by governments, businesses, families, and volunteer organizations such as the American Red Cross. The chapter also illustrates the responsibilities of government and individuals for preparedness by focusing on an evacuation scenario. The chapter concludes with a discussion of various preparedness programs that help make communities and individuals ready for many types of hazard situations.

11.1 PREPAREDNESS IN A NUTSHELL

When a community receives word that a hurricane is approaching, a frenzy of activity takes place to ensure that citizens and businesses are warned and, depending on the projected impacts, an attempt is made to move the vulnerable populations out of harm's way. In the

 DOI: 10.4324/9781003123897-11

midst of these activities, it is to the advantage of the community to have planned out a course of action ahead of time. Determining the most efficient methods for communicating warnings, evacuating large numbers of people, and setting up shelters is not something community officials should do on the fly, especially when it is possible to make these preparations in advance with thoughtful detail.

In essence, this planning for the activities that will take place immediately before, during, and immediately after a disaster occurs is described as preparedness. It is a vital portion of the disaster management cycle discussed in Chapter 2.

Preparedness is a state of readiness to respond to any emergency or disaster. It involves anticipating what might happen during different sorts of hazard events, making sure that plans are in place to deal with those possibilities, and training and educating everyone involved about what their various roles will be as the situation evolves. Along with mitigation, preparedness focuses on the future and is one of the building blocks of a resilient community.

As described by the Federal Emergency Management Agency (FEMA), preparedness includes:

> Actions that involve a combination of planning, resources, training, exercising, and organizing to build, sustain, and improve operational capabilities. Preparedness is the process of identifying the personnel, training, and equipment needed for a wide range of potential incidents, and developing jurisdiction-specific plans for delivering capabilities when needed for an incident.

Preparedness plays a vital role in the emergency management cycle. Preparedness not only involves pre-disaster readiness and planning for the immediate emergency response but also restoration of government services, utilities, and businesses to pre-disaster status as quickly as possible. Preparedness is a concept that overarches most aspects of emergency management. It entails coordination between many government officials, emergency workers, volunteers, and citizens. Emergency management agencies, businesses, and residents alike need to have preparedness capabilities. These capabilities can only come about through planning, training, and performing emergency exercises ahead of a disaster. Knowing what to do in a disaster can reduce the confusion, anxiety, fear, and even panic that often occur as a disaster unfolds. Most significantly, pre-disaster preparedness planning can save lives and minimize injuries.

11.1.1 The Role of Preparedness in Comprehensive Emergency Management

Preparedness is an integral part of the comprehensive emergency management system. **Comprehensive emergency management** is a widely used approach at the local, state, and federal levels to deal with the inevitability of natural hazards and the possibility of human-made hazards and their potential to cause disasters in a community. As discussed in Chapter 2, the four phases of a comprehensive emergency management system are **Preparedness, Response, Recovery,** and **Mitigation**. We prepare for disasters before they occur. When a disaster happens, a community must first respond to that particular event, and soon thereafter begin recovery. But even while the community is still recovering from one disaster, we begin the process of mitigating the impacts of the next disaster.

The Difference Between Preparedness and Mitigation

While there are some overlaps between mitigation and preparedness, there are also some key distinctions. Although preparedness activities are carried out in advance of a hazard event, they are generally directed to the response and recovery phase. During preparedness, we gather our supplies and make plans for what to do prior to impact and immediately thereafter to recover from the effects of the disaster. Mitigation, in contrast, is the ongoing effort to lessen the impacts of disasters on people and property through pre-disaster activities. Mitigation can take place months, years, and even decades before a hazard event and continues after a disaster occurs with an eye to the future. In sum, the difference between these two pre-disaster phases is mainly temporal. Mitigation involves a long-term commitment that ensures fewer people are victims of disasters in the future, while preparedness is planning for emergency services that must be delivered prior to and following a specific event.

To conceptualize the difference between the two, imagine that a major snowstorm is predicted to dump 2 feet of snow on a city with gale-force winds. Mitigation efforts that could have been implemented to reduce damage include burying power lines, providing backup generators to hospitals and shelters, and developing building codes that require reinforced roofs for new buildings. Preparedness efforts to effectively respond to the storm would include spreading sand and salt on roads before the blizzard hit, mobilizing electrical utility repair units from the surrounding region to quickly restore outages, and closing schools to reduce the number of people attempting to drive as the snow arrives.

Relationship Between Preparedness and Response

Preparedness is directly related to response—the phase of the emergency management cycle that occurs immediately after a disaster. To experience a successful response to a disaster, the plans for the response must be in place prior to the response effort. Preparedness takes care of much of the preplanning for response. There are many activities to coordinate in a response effort. The more planning that can be done ahead of a disaster, the more efficient the response to that particular disaster will be. Without preparedness, a timely, coordinated response would not be possible.

11.1.2 Preparedness for a Changing Climate

Many scientists and emergency managers recognize that climate change is shifting the hazard profile and vulnerability of their communities, with effects including intensified wildfires, higher sea levels, extreme rainfall, windstorms, disease spreading to new areas, heat waves, and drought. There have been a number of record-setting severe weather events, from the May 2010 flooding in Tennessee, which was the highest since recordkeeping began there in the 1880s, to the 2013 Colorado Floods, in which 17 inches of rain fell in a few days, comparable to Boulder County's average *annual* precipitation (20.7 in.)! The 2020 California wildfire season was yet another example of record-setting hazards linked to climate change, when nearly 4% of the state's land burned during a single year.

Anticipated climate change implications such as more intense storms and rising sea levels could demand preparedness efforts that support more elaborate and extensive emergency response. More frequent heavy downpours and floods in urban areas and more extensive coastal flooding will cause greater property damage, thus creating a heavier burden on emergency responders and a growing financial toll on businesses and homeowners. Flood insurance policies may have to be reevaluated. Higher threats of infectious diseases will likely require better coordination of emergency management and public health efforts—a reality made all too real during the COVID-19 pandemic, as communities in the United States and across the globe struggled to reduce the spread of the virus. Emergency managers may have to be poised to preposition more stocks to be responsive to potentially catastrophic events. In short, the emergency management community may be required to reevaluate how services are provided to accommodate the potentially hazardous impacts of climate change and implement comprehensive changes to strategic plans.[1]

SELF-CHECK

- List examples of response activities that involve preparedness.
- Explain how climate change may require a shift in preparedness policy and practice.

11.2 PREPAREDNESS IS EVERYONE'S RESPONSIBILITY

Although there are a number of different organizations involved in potential preparedness activities, it is important to realize that every individual, whether as family member or business owner, must accept responsibility for his or her own readiness for disaster. Government agencies and volunteer organizations have a significant role to play, but responsibility lies with each citizen to take these preventative actions as well. Working together to achieve preparedness at each level is the key to any successful response effort.

HURRICANE PAM: A PRE-KATRINA PLANNING AND PREPAREDNESS EXERCISE

Hurricane Pam was a planning and preparedness exercise that took place in July 2004 at the Louisiana State Emergency Operations Center in Baton Rouge. The five-day exercise was based on a hypothetical scenario named Hurricane Pam, a storm conceptualized as a slow-moving, strong Category 3 hurricane that would hit the city of New Orleans at some undetermined time in the future. FEMA provided funding for the exercise because, out of 25 disaster scenarios nationwide, a hurricane hitting New Orleans was selected as one of the most disastrous scenarios possible. The exercise was designed and facilitated by the private contracting firm Innovative Emergency Management Inc. and involved emergency management officials from over 50 parish, state, federal, and volunteer organizations located throughout southeastern Louisiana. The purpose of Pam was to facilitate the development of joint disaster response plans between all of the participants and determine what should be done to prepare and respond to this type of disaster.

The outcomes of the hypothetical scenario were amazingly similar to the actual conditions wrought by Hurricane Katrina a little over a year later in August 2005. Models run during Hurricane Pam visualized sustained winds of 120 miles an hour, up to 20 inches of rain in some areas of Louisiana, and storm surges that topped the levee system in New Orleans. Additionally, the scenario specified that 300,000 people would not evacuate, over 500,000 building would be destroyed, sewer services and communications would be knocked out, about 1000 shelters would be needed, boats and helicopters would be required to rescue stranded residents, and flood waters would create large uninhabitable areas across the southeast.[2] The predicted consequences also included over 175,000 injured, over 200,000 ill, and over 60,000 dead. In this respect, the resemblance of Hurricane Pam to Hurricane Katrina was fortunately not too close.[3]

During the Hurricane Pam exercise, the 300 workshop participants were split into groups and asked to devise responses to each part of the scenario as it unfolded, focusing on search and rescue, sheltering, debris removal, and medical care. Post-landfall and recovery issues were emphasized. The outcome of the exercise was formulated into a to-do list consisting of 15 guiding principles that each level of government should use to revise their plans. The list includes diagrams for distribution of supplies to storm victims; action plans for debris removal, shelter, and search and rescue; and ideas of evacuation plan revisions. The detailed workshop summary also identifies the appropriate lead and support agencies for each of the tasks mentioned.[2]

After Katrina, a number of Hurricane Pam participants reported that the workshop had increased their ability to respond to the real-life disaster by anticipating some of the most critical problems in advance. However, the aftermath of the Katrina disaster also exposed many more lessons that were not heeded.[2] Although history provides the benefit of 20/20 hindsight, it is indeed unfortunate for those who died and whose lives were disrupted so brutally that more of the lessons learned during the Hurricane Pam exercise were not fully implemented before the 2005 hurricane season arrived. The funding for the second planned phase of the Pam exercise was cut by Congress before it could take place.

11.2.1 Federal Coordination of Preparedness Activities

Preparedness responsibilities are shared by individuals, nongovernmental organizations, the private sector, local governments, and state and federal agencies. However, the federal government plays a key role in creating a coordinating structure for preparedness activities and defining roles and responsibilities to be more disaster resilient. The Presidential Policy Directive (PPD) 8: National Preparedness, released in March 2011, led to the development of a systematic process to prepare for threats that pose the greatest risk to the security of the Nation. PPD-8 defines the following five preparedness mission areas and mandates policy and planning documents (described later) to guide the Nation's approach for ensuring and enhancing national preparedness: Prevention, Protection, Mitigation, Response, and Recovery.

National Mitigation Framework

The **National Mitigation Framework** establishes a common platform for coordinating and addressing how the United States manages risk through mitigation. It describes mitigation roles and addresses how the nation will develop and coordinate mitigation capabilities to reduce loss of life and property. The Framework focuses on creating a national culture shift that embeds risk management and mitigation in all planning, decision-making, and development. The National Mitigation Framework discusses seven core capabilities required for entities involved in mitigation:

- Planning
- Public information and warning
- Operational coordination
- Community resilience
- Long-term vulnerability reduction
- Risk and disaster resilience assessment
- Threat and hazard identification

National Response Framework

During a response effort, many activities must be coordinated. The second edition of the **National Response Framework (NRF)**, updated in 2013, provides context for how the response stakeholders should work together and how response efforts relate to other parts of national preparedness. The NRF is built on scalable, flexible, and adaptable concepts identified in the National Incident Management System (NIMS) (discussed later in this chapter) to align roles and responsibilities across government agencies, local communities, the private sector, nongovernmental organization, and individuals. The NRF describes specific authorities and best practices for managing incidents that range from serious but purely local to large-scale catastrophes.

The NRF emphasizes a tiered response so that incidents are handled at the lowest jurisdictional level capable of handling the mission (for example, a county or municipality). The NRF is always in effect, and elements can be implemented at any time. The structures, roles, and responsibilities described in the NRF can be partially or fully implemented in the context of a threat or hazard, in anticipation of an event, or in response to an incident. Because structures and procedures can be selectively implemented, the NRF allows for a scaled response, delivery of the necessary resources, and a level of coordination appropriate to each incident.

National Disaster Recovery Framework

The National Disaster Recovery Framework (NDRF), finalized in September 2011, is a guide to promote effective recovery, particularly from large-scale or catastrophic events. The NDRF defines core recovery principles, roles and responsibilities of recovery coordinators and other stakeholders and lays out a coordinating structure to facilitate communication and collaboration during recovery. The NDRF also provides guidance for pre- and post-disaster recovery planning and describes the overall process by which communities can capitalize on opportunities to rebuild stronger, smarter, and safer.

By emphasizing a process to plan for disaster recovery so that communities can not only rebuild, but reduce vulnerability to future hazards, the NDRF also serves an important role in hazard mitigation. In this respect, preparedness, response, recovery, and mitigation are all mutually reinforcing phases of emergency management.

National Incident Management System

The National Preparedness System requires consistent implementation of the **NIMS**. Established in 2003, NIMS provides a consistent, nationwide approach and vocabulary for multiple agencies or jurisdictions to work together to build, sustain, and deliver the capabilities needed in all phases of emergency management. NIMS is directed under the Department of Homeland Security and described as follows:

> This system will provide a consistent nationwide approach for Federal, State, and local governments to work effectively and efficiently together to prepare for, respond to, and recover from domestic incidents, regardless of cause, size, or complexity. To provide for interoperability and compatibility among Federal, State, and local capabilities, the NIMS will include a core set of concepts, principles, terminology, and technologies covering the incident command system; multiagency coordination systems; unified command; training, identification and management of resources (including systems for classifying types of resources); qualifications and certification; and the collection, tracking, and reporting of incident information and incident resources.[4]

Standardized guidance for federal agencies in terms of preparedness is established through NIMS and includes instructional components of planning, training, exercises, personnel qualifications and training, equipment acquisition and certification, mutual aid, and publications management. NIMS encourages integrating all preparedness components and conducting activities regularly at the federal level to ensure preparedness for an **incident of national significance**. Incidents of national significance are declared as such after meeting any of the following four criteria:

- A federal agency has requested the help of the Secretary of Homeland Security.
- A state or local government has requested the help of the federal government because its capabilities to respond to a disaster are overwhelmed.
- Multiple federal agencies have become involved in a response effort.
- The President requests the involvement of the Department of Homeland Security.

To prepare for an incident of national significance, federal agencies are responsible for meeting the requirements of the NRF during a disaster and the requirements of the more steady-state NIMS. Yet, in general, the federal government's contribution to preparedness is to make available adequate resources to augment state and local efforts. These resources include public outreach materials on hazard preparedness; grants for training, personnel, programs, equipment, and exercises; grants for response and recovery efforts during a disaster that is beyond the capability of local and state governments; and technical assistance to help build stronger programs.

National Prevention Framework

The **National Prevention Framework** describes what the whole community—from community members to senior leaders in government—should do regarding information about imminent threats to the Nation, primarily focused on terrorism. This Framework describes the following core capabilities needed to prevent an act of terrorism and establishes a coordinating structure to enable stakeholders to work together:

- Planning
- Public information and warning
- Operational coordination
- Forensics and attribution
- Intelligence and information sharing
- Interdiction and disruption
- Screen, search, and detection

11.2.2 Key Federal Preparedness Resources

NOAA Weather Radio

One of the most significant federal resources that is made available to the public for hazard preparedness efforts is provided by the National Oceanic and Atmospheric Administration (NOAA). NOAA's National Weather Service is responsible for the **NOAA Weather Radio (NWR) All Hazards Network**. This network of radio stations across the country broadcasts continuous weather and hazards information. Warnings, watches, and forecasts are transmitted directly from the closest National Weather Service office in a local area. The network is called "All Hazards" for a reason—it includes warnings and post-event information for all hazards, even non-meteorological hazards that are not under the purview of the Weather

Service (such as earthquakes or oil spills).[5] Information on purchasing a NWR receiver that is configured specifically to the NWR can be found at https://www.weather.gov/nwr/

Ready.gov Campaign

Ready is a national public service advertising campaign developed by FEMA to educate and empower Americans to prepare for and respond to emergencies including natural and human-caused disasters. The goal of the campaign is to get the public involved and ultimately to increase the level of basic preparedness across the nation.

Ready and its Spanish language version *Listo* ask individuals to do three key things: (1) build an emergency supply kit, (2) make a family emergency plan, and (3) be informed about the different types of emergencies that could occur and their appropriate responses. In addition to the website www.ready.gov, the campaign messages have been distributed through: television, radio, print, and brochures, and increasingly through social media.

Climate Data Initiative

As part of the President's Climate Action Plan released in 2013, the Climate Data Initiative is a broad effort to make climate-relevant data resources freely available to stimulate innovation and private-sector entrepreneurship in support of national climate change preparedness.

The website www.climate.data.gov, a key component of the Climate Data Initiative, makes federal data about our climate more open, accessible, and useful to citizens, researchers, entrepreneurs, and innovators. The website includes curated, high-quality datasets, web services, and tools that can be used to help communities prepare for the future. Initially focused on coastal flooding and sea level rise, these datasets and resources are being expanded over time to provide information on other climate-relevant threats, such as to human health, energy infrastructure, and our food supply.

11.2.3 State-Level Preparedness

State governments are responsible for assisting their local governments when support and resources are needed beyond what the local level can provide. These resources include money, personnel, and equipment to supplement the capabilities of local-level response. State-level responsibilities also include the coordination of planning and preparedness efforts among local jurisdictions such that they do not conflict with each other and the coordination of training and exercising programs among multiple jurisdictions. The states must also coordinate activities of state agencies outside of emergency management that are involved in response efforts, similar to the coordination of federal-level agencies by the Department of Homeland Security.

Each state maintains an emergency management office. The following are examples of the emergency management offices for various states:

- North Carolina Division of Emergency Management within the Department of Public Safety
- Louisiana Governor's Office of Homeland Security and Emergency Preparedness
- Colorado Division of Emergency Management within the Department of Local Affairs
- Mississippi Emergency Management Agency
- Washington Military Department's Emergency Management Division

Regardless of which department each state emergency management office is housed in or the name of the division, they all perform similar functions. All emergency management agencies must have well-maintained emergency plans for facilities and equipment, oversee the development of local hazard plans, and provide funding for training and assistance to local governments. To carry out these functions, state emergency management offices receive funding for preparedness activities, primarily from FEMA and state budgets.

The governor of each state also has responsibility to coordinate with the state emergency management office. As the chief executive of the state, the governor has final word on ordering mandatory evacuations, calling in the National Guard, and communicating with the federal government about state and local capabilities.

A governor's prime resource is the **National Guard**. When called upon, the National Guard provides the capability to greatly assist in disaster response in terms of providing communications systems; construction equipment; emergency supplies such as medical supplies, beds, food, water, and blankets; as well as personnel to assist with distribution. Upon calling in the National Guard, the governor becomes commander in chief of state military forces. The governor also has police powers to amend, rescind orders or create regulations during a declared state of emergency and must also be involved in evacuation coordination between intrastate agencies, local-level governments, and interstate agencies. Although these are largely response-related activities, the governor's office must participate in preparedness activities to ensure the state's readiness to carry out these functions and respond to disasters.

11.2.4 Local Preparedness

Just as a governor has chief executive responsibilities for the state, the city or town manager or mayor has responsibility as leader of the jurisdiction to provide for the welfare and safety of its residents. The mayor must coordinate the local resources available to ensure preparedness and communicate with the governor when those resources are exhausted during an emergency. Local law determines the powers of the mayor to establish curfews, order quarantines, direct evacuations, or suspend local laws. In addition, the mayor is also responsible for communicating warnings to citizens, working with the local emergency manager, and facilitating resource sharing with other jurisdictions.

Each local jurisdiction also has some form of emergency plan that assigns the responsibilities of **first responders** such as police, fire, and paramedics for a variety of emergency scenarios, including natural hazard events and technological emergencies. These first responders each have their own protocols and preparedness activities. Similar to other levels of government, these procedures can be detailed and coordinated in the local **emergency operations plan**, which is usually developed and maintained by local emergency managers, often at the county level.

There are many activities to coordinate and prepare logistically in addition to the deployment of first responders. Communications, notifications and warnings, search and rescue, shelter and mass care, traffic detours, evacuations, law enforcement, and power failure are a few of the issues emergency managers face. The numerous details for which local governments are responsible highlight the critical need for preparedness and emergency operations plans that are developed in advance of a disaster.

FEMA has developed the following list of some of the emergency management responsibilities of local governments:

- Identifying hazards and assessing potential risk to the community
- Enforcing building codes, zoning ordinances, and land use management programs
- Coordinating emergency plans to ensure a quick and effective response

Figure 11.1 The Emergency Management Department in Dare County, North Carolina connects with citizens using a range of communications methods, including actively using Twitter and other forms of social media.

- Fighting fires and responding to hazardous materials incidents
- Establishing warning systems
- Stocking emergency supplies and equipment
- Assessing damage and identifying needs
- Evacuating the community to safer locations
- Taking care of the injured
- Sheltering those who cannot remain in their homes
- Aiding recovery efforts[6]

The local emergency manager is in the unique position of being able to coordinate these aspects of preparedness and can establish and maintain personal contacts with partners outside the emergency management office. Maintaining and implementing the local emergency operations plan is greatly facilitated by an understanding of various agencies, organizations, and individuals involved.

A very important, but often overlooked, responsibility of local emergency management officials involves educating the public about preparedness activities and providing information to citizens about the safest course of action to take during different disaster scenarios. Heightened awareness within the community plays a critical role in implementing a local emergency plan for effective response. The best possible preparation for any community is to have a populace that is prepared to act in its own best interest. Public announcements about weather conditions, emergency care kits, safe water and food handling practices, and other emergency-related information can be very effective for educating the community. Local governments have used a variety of methods to get the word out, including public access to websites, newspaper and radio announcements, social media, brochures, flyers, and school children's educational materials (see Figure 11.1).

11.2.5 Families and Individuals

In addition to the emergency management functions carried out by local, state, and federal governments, each of us plays an important role in preparedness at an individual level as well. Those who are well prepared can be proactive, rather than reactive, during a disaster. It is our individual responsibility to know what hazards could potentially affect us and our families and take action in preparation.

In 2004, FEMA published an informative handbook targeted to citizens entitled *Are you Ready? An In-depth Guide to Citizen Preparedness*. This handbook can be found online at https://www.fema.gov/pdf/areyouready/areyouready_full.pdf. An accompanying video, entitled *Getting Ready for Disaster—One Family's Experience*, is downloadable from the FEMA website or can be accessed through YouTube. These resources provide details for how to:

- Get informed about hazards and emergencies that may affect you and your family
- Develop an emergency plan
- Collect and assemble a disaster supplies kit
- Learn where to seek shelter from all types of hazards
- Identify the community warning systems and evacuation routes
- Include in your plan required information from community and school plans
- Learn what to do for specific hazards
- Practice and maintain your plan[6]

Additionally, the handbook lists suggestions for actions to take during each stage of preparation. Before the disaster, the guide suggests that individuals know their risks and learn to recognize signs of danger, purchase insurance, including additional insurance not covered by traditional homeowner's insurance policies (such as flood insurance), develop disaster plans, assemble a kit of supplies, and volunteer to help others. During the disaster, plans can then be put into action, and citizens can help others while heeding advice of emergency officials. Families should prepare escape routes and make advance plans for communicating among family members during emergencies, for shutting off utilities, protecting vital records, and caring for pets. Knowing the emergency plans for local schools can also assist in making preparations for families with children in terms of communication, safety, and evacuation measures.

All of these are important responsibilities for individuals to take seriously. Those who are well prepared will be more available to help others, becoming part of the solution rather than part of the problem. FEMA lists the following items that should be included in any family's basic disaster supplies kit:

- Three-day supply of non-perishable food
- Three-day supply of water—1 gallon of water per person, per day
- Portable, battery-powered radio or television and extra batteries
- Flashlight and extra batteries
- First aid kit and manual
- Sanitation and hygiene items (moist towelettes and toilet paper)
- Matches/lighter and waterproof container
- Whistle
- Extra clothing
- Kitchen accessories and cooking utensils, including a can opener
- Photocopies of credit and identification cards
- Cash and coins
- Special needs items, such as prescription medications, eyeglasses, contact lens solutions, and hearing aid batteries
- Items for infants, such as formula, diapers, bottles, and pacifiers
- Blankets, sleeping bags, and warm clothing such as jackets, pans, hats, gloves, scarves, and sturdy shoes if in a cold climate[6]

Preparedness for Vulnerable Populations

Many communities have a significant number of residents who are exceptionally vulnerable to the impacts of hazard events. Vulnerable populations may include those living in poverty, the elderly, disabled, non-English speakers, people living in isolated or remote areas, and those individuals and families who are compromised in multiple other ways. In general, these populations have little or no ability to prepare in advance for disaster; imagine, for example, the difficulty of stockpiling three days' worth of food and water when day-to-day living is a struggle. As a result, these populations require additional attention when planning for disasters because their vulnerability necessitates a higher level of response than populations that have greater capacity for self-sufficiency.

11.2.6 Business and Commercial Preparedness

As members of the community, local businesses and commercial operations are also responsible for preparedness. Chapter 9 covers in detail the risks businesses face and the mitigation and preparedness measures they can use to reduce the risks from hazards. This chapter discusses strategies to meet the responsibilities of property protection, business contingency planning, business relocation planning, protecting employees and their families, and purchasing adequate insurance coverage.

In addition to protecting their own assets and investments, businesses can also contribute to preparedness efforts of the wider community. Providing adequate supplies for families in the community takes preparation and coordination on the part of local businesses. For example, families interested in securing their properties from damage, such as boarding up their houses for a hurricane, need to be able to purchase plywood, nails, and hammers. Citizens evacuating the area prior to a wildfire need to fill up their gas tanks. Prior to an oncoming winter storm, individuals flock to grocery stores to buy milk, bread, and canned goods. Businesses are not usually accustomed to accommodating large influxes of customers and in these special instances need to be prepared for bringing in additional supplies if possible.

POP TART PREPAREDNESS

The retail company Wal-Mart implemented many disaster preparedness strategies to safeguard the business from the impacts of hazards, particularly in stores located in hurricane-prone Florida. In addition, the corporation has also focused its preparedness efforts toward shipping targeted items that will be of assistance to local stores and customers. Prior to a hurricane, the company has historically sent trucks full of dry ice and backup generators to protect frozen food from power outages. After studying customer buying patterns in hurricane hazard areas, Wal-Mart was able to determine that before a hurricane, customers typically raid the shelves for certain items. Based on these consumer studies, Wal-Mart has contingency plans in place to deliver additional shipments of items shown to be in high demand, including bottled water, flashlights, generators, tarps...and strawberry pop tarts.[7]

11.2.7 Bringing it all Together: Highlight on Evacuation

Evacuation is a prime example of an emergency-related action that involves preparedness at all levels of responsibility. Evacuation can be planned far ahead of time at the individual, business, local, state, and federal levels, although its execution takes place just before an event. Thus far, this chapter has identified roles and responsibilities of these different levels separately, but in this section, we will tie all of them together in a specific evacuation situation to highlight the degree of coordination necessary.

Imagine you are a resident of a town on a barrier island. While making dinner in the early evening of a lazy summer day, you are keeping an eye on your children playing outside and you have the television on in the background. Suddenly, you hear on the newscast that there is a tropical storm gaining strength in the Atlantic Ocean. NOAA NWS forecasters are predicting that it will turn into a hurricane and your barrier island is within the projected path. Of course, there is only a certain amount of reliability to their predictions, but over the next two days, it is still heading in your direction and has become a Category 3 hurricane. What do you do?

Now imagine you are the local emergency manager for the same town and are receiving frequent hurricane condition updates from the National Weather Service. You have the community's emergency plans at hand. You also know that you will need to recommend a mandatory evacuation to the mayor and governor with adequate notice to ensure there is enough time for citizens and visitors to evacuate. Grounded in prior research and data gathering, your plans show that for a town of your size to evacuate during the peak of the tourist season, it will take at least two days' notice prior to landfall to successfully move the entire population off the island. Yet, you feel the pressure from local businesses, many of whom cater to tourists, to wait until the hurricane is predicted to make landfall in the area with greater certainty before asking the mayor and governor to call for a State of Emergency and mandatory evacuation. The two-day evacuation window is quickly approaching. What do you do?

As an owner of a local hardware store, what do you do? As governor, what do you do? As resident or visitor, what do you do? Luckily, you are prepared.

As a hardware store owner, you called for extra shipments of plywood and other supplies at the first notification of a hurricane. You ensure that your employees are aware of the situation and are preparing for the safety of their families. You have a business contingency plan in place and have purchased flood insurance.

As the emergency manager, you alert citizens and tourists about impending hurricane conditions, encouraging them to evacuate voluntarily several days ahead of expected landfall. When the NWS predictions indicate the hurricane will make landfall in two days' time, you advise a mandatory evacuation. You contact the mayor, who calls the governor, who enlists the National Guard to assist with the reverse traffic flow and set up shelters according to the state's evacuation plan. The governor commands the local police, state police, and the National Guard, including those requested from other states, to enforce the evacuation order. The governor also is working in coordination with federal officials to guide evacuation activities. The NRF is invoked because of the large number of people evacuating from along the coastline of the surrounding areas and states. Your local emergency officials are ready and start assisting with door-to-door notifications of mandatory evacuation and helping those that have special needs. The local chapter of the American Red Cross is gearing up its volunteers and supplies and moving them out of harm's way. The hospitals and nursing homes are preparing to evacuate all of the patients they can according to their emergency plans. And the local utility companies are preparing for power outages.

As a resident, you are boarding up your windows, have ensured that gasoline is in your car, your cellphone is fully charged, and you have identified several locations you can go before the mandatory evacuation is called. You have detailed maps of the area ready in case the traditional roads are overwhelmed and a NWR to receive updates on the path of the hurricane and local evacuation instructions. You have your children's medicines, a suitcase of extra clothing, copies of important documents such as identification and insurance papers, as well as food and water for the car trip ready to go. When the evacuation is called, you are ready to leave immediately to avoid being trapped by any severe weather and know your children's school emergency plan so picking them up does not slow things down. The single bridge leaving the island is crowded, but traffic is moving, and you and your neighbors are able to successfully evacuate.

Without preparation and coordination in advance of the evacuation, however, it is evident that the evacuation process could easily become a nightmare. If the citizens, local emergency officials, business owners, governor's office, and federal weather forecasters did not all work together and know their individual responsibilities through education, exercises, and training, many parts of the evacuation would fail to be executed successfully.

Without warning systems alerting citizens and officials of an approaching hurricane, no one would know to be concerned or begin the evacuation process. Without the local residents having the knowledge of what to do upon hearing that a hurricane is approaching, they would not make early preparations for a mandatory evacuation or initiate their family disaster plans. Hardware stores would be overwhelmed with residents waiting until the last minute to purchase supplies to secure their homes, and inventories would be depleted quickly. If the emergency manager waited too long to recommend a mandatory evacuation, the governor could not activate the National Guard with enough time to provide quality pre-hurricane assistance. The highways would turn into a parking lot with cars attempting to cross the lone bridge off the island. Hospitals and nursing homes would not have time to evacuate and they would have no choice but to keep patients in place. Traffic conditions would discourage other residents from evacuating, and they would stay in their homes to ride out the storm, placing themselves and rescue workers in danger. All this commotion would happen while the hurricane continues to barrel down upon the community with ever-increasing speed and force.

Each of the participants described in this scenario plays an important role in the evacuation process. The better prepared each is, the more efficient and effective the evacuation can be. Yet, if only one of these participants is not prepared, a domino effect can result. Other community members, no matter how well prepared as individuals, will not be able to perform their functions because of a broken link elsewhere in the chain of interdependence. Personal responsibility to take preparedness seriously is essential in an evacuation situation, for ourselves and for the safety and welfare of others around us.

SELF-CHECK

- Describe the **National Response Framework** and the **National Incident Management System**.
- Give a summary of what can be found in the FEMA handbook: *Are You Ready? An In-depth Guide to Citizen Preparedness*.

11.3 PREPAREDNESS PROGRAMS

There are a number of programs, training activities, and exercises available, each of which plays an important role in preparedness. These ensure that the best possible instructions are in place when a disaster occurs and a response effort is necessary. Activities include, but are certainly not limited to, planning for warning systems and evacuations, providing training for emergency response officials, evaluating the efficiency of response exercises, anticipating population trends and special needs, and detailing the coordination between numerous organizations involved. This section highlights several volunteer programs, education programs, and hazard-specific exercises to demonstrate the many preparedness resources available to citizens, families, businesses, and government officials.

11.3.1 Volunteer Programs

There are a large number of volunteer programs throughout the United States that make lasting contributions to preparedness. These included nationally known organizations such as the American Red Cross, Salvation Army, Second Harvest, Catholic Charities, Mennonite Disaster Service, and others that are a part of the National Voluntary Organizations Active in Disasters (NVOAD), as well as numerous locally driven groups.

The American Red Cross

The American Red Cross was created by Clara Barton in 1881 to aid the victims of disaster. Ninety-five percent of the Red Cross is composed of volunteers. These volunteers provide humanitarian aid to people all over the United States and internationally. Key activities carried out by the ARC include the following:

- Responding to approximately 70,000 disasters in the United States each year, ranging from home fires to earthquakes
- Supplying more than 40% of the American blood supply from the nearly 4 million people who donate blood through the ARC
- Training more than 9 million Americans in health and safety courses, such as CPR, First Aid, and Lifeguarding

The American Red Cross provides shelter and supplies, helps people contact their loved ones, and has local chapters ready to mobilize quickly and efficiently in the event of a disaster. In addition, the Red Cross contributes to community preparedness through education and outreach materials and training courses for its volunteers. The Red Cross partnership with FEMA in the Community and Family Preparedness program is only one example of preparedness activity. Other publications can be found online as well (http://www.redcross.org/prepare/location/home-family), including *Preparing for Disaster for People with Disabilities and other Special Needs*.

Community Emergency Response Team

The Community Emergency Response Team (CERT) was formed to support local response capabilities. Through the CERT, local volunteers receive training to learn how to provide immediate assistance to victims and to assist responders' efforts when they arrive on the scene. This way, following a disaster, individuals that are trapped in an area without communications can be educated ahead of time on how to help themselves and others until help can reach them. Local emergency management offices sponsor most CERT training courses, which include 20 hours of instruction in disaster preparedness, fire safety, disaster medical operations, light search and rescue, team organization, and disaster psychology.[6] For more information on CERT training courses, visit http://www.fema.gov/community-emergency-response-teams.

11.3.2 Education and Training Programs

The following are examples of the many education and training programs that focus on disaster preparedness, including the Emergency Management Institute (EMI) and FEMA's Ready Kids Program.

Emergency Management Institute

The EMI was created in 1979 by FEMA to provide emergency management courses for students and working professionals. The Institute has assisted the establishment of numerous degree programs across the United States in emergency management and also provides distance learning programs. Its mission is to enhance U.S. emergency practices through a national training program. EMI is described by FEMA as the national focal point for the development and delivery of emergency management training to enhance the capabilities of federal, state, local, and tribal government officials, volunteer organizations, and the public and private sectors to minimize the impacts of disasters on the American public. EMI curricula are structured to meet the needs of this diverse audience with an emphasis on how various elements work together in emergencies to save lives and protect property.[8]

Thousands of participants attend courses at the EMI campus located in Emmitsburg, Maryland, every year, while many more participate in EMI supported exercises, non-resident programs run cooperatively by EMI, FEMA, and state emergency management agencies, and the EMI Independent Study program. The Independent Study program, EMI's free distance learning program, provides training to professionals and volunteers to promote disaster preparedness. For a listing of the courses and how to enroll, see the EMI program website at http://www.training.fema.gov/EMI/.

Ready Kids!

The U.S. Department of Homeland Security launched a program called *Ready Kids!* in the spring of 2006 to educate children about emergencies. Parents and teachers can point their children to a website (www.ready.gov/kids) that is understandable and appropriate for several age groups. The site features games, puzzles, and in-school lessons developed by Scholastic, Inc. that focus on steps children can take with their families to prepare for emergencies while learning important language arts, geography, and social studies skills. The *Ready Kids!* mascot, Rex the mountain lion, is designed to engage children in active learning for their role in preparedness activities. The American Psychological Association, American Red Cross, National Association of Elementary School Principals, National Association of School Psychologists, National Parent Teacher Association, National Center for Child Traumatic Stress, U.S. Department of Education, and U.S. Department of Health and Human Services all contributed to the design of the *Ready Kids!* program. *Ready Kids!* is part of the larger public service *Ready* campaign, designed to educate all citizens, young and old, about how to prepare for emergencies.[9]

11.3.3 Exercise Programs

Adequate preparedness depends on solid training and exercises that mimic real-life emergency scenarios in a controlled setting, such as the Homeland Security Exercise and Evaluation Program (HSEEP) carried out by the Department of Homeland Security.[10] Many other government agencies also carry out routine exercises to prepare officials, volunteers, and responders for various types of hazards and emergency incidents. The following sections describe some examples of hazard-specific exercise programs.

Great ShakeOut Earthquake Drills

The ShakeOut began in Southern California in 2008 as a drill designed to educate the public about how to protect themselves during a large earthquake, and how to get prepared. Great Shakeout Earthquake Drills are now held on the third Thursday of October every year in more than 20 official ShakeOut Regions, with an option for people in any other state or country to also register and be counted in the global total. In 2013, approximately 24.9 million people registered for the ShakeOut worldwide. New ShakeOut Regions are established each year.

National sponsors of the annual ShakeOut drills include the Federal Emergency Management Agency, U.S. Geological Survey, and the National Science Foundation, as well as the Red Cross and other organizations. The Southern California Earthquake Center, an earthquake science and education center headquartered at the University of Southern California oversees global coordination and manages all ShakeOut websites (except in Japan). Additional sponsors at the regional and local level help organize and implement the drill in in homes, schools, and businesses to practice what to do during earthquakes.

The first ShakeOut drill in 2008 was based on the Shakeout Scenario, a comprehensive description of a magnitude 7.8 earthquake on the San Andreas fault in southern California and the destruction it would cause. Such an earthquake would create unprecedented damage to Southern California—greatly dwarfing the massive damage that occurred in Northridge's 6.7-magnitude earthquake in 1994. The ShakeOut Scenario estimates this earthquake would cause over 1800 deaths, 50,000 injuries, $200 billion in damage and other losses, and severe, long-lasting disruption. To learn more about the Shakeout program, visit https://www.shakeout.org/

Tornado Exercises

Every year during the month of March, in partnership with the National Weather Service, the state of Missouri conducts a statewide tornado drill.[11] All citizens, businesses, and schools are invited to participate. Members of the Missouri General Assembly also participate in the drill, where all taking part in the exercise are encouraged to respond to the storm sirens by seeking a safe place and tuning to their NWRs to wait for further instruction.

The American Red Cross also conducts tornado exercises to test their response capabilities to tornado events. In one example, volunteers from the Jefferson County, Florida, chapter of the Red Cross coordinated tornado efforts with the Jefferson County Emergency Operations Center and state emergency management officials by setting up mock shelters in schools, providing hot meals to mock disaster victims, and identifying areas needing mass care.

Terrorism Exercises

The city of Nashville, Tennessee, and the Greater Nashville Homeland Security District (District 5) conducted an Emergency Preparedness Challenge in April 2006. This exercise was intended to test the abilities of the local first responders to respond to a full-scale terrorist attack on the city. It involved responders at every level of government in Nashville and its four surrounding counties. The challenge was one of the nation's largest local disaster response exercises. Through the recruitment of over 3000 volunteers who played the role of the sick, injured, or dead, or the role of volunteer coordinators of food and beverages, local emergency teams, law enforcement agencies, and 14 area hospitals were able to evaluate their capability to respond to this type of terrorist event. The exercise examined District 5's strategies for "responding to mass casualties, search and rescue for victims, triage and transportation preparation of survivors, hospital processing and treatment, processing of deceased victims and other disaster management efforts."[12] The exercise was also intended to educate the volunteers involved as to their role in participating in preparedness.

SELF-CHECK

• Describe the role of the American Red Cross.
• Describe the EMI Program.
• Select a natural hazard and give an example preparedness exercise for that hazard.

SUMMARY

Preparedness is a continuous process that requires constant updating and revision to remain current. Updates to preparedness activities can be implemented after a disaster, when emergency managers can incorporate lessons learned from the event, as well as after organizational or administrative changes in preparedness functions. Preferably, our preparedness actions are proactive rather than reactive, but in understanding the role of preparedness within the emergency management cycle, we realize that emergency managers must be flexible to adapt established plans and protocol to meet emergency situations as they arise. This chapter described the framework within which preparedness functions are carried out at all levels of government, within the business sector, and by private citizens. All citizens are responsible for continuing preparedness education and for contributing to improvements in governmental, community, and individual readiness.

KEY TERMS

Comprehensive emergency management: A widely used approach at the local, state, and federal levels to deal with the inevitability of natural hazards and their potential to cause disasters in a community.

Emergency operations plan: Contains procedures that can be detailed and coordinated for emergency responders; developed and maintained by local emergency managers.

First Responders: Groups that are the first to arrive at the scene of the emergency, such as police, fire, and paramedics.

Incident of national significance: Declared after a federal agency has requested help from the Department of Homeland Security, a state or local government has requested help from the federal government, multiple federal agencies have become involved, or the President requests the involvement of the Department of Homeland Security.

Mitigation: Any sustained action to reduce or eliminate long-term risk to people and property from hazards and their effects.

National guard: Provides the capability to greatly assist in disaster response in terms of providing communications systems; construction equipment; emergency supplies such as medical supplies, beds, food, water, and blankets; as well as personnel to assist with distribution.

National preparedness assessment and reporting system: Provides a report of the nation's level of preparedness to the President and gives guidance to participating agencies on adopting quantifiable performance measures of preparedness in the areas of training, planning, exercises, and equipment.

National Incident Management System (NIMS): Provides guidance to the federal agencies participating in the National Response Plan in disaster preparedness.

National Response Plan (NRP): Serves to coordinate response responsibilities and logistics at the federal level. Represents a binding agreement among 27 government agencies and the American Red Cross.

NOAA Weather Radio All Hazards Network (NWR): A network of radio stations across the country that broadcasts continuous weather and hazards information.

Preparedness: Activities to improve the ability to respond quickly in the immediate aftermath of an incident. Includes development of response procedures, design and installation of warning systems, evacuation planning, exercises to test emergency operations, training of emergency personnel.

Recovery: Phase in the emergency management cycle that involves actions that begin after a disaster, after emergency needs have been met; examples include road and bridge repairs and restoration of power.

Resilient communities: Towns, cities, counties, Native American tribes, states, and other communities that take action prior to a hazard event so that a disaster does not result.

Response: Phase in the emergency management cycle that involves activities to meet the urgent needs of victims during or immediately following a disaster; examples include evacuation as well as search and rescue.

ASSESS YOUR UNDERSTANDING

Summary Questions

1. Preparedness overlaps with all phases of the emergency management cycle. True or False?
2. Which of the following is not a true preparedness activity?
   a. Training
   b. Exercises
   c. Emergency response planning
   d. Land use planning
3. Preparedness is
   a. First response by paramedics
   b. A long-term activity
   c. Preplanning for response
   d. Building levees or retrofitting houses
4. The National Response Plan has ten emergency response functions. True or False?
5. Emergency response functions are independent of each other. True or False?
6. The All Hazards Network is broadcast over the
   a. NOAA Weather Radio
   b. USGS hazards radio
   c. The Weather Channel
   d. FEMA Weather Radio
7. State-level emergency management offices have different office or agency names, but perform similar functions. True or False?
8. During an incident of emergency, a governor's prime resource is
   a. The local police station
   b. The President
   c. The hardware store owner
   d. The National Guard

9. Local governments do not share in which of the following preparedness responsibilities?
   a. Calling for the help of the Department of Homeland Security
   b. Providing warning systems
   c. Stocking emergency supplies and equipment
   d. Evacuating the community
10. Business owners hold preparedness responsibilities within your community. True or False?
11. The *Are You Ready? An In-depth Guide to Citizen Preparedness* describes where to seek shelter from all types of hazards. True or False?
12. Evacuation involves which of the following:
    a. The local police station
    b. The governor
    c. The national guard
    d. All of the above
13. Which of the following is not a volunteer agency involved in preparedness and response:
    a. The American Red Cross
    b. Catholic Charities
    c. The Emergency Management Institute
    d. All of the above are involved in preparedness and response
14. The Department of Homeland Security does not want to involve children in preparedness because it is too scary. True or False?
15. There are preparedness exercises that can be done for every hazard. True or False?

Review Questions

1. Name ten federal departments or agencies that participate in the National Response Plan.
2. Describe an example of mitigation.
3. Describe an example of preparedness.
4. Describe an example of response.
5. Explain why preparedness is everyone's responsibility.
6. What are some of the ways citizens can participate in preparedness activities?
7. What other volunteer organizations are out there other than The American Red Cross?
8. What is an example of a preparedness exercise using a warning system?
9. Describe the function of CERTs at the local level, how they are formed, and who is involved.

Applying This Chapter

1. Imagine that you are the mayor of a town that is prone to wildfires. What are the different preparedness activities that you can participate in to improve your town's state of readiness? What are other examples from other local warning systems that you could apply to your town? What exercises would you want to employ and who would be involved?
2. Set aside time to create a preparedness plan with your family or roommate. What would you include? Where would you start to look for good examples? Consider encouraging others to use your plan as a template?
3. What are ways that you, as a citizen, can persuade others in your community to get involved in preparedness activities taking place in the area?

You Try It

The American Red Cross

The American Red Cross relies on volunteers to carry out most of its programs. Following every disaster in the United States, ARC chapters spring into action to provide emergency aid, care, and comfort. To contact a local Red Cross chapter near you, follow the instructions on the Red Cross Web site: www.redcross.org/where/chapts.asp. Describe the specific programs and resources that the American Red Cross has in place to help your community after a disaster.

READY? ... Set ... Go!

There are so many responsibilities for emergency managers that vary from place to place. Look on your local government website for the emergency plan in your locality. Check to see if disaster response responsibilities are clearly described, delineated, and coordinated for the officials that are there to protect you and your community—and see what you can do to get involved.

REFERENCES

1. FEMA Strategic Foresight Initiative. 2011. *Climate Change: Long Term Trends and their Implications for Emergency Management.* http://www.fema.gov/pdf/about/programs/oppa/climate_change_paper.pdf
2. U.S. House of Representatives. 2006. A Failure of Initiative: Final Report of the Select Bipartisan Committee to Investigate the Preparation for and Response to Hurricane Katrina. Available at katrina.house.gov.
3. Beriwal, M. 2005. Hurricane Pam and Katrina: A Lesson in Disaster Planning. *Natural Hazards Observer* 30 (November) (2): 8–9.
4. U.S. Department of Homeland Security. 2004. *National Information Management System.* Available at NIMS online: www.nimsonline.com/nims_3_04/introduction_and_overview.htm.
5. NOAA. 2013. *National Weather Service: NOAA Weather Radio All Hazards.* www.nws.noaa/gov/nwr.
6. Federal Emergency Management Agency. 2004. *Are you Ready? An In depth Guide to Citizen Preparedness.* IS-22. FEMA.
7. Leonard, D. 2005. The Only Lifeline Was the Wal-Mart. *Fortune,* 3 October, 2005.
8. Emergency Management Institute. 2006. *Welcome to the Emergency Management Institute (EMI).* www.training.fema.gov/EMIweb.
9. *DHS Wants Kids to Get Ready!* 2006. Natural Hazards Observer. Vol. 30 (March) (4): 5–6.
10. Homeland Security Exercise and Evaluation Program. 2006. *Welcome to the HSEEP Website.* Hseep.dhs.gov.
11. State of Mississippi Emergency Management Agency. 2004. *Informational Notes for First Responders and Officials.* Bulletin #4 5 (20 February). Available at sema.dps.mo.gov/Bulletin45.pdf.
12. Metropolitan Nashville and Davidson County, TN, Mayor's Office of Emergency Management. 2006. *Office of Emergency Management Home.* www.nashville.gov/oem.

12

Hazard Mitigation Planning
Creating Strategies to Reduce Vulnerability

What You'll Learn

- The major categories of mitigation strategies
- Examples of funding sources for mitigation
- Important factors in choosing a mitigation strategy
- The steps to develop a hazard mitigation plan

Goals and Outcomes

- Master the terminology, understand the procedures, and recognize the strategies to reduce vulnerability to hazards
- Evaluate the pros and cons of various mitigation tools
- Understand the relationship between risk assessment and strategy selection
- Learn the basic components of a hazard mitigation plan

INTRODUCTION

This chapter introduces strategies that can increase the resiliency of a community, beginning with an outline of five broad approaches to mitigation. The chapter details some of the advantages and disadvantages of structural engineering projects, with attention given to projects used to protect shorelines from coastal hazards. The chapter then discusses preventative mitigation strategies, using examples such as acquisition of properties located in hazard areas and land use regulatory techniques such as zoning. The chapter next describes property protection, followed by a discussion of various tools for natural resource protection and ways of informing community members about potential hazards through public education and awareness programs. In addition, this chapter reviews some of the sources of funding that are available to communities to implement mitigation efforts at the local level. The chapter also contains a short description of some of the methods that can be used to deal with various human-made hazards. The chapter concludes by describing how a community can incorporate its mitigation strategies and actions into a local hazard mitigation plan to provide a cohesive and coordinated approach to reducing vulnerability.

12.1 TYPES OF MITIGATION TOOLS AND TECHNIQUES

Mitigation tools and techniques can be as varied as the communities that use them, and no two will use the exact same set of strategies. In general, there are five broad approaches to mitigation, as shown in the following table. Within each of these categories, different mitigation actions target specific types of problems. Some communities may choose to focus on one type of mitigation strategy, while other communities may use a mix and match approach. Whatever strategy (or combination of strategies) is used depends on various factors, such as the cost of each type of action, the technical ability of the community to put the strategy into place, and the benefit that the community will receive once the strategy is implemented. Some mitigation techniques are best suited to prevent future disasters by keeping people and property out of harm's way before development occurs (these are strategies in the prevention category). Other categories of mitigation are more effective for protecting existing structures (such as the strategies in the property protection group) and are appropriate for areas where development has already occurred. Table 12.1 summarizes the types of mitigation strategies that communities can use as part of a comprehensive mitigation program and provides a few examples of each.

As you can see, there can be a bit of overlap between some of the categories in the chart above. Further, some strategies may fall into more than one category, while other strategies may not fit squarely into any one group. Nevertheless, while we can quibble about the details, the groupings laid out here can provide a common vocabulary to use during discussions about the wide variety of options available.

Table 12.1 Types of Mitigation Strategies.

Type of Strategy	Purpose and Critique	Examples
Structural Engineered Project	Lessen the impact of a hazard by modifying the environment or progression of the hazard event. Can have the potential to increase vulnerability over the long term and/or cause environmental degradation	• Dams and reservoirs • Dikes/levees/floodwalls/berms • Diversions • Seawalls/groins/jetties • Revetments • Beach nourishment • Storm sewers/drainage system • Vegetative buffers
Prevention	Avoid hazard problems or keep hazard problems from getting worse. Most effective in reducing future vulnerability, especially in locations where development has not yet occurred	• Land use planning • Zoning/subdivision • Floodplain regulation • Acquisition and relocation • Shoreline/fault-zone setbacks • Capital improvement programs • Taxation and fees
Property Protection	Protect structures by modifying/strengthening the building to withstand hazard impacts. Effective for protecting existing structures in hazard areas	• Building codes/construction standards • Building elevation • Floodproofing/windproofing • Seismic retrofit • Safe rooms • Fire retardant construction materials

(Continued)

Table 12.1 (Continued)

Type of Strategy	Purpose and Critique	Examples
Natural Resource Protection	Reduce the impacts of natural hazards by preserving or restoring natural areas and their mitigation functions. Can also serve other community interests of providing open space/recreation areas/ greenways	• Floodplain protection • Beach/dune preservation • Riparian buffers • Fire-resistant landscaping • Erosion/sediment control • Wetland conservation and restoration • Habitat protection • Slope stabilization
Public Information	Advise residents, business owners, potential property buyers, and visitors about hazards, hazardous areas, and mitigation techniques to protect themselves and their property	• Outreach projects • Hazard map information • Real estate disclosure • Warning systems • Education programs for schoolchildren

12.1.1 Choosing the Right Mitigation Strategy to Fit the Problem

It is important to remember that mitigation strategies are not selected in a vacuum. We will discuss the process of selecting and applying mitigation strategies later in the chapter when we introduce the concept of hazard mitigation planning. For now, keep in mind that we choose a mitigation technique to solve a predetermined problem. In other words, a mitigation strategy is only effective if it actually serves to reduce a risk that has been identified during a careful, data-informed risk assessment.

12.1.2 Using Hazard Mitigation to Prepare for Climate Change

Climate change is resulting in far-reaching differences in the frequency, intensity, and variability of many natural hazards, such as flooding, drought, severe storms, and hurricanes. As we take action to reduce the risk of disasters caused by these events, we are also improving our ability to prepare for and adapt to the impacts of climate change. For example, if a community knows that they have experienced drought in the past and, because of climate change, are likely to have more severe droughts in the future, hazard mitigation techniques to address this changing vulnerability are also a form of climate change adaptation. While this chapter focuses on hazard mitigation, keep in mind the ways that hazard mitigation may also be effective in enhancing community resilience as our climate and associated weather events continue to shift.

SELF-CHECK

- Cite five types of mitigation strategies.
- Discuss the factors involved in choosing a mitigation strategy.
- Describe how a risk assessment relates to the selection process.

12.2 MITIGATION THROUGH ENGINEERING PROJECTS

For many years in the United States, the favored technique for preventing disasters was to try and control the hazard itself. It was assumed that engineering and technology could be used to armor against the forces of nature. State and federal agencies, communities, and even individual property owners have built dams, levees, seawalls, and other large projects throughout the country designed to make communities resistant to natural hazards. In many cases, these hard structures do indeed protect people and property from rising floodwaters, erosion, wave action, and other natural hazards. When communities are located in an area that depends on a particular natural resource, such as a river, it may make sense to protect residents in this way. In some places, structural projects have been in place so long that they must be maintained in order to keep the community intact. In other places, the existing investments in an area or the cultural importance of the location make it difficult or unthinkable to use an approach other than engineered barriers. However, structural mitigation also has its drawbacks, and many communities have experienced serious disadvantages associated with these projects.

12.2.1 Disadvantages of Structural Engineered Mitigation Projects

While structural engineered projects are appropriate in some locations, in general, this approach to mitigation is based on a flawed assumption. By armoring communities to resist hazards, it is assumed that these communities can defeat the forces of nature. This is a never-ending proposition, one with few guarantees of success and the potential to lead to a false sense of security.

Providing a False Sense of Security

The major drawback of many structural mitigation projects is that in the process of reducing short-term risk, they can actually make future disasters worse, particularly by encouraging development in hazard-prone areas when residents feel a false sense of security. Civil engineers, planners, and others interested in flood-control management have observed that damage from floods in this country has actually gone up despite our huge investment in flood-control infrastructure.

Reducing the Mitigation Function of Natural Resources

Structural engineered projects can also reduce nature's ability to mitigate the impacts of storms and floods. Often these negative effects are experienced at some distance from the site of the project itself. For example, levees may worsen upstream or downstream flooding by changing the natural flow and volume of a river. Groins, which are meant to protect the shore from erosion by trapping sand, can worsen erosion on neighboring beaches. Channel diversions that are built for flood-control purposes can rob surrounding wetlands and marshes of silt deposits and starve them of nutrients, reducing the floodplain's natural capacity to absorb floodwaters. It is important to consider the wider region when thinking about structural mitigation projects to avoid simply shifting problems from one neighborhood to another.

The Potential Expense of Structural Mitigation Projects

Armoring against nature can be very expensive. Many structural projects are technically difficult and costly to build and their benefits may be short-lived. When budgets are tight, routine maintenance and repairs to levees, seawalls, and other large projects may be postponed, increasing the likelihood of failure. Few local governments can afford to build and maintain big mitigation projects, and most large-scale engineering works are funded by the federal and state governments. Federal funds are most often used for mitigation projects in areas that are of national interest, such as large ports or shipping channels, or where significant tax revenues and jobs are created, such as along the oceanfront where property values are high. Unfortunately, some of these projects are funded through "pork barrel" appropriations of federal tax dollars—when a member of Congress is able to direct large amounts of money to his or her own district, even though there may only be a direct benefit to relatively few people.

These disadvantages apply to mostly very large-scale structural projects that require complicated engineering plans and millions of dollars to construct. A description of large structural projects follows, along with potential advantages and disadvantages of each project. Not all structural projects are carried out on this scale, however. Some of the smaller projects that are carried out at the local level will also be discussed, such as storm sewers and drainage systems, where many of these disadvantages do not apply.

12.2.2 Dams and Reservoirs

A dam is an artificial barrier designed to impound water, wastewater, or any liquid-borne material for the purpose of storage or flood control. Dams can be effective flood-control devices by retaining water and releasing it at a controlled rate that does not overwhelm the capacity of downstream channels. Dams are also used to maintain water depths for navigation, irrigation, water supply, hydropower, and other purposes. Reservoirs are water storage facilities that are located behind dams and used to hold water during peak run-off periods, to serve as sources of drinking water, and to provide recreational and fishing opportunities.

Dam Ownership in the United States

Although very large dams are often owned, operated, and regulated by state or federal agencies, the majority of dams in the United States are privately owned. Dam owners are responsible for the safety and the liability of the dam and financing its upkeep, upgrade, and repair. Most states have a dam safety program that helps monitor dams and carries out inspections on a regular basis, yet the large number of dams that are owned and controlled by private landowners makes it difficult for state and local officials to ensure their safety. In many states, the dam safety office is understaffed and underfunded, and dam officials cannot inspect all privately owned dams in the state. Dam repair and maintenance can be costly, and many state dam safety programs do not have enforcement authority to require private dam owners to make repairs.

Environmental Costs Associated with Dams

As with some other types of structural projects, dams and reservoirs are expensive and land-consumptive, which require regular maintenance, and only prevent damage from floods for the capacity that they are designed to handle. Dams and reservoirs can have many environmental costs, such as the flooding of natural habitat when the reservoir is filled or barriers to migration of species such as salmon. Dams can eliminate the natural and beneficial function of the floodplain, including its ability to absorb floodwater. Dams can also change the hydrology of an entire watershed, causing negative impacts in areas far from the dam itself.

Dam Break Hazards

The potential for dam failure is an extremely serious hazard in many states. Leaks and cracks that form in ill-maintained dams can cause dam failure, resulting in very rapid flooding downstream, often with little warning, putting property and human life in grave danger (see Photo 12.1). Dams can fail for one or more of the following reasons:

- Overtopping caused by floods that exceed the capacity of the dam
- Deliberate acts of sabotage
- Structural failure of materials used in dam construction
- Movement and/or failure of the foundation supporting the dam
- Settlement and cracking of concrete or embankment dams
- Piping and internal erosion of soil in embankment dams
- Inadequate maintenance and upkeep[1]

Dam Failures in the United States

A series of dam failures in the 1970s caused the nation to focus on inspecting and regulating dams.

- On February 26, 1972, a tailings dam owned by the Buffalo Mining Company in Buffalo Creek, West Virginia, failed. In a matter of minutes, 125 people were killed, 1100 people were injured, and over 3000 were left homeless.
- On June 5, 1976, Teton Dam, a 123-meter high dam on the Teton River in Idaho, failed, causing $1 billion in damage and leaving 11 dead. Over 4000 homes and 4000 farm buildings were destroyed as a result of the Teton Dam failure.

Photo 12.1 View from below Lake Delhi Dam shows the force of rushing water after a breach in 2010. (Image courtesy of Josh deBerge, FEMA.)

- In November 1977, Kelly Barnes dam in Georgia failed, killing 39 people, most of them college students.

12.2.3 Dikes, Levees, Floodwalls, and Berms

The terms dike and levee are often used synonymously. Dikes are usually earthen or rock structures built partially across a river for the purpose of maintaining the depth and location of a navigation channel. Levees are earthen embankments used to protect low-lying lands from flooding. A floodwall is a reinforced concrete wall that acts as a barrier against flood-waters. Berms are barriers created by grading or filling areas with soil and are meant to keep floodwaters from reaching buildings.

To be effective, levees and similar flood-control structures must be located outside of the floodway and must make up for the flood storage they take up. Levees, dikes, and floodwalls should not be used to reclaim land in the floodplain for development.

Environmental Damage Caused by Flood-Control Structures

Dikes, levees, floodwalls, and berms can cause environmental damage similar to that of dams and reservoirs. These structures can interfere with the environment's ability to naturally miti-gate floods, which it can do under normal circumstances by absorbing excess water into wet-lands and low-lying areas. Levees and other floodwalls prevent floodwaters from flowing into the natural floodplain. As a result, they frequently concentrate flooding in locations upstream and downstream. These flood-control structures can also deprive wildlife and fish habitats, such as marshes and estuaries, of the water and nutrients they need to function properly.

THE FAILURE OF NEW ORLEANS LEVEES FOLLOWING HURRICANE KATRINA

For many successive generations, the tools and techniques used in New Orleans, Louisiana, for flood hazard prevention have focused on structural means through the construction of levees. Historically, the levees surrounding New Orleans and those built along the banks of the Mississippi River have repeatedly failed to keep flood-waters out.

After each successive flooding event, the levees of New Orleans have simply been built higher as a preventative measure against the next flood. The levees also work to increase the volume of water by channeling river flow into a concentrated area. These factors combine with the routine subsidence that occurs in the area due to natural soil conditions, effectively creating a never-ending challenge for the protection of New Orleans. The fact that the levees of New Orleans were breached by the forces exerted by Hurricane Katrina in 2005 is a dramatic demonstration of how levees in general are not foolproof flood protection measures. What happened in New Orleans after the levees breached is an even more telling example of the worst-case scenario, with excessive inundation of most of the city and devastation of the neighborhoods in the vicinity of the levee breaches.

As Katrina passed through the area in and surrounding New Orleans, bringing high storm surges and large amounts of rainfall, the level of Lake Pontchartrain rose rapidly, straining the entire levee system in the New Orleans area, especially in the 17th Street Canal and London Avenue Canal. On August 29, the surging water over-topped the eastern levees around New Orleans, spilling into Orleans Parish and St. Bernard Parish and pushing water up the Industrial Canal and Intracoastal Water-way.[2] There were breaches along the 17th Street Canal and the London Avenue Canal that day as well, resulting in flooding of 80% of New Orleans with floodwaters reaching up to 20 feet in parts of the city. It was difficult and time-consuming to repair the breaches, especially with the arrival of Hurricane Rita a short time later. The U.S. Army Corps of Engineers was not able to drain all of the floodwaters out of the city until October 11, 43 days after Katrina's landfall.

There is considerable speculation as to exactly why and how the levees of New Orleans failed so completely. What is known for certain is that the Army Corps of Engineers had purposefully built the levees to a specified level known as the "Standard Project Hurricane."[3] This standard is designed to withstand up to and including a Category 3 hurricane in terms of storm surge levels and a Category 2 hurricane in terms of wind speed. As a consequence, the levees of New Orleans were not designed or constructed to withstand a strong Category 3 hurricane like Katrina. Further complications arose due to the numerous agencies that were responsible for managing the levee system after it was built, resulting in variable maintenance and repair policies and practices, and weaknesses in transition areas between jurisdictional responsibilities. These issues are in addition to the basic problems encountered by building levees on deltaic soils that are prone to subsidence, which causes levees to sink and become unstable over time. Leaks in the 17th Street Canal levee that were reported before Katrina may have been due to weakened structural components caused by this subsidence.

Continuation of a system of levees is not the only mitigation technique that is available to the City of New Orleans, although efforts to strengthen and increase the height of the levees are ongoing. The following adaption strategies were recommended for New Orleans in an article in the 2002 Natural Hazards Observer, a publication of the Natural Hazards Research and Applications Information Center at the University of Colorado. At that time, the article recommended a variety of tools and techniques to mitigate future flood hazards, including the following:

- Protect and restore natural coastal defenses
- Upgrade levees and drainage systems to withstand Category 4 and 5 hurricanes
- Develop maps of potential flood areas that integrate local elevations, subsidence rates, and drainage capabilities
- Design and maintain flood protection based on historical and projected rates of local subsidence, rainfall, and sea level rise
- Minimize drain and fill activities, shallow subsurface fluid withdrawals, and other human developments that increase subsidence
- Improve evacuation routes to increase the ability of residents to escape an approaching hurricane
- Encourage floodproofing of buildings and infrastructure
- Encourage more homeowners and business owners to purchase National Flood Insurance Program policies[4]

12.2.4 Reducing Coastal Hazard Impacts through Structural Engineered Projects

A traditional approach to hurricane and coastal storm mitigation is to strengthen, reinforce, or replenish the natural environment so that it is less susceptible to the damaging forces of storms. Most hurricane-related deaths and property damage are a result of storm surges. Shoreline protection works are designed to combat storm surge and storm-induced waves. Some shoreline protection works are also designed to protect existing development from ongoing coastal erosion. However, these measures often have high costs, both in monetary and environmental terms, and should primarily be used as the last defense before abandoning existing major buildings. Some coastal states, mindful of the environmental damage and high cost of these projects, have passed legislation that prohibits most shore-hardening devices.

Sediment-Trapping Structures

Beaches and dunes are the coast's first line of defense against storm winds and waves. The sand that provides this defense is constantly moving from offshore bars to channels, to beaches and dunes, and back again in response to the natural forces of wind, waves, currents, and tides. Sand-trapping structures are designed to protect, maintain, or enhance beaches and dunes by interrupting this cycle as sand is deposited on the beaches or dunes. Some structures, such as groins or jetties, are designed to capture sand as it flows parallel to the shore, a natural process known as littoral drift. Planting and fencing are designed to capture sand as it is blown through the air. However, by interrupting the natural cycle of sand flow, these techniques can create unintended negative consequences. They may starve downstream beaches or create currents that swish sand away from the shore.

Groins

Groins are wall-like structures, built of timber, concrete, metal sheet piling, or rock placed perpendicular to the beach to capture sand moved by currents that run parallel to the shore. Usually constructed in groups called groin fields, their primary purpose is to trap and hold onto the sand, filling the beach compartments between them.

Groins are mainly designed to create a wider beach for recreational purposes and reduce the need for sand replacement on beaches. A wider beach can help slow erosion by making storm waves break further out to sea, but it is not an effective means of protecting shorefront buildings from coastal surges or high winds. By interrupting the normal patterns of drift, groins starve downstream beaches of their diet of sand and may worsen a shoreline's overall erosion problem.

Jetties

Jetties are wall-like structures perpendicular to the coast, often in pairs, to keep sediment from building up in inlets. Inlets are natural waterways that run between barrier islands and connect the ocean to the sound and are very important to navigation. The main function of jetties is to allow safe passage for boats.

While the primary function of jetties is to protect navigation channels, they can restrict the movement of sediment traveling parallel to the shore, even more so than groins. Jetties can also create currents that transfer sand offshore, leading to net sand loss from the beach. The effects of jetty systems are sometimes difficult to predict and are frequently not evident until years or decades later.

Seawalls and Bulkheads

Seawalls are vertical coastal walls designed to protect buildings from shoreline erosion. They may or may not also protect against storm wave attacks. Bulkheads are vertical walls set back from the shoreline, often constructed of wood or steel. Unlike seawalls, bulkheads are designed to *retain* loose fill and sediment behind them. Despite their differences, the terms seawall and bulkhead are often used interchangeably.

Seawalls are costly to build and can block public access to the shoreline. They reflect waves and make currents more intense, which can make the profile (slope) of the beach steeper and actually make erosion in front of the wall and on the property at both ends of the wall worse. Seawalls require continual maintenance and investment since loosened materials can become a hazard during storms. Temporary seawalls constructed from sandbags are unlikely to withstand the force of a storm and should be used only to repel normal erosion until the structure they are protecting can be relocated.

Construction and Stabilization of Sand Dunes

Dunes are naturally very useful to protect buildings from damage during severe storms and long-term erosion. They also prevent overwash flooding (when oceanside waves are driven onto an island, usually through gaps in the dune field) during storms and minimize the scouring that occurs when the overwash water flows back to the sea. Dunes also shelter buildings from high winds. Dunes can be constructed artificially by trapping sand with fences or piling sand into dunes with bulldozers. Dune stabilization is a technique for anchoring sand in dune form using plants.

Dune fields can be difficult to place in between existing beachfront homes. To provide any storm protection, dune fields must be wide, about 100 feet, and the dunes must be as high as 10 feet. There also must be no gaps between the dunes, which limits oceanfront views and public access to the beach. Dunes migrate as part of their natural life cycle. Attempts to anchor dunes in place generally result in "seawall" dunes that narrow beaches and can cause erosion at their ends. Areas with low sand supplies will have trouble building dunes artificially.

Beach Nourishment

A beach that is relatively stable or growing provides natural protection to structures behind it. Beaches that are losing sand through erosion or starvation cannot provide this natural protection. **Beach nourishment** is the artificial replacement or addition of sand to beaches to widen the backshore and move the high-water line further toward the sea.

Large-scale nourishment programs can be very expensive, on the order of $1–$5 million/mile/application. The frequency of nourishment required to maintain a beach is difficult to predict. Most nourishment projects along the Atlantic Ocean have a life span of two to ten years depending on how often storms occur. Artificially renourished beaches tend to erode more quickly than natural beaches.

While nourishment programs create wider beaches for recreational use, they can also unintentionally worsen the hazard risk. The sand used to nourish beaches is often taken from nearby offshore banks because these banks offer a less expensive source of matching sand. But robbing these banks is shortsighted, since they act as an offshore "speed bump." The result is that larger waves reach the shore, causing more severe erosion. Nourishment programs may also spur oceanfront development, putting even more structures at risk.

SELF-CHECK

- List at least three ways dams can fail.
- Explain how structural engineering projects can encourage the development of hazard-prone areas.
- Discuss the environmental costs of large-scale engineering projects such as dams.

12.3 STORMWATER MANAGEMENT SYSTEMS

Not all structural mitigation projects are huge and expensive. On a smaller scale—at the community level—structural projects are usually designed by engineers and managed by public works staff and include such necessary actions as the construction and maintenance of stormwater and sanitary sewer systems, as well as drainage and pipe systems.

12.3.1 Building Drainage Systems with Adequate Capacity

A number of floods occur in urban areas for the simple reason that drainage systems are not built with the capacity to handle stormwater runoff. **Runoff** is rainwater that does not soak into the soil, evaporate, or become trapped by plant roots and thus flows over the surface of the ground into the first depression, stream, lake, or other low-lying areas it meets. Stormwater systems are designed to catch runoff and channel it into a series of drains and pipes to a catch basin or other containment device. When drainage systems are installed, a community should make sure that culverts, ditches, channels, pipes, and all other components are built with enough capacity to meet the volume of stormwater that is expected during normal above-average rainfalls.

When designing a new or updated stormwater system, a community would do well to anticipate any changes that could occur to flood levels due to future development and growth. Increased development usually brings an increase in **impervious surfaces**—paved areas that rainwater cannot soak through, such as parking lots, roofs, streets, and other non-porous surfaces—resulting in a greater volume of water entering the stormwater system. Rapid urbanization that is not well planned can quickly overwhelm a community's ability to manage increased levels of stormwater runoff.

12.3.2 Drain System Maintenance

Drainage systems will not continue to function properly without a well-planned, ongoing preventive maintenance program of inspection, desilting, and repair. Maintenance work can be expensive but not nearly as expensive as fixing flooding problems. Problematic roadside ditches, stormwater intakes, drains, and watercourses should be inspected on a regular basis, especially before and during the rainy season. Some municipalities use closed-circuit television to monitor existing drains where human-entry inspections are not possible.

12.3.3 Nontraditional Stormwater Management

Traditional municipal stormwater management and flood-control projects involve hard, invasive techniques that disturb natural urban stream channels. Some communities are choosing alternative methods, typically referred to as Green Infrastructure or Low-Impact

Development techniques, including soil bioengineering, the use of vegetation along streams to slow runoff, and other nontraditional ways to stabilize stream banks and control floodwaters. Some communities also restrict the amount of impervious surface and encourage innovative solutions such as green roofs, where small trees, shrubs, and other plantings are grown on rooftops to filter and soak up rainwater before it meets the drainage system. These and other types of approaches can improve water quality as they reduce flood hazards and also add to the beauty of a community.

Moving Away from Structural Engineered Mitigation Projects

Mitigation practice is moving away from focusing only on engineering approaches as a way of reducing hazard impacts. Experience has shown that while the actions described above might work in the short term, their long-term effectiveness is often questionable. Many structural projects are expensive to build and maintain. They can be vulnerable to sudden failure, and they encourage development to take place in their shadow. Structural approaches can cause unintended damage to the environment or people downstream. Strategies with long-term costs that outweigh their benefits are unsustainable, and over the long run, such actions can decrease rather than increase community resiliency. Mitigation experts are tending toward activities that are more sustainable, such as the prevention, natural resource protection, and property protection strategies that we will discuss next.

SELF-CHECK

- Define runoff and impervious surface.
- Explain the relationship between urban flooding and maintenance of drainage systems.
- Discuss the long-term effectiveness of structural engineering projects.

12.4 MITIGATION THROUGH PREVENTION

Over the long term, the most sustainable approach to minimize damages and losses from natural hazards is to guide development away from hazard-prone areas. This means not building in floodplains, avoiding steep slope and landslide areas, and setting development back from high-erosion coastal areas. In other words, we try to avoid disasters altogether by removing people and property from the location where the built environment intersects with hazard events. This section described three ways of preventing disasters:

1. The most direct way to prevent future disasters is through public acquisition of hazard land: paying the owners to leave and then demolishing or relocating any buildings located on the site.
2. A second method to prevent disasters involves local land use regulations, such as zoning, subdivision ordinances, and setback regulations to prohibit future building in known hazard areas.
3. A third method involves the community's power to spend public money for capital improvements in order to discourage development in hazard areas and encourage development in safer areas.

The prevention approach is most useful when other, safer development locations are available in the community to which growth can be steered. Communities that have reached **build-out**—the upper limit of the area's capacity to absorb additional development—are more limited in their options for using prevention strategies, although there are ways that the local government can encourage new structures to be built on existing lots (a practice called **infill**) in safe locations. Prevention techniques apply only to hazards that can be geographically delineated and located on a map (flooding, for example). They are less effective for hazards that are not locally geographically specific. These hazards require different types of mitigation strategies, since the hazard might occur anywhere (tornadoes) and everywhere (ice storms) in the community.

12.4.1 Acquisition and Relocation

By acquiring property in hazardous areas, a community can ensure that the land will be used only for purposes that are compatible with the hazard. Picnic shelters and dog parks, for example, are a better choice for the floodplain than homes and shops. Although acquisition is typically one of the most expensive mitigation tactics, in the long run, acquisition can be very cost-effective. Through acquisition, the local government takes ownership of privately held residential or business property that has been subjected to repeated hazards, most often flooding. Acquisition can be accompanied by relocation, when the owner's home is moved to a safer location, or demolition, if the structure cannot be moved or it is not cost-effective to do so.

Saving Money through Acquisition

Although buyout programs require an initial outlay of thousands, sometimes millions, of dollars depending upon the price and number of homes involved, over the long term these funds are paid back in full through cost savings realized by avoiding future disasters. Initially, since the title to the acquired property is transferred to the public domain, acquisition can remove properties from the tax rolls, so that the local government can no longer collect real estate taxes on that property, a major source of revenue for most communities. However, the cost of losing tax revenue from these properties is usually much lower compared to the cost of repairing and rebuilding homes repeatedly after they are damaged during hazard events. The local government also avoids the expense of rescue and recovery operations, emergency sheltering, and financial assistance that arises when residents are displaced due to a disaster. Cost savings are also realized since the local government no longer is responsible for providing municipal services (such as garbage pickup and road maintenance) to these properties once they are acquired. Over the long term, acquisition allows communities to save a great deal by preventing repetitive losses.

Communities have put their acquired properties to any number of uses, such as parks, greenways, open space, tennis courts, ball fields, nature preserves, and community gardens. These new uses can serve the community in multiple ways, including protecting habitat, enhancing water quality, conserving open space, and contributing to the beauty and recreational opportunities of the area.

Acquiring contiguous lots—for example, all the parcels on a street or in an entire neighborhood—provides the greatest long-term benefit to the community. A piecemeal approach, where properties are acquired in a higgledy-piggledy fashion, may not lend itself to an effective reuse of the land. But since buyout programs that are supported by federal funds (which covers the vast majority of buyout projects nationwide) involve willing sellers who voluntarily commit to the acquisition and relocation process, there have been some unfortunate cases where a lone structure remains in the midst of otherwise open space. This "snaggle-tooth" approach can diminish the overall reduction in the vulnerability of the hazard-prone area. In general, however, a well-crafted acquisition program can serve as a very effective mitigation strategy for communities that have experienced repeated flooding.

12.4.2 Land Use Regulation

Another effective method of preventing disasters is to keep people and property from locating in known hazard areas *before* these areas become developed. Communities carry this out by adopting a land use plan or comprehensive plan that creates a vision of how the community wants to grow and then passing ordinances that follow the plan to control where and how property can be developed. The ordinances are typically implemented through the permitting process, whereby the landowner or developer must abide by the rules in exchange for a permit that allows the development to take place. This section discusses some of the more commonly used types of regulation that local governments can use to control growth in hazardous locations, including zoning ordinances, subdivision ordinances, and setbacks.

Zoning Ordinances

The majority of local governments in the United States use **zoning** as a tool to control the use of land within their jurisdiction. The local government is authorized to divide its jurisdiction into districts and regulate and restrict the construction and use of buildings within each of those districts. Land uses controlled by zoning include the type of use (residential, commercial, industrial, etc.) as well as minimum specifications such as lot size, building height, street setbacks, density of population (how many people can be accommodated in one area), and other elements of development.

   A local zoning ordinance consists of maps and written text. Some communities have made good use of their zoning ordinances by showing hazard areas on the map. The corresponding text of the ordinance may require that these areas permit low-intensity uses such as recreation, open or green space, or agriculture. Zoning can also be used to prohibit environmentally hazardous uses, such as junkyards and chemical facilities in areas exposed to natural hazards. At the same time, a zoning ordinance can be used to encourage development in safe areas, by allowing greater density in parts of the community that are not subject to hazards.

Subdivision Ordinances

Subdivision regulations control land that is being divided into smaller parcels for sale or development. Subdivision ordinances typically set out construction and location standards for lot layout and infrastructure such as roads, drainage systems, sidewalks, and lighting. Subdivision ordinances are not as broad as zoning and only indirectly affect land use. Nonetheless, subdivision regulations have been used to limit development on hazardous land, especially flood-prone property and wildfire hazard areas. Subdivision ordinances can require increased distances between structures and hazard areas and set limits for the amount of impervious surfaces to control stormwater flow. Subdivision ordinances are also useful for clustering development, so that homes are more densely located in safer areas, while floodplains, high-erosion areas, and firebreak zones are left clear of development.

SUBDIVIDING IN COLORADO, CALIFORNIA, AND OREGON

In Colorado, local governments require subdivision applicants to prepare drainage plans to prevent flooding and erosion. In California, municipalities require subdividers to incorporate wildfire suppression facilities into the development plans. In Portland, Oregon, developers must locate public facilities and utilities, such as sewer and water systems, in a way that minimizes flood damage.

12.4.3 Setback Regulations

Setback regulations establish a minimum distance between a hazard area and the portion of the lot that may be built upon. Ocean shoreline setbacks are designed to prevent damage to structures from coastal storms and regular erosion. Fault-zone setbacks work in a similar fashion, establishing the distance that construction can take place from a known fault line to prevent damage to structures from earthquakes.

A major problem with setbacks is that some communities grant too many **variances** (exceptions that allow development to go ahead, even though the rules prohibit it), which weakens the regulations' effectiveness. Some variances are granted to homeowners who want to rebuild their oceanfront homes after a major storm has reduced the amount of beachfront on the lot. Constitutional issues can arise when state and local officials deny a permit to build or rebuild based on the setback. Some of the constitutional issues associated with setback regulations are discussed in earlier chapters.

12.4.4 Capital Improvement Programming

Local governments are empowered to spend public money for public purposes such as capital improvements, which include physical projects such as bridges, police stations, schools, recreation centers, and other community facilities. Most local governments plan for these big-ticket items with a capital improvement program (CIP). The CIP lays out the government's intentions to provide public facilities over the next five to ten years and specifies where they will be located and when and how they will be built, renovated, and maintained.

Using Capital Improvement Plans to Protect Public Facilities from Hazards

Communities can protect public facilities by requiring that capital improvements not be built in known hazard areas. Such careful siting can protect lifelines and critical facilities and also reduce public expense for repair and reconstruction of public structures that might be damaged during hazard events. Local governments can also use capital improvement and maintenance programs to require that public facilities be built using durable materials and constructed in ways that make them strong enough to withstand the impacts of hazards.

Using Capital Improvement Plans to Steer Private Development from Hazard Areas

In addition to using the capital improvement plan to limit damage to public structures, local governments can also use the spending power to discourage growth and private development in hazardous areas. By limiting the availability of public services such as roads, schools, water and sewer lines, and other infrastructure that is necessary to support development, the community can make it much more expensive and difficult for a developer to build in hazardous areas. Many communities enact prohibitions on extensions of services to outlying areas in an attempt to curb urban sprawl. Local governments can also use capital improvement planning to encourage growth and development to take place in desirable sections of the community where hazards are not present. However, CIPs have not been used extensively for hazard mitigation purposes, even in highly hazardous, fast-growing areas. In the rare instances that capital improvement spending has been used as a mitigation tool, it is only effective when used in combination with other land use regulations and planning.[5]

SELF-CHECK

- Define **variance**
- Describe three disaster-preventive tools
- Explain the costs and benefits associated with land acquisition as a mitigation strategy

---

12.5 MITIGATION THROUGH PROPERTY PROTECTION

In a perfect world, communities would be built in locations that are never exposed to the impacts of hazards. But when hazards cannot be avoided, it is imperative to reduce potential disaster losses by strengthening buildings and facilities so they can better withstand hazard impacts. Local governments can encourage or in some instances require property owners to take steps that will improve the hazard resilience of homes and businesses. Local governments can also make sure that public facilities, such as sewage treatment plants, fire and police stations, schools, libraries, government buildings, water and power distribution lines, roads, bridges, and other infrastructure, are built to high standards that make them less vulnerable.

From studying structures that were damaged during past disasters, we now understand many of the factors that can contribute to property damage, including the following:

- Ground-level construction (makes structures more susceptible to flooding)
- Poor framing (causes structures to be vulnerable to high winds, snow loads, and earthquakes)
- Inadequate anchoring (contributes to instability during earthquakes and susceptibility to high winds)
- Pilings and supports that are not buried deep enough (making structures vulnerable to erosion and the scouring action of storm surge)
- Low-quality building materials (increasing vulnerability to multiple hazards)
- Shoddy workmanship (significantly weakens structures against all types of hazards)

Some of the ways that communities can combat these deficiencies and make sure that buildings are able to withstand hazard conditions include strengthening buildings and facilities, enforcing building codes, and municipal improvements. The following sections explore these methods of property protection.

12.5.1 Strengthening Buildings and Facilities

Among the many types of mitigation strategies that are used to strengthen buildings and facilities, four techniques are described in this chapter: (1) elevation, (2) floodproofing, (3) windproofing, and (4) seismic retrofitting.

Elevating Buildings above Flood Level

Many communities have successfully used elevation to reduce future flood losses while allowing property owners to remain in the same location. Elevation-in-place also works for some public facilities and infrastructure. Elevation is most commonly done by placing a building on stilts or piles, with open space underneath. The lowest habitable floor of an elevated building is typically raised above the 100-year flood level, so that rising water flows under the building without harming the structure. Many building codes will allow minor storage and parking and other similar activities to occur below the 100-year flood level. Along the oceanfront, elevation may also mean raising the building above expected storm surge and wave heights.

One less expensive way to reduce flood damage is to elevate just mechanical and electrical equipment in buildings, such as the heating, ventilating, and cooling (HVAC) equipment-like furnaces and hot-water heaters. This equipment can often be moved to an upper floor or attic. However, relocating HVAC systems is likely to involve plumbing and electrical changes. Electrical system components, such as service panels (fuse boxes and circuit breakers), switches, meters, and outlets should also be elevated at least 1 foot above the 100-year flood. These components easily suffer water damage and can short and cause fires. By elevating electrical and mechanical equipment, buildings can often be habitable more quickly and less expensively after a flooding event.

The level that one may choose to elevate a building depends on a number of factors. For buildings where the possibility of flooding would have more catastrophic impacts, it may be wise to elevate far above the 100-year flood level. For example, hospitals or industrial facilities that have large quantities of hazardous materials should be elevated several flood above the floodplain.

Floodproofing

There are two major types of floodproofing. Dry floodproofing means that all areas below flood level are made watertight. With wet floodproofing, floodwaters are intentionally allowed to enter a building to reduce the pressure exerted by deep water. The property owner floodproofs the interior by removing water-sensitive items from parts of the building that are expected to flood. Backflow valves (also referred to as "check valves") can help homeowners prevent the reverse flow of sewage into the house by temporarily blocking drainpipes.

Although floodproofing makes construction more expensive, it can be an effective mitigation tool and provides a high level of protection from water damage. Dry floodproofing is typically done by coating walls with waterproof compounds of plastic sheeting and protecting building openings with removable shields or sandbags. Dry floodproofing cannot extend more than 2 or 3 feet above the foundation of the building because the pressure exerted by deeper water would collapse most walls and floors.

Windproofing

Windproofing involves designing and constructing buildings to withstand wind damage. Windproofing typically involves improvements to the aerodynamics of a structure, the materials used in its construction, or adding features such as storm shutters and shatter-resistant windowpanes. Windproofing can also help protect a building's occupants and their possessions from broken glass and flying objects.

Residential structures are never completely windproof but can be made wind-resistant. Construction techniques that can increase resistance without significantly increasing the cost include fairly simple techniques such as using larger than usual timbers, using bolts instead of nails, and installing hurricane clips or reinforcing roof braces. These techniques can help prevent roofs or even entire buildings from coming loose during high-wind events and becoming flying projectiles that cause further damage to neighboring structures and endanger human life.

Seismic Construction and Retrofitting

Seismic construction involves designing and building new structures to withstand the shaking force of an earthquake. It also includes nonstructural improvements to the inside of buildings to reduce earthquake damage. The cost of including seismic techniques during the building process can be relatively minor, such as adding reinforcing rods to concrete or using a wood frame with brick veneer rather than all brick when building new homes.

In contrast, **retrofitting** existing buildings is often a more challenging process. Rebuilding is vastly more expensive than incorporating design improvements during initial construction. Seismic retrofitting may be a low priority for the public in areas that are rarely affected by serious earthquakes. But even in these areas, fairly inexpensive tactics can go a long way to reducing earthquake risk.

Structural improvements to buildings typically include adding braces and removing overhangs. Bridges, water towers, and other non-occupied structures can also be retrofitted with earthquake-resistant materials. Sources of secondary damage, such as sprinkler pipes, water connections, and gas service lines, that can rupture during a quake should be secured or fitted with shutoff valves. Fuel tanks and their supply lines should be securely anchored so that they do not become dislodged by earthquakes.

Nonstructural mitigation techniques include securing bookcases, computer monitors, and light fixtures to the wall; covering glass windows with shatter-resistant film; and locating hazardous materials where they are less likely to be spilled during an earthquake.

12.5.2 Building Codes: Requiring and Enforcing Safe Construction

An effective way of protecting buildings from hazard impacts is through strict enforcement of a stringent building code. **Building codes** are laws, ordinances, and regulations that set forth standards and requirements for the construction, reconstruction, maintenance, operation, occupancy, use, and appearance of buildings. Building codes usually require a certain level of fire resistance and also regulations for earthquake, flooding, and high wind impacts in order to save lives and reduce building collapse.

Strict compliance with the letter as well as the spirit of the building code is essential so that structures are built as safe as possible. Strict enforcement is especially critical in the aftermath of a disaster. It is understandable that residents and property owners want to rebuild their homes and businesses as quickly as possible following a hurricane or other large-scale event. Political pressure may be put on building officials in the post-disaster period to expedite the permitting process. However, this urge to get back to normalcy should not be indulged at the sacrifice of public health and safety.

SHODDY WORKMANSHIP MAKES FOR HUGE LOSSES

In August 1992, more than 75,000 homes and 8000 businesses were destroyed or severely damaged by Hurricane Andrew, a storm with sustained winds over 120 miles/hour. Damage reports following the storm showed that Andrew caused more damage to recently built structures than those built before 1980! Much of the damage was attributed to the widespread practice of shoddy workmanship, poor design, and lax enforcement of the building codes. Following Hurricane Andrew, Florida's building code was modified to require glass that can withstand high-velocity impact from wind-borne debris and hurricane-strapped roof tresses to make structures more resistant to wind-related damage.

12.5.3 Other Municipal Improvements

In addition to strengthening buildings and facilities, there are other techniques communities can use to protect public facilities, such as burial of utilities and routine pruning. These steps are described below.

Burying Utility Lines

Burying utility lines underground can help keep power and telecommunications running during a hazard event, particularly during high winds and winter storms. During normal weather conditions, underground systems can also be more reliable than overhead systems, with fewer interruptions. However, the gain in reliability is offset by an increase in repair time, because specialized crews must identify and locate the problem, dig the area, and repair the cable. During severe weather events, such as hurricanes and ice storms, customers with underground facilities are less likely to be interrupted but may be among the last to have power restored when there is an underground failure.

Burying existing overhead lines is often expensive and can take years to complete. Customers might see their utility bills go up as much as 125% to cover the cost of burial and the higher operation and maintenance costs. However, the costs of burying utility lines in newly developed areas can be a cost-effective alternative.

Pruning and Planting

Pruning is the thinning of trees and tall bushes that interfere with utility lines. Pruning not only removes branches that pose an immediate threat to power lines, but it also strengthens trees and makes them less likely to topple over or drop heavy branches on power lines, cars, and buildings during high winds or ice storms. Pruning requires near constant effort to keep up with the rate of new growth. Where the public right-of-way is not wide enough to allow for sufficient pruning, communities can purchase or lease additional rights-of-way. Communities can choose to plant wind-resistant species of trees and plants and larger stands of trees, which are less vulnerable to windfall than widely separated trees.

SELF-CHECK

- Define retrofitting.
- List three ways of protecting property from hazards.
- Cite four strategies used to strengthen buildings.
- Discuss ways of protecting utilities and public facilities.

12.6 MITIGATION THROUGH NATURAL RESOURCE PROTECTION

A community's wetlands, hillsides, shorelines, floodplains, riparian areas, forests, and habitats can provide important and cost-effective eco-services and benefits, not the least of which is hazard mitigation. Often, the best way to reduce vulnerability of people and property is to preserve a healthy, well-functioning ecosystem.

12.6.1 Preserving Wetlands

Wetlands are areas that naturally flood with water at least a portion of the year and are some of the most dynamic, valuable, and diverse ecosystems on earth. Wetlands serve as natural flood controls by storing tremendous amounts of floodwaters and slowing and reducing downstream flows. The federal government, along with state and local governments, protects wetlands through regulations and permitting requirements for dredge and fill activities, as well as acquisition and purchase of easements in wetland areas. For further discussion of wetland regulation, see Chapter 7.

The Demise of the Nation's Wetlands

Over the past century, coastal and inland watersheds of the United States have changed dramatically. Up to 80% of wetlands in some locations have been converted to agriculture and urbanization. In other areas, the construction of massive flood-control structures designed to keep rivers from switching channels in their natural meandering patterns has resulted in a restriction of sediment flow and freshwater supplies to many floodplains and deltas.

Among the human actions that physically alter, degrade, or destroy wetlands are conversion to agriculture; clearing for development; draining for irrigation; dredging for navigation, energy exploration, and extraction; and the construction of levees, dikes, and dams. Wetlands are also commonly degraded through water and air pollution, introduction of invasive (non-native) species, sedimentation, and changes in temperature and salinity. In the future, sea level rise may be the most serious long-term threat to wetlands in the coastal zone, due to inundation as well as saltwater intrusion caused by a rising water table. A sizable portion of coastal wetlands may be inundated if even the mildest of sea level predictions comes true.

12.6.2 Soil Conservation and Steep Slope Preservation

Most slopes greater than 15 degrees have enough soil and loose rock to cause a landslide. Landslide risk greatly increases when steep slopes and loose soils are drenched with water, either from torrential rainfall, broken water pipes, or misdirected runoff.

Soil conservation and steep slope preservation are measures that place restrictions on the grading of hillsides and impose limits on the development of landslide-risk areas. Some methods of slope stabilization involve changes to the structure of the slope, such as reducing the steepness of the grade. Other techniques involve planting vegetation to help anchor loose rubble and soil. Because water greatly increases the risk of landslides, wise water management can help reduce the hazards associated with steep slopes. One method is to cover the surface with impermeable material to prevent water from reaching the loose material beneath it. However, this technique will increase stormwater runoff and may create flood hazards downhill. A better approach is to redirect stormwater or install a subsurface drainage system.

SELF-CHECK

- Name two ways of using natural resource protection as a mitigation strategy.
- Explain the mitigation benefit of wetland preservation.

12.7 MITIGATION THROUGH PUBLIC INFORMATION

Often, the key to building a resilient community is educating the public about the nature and consequences of hazards. As citizens, elected officials, planners, builders, emergency managers, school children, and others in the community learn about the hazards around them, they can also learn about the steps that can be taken to minimize injuries and death, damage to property, and economic losses. There are many methods for informing the public about hazards and mitigation, including hazard mapping, disclosure requirements during real estate sales, disaster warning systems, and community awareness campaigns.

12.7.1 Hazard Mapping

Some communities choose to relay information about local hazards by publishing maps. Mapping of hazards includes inventories of at-risk populations, hazardous areas, hazardous structures, and environmentally sensitive areas. Hazard maps can range in sophistication from simple paper maps that show the outlines of hazardous areas (storm surge inundation zones, for example) to multilayered computerized maps created through a geographic information system (GIS). GIS supports the inventory and analysis of spatial data related to the location and characteristics of hazardous areas, demographic data, characteristics of the built environment, and other factors that are necessary to mitigation and preparedness efforts.

Hazard maps are often made available to the public for viewing in local government offices. Many communities make their maps accessible over the internet through links from a municipal or county website so that new and current residents have access to the maps at any time at relatively little cost. Using web-based maps also facilitates dissemination of up-to-date and interactive mapping information. Maps that clearly portray the extent of hazard exposure a community faces can create an awareness and understanding among local officials, as well as the general public, that often is more vivid than other methods of information dissemination. These graphic depictions of community vulnerability can be worth a thousand words and can serve to notify residents of where the dangers lie in relation to both public and private property. A map of the town's property tax base overlaid with hazard maps of storm surge or flood zones, for example, can be a real eye-opener. When the intersection of the built environment with the potential hazard area is illustrated on a map, it can highlight the need for management practices that will reduce the community's level of vulnerability.

USING GIS TO PROJECT FLOODING FROM FUTURE DEVELOPMENT

Planners and engineers of the Charlotte-Mecklenburg Storm Water Service in North Carolina use GIS technology to create computer models of the impact of future flood events and assess the impact of various land use, development patterns, and growth scenarios. In fact, by conducting a build-out analysis, they are able to predict the floodplain assuming the city is fully developed based on current zoning. The department uses the GIS data to choose the most appropriate stormwater flood-control measures in the floodplains of the metropolitan area.

12.7.2 Real Estate Disclosure Laws

Hazard Maps can be used to define the boundaries within which hazards must be disclosed during real estate transactions. Real estate disclosure laws require that the buyer and lender be notified if a property is located in a hazard-prone area. Supporters of disclosure laws claim that a better informed marketplace should result in better decision-making. For example, lenders would be hesitant to extend credit in hazard areas, and well-informed purchasers would choose to avoid purchasing in hazardous areas, demand a lower price, or require mitigation as a bargaining chip. Only a handful of states have mandated real estate disclosure about natural hazards. Federally regulated lending institutions (which include the vast majority of banks and mortgage issuers in the United States) are required to advise applicants for a mortgage or other loan if the building is in the floodplain as shown on an official Flood Insurance Rate Map.

Notification may not have much of an impact on home buyers if the notification of the hazard risk occurs too late in the real estate process. For instance, federal lending laws require that flood hazard notification must be made five days before closing, by which time the applicant has usually signed a contract or has otherwise committed to purchasing the property.

Local real estate boards can help make notification practices more effective by requiring that newcomers be advised about hazard risks thoroughly and early in the home-buying process. Real estate boards may also require homeowners to disclose past disaster events, whether or not the property is in a mapped high-risk zone. However, sellers in many states retain the option to make no representation about the hazard risks or past hazard events, including flooding, erosion, or coastal storms that have affected the property.

12.7.3 Disaster Warning

Disaster warnings are critical for protecting residents from flash floods, dam breaks, thunderstorms, winter weather, tornadoes, and other rapid-onset hazards. Many disaster warnings are issued through the National Weather Service and disseminated to the public in numerous ways, including sirens, radio, television, mobile public-address systems, telephone trees, reverse 911 systems, and door-to-door contact. Posted signs can be used to identify risks at a particular site. Informational signs have been installed in riptide areas along the coast, tsunami inundation areas, falling rock and landslide-risk zones, areas of localized flooding, and other hazard areas.

Many people fail to respond to emergency warnings of imminent disaster, and even fewer residents heed warnings that are projected further into the future. Individuals ignore warnings for a variety of psychological or social reasons, including:

- Misperception of disaster probability
- Underestimation of the effectiveness of mitigation measures
- Fatalistic belief that it is impossible to control one's destiny
- Refusal to believe hazards are present
- Assumption that after a hazard occurs once, it will never recur
- Warnings in the past might have proven unwarranted (i.e., the hazard they were warned about never actually happened)[5]

12.7.4 Community Awareness Campaigns

Even though communities cannot single-handedly change the fatalistic outlook or combat all of the psychological factors that lead people to ignore warnings and cautionary words, community awareness programs can be used to directly educate the general public about hazard risks and mitigation strategies. Information can be presented in a number of ways, including outreach projects, hazard information centers and kiosks, school-age education workshops, and other means of spreading the word.

General awareness campaigns can include a wide variety of topics, such as practical information specific to the community and individual households. Residents should be informed about ways they can limit exposure, how they can retrofit their property to reduce damage, items to pack for any type of emergency, and local evacuation routes and procedures. Awareness campaigns can also cover information that the public should know about how their community fits into a larger environment, such as how uncontrolled floodplain use impact downstream neighbors, the ways in which wetlands naturally absorb and filter floodwaters, barrier island and inlet migration, and how dunes protect inland areas from wave action and storm surge.

General awareness programs have a mixed record for building public support for hazard mitigation and preparedness activities. More successful are self-help programs with a narrow scope, such as residential floodproofing workshops or property insurance informational sessions. Some communities have successfully teamed with local building supply and home improvement stores to provide consumers with information about mitigation building techniques. For example, large retailers, including The Home Depot and Lowes, have held mitigation expos and preparedness fairs in several coastal areas. These events are often strategically timed to take place in early summer, just before hurricane season begins. Demonstrations of mitigation techniques—for example, how to place plywood sheets over windows to protect glass against high winds—highlight supplies available for sale in the store, while educating and motivating customers to turn their DIY energy toward home protection, as well as home improvement.

SELF-CHECK

- Explain how public information is an effective hazard mitigation technique.
- Discuss obstacles to disaster warning systems.
- Give an example of a community awareness campaign.

12.8 MITIGATION FUNDING

There is no doubt that communities can incur significant costs in implementing many of the mitigation tactics mentioned in this chapter. Local government officials must balance many competing interests when deciding how to distribute limited resources. Hot-button issues such as crime control, education, affordable housing, public transit, homelessness, and health services often grab the immediate attention of voters. Many local government budgets are stretched thin in meeting the urgent needs of citizens, and mitigation may receive low priority, particularly if the community has not experienced a hazard event in the recent past. However, it is a well-accepted principle in planning and emergency management circles that current dollars invested in mitigation greatly reduce the demand for future dollars by reducing the amount needed for emergency response, recovery, and reconstruction following a disaster. Keeping businesses open, residents in their homes, and basic services operating following an emergency results in economic security and social stability for local communities. Financial resources that are directed toward lowering risk represent money well spent.

12.8.1 State and Federal Funding Sources

State and federal aid is a large part of many local government revenue streams. The vast majority of buyouts, elevation projects, and other expensive mitigation activities are paid for with federal funds, through programs such as the Hazard Mitigation Grant Program (HMGP), the Building Resilient Infrastructure and Communities (BRIC), and the Flood Mitigation Assistance (FMA) Program. Other funding sources include the Small Business Administration Disaster Assistance Program and Community Development Block Grants issued by the Department of Housing and Urban Development. Most of these programs are available to communities after the President of the United States has issued a disaster declaration for the area. Some programs, such as the BRIC and FMA programs administered by FEMA, are not tied to a disaster declaration, and local governments may apply for this funding annually. You can find descriptions of these and other federal programs in Chapter 6.

12.8.2 Combining Mitigation with Other Goals

In addition to disaster assistance programs, other federal and state programs may fund mitigation activities, even though the programs are not directly related to hazards. Mitigation goals can often be coupled with other objectives, such as affordable housing, pollution prevention, water quality protection, natural resource preservation, wildlife conservation, and other mutual interests. For instance, wetland restoration funding may be available from the federal Environmental Protection Agency (EPA), soil and water loans may be granted by the U.S. Farm Service Agency, and watershed protection grants may come from the Natural Resources Conservation Service. Although these programs may not have natural hazards mitigation as a primary objective, they can often provide an opportunity to fund hazard mitigation as a side benefit.

12.8.3 Finding Matching Funds

Many federal grant programs require the local government to contribute what is known as a **nonfederal match**—usually a percentage of the total grant amount awarded—that must come from another source. This is true of many federal hazard mitigation grants. Local or state funds can be used to meet the match, although federal funds from another source cannot.

When the state does not provide the needed match, local governments applying for grants can often meet the nonfederal match with **in-kind contributions** instead of cash outlays. In-kind resources can consist of labor or salaries paid to local staff to carry out the mitigation activities (such as project managers, engineers, planners, public works crews, etc.). In-kind contributions can also include donated services, supplies, equipment, and office space. Partnerships and coalitions formed with other organizations can also be a source of in-kind resources.

PAY AS YOU FLOW

Tulsa, Oklahoma, has established a stable financing source to pay for its stormwater management program. Each home and business in the watershed is assessed a monthly stormwater fee as part of its utility bill. Businesses are assessed based on the amount of impervious surface. The fee raises over $8 million a year, which the city uses to pay for the enforcement of regulations on new development, a master drainage plan for the city, and acquiring lands along creek beds to be used as biking and hiking trails.

12.8.4 Finding Mitigation Funds at Home

Although outside sources of funding pay for the bulk of large mitigation projects, many creative local governments are becoming more self-reliant when it comes to paying for mitigation activities. Local governments have used a variety of sources, including capital budgets, taxation and special assessments, municipal bonds, utility and permitting fees, and partnerships with nonprofit organizations to fund mitigation activities.

Local governments can also study their annual operating budgets carefully to see where mitigation can fit into ongoing community programs. Often a change in spending priorities is all that is needed to finance some mitigation ideas. And sometimes, the most effective mitigation activities require no new money at all, just a shift in thinking so that the community includes mitigation principles in day-to-day operations and decision-making.

SELF-CHECK

- Define nonfederal match and in-kind contribution.
- List three local sources of mitigation funding.
- Cite three sources of federal and state funding for mitigation.

12.9 MITIGATION STRATEGIES FOR HUMAN-MADE HAZARDS

Instead of preventing human-made disasters by avoiding hazardous locations, it is necessary to create a built environment that is protected from attack or is better able to withstand an attack or hazardous materials accident. This can be achieved through target hardening and other strategies. It is also possible to carry out public awareness campaigns so that members of the community are better informed about ways to protect themselves, their families, and their businesses from various types of human-made hazards.

Target-hardening strategies can be fairly simple—for example, installing security fencing around an HVAC system's air intake to avoid the insertion of poisonous gas. Target hardening can also be more elaborate, such as blocking off large areas as buffer zones around particularly sensitive buildings. Some of the strategies that are appropriate for mitigating natural hazard impacts can also be used to increase protection against man-made hazards. For example, some types of earthquake mitigation techniques may also strengthen a building against the effects of a bomb blast. Mitigation against wildfire can protect structures from incendiary devices. And property protection measures that strengthen buildings against high winds may help mitigate the impact of an explosion. Table 12.2 gives a few examples of the type of strategies that can be used to mitigate the impacts of human-made hazards.[6]

SELF-CHECK

- Define **target-hardening** strategies.
- List seven mitigation techniques for terrorism and technological hazard mitigation.
- Explain a key difference between man-made and natural disasters.

Table 12.2 Terrorism and Technological Hazard Mitigation Strategies.

Type of Mitigation Technique	Sample Action
Site planning and landscape design	• Minimize concealment opportunities such as hedges, bus shelters, trash cans, mailboxes, etc. • Limit entrances/exits • Provide adequate lighting
Architectural and interior design	• Avoid locating toilets and service spaces in nonsecured areas • Locate delivery/mail service facilities at remote locations • Prevent vehicles from driving into or under a building • Restrict roof access
Structural engineering	• Create blast-resistant exterior envelope • Ensure structural elements can withstand blast loads • Enclose critical building components within hardened floors, walls, and ceilings
Security	• Develop backup control center capabilities • Implement intrusion detection systems • Install screening systems (metal detectors, X-ray machines, etc.)
Mechanical engineering	• Protect utility lifelines (water, power, communications) by concealing, burying, and encasing • Locate air intakes on roof with restricted access • Provide filtration of intake air
Electrical engineering	• Secure primary and backup fuel supply areas • Implement separate emergency and normal power systems • Locate utility systems away from entrances, loading areas, etc

12.10 PUTTING IT ALL TOGETHER: LOCAL MITIGATION PLANNING

All of the mitigation strategies described in this chapter are put to their best advantage as part of a comprehensive mitigation plan. Hazard mitigation planning is the most effective way of establishing a community's commitment to mitigation goals, objectives, policies, and programs. By expressing what a community hopes to achieve, the plan can be an important connection between the public interest that is being served and the mitigation strategy to be put in action. A plan can help a local community avoid the uncoordinated and often inconsistent results of an ad hoc, project-by-project attempt at mitigation by identifying what it wants to do before a hazard event occurs. That way, as soon as money is available and the opportunity arises, the community can implement mitigation strategies more efficiently.

Not only does a local mitigation plan make sense, but it is also required by law that local governments have an approved mitigation plan in place before they can receive certain types of federal disaster assistance. This includes funds from the HMGP and the BRIC Program, two significant FEMA funding sources.

According to the Disaster Mitigation Act, the primary purpose of hazard mitigation planning is to identify community policies, strategies, and tools for action over the long term that will reduce risk and the potential for future losses throughout the community. The FEMA Local Mitigation Planning Handbook lays out nine tasks that comprise this process:

1. Determine the planning area and resources
2. Build the planning team
3. Create an outreach strategy
4. Review community capabilities
5. Conduct a risk assessment
6. Develop a mitigation strategy
7. Keep the plan current
8. Review and adopt the plan
9. Create a safe and resilient community

Each of the nine major steps in the hazard mitigation planning process is described in the following section of this chapter. For a more detailed description of these steps, you can download the planning guidance from the FEMA website.[7] In addition to the FEMA Handbook, the *Beyond the Basics* website (www.mitigationguide.org) provides guidance and examples from a variety of communities around the country of high-quality mitigation planning.

12.10.1 Determine the Planning Area and Resources

Local governments can prepare a mitigation plan for their jurisdiction independently, known as a **single-jurisdictional** plan. Alternatively, communities may develop a mitigation plan in conjunction with other communities in a **multi-jurisdictional** planning process. In many cases, multi-jurisdictional plans are coordinated at the county level. Multi-jurisdictional plans are acceptable under the FEMA requirements as long as each jurisdiction participates in the process and officially adopts the plan. Both single and multi-jurisdictional plans present their own benefits and challenges, so in deciding which approach is right for your community, it will be important to weigh the costs versus the opportunities.

Establishing a mitigation plan in conjunction with other jurisdictions may increase the pool of resources—human, technical, and financial—available to complete the planning effort. But regardless of whether your community pursues a single- or multi-jurisdictional plan, many external resources exist to facilitate the process. For example, many regional planning agencies can provide expertise, as can local universities with planning or emergency management degree programs. Private consultants are also available to assist in the coordination, facilitation, and execution of the mitigation planning process. See the FEMA Handbook for criteria to weigh when selecting a consultant.

12.10.2 Build the Planning Team

Before embarking on the planning process itself, the community must establish the commitment and political will to see the plan through to the end. Planning can be a protracted procedure, and sustaining support is critical to its success. An important component of garnering the necessary support depends on the knowledge base of the community at large. A certain level of understanding about hazard mitigation planning and risk reduction is necessary for a successful outcome. There must also be a general awareness of the hazards the community faces and of the need to do something about them. Of course, the planning process itself will serve an educational role as participants in the process become more knowledgeable about their community's vulnerability and ways to decrease it, but an assessment of how much citizens and elected and/or appointed officials actually know about hazards from the outset can help direct later steps in the most efficient and effective manner.

The planning team that will develop the hazard mitigation plan should be made up of local staff who have the authority to carry out the detailed studies as well as the analysis and policy recommendations that are part of the planning process. Many communities establish an advisory committee or task force to meet regularly and oversee the mitigation planning process. It is also important to coordinate with other agencies within the local government and other jurisdictions. This is particularly important if the plan is to be a multi-jurisdictional plan, that is, one that covers all the local governments in a county or region.

12.10.3 Create an Outreach Strategy

In order to solicit adequate public participation in the mitigation planning process, it is critical for a community to express what it wants to accomplish through its outreach efforts, who to involve in the hazard mitigation plan, and how and when to effectively engage the community. An outreach strategy will help pinpoint the stakeholders and members of the public to target and identify methods of bringing them into the planning process.

FEMA recommends that, at a minimum, the stakeholders that must be included in the planning process are neighboring communities, local and regional agencies involved in hazard mitigation activities, and agencies that have the authority to regulate development, as well as businesses, academia, and other private and nonprofit interests. Moreover, FEMA recommends soliciting participation from local cultural institutions and elected officials and planning commission members.

In addition to these key stakeholder groups, the general public must also be given an opportunity to be involved in the planning process. Beyond simply keeping citizens abreast of how the mitigation plan is developing, community members, though not necessarily technical experts, can help shape the content of the plan itself, identifying assets and problem areas, narrating threat and hazard history, and prioritizing proposed mitigation alternatives.

Promoting public participation not only ensures that the mitigation plan represents the goals and priorities of the community but also increases buy-in from stakeholders whose support will help implement the plan. FEMA requires that the public be invited to participate in the process when the plan is in draft stages and prior to plan approval. Public meetings, workshops, informational presentations, websites, resident mailings, and other forms of communication are often effective ways to solicit citizen participation.

While actual methods of outreach will vary from community to community, many tactics are common across the United States. For example, presentations to governing bodies like a board of commissioners can help secure participation from those key stakeholders. Meetings and workshops where the mitigation plan is discussed are often advertised through the news media, social media, municipal website, or at community events such as fairs or sporting events. Jurisdictions can also host informal roundtables and forums at strategic locations to solicit public participation.

12.10.4 Review Community Capabilities

Part of hazard mitigation planning is knowing what strengths, in the form of existing policies, programs, and resources, are already available to a community. These assets should be documented in a capability assessment. The capability assessment describes the legal authority vested in local governments to pursue mitigation measures. The assessment also evaluates the community's institutional framework, technical know-how, and ability to pay for mitigation. The capability of all levels of government (local, state, tribal, federal, and regional), as well as the contributions made by nongovernmental organizations (churches, charities, community relief groups, the Red Cross, hospitals, for-profit- and nonprofit businesses), should be included, with a description of their utility to the community in terms of hazard mitigation. Preparing a capability assessment assures that local mitigation strategies will be based on existing authorities, policies, programs, and resources, and that the community's ability to expand on and improve its existing tools is duly noted.

The political willpower necessary to carry out mitigation strategies should not be underestimated. In some communities, the most difficult hurdle to overcome may be reluctance on the part of citizens or local officials to engage in something new. Some property owners may view hazard mitigation as a restriction of their rights. Other community members may mistakenly think hazard mitigation will pose an impediment to growth and economic development. In times of fiscal restraint, expenditure of limited resources may be a challenge. On the other hand, some residents and elected officials may have experienced personally the devastation of a past disaster and will support local hazard mitigation efforts wholeheartedly. The planning team should consider the local political climate carefully when assessing the community's capability.

12.10.5 Conduct a Risk Assessment

The risk assessment task is the backbone of the hazard mitigation plan, providing the factual basis that allows communities to identify and prioritize appropriate mitigation actions. The risk assessment process includes an identification and profile of hazards, an assessment of vulnerable assets and populations, an estimate of potential losses, and a description of future land use and development trends. These steps are described in detail in Chapter 10.

12.10.6 Develop a Mitigation Strategy

The previous steps identified the populations and assets that are vulnerable to specific identified hazards and the capabilities of the community to address its hazard threats. The planning team must then develop appropriate mitigation actions to reduce vulnerability. Goals and objectives are useful for guiding mitigation decisions and developed to address the hazard and risk assessment findings.

- **Goals** are general guidelines that describe what the community hopes to achieve.
- **Objectives** provide a more specific way to achieve the goals. In general, each goal statement will have three or four objectives that spell out steps to reach that goal.
- **Mitigation actions** are developed later and are the most specific proposals for reaching goals.

Together, goals, objectives, and actions make up a mitigation strategy that is designed to increase community resiliency. Goals establish a vision of how the community wants to protect itself from hazards and how the community wants to grow and develop in the future.

Objectives are more specific and narrower in scope than goals and are usually phrased so that it is easy to see when (or if) they have been reached.

Once the community has concluded that it faces an unacceptable risk to certain identified hazards and has made the commitment to reducing its level of vulnerability by establishing meaningful goals and objectives, it is time to formulate a plan that meets those goals. This is the action part of the planning process, where the planning team establishes what will be done, and where, to reduce vulnerability. This section of the plan involves the identification, evaluation, and prioritization of a comprehensive range of specific mitigation actions and projects to reduce the effects of each hazard identified earlier. The policies created will help guide both the day-to-day and long-range decision-making of the community.

The mitigation actions considered should cover a wide range of options to reach the objectives laid out previously. Every single action may not necessarily be acted upon, but the planning team should think of multiple alternatives, each with its own set of relative merits. Some of the actions that are identified may be "brick and mortar" projects, such as constructing tornado-safe rooms or retrofitting existing school buildings to withstand earthquake shaking. Other mitigation actions may be nonconstruction projects, such as acquisition of flood-prone properties or changes to the zoning ordinance or building code. In general, mitigation actions should cover each of the six broad categories of mitigation activities, including prevention, property protection, natural resource protection, structural projects, and public education and awareness strategies as well as emergency operations. It is important that the identified actions and projects address both reducing the effects of hazards on new buildings and infrastructure, as well as existing buildings and infrastructure. In addition, the actions should include some that are appropriate to carry out after a disaster has occurred, while others can be instituted at any time, including in the pre-disaster period.

Benefit-Cost Analysis

The regulations that accompany the Disaster Mitigation Act require that the prioritization process for selecting mitigation actions include an emphasis on the use of a cost-benefit review to maximize benefits. All projects using federal funds must be justified as being cost-effective. This can be determined through the use of various benefit-cost analysis (BCA) methodologies.

A **BCA** is a quantitative procedure that assesses the desirability of a hazard mitigation project by taking a long-term view of avoided future damages to insurable structures as compared to the cost of the project.

A **Benefit-Cost Ratio (BCR)** is the outcome of the analysis, which demonstrates whether the net present value of benefits exceeds the net present value of costs.

FEMA's BCAs are governed by guidance from the Office of Management and Budget (OMB). A BCA is required for all mitigation projects submitted to FEMA for funding, and mitigation projects with a BCR less than 1.0 will not be considered for funding under most programs. Mitigation projects with higher BCRs will be more competitive to receive federal funds.

12.10.7 Keep the Plan Current

Mitigation is an ongoing process. Effective plans are dynamic and evolving and must be continually tested. Therefore, an essential element of the written mitigation plan is a section that spells out in detail the procedures to monitor and evaluate the plan's progress on a regular basis. The plan should designate a specific person or position within the local government to perform these functions.

The primary question to be addressed in monitoring and evaluating a hazard mitigation plan, is, "Has the area's vulnerability increased or decreased as a result of planning and mitigation efforts?" Where vulnerability has decreased, the planning team should determine if other methods could be used to achieve even greater improvement in reducing the area's vulnerability. Where vulnerability has increased, or has not decreased as projected, mitigation efforts must be evaluated to determine if other mitigation strategies might provide greater effectiveness than those currently in use.

Regularly scheduled updates to the hazard mitigation plan address changes that have taken place in the local area. This schedule can be quarterly, semiannually, or annually—whatever best suits the needs and ability of the local government to stay on top of things. At a minimum, under the Disaster Mitigation Act, local mitigation plans must be updated within a five-year cycle. The plan should include a statement that declares the community will review and update the plan every five years, and that it will resubmit the plan to the State Hazard Mitigation Officer and FEMA for review and approval. The planning team should also set a regular schedule for monitoring implementation of the plan.

12.10.8 Review and Adopt the Plan

The governing body of the local government must officially adopt the hazard mitigation plan in order to make the plan enforceable. A series of recommendations made by planning or emergency management staff does not have nearly the impact as an official document that clearly lays out the government's policies for dealing with hazards and reducing vulnerability. In fact, adoption of the plan is a prerequisite for plan approval by FEMA.

The final version of the plan should be presented to the lead governing body of the community, usually at a regularly scheduled meeting that is open to the public. Depending upon the structure of the local government, this may be a meeting of the city council, board of supervisors, county commissioners, board of aldermen, or other official policy-making groups (see Chapter 8 for a discussion of the various forms of local government in the United States). The mitigation plan must be adopted through the government's normal legal process. Generally, most local governing bodies adopt a hazard mitigation plan by resolution. A **resolution** is an expression of a governing body's opinion, will, or intention that is usually legally binding. Depending upon the laws of the state and the local jurisdiction, adoption of the plan gives the local government legal authority to enact ordinances, policies, or programs to reduce hazard losses and implement the recommended mitigation actions contained in the plan.

12.10.9 Create a Safe and Resilient Community

Once adopted, communities must work to implement the actions developed in the hazard mitigation plan. Communities typically face challenges in effectively carrying out the strategies described in the plan, including a lack of funding or other resources, a loss of interest after the mitigation planning process is over, and a disconnect between the mitigation strategy and day-to-day operations and governmental programs.

The following approaches may be helpful for communities seeking to successfully implement hazard mitigation plans.

- **Use the post-disaster window of opportunity.** The post-disaster recovery period offers unique opportunities to accomplish mitigation goals. Public support and political will to change policies and invest in long-term risk reduction may be at their highest. In addition, funding sources may become available for mitigation, such as FEMA's HMGP and Public Assistance.

- **Focus on quality over quantity.** By implementing a plan, it helps to achieve a few "early wins," or successfully complete some initial mitigation actions. These could be low-cost actions that can be implemented quickly or a single high-priority project. Demonstrating progress can go a long way in gaining the support needed to implement more complex actions in the future.
- **Encourage local champions.** Successful projects often involve a strong local champion. Champions are leaders who understand the mitigation vision, can clearly communicate it, and can engage others to get buy-in.
- **Identify a mentor.** Community officials can learn from other communities that have successfully implemented mitigation actions. Other communities may be willing to share experience and lessons learned. The FEMA Best Practices Portfolio (http://www.fema.gov/mitigation-best-practices-portfolio) or State Hazard Mitigation Officers can provide ideas and advice.

SELF-CHECK

- Explain the role of a local hazard mitigation plan.
- Discuss the importance of a mitigation plan in regards to federal disaster funding.
- Describe the steps involved in developing a mitigation plan.

SUMMARY

This chapter describes some of the many tools and techniques that local communities can use to reduce vulnerability to natural and human-made hazards. These tools include a variety of structural engineering projects, ways of strengthening buildings and facilities to withstand hazard impacts, land use regulations and building codes, natural resource and wetland preservation strategies, techniques for informing the public and increasing community awareness of hazards, as well as mitigation strategies aimed at reducing the impacts of human-made hazards. Additionally, the chapter provided examples of funding sources for mitigation, including federal and state resources, and ways that local governments can fund mitigation activities using internal revenue sources. The chapter concluded with a discussion of hazard mitigation planning as a way to coordinate and integrate resilience into all community programs and policies.

KEY TERMS

Beach nourishment: The artificial replacement or addition of sand to beaches to widen the backshore and move the high-water line further toward the sea.

Building codes: Laws, ordinances, and regulations that set forth standards and requirements for the construction, reconstruction, maintenance, operation, occupancy, use, and appearance of buildings.

Build-Out: The upper limit of a community's capacity to absorb additional development.

Impervious surfaces: Paved areas that rainwater cannot soak through, such as parking lots, roofs, streets, and other nonporous surfaces.

Infill: The practice of building new structures on existing lots.

In-kind contributions: Noncash contributions of goods and/or services. Can include items such as equipment, technical or consulting services, furniture, office supplies, etc. May also include donated staff or volunteer time.

Nonfederal match: The amount of funds, usually a percentage of the total grant amount awarded, required by many federal grant programs that must come from a source other than the federal grant program.

Retrofitting: Rebuilding existing buildings to withstand the shaking and ground movement associated with an earthquake.

Runoff: Rainwater that does not soak into the soil, evaporate, or become trapped by plant roots and thus flows over the surface of the ground.

Subdivision ordinance: Regulations that govern the division of larger tracts of land into smaller parcels. Subdivision ordinances dictate the land uses that are permitted on the parcels and are often accompanied by conditions that require the developer to provide adequate amenities to support the new development in exchange for a permit.

Target-hardening strategies: Methods of protecting structures from man-made hazard impacts.

Variance: Exception that allows development to proceed, even though the rules prohibit it.

Zoning: The process of dividing a local community into districts, or zones. Zoning regulations control the type and amount of development and land uses that are permitted in each zone.

ASSESS YOUR UNDERSTANDING

Summary Questions

1. Mitigation is based on short-term preventative measures. True or False?
2. Which of the following is an example of a property protection mitigation strategy?
   a. Safe room
   b. Capital improvement
   c. Hurricane shutters
   d. Vegetative buffer
3. Levees are an example of which type of mitigation strategy?
   a. Natural resource protection
   b. Property protection
   c. Prevention
   d. Structural engineered project
4. A hazard mitigation plan is the first step of a risk assessment. True or False?
5. Which of the following is an example of a public information strategy?
   a. Taxes and fees
   b. Building codes
   c. Warning system
   d. Diversions
6. Wetland conservation is an example of a structural engineered project. True or False?
7. Dams increase the natural function of a floodplain. True or False?
8. Which of the following is used to reduce coastal hazard impacts?
   a. Riparian buffer
   b. Groin
   c. Seismic retrofit
   d. Slope stabilization
9. Groins are hardened materials on the shore to protect against erosion. True or False?

10. Stormwater systems should have the capacity to meet the volume of stormwater expected in a lower than normal rainy season. True or False?
11. Keeping development out of hazard-prone areas is the most sustainable approach to hazard mitigation. True or False?
12. A buyout program is one method of
    a. Public information.
    b. Property protection.
    c. Prevention.
    d. Natural resource protection.
13. Acquisition is only used in cases where property owners are willing to sell. True or False?
14. A land use plan and the resulting zones and ordinances can be used to keep people and property from locating in hazard areas. True or False?
15. Setback regulations can be used to
    a. Build capital improvements.
    b. Reuse acquired properties.
    c. Establish the distance between building zones.
    d. Establish the distance between construction and a fault line.
16. In situations where communities cannot avoid hazards, they must then protect property from as much damage as possible. True or False?
17. Wet floodproofing uses special paints and compounds to protect walls from water damage. True or False?
18. Seismic construction includes structural and nonstructural improvements to reduce earthquake damage. True or False?
19. Wetlands reduce pollution by
    a. Increasing floodwaters.
    b. Filtering pollutants.
    c. Reducing floodwaters.
    d. Diluting pollutants.
20. Which of the following is an example of a mechanical engineering mitigation technique?
    a. Filtration of intake air
    b. Intrusion detection systems
    c. Metal detectors
    d. Blast-resistant exterior

Review Questions

1. Mitigation is a long-term approach to reducing hazard risk. List five different mitigation strategies that communities can use to control hazards and disasters.
2. Dams, seawalls, and vegetative buffers are all examples of structural engineered projects. Describe the purpose of this type of strategy.
3. A risk assessment can help a community choose a mitigation strategy. How?
4. By building dams, levees, and seawalls, humans assume that they can defeat the powers of Mother Nature. What are three disadvantages to such projects?
5. List two ways that communities can reuse acquired properties.
6. Discuss the role of setback regulations in preventative mitigation.
7. What is a buyout program, and why does it work best when it involves blocks of homes or a neighborhood?
8. Wetlands are a valuable part of the environment. How do they contribute to flood control?

9. What are some ways humans have damaged our wetlands?
10. Whose responsibility is it to determine a property's vulnerability to hazards—potential buyers, sellers, or mortgage companies?
11. List three different funding sources available to communities that wish to carry out mitigation strategies.
12. Which of the state and federal aid programs does not require a disaster situation?
13. Define target hardening to mitigate against human-made hazard threats.
14. Law requires that local governments have an approved mitigation plan before they can receive federal disaster money. Explain why.

Applying This Chapter

1. Explain how a mitigation plan can help a community in an earthquake-prone area carry out mitigation strategies.
2. What rationale would you give to support a proposal to remove a dam on a river in Minnesota? Opponents of the proposal claim that the loss of hydropower and flood control will negatively affect the area.
3. A small coastal town in Georgia is exploring the idea of using a seawall to protect a stretch of shoreline where a dozen homes and several small businesses are located. What factors determine the effectiveness of such a seawall? What are other options available to this community?
4. As a mitigation planner in a tornado-prone area of Kansas, what property protection mitigation measures would you recommend to protect the homes in the community? What resources would you use to research the potential strategies?
5. Look around your community and think about the wetlands that have been impaired or destroyed because of development or other means. What impact, if any, has that had on flooding in the area? Are there wetlands that are still vulnerable?
6. What disaster warning systems are in place for your community? How do they compare to another community, one with different hazard issues?
7. As the owner of a warehouse in an industrial area, you've decided to build an adjacent building to house part of your business. A chemical explosion at the other end of the industrial park has caused you to think about protecting your new building and investment. What types of mitigation strategies could you put to use in the design, construction, and security of the building?
8. Assume you are the emergency manager in a town that has experienced major flooding for the fourth time. Homes in several neighborhoods located in the floodplain were damaged severely, and many people are living in trailers and other types of temporary housing. The mayor of your town asks you to seek funding from FEMA to carry out some mitigation projects. What would you advise the mayor and the town council to do? What factors would you consider as you propose your ideas?

You Try It

Savings Plan

Think about any areas or neighborhoods in your community or county that should not be developed or that cannot be protected well enough from hazards. Come up with an acquisition plan that would protect this area from development and protect residents and property from injury or damage. How would you defend the high cost of such a strategy?

Public Support

Think about some mitigation action that has been proposed for your community (or one that you believe would be beneficial). What is the general sentiment of the community about the action? What could be done to gain more support for the mitigation?

Going for the Green

Choose a particular mitigation action for your community and consider the funding options available to pay for it. What resources would you investigate?

REFERENCES

1. FEMA. 2016. *Be Aware of Potential Risk of Dam Failure in Your Community.* National Dam Safety Program.
2. Knabb, R.D., J.R. Rhome, and D.P. Brown. 2005. *"Tropical Cyclone Report, Hurricane Katrina, 23-30 August 2005."* National Hurricane Center. www.nhc.noaa.gov/2005atlan.shtml.
3. U.S. House of Representatives. 2006. *A Failure of Initiative: Final Report of the Select Bipartisan Committee to Investigate the Preparation for and Response to Hurricane Katrina.* Available at katrina.house.gov.
4. Leatherman, S.P. and V.R. Burkett. 2002. *Sea-Level Rise and Coastal Disasters: Lessons from the East Coast and New Orleans. Natural Hazards Observer 26* (March) (4): 10–11.
5. Buby. R.J., ed. 1999. *Cooperating with Nature: Confronting Natural Hazards with Land Use Planning for Sustainable Communities.* Washington, DC: Joseph Henry Press.
6. FEMA. 2003. *State and Local Hazard Mitigation Planning How-To Guide: Integrating Manmade Hazards into Mitigation Planning.* Publication 286-7.
7. FEMA. 2013. *Local Mitigation Planning Handbook.* Publication 302-094-1.

Section IV

The Future of Disaster Management

Chapter 13 Disaster Resilience

In the final chapter of the book, we tie together all we've learned about managing disasters and climate change in the United States by exploring the concept of disaster resilience. How can we build a culture of disaster prevention and ensure that, when disasters do occur, we are prepared for them and have a plan to recover and successfully rebound? What is the role of emergency managers in shaping disaster planning to lessen our communities' long-term risk? When disasters do impact our communities, how can we embrace resilience and build back in a way that mitigates future disasters? These and other questions are the focus of this chapter.

A central goal of this textbook is to frame hazard mitigation and preparedness as ongoing, iterative processes. The work of assessing and managing risk should evolve as the social, environmental, and economic realities of our communities change over time. In addition to describing how resilient communities use adaptive learning to plan for climate change, this chapter highlights key resources to aid emergency managers, resource planners, and others to incorporate the best information and tools to reduce hazard vulnerability:

• U.S. Census Bureau	(*factfinder.census.gov*)
• Hazus-MH	(*fema.gov/hazus-software*)
• Disaster Data	(*disaster.data.gov*)
• National Climate Assessment	(*nca2018.globalchange.gov*)
• Climate Data Initiative	(*climate.data.gov*)
• Digital Coast	(*coast.noaa.gov/digitalcoast*)
• Beyond the Basic Mitigation Guide	(*mitigationguide.org*)
• Ready.gov	(*ready.gov; listo.gov*)
• State Hazard Mitigation Officers	(*fema.gov/state-hazard-mitigation-officers*)
• State Climatologists	(*stateclimate.org*)

13

Disaster Resilience
Living with Our Environment

What You'll Learn

- How mitigation and preparedness support the concept of resilience
- Effective risk communication strategies
- The role of the private and nonprofit sectors in creating resilient communities
- Useful sources of information about hazards, risk, and climate change
- The value of using post-disaster redevelopment as an opportunity to enhance resilience

Goals and Outcomes

- Assess the opportunities available for mitigation and preparedness actions that create greater community resilience
- Develop a more nuanced understanding of the role of emergency management in the pursuit of resilience
- Learn known techniques for effectively communicating information about hazards and risk
- Explore datasets, tools, and resources that contain information about disasters, vulnerability, and climate change
- Consider the level of risk that you deem acceptable for natural and human-made hazards
- Appraise the role of personal responsibility in preventing disaster
- Collaborate with others to develop strategies to incorporate mitigation into post-disaster recovery

INTRODUCTION

While hazards are a function of the natural world, vulnerability to disasters is largely a function of human actions and behaviors. The ways in which we create our communities and choose to live determine how resilient we are to the impacts of hazards and climate change. Infusing an ethic of mitigation—a culture of prevention—and a commitment to fully prepare for events that do occur can help us achieve a more sustainable and resilient future. This chapter describes the emergency manager as a communicator, a coordinator, and a facilitator of a community action. The chapter also discusses key sources of reliable information that undergird mitigation, preparedness, and climate change adaptation in the United States. The chapter concludes with a discussion of strategies and approaches to create more resilient

  DOI: 10.4324/9781003123897-13

communities in the face of hazards and help lead communities toward a safer and more resilient tomorrow.

13.1 EMBRACING DISASTER RESILIENCE

The United States has witnessed an extraordinary increase in material losses due to disasters over the past several decades. While the number of deaths has not equaled those experienced in other nations that have suffered natural or human-made disasters of similar or greater proportions, the extent of property damage has been astronomical and has outstripped that of other developed countries.

Between 1980 and 1989, 27 weather and climate disasters in the United States cost more than $1 billion (adjusted for inflation). In the following decade, between 1990 and 1999, this number soared to an astounding 48 disasters with losses totaling more than $1 billion. The trend continued between 2000 and 2009 with 54 weather and climate disasters exceeding $1 billion. Incredibly, between 2010 and 2019, the tally of billion-dollar disasters reached 119.[1]

These numbers paint a staggering picture of the rising disaster losses in the United States. In addition to more people and investments in vulnerable areas, we also know that "climate change, once considered an issue of a distant future, has moved firmly into the present."[2] Average temperatures in the United States have risen nearly 2°F over the past century, with much of that change occurring during the last four decades. In the coming few decades, we can expect average temperatures to increase another 2–4°F, and possibly as much as 9°F by the end of this century without very significant reductions in greenhouse gases.[2]

With these changes in global temperatures come regional and local variations in climate, leading to more extreme weather events. According to a 2018 study by the National Oceanic and Atmospheric Administration, by 2050 a majority of U.S. coastal areas are likely to be threatened by 30 or more days of flooding each year due to dramatically accelerating impacts from sea level rise.[3] Major hurricanes and their destructive storm surge are likely to become more common in the Atlantic, at a time when roughly 39% of the U.S. population lives in coastal counties.[4] What is considered an extreme drought or an unusually powerful thunderstorm today may be the norm in coming years.

Traditional development patterns and urban growth in the United States have created communities that fail in some very fundamental ways. When development patterns do not take hazards into account, the social, economic, and environmental fabric of communities becomes brittle. The traditional approach to preventing disasters was to contain or control the hazard itself, often through the construction of large-scale engineering works, such as dams, dikes, levees, seawalls, and similar projects. In many instances, these structural mitigation projects have provided a false sense of security, leading to massive displacement and property damage when they ultimately fail. Nothing points to this troubling reality more than the damage in New Orleans when Hurricane Katrina's floodwaters broke and overtopped levees. Large-scale protection works can also impair nature's ability to mitigate against extreme events. Numerous studies provide examples of engineering works that have been counterproductive at the best or have even exacerbated vulnerability by interfering with natural processes. Events such as hurricanes, earthquakes, and floods are natural (although they may be worsened by human activities) and inevitable phenomena, and only when we choose to build structures and place settlements in their paths do they become disasters.

13.1.1 Investing in Our Future

These trends of rising vulnerability and extraordinary disaster losses are fundamentally unsustainable for our communities and our nation as a whole. A change in thinking is needed about where and how we want to live. We must consider the natural world and the threats and opportunities it presents when we build or rebuild our neighborhoods and city centers. The objective of preventing or lessening the impact of disaster must permeate all of our actions and behaviors to promote safer living conditions. Yet, as the former Secretary-General of the United Nations, Kofi Annan, has noted,

> Building a culture of prevention is not easy. While the costs of prevention have to be paid in the present, its benefits lie in a distant future. Moreover, the benefits are not tangible; they are disasters that did **not** happen.[5]

Despite this challenge in taking action today for future benefits, we know that preparedness and mitigation are proven to save lives and money. In fact, research about the value of mitigation showed that, on average, each dollar spent on mitigation saves society of four dollars in avoided future losses![6] And for flood risks, the return on investment is nearly five dollars for every dollar spent on mitigation. As we look to the future, a culture of resilience is needed—one in which we all share responsibility for understanding our environment and taking long-term action to ensure that communities are able to resist and bounce back when faced with natural and human-made hazards.

13.1.2 Resilience Defined

The National Academy of Sciences defines **resilience** as *the ability to prepare and plan for, absorb, recover from, and more successfully adapt to adverse events.*[7] Embracing disaster resilience requires us to better anticipate and plan for disasters to reduce losses before an event takes place. Resilience is not a one-time investment; it is an ongoing goal for policy-makers, resource managers, emergency managers, families, and even individuals to continually work toward. Understood in this context, resilience is both a process and an outcome. A report by the National Research Council described the characteristics of a resilient nation using the following statements:

- Every individual and community in the nation has access to the risk and vulnerability information they need to make their communities more resilient.
- All levels of government, communities, and the private sector have designed resilience strategies and operations plans based on this information.
- Proactive investments and policy decisions have reduced loss of lives, costs, and socio-economic impacts of future disasters.
- Community coalitions are widely organized, recognized, and supported to provide essential services before and after disasters occur.
- Recovery after disasters is rapid and the per capita federal cost of responding to disasters has been declining for a decade.
- Nationwide, the public is universally safer, healthier, and better educated.[7]

What does this look like on the ground? A resilient community cannot stop a hurricane from coming ashore, summon rain to forestall drought, or prevent a fault from slipping and shaking the earth. And a resilient community may not be able to fully prevent damage from these hazards. But its lifeline systems—transportation, communication, healthcare, etc.—are designed to continue functioning in the face of stress. Neighborhoods and businesses are located in safe areas of town, leaving known high-hazard areas for recreational or natural uses. Businesses that are damaged have plans in place to support their employees and continue or resume operations as soon as possible. Historic buildings have been retrofitted to meet current codes. And vital environmental protective features like wetlands and dunes are protected, serving as buffers that reduce the impact of the built environment when extreme weather events do occur.[8] Community members are informed about their risk and the many actions they can take to keep themselves, their families, and their friends safe. When a disaster does strike, communities learn from the past, continually adapting and evolving to become more secure and use the best available information as they plan for the future.

SELF-CHECK

- Define disaster resilience.
- Describe several characteristics that are essential for more resilient communities.
- Explain why the benefits of disaster reduction or prevention are difficult to measure.

13.2 SHARED RESPONSIBILITY

As we have discussed throughout this book, reducing disaster risk and building more resilient communities rely on a wide range of actors—from multinational organizations to individual citizens. Policies and investments that promote or hinder hazard management occur throughout the public sector at local, state, and federal levels. Developers, insurers, banks, and nonprofit organizations all have the power to embrace resilience and mitigate losses before a disaster takes place. Emergency managers, firefighters, police, hospitals, and others that play central roles providing services during disasters are also critical in the endeavor to create communities that may bend, but do not break, when faced with extreme events. And in the long run, resilience also relies on those who research innovative methods for understanding risk, designing infrastructure, and managing resources. Table 13.1 summarizes some of the many responsibilities, challenges, and opportunities facing some of these key actors in our quest for greater disaster resilience.[7]

13.2.1 The Art of Emergency Management

We have discussed throughout this book how mitigation can lower risk and reduce vulnerability to hazards, thereby contributing to a community's overall resilience. Emergency managers have a unique opportunity within communities to convene the whole community and set a direction that promotes resilience. Rather than focusing solely on response, an effective emergency manager serves as a communicator, a facilitator, and a coordinator—infusing an ethic of resilience in the many decision-makers and actors that are required to plan for the future, reduce disaster losses, and save lives. The skills necessary to balance priorities and promote resilience across a community highlight the function of emergency management as an art form and illustrate how emergency managers serve multiple and ongoing roles to guide a community toward a safer, healthier, and more sustainable path.

Many of the mitigation functions carried out by emergency managers are technical. We need meteorologists and geologists to inform us of the likely hazard events in our area and how they can affect people and property. We rely on civil engineers and architects to develop building codes and to design structurally sound buildings and infrastructure that can resist hazard impacts. We need GIS technicians to gather data and display it in a geospatial format that captures the intersections between the built environment and potential impacts. We need hydrologists and hydraulic engineers to create flood maps that indicate where structures are at risk of flooding and to establish flood heights on which to base regulatory requirements

Table 13.1 Responsibilities, Challenges, and Opportunities of Key Interacting Parties in Risk Management.

Interested Party	Responsibility	Challenges	Opportunities
Federal government	Provides and operates protection structures for communities; supports National Flood Insurance Program; provides disaster assistance	No comprehensive or coordinated approach to disaster risk management	Stemming the growth in outlays of post-disaster recovery funds
States and local governments	Ensure public health and safety in use of land, zoning, land-use planning, enforcement of building codes, development of risk management strategies	Reluctance to limit development; difficulty in controlling land use on privately owned land	Reaping benefits of multiple ecosystem services by investing and strengthening natural defenses
Homeowners and businesses in hazard-prone areas	Take action to reduce vulnerability and increase resilience of property	May be unaware of or underestimate the hazards that they face	Creating demand for disaster-resistant or retrofitted structures with increased value
Emergency managers	Oversee emergency preparedness, response, recovery, and mitigation activities	More focused on immediate disaster response than risk management	Reorientation of training and roles to balance focus toward prevention and disaster resilience
Construction and real estate	Incorporate resilience into designs; inform clients of risk	Actions may increase cost and reduce the likelihood of sales	New opportunities in niche markets
Banks and financial institutions	Require hazard insurance	No incentives given to require insurance	Reduce overall risk in their portfolios
Private insurers and reinsurers	Offer hazard insurance at actuarial rates; identify risks	Limits may be placed on rate structures	Greatly expanded incentives such as premium reductions for retrofit measures
Researchers	Collect, analyze, and communicate data, forecasts, and models about risk, hazards, and disasters	Insufficient or dispersed datasets; knowing how to share research with broad audiences	Increased forecasting and modeling capability

for building in the floodplain. We need planners and resource managers to direct growth and development out of hazard areas and to encourage more sustainable patterns of land use.

The science of emergency management relies on good data, accurate mapping, and the expertise to interpret them. But emergency management also involves extensive critical thinking, application of that knowledge to practice, and effective communication of sound, data-driven advice to decision-makers. Ultimately, it is not until the data is interpreted and translated into policy that mitigation will make a difference. It is here, at the juncture of science and policy, that emergency managers build resiliency.

13.2.2 Risk Communication: Getting the Message Across

A major obstacle to implementing hazard reduction measures involves the public's misunderstanding of risk and the fact that most people do not want to believe that their community will ever experience a disaster, much less experience another if they've already been through one. All people, no matter where they live, deserve to know the level of risk they are undertaking by living in a particular place, and the art of emergency management involves understanding how to communicate risk in ways that are understandable to the public and connect the messaging with people's values to spur action.

Communication for resilience goes beyond tactical communication—such as warnings and emergency messaging. Resilience communication shapes "how people see their roles in disasters, build the resolve necessary to endure, and encourages learning from historical precedent."[7] Effective risk communication that drives resilience is no small feat; yet social science research provides evidence-based strategies that emergency managers can use to convey information about hazards and encourage mitigation and preparedness. The following concepts summarize key techniques to effectively communicate about hazards and risk to promote resilience.

Preserve the Social Memory of Disasters

Educators, emergency managers, and professional communicators should find creative ways to draw on past events to help community members and organizations learn from previous disasters and retain skills and knowledge needed for response and recovery. And as an example, older members of the Vietnamese-American community in New Orleans East passed along to the younger generation lessons learned from previous adversity, such as pooling resources and home construction, which ultimately helped their community recovery from Hurricane Katrina more quickly than other parts of the region.[9]

Highlight Communities and Individuals as Primary Problem Solvers

Approaches to disaster management that focus only on aid and service provision coming from outside the community discourage individual action and community involvement. Since resilient communities take responsibility for their own health and safety, communication efforts should be framed in a way that places the onus to prepare for and mitigate hazards on everyone, rather than setting an unrealistic expectation that government or other outside organizations will simply restore communities to their pre-event state if a disaster takes place.

Identify a Sense of Community and Social Linkages

Resilient communities are characterized by shared connections among their citizens who demonstrate respect for and service to others. Effective communication should emphasize and strengthen a sense of community to promote norms of helping, cooperation, and reciprocity. Ideally, messaging that fosters social cohesion can help community members make complex policy choices despite competing interests.

Understand What People Need and Want to Know

All communities are different, and communications strategies should be grounded in the unique desires of a community. Rather than making assumptions about what information citizens need, audience research techniques such as focus groups, interviews, and surveys can help focus communication strategies on topics and concerns that are common in a given community. Similarly, understanding the shared perceptions, beliefs, and values of a community will aid in the design of messages more likely to motivate behavior change.[10]

Emphasize the Benefits of Personal Actions Rather Than Risk Alone

People are more likely to take actions to prepare for and mitigate hazards if they believe they can influence the consequences of a disaster. Scaring people with the potential for catastrophe without focusing on solutions creates a belief that a threat is too great for personal action to make a difference.

Lead People to Consider Helping Those More Vulnerable Than Themselves

Drawing on people's compassion for others, especially those more vulnerable such as children and the elderly, is a powerful motivator to inspire actions to make communities more resilient. This messaging can also be valuable in helping communities create mitigation and preparedness strategies that address broader social needs.

Start with Small Actions That Are Easy to Adopt

Providing specific information and steps that people can take to reduce risk helps convince people that preparedness and mitigation are worth the effort. If people are given a small list of actions they can take to prepare for disasters, starting with those that are easiest to adopt, they are more likely to feel motivated to act.

Connect Probabilities and Data to People's Lives

Risk is often couched in terms that are difficult to interpret and understand, especially when thinking about a timescale of years or decades. Effective communication about levels of probabilities and risk should go beyond mere statistics and ensure that numeric information is presented in a way that is understandable and relevant to the decisions that need to be made, whether that is deciding what property insurance is adequate or what the base elevation of a new house should be.

WHAT DOES A 100-YEAR FLOODPLAIN REALLY MEAN?

Our standard method of describing flood risk is through the delineation of the 1% annual chance floodplain as shown on a local map illustrating the 100-year floodplain. The all-or-nothing quality conveyed by the delineation of a 1% annual chance floodplain is a continuing and insidious problem. The public, local officials, and insurance agents usually interpret the flood map to mean that there is no flood risk whatsoever just outside the line showing the 1% zone. The terms "1% annual chance flood" and "100-year flood" have been sources of continual misunderstanding for the public and decision-makers.

In recent years, efforts have been made to connect statistics such as the 100-year floodplain to timescales that are more relevant to those using the information. For example, describing the likelihood of flooding occurring over the life of a 30-year mortgage may be much more relatable and useful for many people. While building a home just beyond the 100-year floodplain may sound like a completely safe choice, there is still a 26% chance of flooding before the mortgage is even paid off! After looking at the information in this way, a homeowner may think twice about the level of protection they are comfortable with before building or purchasing a home.

13.2.3 Individual Responsibility: Resilience from the Bottom Up

A discussion of resilience as it relates to hazards management would not be complete without reference to the issue of personal responsibility. Assuming that individuals and their families, businesses, and local government officials have accurate, reliable, and clearly communicated information regarding hazards in the community, a certain level of responsibility comes into play for addressing those hazards in the way we live.

At the individual and family level, we must assume that one cannot completely rely on others. Even the government, first responders, the Red Cross, one's neighbors, or church cannot always be there to help in times of disaster—ultimately, we all are responsible for our own safety. Having said that, we live in a society that recognizes that some do not have the capacity to help themselves (the young, the old, the poor, the dispossessed and disenfranchised, the mentally ill, those who are sick and infirm, and others less fortunate in their life circumstances). Therefore, while personal responsibility and independence are highly valued, responsibility also lies with the community as a whole to prepare for and mitigate hazards, both because this is the more socially acceptable approach as well as the more efficient and cost-effective means of addressing issues of hazard vulnerability.

It is not always law and governments that encourage adoption of risk reduction practices. A certain level of engagement by the citizenry who is able and willing to take action is needed. The vision of resilience in part embodies a spirit of responsibility and self-sufficiency, and heavy reliance on outside resources (i.e. federal and state funding) for disaster resistance is inconsistent with this. Communities must be better prepared to cope with the financial implication of disaster events and should be expected to utilize more of their own resources, at least in all but the most catastrophic of disaster events. Partly this means accepting more responsibility for allowing, or even actively promoting, development in vulnerable places and striving to reduce this over time.

By sharing the responsibility for a community's all-hazards preparedness and disaster prevention efforts, community involvement is the key to successful emergency management programs. Government will never have enough resources or money to mitigate alone and certainly not to fund a full recovery in the absence of mitigation. A model of resilience based on personal and community responsibility requires that government not be the sole source for mitigation action. Businesses, nonprofit organizations, professional associations, neighborhood activists, and other members of a community can become more involved and make a difference. Every level and individual in a community is ultimately responsible for their community's resilience, first by taking care of themselves and their family, and then by participating in taking their community to the next level of resilience.

13.2.4 Building a "Whole Community" Coalition

In addition to individual citizens taking personal responsibility to create safer, more equitable places, resilient communities engage a broad coalition of community groups, private sector organizations, and nonprofits to become key partners and stakeholders in disaster risk reduction. After all, in the United States, the public sector only makes up 10% of the total workforce, the remaining 90% work in the private sector and nongovernmental organizations. As we discussed in Chapter 9, the private sector plays an essential role in mitigation and preparedness activities, both as a form of individual business protection and as a way of creating economic stability within the community at large. Nongovernmental organizations, such as environmental groups, faith-based organizations, and groups that provide social services or support indigent populations, should also be included in a broader coalition to help communities lessen and prepare for the impacts of hazards. Table 13.2 summarizes

Table 13.2 Mechanisms for Community Engagement in Disaster Policy-Making.

Mechanism	Purpose
Development of broad-based community coalitions	Rather than just an instrument to secure a community's commitment to disaster resilience, the development of a broad-based community coalition is itself a resilience-generating mechanism in that it links people together to solve problems and builds trust.
Involvement from a diverse set of community members—the "full fabric" of a community	Because no single entity can deliver the complete public good of resilience, it becomes a shared value and responsibility. Collaboration in fostering interest in resilience in the community can ensure that the full fabric of the community has the opportunity to be included in the problem-solving endeavor— and that it represents public and private interests and people with diverse social and economic backgrounds.
Building organizational capacity and leadership	Meaningful private-public partnerships for community resilience depend upon strong governance and organizational structures, leadership, and sustained resources for success.
Resilience plan	A priority activity for a local disaster collaborative is planning for stepwise improvements in community resilience.

key mechanisms to further resilience by creating a broader coalition to support disaster policy-making.[7]

Conservation and Environmental Protection Organizations

Whether through floodplain preservation, river basin planning, or green infrastructure initiatives, hazard reduction and environmental protection are mutually reinforcing activities that often promote more sustainable communities. In many communities, the job of preservation and conservation of natural areas is undertaken by nongovernment organizations (NGOs). The growing nonprofit sector encompasses environmental activist groups, land trusts, conservancies, recreational clubs, watershed protectionists, hunting and fishing associations, watchdog groups, and other organizations focused on environmental quality and resource protection. They range in size from large-scale, nationally recognized organizations such as the Sierra Club, Nature Conservancy, and the Natural Resources Defense Council, to local grassroots volunteer groups with shoestring budgets and tiny resource pools. These NGOs, also known as the third sector, are a growing and powerful force in our society and often quite visible and vocal in presenting and furthering their agenda.

Each type of nonprofit environmental organization pursues its own priorities, but many of its objectives overlap with local or state management goals for hazard mitigation in environmentally sensitive or ecologically fragile lands. Even though environmental organizations may not target their efforts to natural hazards *per se*, many of their resultant outcomes can have the effect of reducing natural hazard impacts. For instance, purchasing acreage for conservation and environmental protection purposes may also result in increasing the hazard mitigating function of these natural areas. Wetlands, for example, can reduce flood losses while also providing important habitat and breeding grounds for fish and wildlife. Placing land under conservation easements or in permanent holding will also keep these areas out of the development stream, thereby preventing structures from being built in hazard areas. The complementary relationships between hazard mitigation efforts, environmental protection, sustainability, and, ultimately, community resilience become clear when consideration is given to how healthy natural systems often serve to protect communities from hazards and how land use strategies in turn often serve to keep those natural systems healthy.

SELF-CHECK

- Provide at least three strategies to communicate more effectively about disaster risk and resilience.
- List some of the other groups, organizations, and professional fields that can contribute to emergency management functions.

13.3 KNOWING OUR ENVIRONMENT

At its foundation, resilience requires us to understand the world we live in so that we can manage the built environment and social systems in ways that are sensitive to current and future conditions of the natural environment. How should a small business owner know which hazards to anticipate and adequately prepare her continuity of operations plan? Where does an emergency manager look for the latest information about expected impacts of climate change when updating the community's hazard mitigation plan? What information can a civil engineering firm use to properly size a culvert beneath a newly constructed bridge?

If anything, the challenge that many people confront is not a lack of information and data about hazards, climate, and economic and social trends. Rather, the internet has put unending amounts of information at our fingers, and finding trusted resources and the best curators of reliable information is an important step in creating data-driven policies and making the best decisions. The following section summarizes key resources, tools, and organizations that provide valuable information to serve as the basis for mitigation and preparedness actions.

13.3.1 U.S. Census

The U.S. Census Bureau provides a wealth of information about population and economic characteristics in every community around the country. In addition to an actual count of every person each decade, the American Community Survey (ACS) provides an ongoing, statistical survey with current information that communities can use. An Economic Census is also conducted every five years, providing information about American business and the economy.

Data from the census undergirds hazards management, providing information about where people live, how populations are changing, economic and social vulnerability, and the makeup of businesses in a community. Census data can be accessed through factfinder.census.gov.

13.3.2 Hazus

Hazus (Hazards U.S.) is a computer modeling system developed and made freely available from FEMA that can be used to gather and analyze data for many of the steps in the risk assessment process. The latest version, Hazus-MH (Multi-Hazard), is used to estimate losses from earthquakes, hurricanes, and flooding. The software also contains useful information for preparing inventories and mapping community features vulnerable to other hazards as well.

Potential loss estimates analyzed in Hazus include:

- **Physical damage** to residential and commercial buildings, schools, critical facilities, and infrastructure
- **Economic loss**, including lost jobs, business interruptions, and repair and reconstruction costs
- **Social impacts**, including estimates of shelter requirements, displaced households, and population exposed to scenario floods, earthquakes, and hurricanes

The latest Hazus software and user manuals can be accessed through https://www.fema.gov/hazus-software.

13.3.3 Disaster Data

Working in collaboration with many federal agencies, the White House released the portal disaster.data.gov as a central location for disaster-related datasets, tools, and other resources to strengthen national resilience to disasters. Just months after its launch in 2014, more than 150 datasets were included in the portal, including the Severe Weather Data Inventory, FEMA Disaster Declarations, Earthquake Feeds, National Integrated Drought Information System, National Fire Incident Reporting System, to name only a few.

13.3.4 National Climate Assessment

The United States Global Change Research Program (USGCRP) coordinates and integrates federal research on environmental changes and impacts for society. Every few years, the USGCRP releases a National Climate Assessment, which integrates and summarizes the latest research about climate changes, including both observations and projections. The assessments include information about climate change impacts for the United States as a whole, as well as specific impacts for each region and various sectors of the economy. The Fourth National Climate Assessment, released in 2018, can be accessed at the following link: http://nca2018.globalchange.gov.

13.3.5 Climate Data Initiative

The Climate Data Initiative makes federal data about our climate more open, accessible, and useful to citizens, researchers, entrepreneurs, and innovators. The website climate.data.gov includes curated, high-quality datasets, web services, and tools that can be used to help communities prepare for the future. Initially focused on coastal flooding, food resilience, water resources, and ecosystem vulnerability, these datasets and resources are being expanded over time to provide information on other climate-relevant threats, such as to human health and energy infrastructure.

13.3.6 Digital Coast

Sponsored by the National Oceanic and Atmospheric Administration, the Digital Coast website, http://coast.noaa.gov/digitalcoast, focuses on helping communities address coastal issues with data, tools, training, and case studies. The website includes historical hurricane tracks, an interactive sea level rise viewer, tools to view land cover change, and many other resources to understand coastal environments and plan for coastal resilience.

13.3.7 Local Mitigation Planning

The "Beyond the Basics" website builds on guidance about local hazard mitigation planning from FEMA with examples and best practices from around the country. The website includes everything an emergency manager or planner needs to know to meet the basic requirements of an approved hazard mitigation plan and provides ideas and examples of how communities may go beyond the requirements to strengthen their plan and ultimately create more resilient communities. The tool can be accessed using the website: http://mitigationguide.org.

13.3.8 Ready.gov

The website Ready.gov is a FEMA-sponsored national public service advertising campaign designed to educate and empower Americans to prepare for and respond to natural and human-made disasters. In both English (www.Ready.gov) and Spanish (www.Listo.gov), the website helps people (1) build an emergency supply kit, (2) make a family emergency plan, and (3) be informed about the different types of emergencies that could occur and their appropriate responses.

13.3.9 State Hazard Mitigation Officers

A valuable resource for mitigation planning within each state is the official point of contact for the FEMA Mitigation Grant Programs, referred to as the State Hazard Mitigation Officer. The State Hazard Mitigation Officers provide support to local communities carrying out mitigation planning and seeking funding for mitigation projects. FEMA maintains an up-to-date list of State Hazard Mitigation Officers and their contact information at the following link: https://www.fema.gov/state-hazard-mitigation-officers.

13.3.10 State Climatologists

Most states maintain climate offices that provide multiple services to the state, including helping to coordinate research, informing resource managers and organizations about climate data and information, and educating citizens. The state climatologist within each of these offices is tremendous resources for those engaged in mitigation, preparedness, and climate adaptation since they can provide information about specific changes and climate vulnerabilities within a given state. The American Association of State Climatologists maintains a list of states that have a climate office and provides contact information for each of the state climatologists: http://www.stateclimate.org.

SELF-CHECK

- Name the most trusted source of socioeconomic data of the United States.
- Explain what hazards and potential losses can be analyzed using Hazus.
- Describe two sources of information about impacts of climate change.

13.4 DETERMINING AN ACCEPTABLE LEVEL OF RISK

One of the ethical issues that emergency managers and communities must deal with when managing hazard impacts is how to define an acceptable level of risk. We cannot eliminate 100% of all risk from natural or human-made hazards, even with the latest technologies, building techniques, or state-of-the-art land use planning practices. There will always be a degree of risk inherent in living anywhere on the Earth. Of course, in some locations, this risk is more prevalent than others. New Orleans is one such place, where much of the city lies below sea level. In many respects, the possibility of a hurricane hitting New Orleans and causing massive damage has been called a disaster waiting to happen. When Hurricane Katrina arrived in 2005, the hypothetical became reality.

Over 169 miles of levees and floodwalls were damaged in New Orleans during and immediately after Hurricane Katrina, causing massive flooding, property damage, displacement of thousands of residents, and the loss of hundreds of human lives. What went wrong? A lethal combination of physical, engineering, and human and organizational factors led to the overtopping and breaching of the protective features surrounding the city. Many of these factors are rooted in happenstance, bad luck, bad timing, or a seemingly random set of coincidences. However, many of the other factors leading up to the devastation of New Orleans were the result of deliberate, well-considered decisions that were based on known facts and established protocols. One such decision involved the level of risk that was considered appropriate for flooding in the city.

13.4.1 Setting the Limit of Acceptable Risk: A Visit to the Netherlands

To understand some of the considerations that are made in setting an acceptable level of risk for a given population in a given area, we can look for a moment at an international corollary of New Orleans—the country of the Netherlands. The Netherlands has, for hundreds of years, designed and built structures allowing the country to maintain an entire nation with much of the land near or below sea level. The Netherlands is one of the lowest geographical countries in the world; its name literally means "low countries," and the first dikes were built as early as the twelfth century. In low-lying peat swamps, a complex system of drainage canals and windmill-powered pumps have been used to keep land dry.

The similarities between the Netherlands and the city of New Orleans are striking in many ways. Roughly a quarter of the Netherlands lies below sea level; New Orleans is approximately 50% below sea level. The Netherlands uses an elaborate system of seawalls and levees to protect the population from the sea; New Orleans relied on a system of levees and dikes to protect its population from the Gulf of Mexico and Lake Pontchartrain. Dutch engineers look to soil samples, engineering techniques, and building materials to construct massive walls and barriers to limit flooding. Engineers and contractors working in New Orleans conduct similar studies and engage in similar tactics to reduce flooding. The differences lie in part in how each community sets an acceptable level of risk and implements the details of construction. Some of the differences may be accounted for by difference in topography, soil types, expertise, exposure to storms, and other issues. But more importantly, the difference between the way in which the Netherlands approaches its task and the situation in New Orleans is rooted in the divergence between the two communities in the definition of risk, the level of protection that is desired, and the experience and longevity with which the flood control has been improved upon over time.

In simple terms, the Netherlands provides a higher level of protection from flooding for its population than that which is provided in New Orleans. The Dutch commitment to flood mitigation is based on a probability of flood occurrence in urban areas of 1 in 10,000 for higher density areas and 1 in 4,000 for less populated areas of the country. This means that the Dutch attempt to protect their cities against an event that could occur once in 10,000 years with regard to the size of event and the pressure exerted on the floodwalls. The United States, as a matter of national policy, does not consider such a level of protection feasible at this time. Instead, we typically focus on a 1 in 100 chance of flooding as the basis of our flood prevention strategies and consider a 1 in 500 flood protection level to be very conservative.

13.4.2 What Does It Take to Have Such a High Threshold?

A simple answer to the question of why the Netherlands provides a higher level of protection than that which is found in New Orleans is a matter of national will and experience addressing flood risks. The Dutch citizens and their elected leaders long ago put the country on its current track of maintaining and even augmenting the dry land—much of it reclaimed over the course of many years from the North Sea. The political will of the people is behind the system of dikes and levees that keep the Netherlands safe from the onslaught of waves, winds, and storm surge. The Dutch have deliberately chosen this course and are willing to continue to pursue the way of life they have known for generations.

The political will of the Dutch is surpassed only by their ongoing diligence. The Dutch not only maintain their dikes and seawalls but also, every year, they seek to improve the system of flood prevention. Dutch engineers are constantly seeking new ways to heighten the structures' integrity and soundness in the face of ongoing hazard risks. Money is certainly a part of this issue. Due diligence is matched by the willingness of the Dutch to expend public moneys, and significant funding is allocated toward the dike system and levees that keep the country safe and dry. The level of risk that is acceptable in the Netherlands drives decisions surrounding the dike system. The choice of materials and techniques fit the risk that the residents are trying to reduce.

In recent years, the flood management strategy in the Netherlands has been shifting in large part due to the effects of climate change and an understanding that effective flood control must work with natural systems rather than only constructing walls to keep water out. In many ways, the changes in flood management are in response to an acknowledgment that protecting some areas will be infeasible, especially given climate change.

The "Room for the River" program, a series of more than 30 distinct projects, was implemented between 2006 and 2015. The projects include moving some dikes, creating and increasing the depth of flood channels, constructing a flood bypass, and other measures to allow flooding in specific areas during extreme weather events while protecting other urban areas. The program is expected to improve environmental quality and reduce the likelihood of catastrophic flooding by dissipating water into known or constructed floodplains.[11]

In the United States, there is no such a long history of flood prevention as exists in the Netherlands. Since adoption of a structural protection approach to flooding nearly 200 years ago, the United States generally takes a "hurry up and wait" approach to maintenance and repair, whereby levees are allowed to decay, sag, collapse, settle, and develop cracks over the course of a decade or more. When a catastrophic event such as Katrina occurs, emergency appropriations from state, federal, and local coffers are required to fund expensive short-term fixes to the problem. Several more years of neglect and decline are allowed, until another hazard event recurs. The Netherlands does not maintain such a cyclical pattern of flood protection. Their national will, funding, and diligence mean that their levees are never considered finished.

SELF-CHECK

- Compare how the Netherlands and the United States approach the determination of what is an acceptable level of risk to flood hazards.
- Discuss why the "Room for the River" project in the Netherlands is a shift in strategy for flood management.

13.5 IMPLEMENTING STRATEGIES THAT PROMOTE RESILIENCE

Throughout this book, we have discussed the *process* of mitigation and preparedness, and the roles of various levels of government and organizations to engage in hazards management. We have intentionally avoided being too prescriptive about specific mitigation and preparedness strategies that should be followed, because the strategies that are effective from community to community vary widely depending on the hazard profile, the natural environment, the capacity of the community, and the values of its citizens. The process of analyzing risk and involving the community in the development of actions that might be taken to enhance resilience is irreplaceable. However, some broad categories of mitigation and preparedness strategies have emerged time and again as ways to protect valuable natural areas while simultaneously reducing the impact of hazards on the built environment. This section summarizes these concepts that often serve as the foundation for resiliency planning and implementation.

13.5.1 Using Land Wisely

In resilient communities, land is viewed as a limited resource and managed thoughtfully. Environmentally sensitive lands (wetlands, shorelines, hillsides, fault zones) are placed off-limits to intensive development. Development patterns promote compact urban areas, curtailing scattered development and sprawl. Resilient communities may take advantage of underutilized urban areas and encourage infill and brownfield development. Energy and resource conservation are high priorities and a greater emphasis is placed on creating options for multiple forms of transportation, including public transit, walking, and bicycling—redundancy that can be vital in the event of a disaster. At its core, a community that is resilient to hazards acknowledges the presence of natural features and processes—such as riverine flooding, wildfires, and barrier island migration—and arranges its land use and settlement patterns so as to sustain rather than interfere with or disrupt them.

Zoning and subdivision ordinances and other land use planning activities that take hazards into account and that disallow building in the most hazardous areas can also help protect the local economic base from disasters. Capital improvement planning and long-range strategic planning for infrastructure can help discourage development in hazard areas by restricting public facilities such as water and sewer in the most fragile areas. Other communities choose to use other innovative strategies to use land wisely, such as cluster development ordinances that attempt to increase density of new development on more suitable land, while leaving vulnerable or sensitive land as open space or farmland.

Resilient communities also recognize that natural systems do not necessarily correspond to political boundaries and approach planning and resource management on a broader scale to account for impacts that cross jurisdictional lines. As an example, **river basin management** is a planning mechanism that is effective, although an underutilized system for addressing issues of water quality, habitat protection, rural land conservation, and flood hazard mitigation on a regional scale. Since a river basin consists of all the land draining to a major river system, the streams, tributaries, and watersheds of a river basin exist as a continuum through many communities, land cover types, and various land usages. Several states use a basin-wide approach to planning for water quality purposes. However, fewer states use the river basin as a unit for planning for flood control purposes, despite the potential utility of such an approach.

13.5.2 Green Infrastructure

Infrastructure is a term that usually encompasses the public works and utilities that serve development, such as roads, sewer lines, and drainageways. However, as we have learned throughout this book, nature can also provide many services for humans such as protecting us from flooding, excessive heat, and improving air and water quality. A healthy sand dune is unmatched when it comes to absorbing the pounding of waves. Similarly, naturally occurring wetlands can often absorb and infiltrate enormous quantities of stormwater runoff while simultaneously filtering and cleaning the water.

The concept of **green infrastructure** views natural areas as another form of infrastructure needed for both the ecological health of an area and for the quality of life that people have come to expect. Green infrastructure is a strategic approach to harnessing natural systems to serve stormwater management, climate adaptation, environmental health, and other social, economic, and environmental goals. Green infrastructure can involve wetlands, natural berms and dunes, urban forests, parks, buffers along waterways, greenways, residential landscaping, and even urban gardens, each of which can serve multiple purposes in the community. Not only can green infrastructure protect natural resources and habitat, but these spaces also act as floodwater storage facilities, water conveyance areas, and runoff filters to reduce the impacts of excess water in the community. Green infrastructure also lessens the amount of impervious surface area in a community, effectively reducing the volume and velocity of stormwater flows.

NASHVILLE USES GREEN INFRASTRUCTURE TO REDUCE FLOOD RISK

Nashville, TN experienced extensive flooding in 2010 after record-breaking rainfall caused the Cumberland River to overflow its banks. To reduce flood risk and restore impaired streams, the "Nashville Naturally" open space plan uses the concept of green infrastructure by calling for the protection of 22,000 acres in hundreds of locations dispersed throughout the city. The land to be preserved, which includes a large stretch along the Cumberland River, is expected to provide a buffer against floodwaters, improve water quality, protect agricultural soils, and offer recreational opportunities. The plan also identifies 50 smaller green infrastructure projects within the city center designed to help reduce sewer overflows and alleviate flood risks.

13.5.3 Incorporating Future Build-Out into Flood Risk Determinations

In addition to problems we discussed earlier associated with communicating the meaning of the 100-year flood risk, the concept itself is also difficult to use proactively because flood levels change due to any number of reasons, including increased development and climate change. Changing conditions in the floodplain and elsewhere in the watershed have profound impacts on flood levels. As watersheds are developed, the increase in impervious surfaces, such as pavement and rooftops, causes more water from a storm to run off the land's surface into the drainage system and streams, and usually at a faster pace, than was the case before development. The flood depths and boundaries that were calculated and mapped before such urbanization took place become inaccurate within a short period of time.

What this means is that today's 1% (100-year) standard, which allows encroachments into the floodplain, in actuality, may be tomorrow's 50-year standard and only a 10-year standard once the watershed is fully developed. And once an area is developed, it is extraordinarily difficult to wind back the clock and remove future development from the area. These trends do not bode well for controlling the escalation of flood damage.

As an alternative to the current method of flood risk determination, changes in development patterns—which result in increases in flood damage, even though the area is being managed—can be accounted for by using a future-condition scenario when determining the expected runoff. As new levels of development are factored into the determination of flood elevations, regulations for the lowest level floor elevations can anticipate where flood heights might be within the lifetime of the structure, greatly increasing the level of protection afforded to a particular residence.

A few communities have made use of development projections when setting flood regulations, such as Charlotte-Mecklenburg in North Carolina. The City-County floodplain management authority stresses identification of the flood hazard area based on future developed conditions. Maps incorporate increased runoff rates from development that has not yet taken place within the watershed, and corresponding regulations reflect these levels.

13.5.4 No Adverse Impact: A Do No Harm Policy

In addition to incorporating the effects of future development into the determination of acceptable flood risks, another approach involves the concept known as **no adverse impact**. The no adverse impact approach to floodplain management strives to ensure that the actions of one property owner do not increase the flood risk of other property owners.

The "no adverse impact" approach focuses on planning for and lessening flood impacts resulting from land use changes. It is essentially a policy to ensure that new development does not exacerbate flood damages. For example, if an empty lot neighboring your house is developed, a "no adverse impact" policy would require that the design should not result in new flooding on your property during rainstorms that did not exist previously. Therefore, the design may need to use a green roof, rain garden, or other mitigation technique to capture and infiltrate stormwater before it makes it to your property. When embraced fully by regulators and residents, no-impact floodplains become the default management criteria and can be extended to entire watersheds. Development is permitted in a way that creates no negative changes in hydrology, stream depths, velocities, or sediment transport functions; impacts are only allowed to the extent they are offset by mitigation. Site-specific mitigation techniques range from the installation of detention and retention basins to adequate drainage channels to improved stormwater management features.

The no adverse impact approach to flood mitigation promotes fairness, responsibility, community involvement, preflood planning, sustainable development, and local land use management. It places responsibility for managing floodplain risks squarely on local governments and individuals, since the specific details for land use are decided at the community level. It also supports private property rights because property owners can have input on management strategies that impact their own property. This approach can especially benefit those property owners who are not currently in regulated flood areas, but who could be in the future.

SELF-CHECK

- Define green infrastructure.
- Discuss the value of using a river basin scale to manage flooding.
- Give an example of a "no adverse impact" mitigation strategy

---

13.6 PRE- AND POST-DISASTER OPPORTUNITIES FOR REDEVELOPMENT

In the best of all worlds, communities strive to become more resilient as part of their daily activities. "Mitigation is most effective when carried out on a comprehensive, communitywide, and long-term basis. Single grants or activities can help, but carrying out a slate of coordinated mitigation activities over time is the best way to ensure that communities will be physically, socially, and economically resilient to future hazard impacts."[12] Any and all selected mitigation measures must be joined with the political will and the institutionalized systems with the power to enforce them. How well a community integrates mitigation objectives with community growth and development, and balances competing priorities, will determine the extent to which the community has a resilient future.

13.6.1 Post-Disaster Redevelopment

Sometimes, the best opportunity for encouraging a resilient and sustainable approach to community life arises after a major disaster. One of the impediments to local implementation of mitigation is the fact that much of the land within a local jurisdiction has already been developed according to practices and traditions that are far from sustainable.

Ironically, the time immediately following a natural disaster may provide a community with a unique window of opportunity for inserting an ethic of resilience in guiding development and redevelopment in high-risk areas. With forethought and planning, communities that are rebuilt in the aftermath of a natural hazard can be built back so that they are more resilient to future hazards, breaking the cycle of hazard-destruction-rebuilding. At the same time, the community is given the opportunity to incorporate other attributes of sustainability into its second chance development, such as energy efficiency, affordable housing, walkable neighborhoods, use of recycled building materials, reduction of water use, and environmental protection.

If a community has not yet formally considered broader issues like environmental quality, economic parity, social equity, or livability, the period of recovery after a disaster can be a good time to start, primarily because disasters "jiggle the status quo, scrambling a community's normal reality and presenting chances to do things differently."[13] Some of the changes that occur in the routine business of a community after a disaster include the following:

- **Hazard awareness increases:** Immediately following a disaster event, people become personally aware of the hazards that can beset the community and the extent of the impact. In other words, suddenly, it becomes real.
- **Destruction occurs:** In some cases, the disasters will have done some of the work already. For example, a tornado, earthquake, or fire may have damaged or destroyed aging, dilapidated, or unsafe buildings or infrastructure.
- **Community involvement increases:** A disaster forces a community to make decisions, both hard and easy. Community involvement and citizen participation in policy formation often increase after a disaster.
- **Help arrives:** Technical assistance and expert advice become available to a disaster-impacted community from a variety of state, federal, regional, academic, and nonprofit sources.
- **Money flows in:** Financial assistance becomes available from state and federal government agencies, both for private citizens and the local government for disaster recovery and mitigation projects; insurance claim payments can also provide a source of funds for recovery and mitigation work.
- **Hazard identification changes:** Sometimes, a hazard may change a community's assessment of where hazard areas are located. A disaster may provide opportunities to update flood maps, relocate inlet zones, reestablish erosion rates, modify oceanfront or seismic setback regulations, and change other indicators of vulnerability to reflect actual hazard risks based on new conditions.

The best way to ensure that a community has a recovery from a future disaster in a way that reduces vulnerability is to prepare a comprehensive, holistic plan in advance of an event. But even if a community has not prepared such a plan, there are many commonsense things that can be done during the recovery process that will make a community more sustainable than it was before. Integrating sustainable development and resilience into disaster recovery requires some shifts in current thinking, land use, and policy. Some broad guidelines for developing recovery strategies that promote hazard mitigation include:

- **Adopt a longer time frame:** Incorporating hazard mitigation calls for the adoption of a longer time frame in recovery decision-making. Particularly, foolhardy are short-term actions that destroy or undermine natural ecosystems and that encourage or facilitate long-term growth and development patterns that expose more people and property to hazards.
- **Consider future losses:** Substantial attention must be paid during rebuilding to future potential losses from hazards, including changes in event return periods or intensity because of climate change.
- **Protect natural resources:** Features of the natural environment that serve important mitigation functions, such as wetlands, firebreak zones, and sand dunes, should be taken into account and protected during rebuilding.
- **Use the best available data:** Scientific uncertainty about frequency intervals, prediction, or vulnerability should not postpone structural strengthening or hazard avoidance during rebuilding.
- **Invest in redevelopment wisely:** Post-disaster reconstruction that does not account for future disasters is an inefficient investment of recovery resources. Communities should seek to learn from disasters and treat recovery as an opportunity to invest in the future safety and vitality of their citizens.

It must be remembered, however, that the post-disaster recovery period is one of high stress and anxiety for the victims of a recent disaster. There may be community resistance to any redevelopment effort that appears to slow the process down. In addition, people whose lives have been disrupted by disaster often want to put their lives back together just the way they were before the hazard event occurred. Such an attitude, while understandable, may prove to be an impediment to changing the community during the redevelopment phase.

13.6.2 Examples of Resilient Redevelopment

Examples of communities that have taken a redevelopment approach that embraces sustainability and enhances resilience following a natural disaster are many and widespread. Among such communities that have taken advantage of the post-disaster window of opportunity to become more sustainable are as follows:

- Located on the Arkansas River, *Tulsa, Oklahoma*, has a history of vulnerability to flooding. After years of repeated flooding, in the 1980s, Tulsa initiated a multipronged approach to mitigation. Projects to reduce flood risks include moving homes out of the floodplain, adopting watershed-wide regulations on new development, developing a master drainage plan for the city, establishing a funding source for stormwater management, and creating open space and recreational areas in the floodplain.
- After the 1993 Midwest Floods, *Soldiers Grove, Wisconsin*, rebuilt the community while following many sustainable development guidelines. Among other activities to promote resilience and sustainability, the town relocated its business district entirely out of the floodplain, required new businesses to obtain at least half their energy from solar, conducted life-cycle analysis of building materials, sited buildings and landscaping based on a detailed site analysis, and mixed housing into downtown development.
- During rebuilding following Hurricane Andrew, Habitat for Humanity constructed an affordable housing complex called *Jordan Commons,* near Homestead, Florida. The

project was designed as a community rather than built as individual housing units. The project incorporated design standards and building practices to withstand future hurricanes while providing affordable housing to low- and middle-income residents who participated in the rebuilding process.

- Following a devastating tornado in the spring of 1997, the city of **Arkadelphia, Arkansas,** used funding from the U.S. Department of Housing and Urban Development (HUD) to develop a comprehensive downtown recovery program as part of a larger community redevelopment initiative. Key projects that were developed in reaction to local commitment to keeping downtown as the heart of the community included the construction of a new city hall and town square complex, implementing streetscape improvements, construction of a new riverfront park, attracting middle-market housing to affected neighborhoods, and the creation of a housing rehabilitation program. In addition, changes to the zoning code encouraged a greater diversity of housing types throughout the city, compact neighborhood design, and energy-efficient home building practices. The city took advantage of the HUD funding after the tornado to develop a sustainable recovery plan that benefited the entire community.

- In the wake of Hurricane Sandy, many communities along the Northeastern coastline are implementing recovery strategies that include efforts to reduce long-term vulnerability to hurricanes, coastal flooding, sea level rise, and other hazards. **Nassau County, New York,** received $125 million in public and private funding from the Rebuild by Design competition to address storm surge flooding and stormwater inundation. The project is designed to enhance environmental, economic, and social resilience by incorporating a mix of green infrastructure, such as marshland restoration and the creation of recreational berms, with zoning changes and infrastructure investments to increase the density and vitality of development in flood-resistant areas.

SELF-CHECK

- What is meant by the post-disaster window of opportunity?
- Provide three strategies to promote mitigation in disaster recovery.

SUMMARY

Taxpayers spend billions of dollars each year helping communities respond to and recover from disasters. Losses continue to rise, and climate change appears to be making what was once an extreme weather event more common. Moreover, these disaster losses and recovery costs are not borne equally. We allow some people to build in environmentally sensitive areas susceptible to natural hazards, and then we as a society pay to help them recover when disaster strikes. This is not a sound environmental or fiscal policy. In many cases, decisions about where to locate development are made because they appear to save money in the short term. Ultimately, these decisions cost more since it is much more cost-effective and sensible to invest in mitigation and preparedness than to pay to clean up after damage occurs. More importantly, lives that are lost in disasters cannot be made whole again.

A more resilient approach to development and hazards management calls on all of us—emergency managers, local elected officials, business owners, churches and religious institutions, nonprofits, homeowners, and state and federal policy-makers. Beginning with clear and reliable information about hazards and climate change, communities can begin to assess vulnerability, make thoughtful decisions about the level of risk they are comfortable with, and consider changes that could be made to become more resilient to natural and human-made hazards. A wide range of mitigation and preparedness strategies have been successfully employed to manage hazards, including engineering approaches, strong building codes, organizational continuity planning, and land use planning. However, it is increasingly clear that preserving and protecting the natural environment, including wetlands, dunes, floodplains, and shorelines, is part of an effective approach to creating a more resilient built environment. While we do our best to prevent disasters from occurring, we know that they are part of the world we live in and do our best to learn from them and rebuild in a better way. In the end, we are all responsible for making our communities more resilient to the impacts of hazards, to ensure a safer tomorrow.

KEY TERMS

Green infrastructure: Views natural areas as a form of infrastructure (public works and utilities such as sewer lines and roads) that supports not only quality of life but also the ecological health of an area.

No adverse impact: An approach to floodplain management that attempts to ensure that the actions of one property owner do not increase the flood risk of other property owners through land use planning and mitigation strategies.

Resilience: The ability to prepare and plan for, absorb, recover from, and more successfully adapt to adverse events.

River basin management: A technique for addressing issues of water quality, habitat protection, rural land conservation, and flood hazard mitigation on a regional scale in recognition of the fact that natural systems do not necessarily correspond to political boundaries.

ASSESS YOUR UNDERSTANDING

Summary Questions

1. Development patterns are brittle when they do not take hazards into account. True or False?
2. Hazard mitigation is the phase of emergency management that is especially dedicated to breaking the cycle of damage, reconstruction, and repeated damage. True or False?
3. Which of the following may serve as a useful communication strategy to encourage citizens to prepare for disasters?
   a. Scare people by talking about the consequences of a disaster
   b. Encourage people to help those more vulnerable than themselves
   c. Assure citizens that emergency responders will be ready to save them
   d. Pretend that disasters have not happened in the community in the past
4. Resilient communities can better withstand which negative economic effects of a disaster?
   a. Displacement of residents and loss of local employment base
   b. Deferment of other publicly funded projects
   c. Loss of major employers
   d. All of the above
5. The simple answer to the question of why the Netherlands provides a higher level of protection than that which is found in New Orleans is a matter of global economics. True or False?
6. The Census counts the population of the United States every year. True or False?
7. Which of the following sources can provide information about the impacts of climate change in the United States?
   a. Climate Data Initiative
   b. National Climate Assessment
   c. Digital Coast
   d. All of the above

8. Which of the following is an example of green infrastructure?
   a. Roads
   b. Farms
   c. Sewer lines
   d. Utility lines
9. Infusing a mitigation ethic into all land use planning and development activities is the best way to increase local vulnerability. True or False?
10. We can rely on others, such as the Red Cross or the federal government to be responsible for our safety. True or False?

Review Questions

1. Define disaster resilience.
2. Why is the standard method of describing flood risk as a 1% chance flood illustrated as the 100-year floodplain a misleading?
3. What are the benefits of a natural floodplain?
4. What are some of the changes that occur in a community after a disaster?
5. List three guidelines communities can use to enhance resilience during the redevelopment following a disaster.
6. List three effective communications strategies to encourage citizens to prepare for and mitigate hazards.
7. What information sources are important for understanding the characteristics of a community's population?
8. Name two sources of information and data about climate change impacts.
9. Describe some of the complementary goals of local governments and nonprofit environmental organizations in reducing hazard vulnerability.
10. Why is the recovery from disaster a potentially valuable time to undertake mitigation?
11. Describe why emergency management can be seen as an art form.

Applying This Chapter

1. What river basin are you located in? Are you upstream near the headwaters, downstream near the outflow point, or somewhere in between? How do the actions of your community affect the entire river basin as a whole?
2. Think of a disaster that could affect your community. After that disaster, if you were an emergency manager, what would you do to insert an ethic of resilience into guiding development and redevelopment in high-risk areas? Would you take advantage of that window of opportunity? And if so, how? What recovery strategies would you use to promote mitigation?
3. Identify some of the natural features of your community. If you live near a river, can you identify the extent of the floodplain? Are there wetlands present or nearby? If so, are they allowed to function in their natural capacity as catchments for excess rainfall? If not, what measures should be in place to protect their mitigation function?
4. Describe how structural engineers in New Orleans might approach levee repair and reconstruction following a major hurricane if they were trained in the Netherlands. What obstacles to their approach might they encounter? Consider the budget they might be allocated. Consider too the traditions of land use planning and development.
5. Outline the strategy you might take to developing floodplain regulations if your community were to take a no adverse impact approach to flood mitigation. How would you assess the boundaries of the floodplain? Would you take into account future development? Why or why not?

6. You are the emergency manager of a small town that has experienced repeated flooding. The town manager has asked you for a report, detailing the costs and benefits of a proposed structural mitigation project. What factors will you consider when compiling your report? What basis of your information will you use?

You Try It

Greening Your Infrastructure

The Maryland Department of Natural Resources is working to identify those undeveloped lands that are most critical to the state's long-term ecological health. These lands, referred to as Maryland's green infrastructure, provide the natural foundation needed to support diverse plant and animal populations, and enable valuable natural processes like filtering water and cleaning the air to take place. Identifying and setting priorities for the protection of the green infrastructure is an ongoing process. A description of Maryland's green infrastructure, including county-by-county maps, can be found at https://dnr.maryland.gov/land/Pages/Green-Infrastructure.aspx. Using Maryland's approach as a guide, find out how your community treats its open spaces. If you live in an urban area, does your city protect urban forests or other natural areas? If your community is suburban or rural in nature, is agricultural land or habitat protected in any way? What water quality protections are in place at the local level? State level?

Environmental Justice at Home

Seeking information from your local planning department, community affairs, or housing agency, or from the U.S. Census, identify where low-income or minority populations live in your community. Now identify the hazards that may be present there. Look at the local flood maps. Are toxic waste sites or local landfills nearby? Are disadvantaged people living in areas that are more vulnerable to hazards than other sectors of society? If so, what might you do as an emergency manager to safeguard all members of your community?

Risky Business

The terms we use to describe risk are often confusing and misleading to the general population. Take an informal poll of friends, colleagues, and family members. Ask them what comes to mind when you mention the "100-year flood risk." How many people respond that it must mean a flood that occurs once every 100 years? Does the phrase "1% chance of flooding in any given year" help clarify the concept of risk for them? Confuse them more? How would you describe flood risk in terms that people who are not in the emergency management field could understand?

REFERENCES

1. National Oceanic and Atmospheric Administration. 2020. Billion-Dollar Weather and Climate Disasters. National Oceanic and Atmospheric Administration. http://www.ncdc.noaa.gov/billions/.
2. U.S. Global Change Research Program. 2018. *National Climate Assessment*. U.S. Global Change Research Program. http://nca2018.globalchange.gov.
3. Sweet, W.V. and J. Park. 2014. *From the extreme to the mean: Acceleration and tipping points of coastal inundation from sea level rise. Earth's Future*, 2(12): 579–600.
4. National Oceanic and Atmospheric Administration. 2018. *Fast Facts: Economics and Demographics*. Office of Coastal Management.

5. Annan, K. 2000. *Facing the Humanitarian Challenge: Towards a Culture of Prevention.* New York, NY: United Nations.
6. Multihazard Mitigation Council. 2005. *Natural Hazard Mitigation Saves: An Independent Study to Assess the Future Savings from Mitigation Activities.*
7. National Academy of Science. 2012. *Disaster Resilience – A National Imperative.* Washington, DC: National Academies Press.
8. Godschalk, D., T. Beathley, P. Berke, D. Brower, and E. Kaiser. 1999. *Natural Hazard Mitigation: Recasting Disaster Policy and Planning.* Washington, DC: Island Press.
9. Kershaw, P.J. 2005. *Creating a Disaster Resilient America: Grand Challenges in Science and Technology: Summary of a Workshop,* edited by National Research Council of the National Academies. Washington, DC: National Academies Press.
10. Mileti, D.S. and L. Peak. 2002. Understanding Individual and Social Characteristics in the Promotion of Household Disaster Preparedness. *New Tools for Environmental Protection: Education, Information, And Voluntary Measures,* edited by T. Dietz and P.C. Stern, pp. 125–139. Washington, DC: National Academies Press.
11. Room for the River Programme. http://www.ruimtevoorderivier.nl/english/room-for-the-river-programme/.
12. Ganderton, P. T., et al. (2006) *Mitigation generates savings of four to one and enhances community resilience. Natural Hazards Review,* 30(4).
13. Monday, J. (2005) *Chapter 1: Introduction to Sustainability. Holistic Disaster Recovery: Ideas for Building Local Sustainability after a Natural Disaster.* Boulder, CO. http://www.colorado.edu/hazards/publications/holistic/ch1_sustainability.pdf.

Index